D1526590

GLOBALYCEUM

World History
1500 to Present

Volume II

Table of Contents

Overview of Era V, 1500-1700

Unit 9: The East, 1300-1700   5

    Reading: China   5

    Reading: New Visions of the City in Early Modern China (Topical Essay)   9

    Reading: Japan   12

    Reading: Korea and Vietnam   16

Unit 10: The Early Modern West, 1500-1700   20

    Reading: The Maritime Expansion of Early Modern Europe   20

    Reading: The Political Economy of Early Modern Europe   23

    Reading: The African Slave Trade

    Reading: The Rise of Muscovy

    Reading: Columbus and Vespucci: A Tale of Two Discoveries

    Reading: The Wars of Religion and the 30 Years' War   28

    Reading: The West Looks East, Again   33

    Reading: The Early Modern Global Travelers (Topical Essay)   38

    Reading: The Intellectual Revolutions and Technology Transfer   41

    Reading: The Reformation   46

    Reading: The Renaissance   52

    Reading: Renaissance Art

    Reading: The Idea of Absolutism

    Reading: Scientific Revolution   59

Overview of Era VI, 1700-1800

Unit 11:The Middle East and South Asia,1500-1900   65

    Reading: The Three Empires at their Apex   65

    Reading: A Reversal of Fortune in the 18th Century   69

    Reading: An Intensification of Challenges   71

    Reading: Iran's Encounter with Modernity in the 19th Century (Topical Essay)   77

Overview of Era VII, 1800-1900

Unit 12: Europe and the world   82

    Reading: The Promises of Enlightenment

    Reading: The French Revolution, 1789-1799

    Reading: Napoleon Bonaparte, 1769-1821   82

    Reading: Industrialization and the Social Question   87

    Reading: Global Migration 1500-1900

    Reading: Europe, 1815-48   91

    Reading The Rise of Nations   97

Reading: The British in India (Topical Essay)

Reading: The Age of Imperialism, 1850 -1914 (Topical Essay)   99

Reading: The Atlantic Revolutions and Independence

Reading: African Scramble

Reading: Imperial Russia and the Making of a Nation (Topical Essay)   105

Reading: Latin America, 1500-1900   111

Unit 13: East Asia, 1700-1919   123

Reading: The Early Qing Empire, 1644-1796   123

Reading: The Meaning of the Bound Feet of Chinese Women (Topical Essay)   127

Reading: The Long 19th Century in China, 1793-1919   132

Reading: The Meiji Restoration

Overview of Era VIII, 1900-present   138

Unit 14: World Wars and Decolonizations , 1900 – 1945   144

Reading: Wars, Mass Violence, and Genocide   144

Reading: The Spanish Republic   148

Reading: World War I: A Military History

Reading: The History of World War II and its Great Battles   151

Reading: The Crisis of Meaning: Artistic, Philosophical, and Political   155

Reading: National Liberation/Decolonization   159

Unit 15:The Bipolar World and its Demise   165

Reading: The Making of the Post-War World Order, 1945-63   165

Reading: Global Institutions and the Stability of the Post-War World (Topical Essay)
                                                                     168

Reading: The Cold War in the Third World and the Non-Aligned Movement, 1949-
1973   173

Reading: Vietnam and the 1960s

Reading: Demise of the Cold War, 1973-present   176

Unit 16: Globalization in the 20th and 21st Centuries   181

Reading: The First Wave of Globalization, 1890s-1914   181

Reading: The Second Wave of Globalization, 1945-75   185

Reading: The Third Wave of Globalization, 1991-Present   190

Reading: From the National to the Global Imaginary (Topical Essay)   195

Our Authors   201

Note: The digital Globalyceum site has hundreds of images, maps, author videos and videos that go along with these texts, as well as dozens of primary source activities and assessments. This paper supplement, however, only contains the text readings. You will have to consult the digital site in order to see the readings and the visuals as they were designed to be read.

Overview of Era 5: Interconnectedness, 1400-1700

Joshua Weiner, American River College

One of the defining features of our contemporary world is interconnectedness. Information, ideas, technology, culture; all of these things flow from region to region, person to person, and from screen to screen. But, let's imagine a different kind of world, a world defined by isolation. In this imaginary world, societies are not just separated by geography and distance but are also confined within giant bubbles making interactions with any outside groups impossible. Within this reality, our common biology would be the only thing that linked these disparate human societies. Other than being the same species, each would develop their own unique survival strategies, political and social organizations, culture, economic systems, and standards of behavior. Of course, human societies rarely develop in total isolation. Interaction over large and small distances has always allowed for, at least, limited sharing of ways of life among human groups.

Yet, as much as the idea of bubbles is silly, it does have some relevance to the world of the 15th century. This was a world that was in many ways more connected than ever, even as significant pockets of isolation continued to exist. Much of Afro-Eurasia was tied together through bonds of exchange that connected an enormous swathe of territory that included the eastern and western halves of Eurasia, North Africa, and most of those societies bordering the Indian Ocean. Within this world of connection, however, not everyone experienced interaction as intensively or even much at all. The historian Janet Abu-Lughod referred to "an archipelago of world cities," marked by the prevalence of long-distance trade, cross-cultural interaction, and cosmopolitanism. The archipelago of world cities contrasted with its alternative -- a vast sea of towns and villages inhabited by people who were much less likely to experience a world beyond their immediate area.

Outside of this Afro-Eurasian core, isolation was even more pronounced. Huge parts of sub-Saharan Africa remained outside the world of long-distance interaction, and the Americas and Oceania remained worlds unto themselves with no connections to Afro-Eurasia and even limited interactions within their regions. So in a sense, and particularly within these seas of isolation, many societies *were* surrounded by protective bubbles within which they were able to develop and maintain their own languages, diets, dress, and philosophical, religious, and political traditions. But this would change. From the 15th to the 18th centuries, exploration would fill in the blank spaces on world maps and help connect previously isolated peoples. Imperial expansion would intensify interactions across large areas, and global trade would help to construct a world of economic interdependence in which conditions on one side of the world could have a massive impact on the other.

Globalization

Globalization is a term we use to describe the effects of growing connections and reduced isolation. It is a concept that is often associated with the contemporary world and therefore is sometimes discussed as if it is a recent phenomenon. There is nothing new about it, however. Globalization has been happening for as long as humans have interacted across distance. What made the globalization of this and later eras distinct from that of earlier periods was the speed, scale and intensity with which it occurred. More interactions across greater distances connect larger numbers of people, and over time, the result is more and more people sharing ways of life that became increasingly less diverse.

That reduction of diversity is a crucial element of globalization. As the bubbles of isolation were punctured, people across the world were exposed to new influences, which in turn reduced or eliminated the importance of local traditions. Indigenous spiritual beliefs across the Americas being influenced or replaced by forms of Christian worship, the spread of Indian cotton textiles to West Africa and Europe, and the Old World's adoption of American domesticates, such as corn, potatoes, sweet potatoes, tomatoes, and chili peppers are all examples of ways in which globalization in this era created a world in which more people, across greater distances, practiced ways of life that were more similar than ever before. Driving this story would be exploration, conquest, and trade.

Exploration

The premodern world was full of monsters. It can be hard for us, living in a time of information overload, to imagine a world where so little was known about so much. In fact, what was unknown far outstripped that which was known, and while the known world is mundane and largely familiar, the unknown world was bounded only by the human imagination. Into that unknown could be projected one's hopes and fears: ferocious horned rabbits (*Al-mi'raj*), humans with dog faces (*cynocephali*), sea monsters that transformed from sparrows to oysters in 1000-year cycles (*shèn*), feathered serpent gods (*quetzalcoatl*), Christian Priest-Kings (Prester John), and cities of gold (Cibola).

One of the reasons that such things could exist is because there were still so many unexplored spaces that they could occupy. Exploration shrunk those spaces and put peoples from around the world in direct contact with each other. Gods and monsters could still exist, but in habitats that seemed to grow smaller by the day. In place of the legendary and mythical stood only plants, animals, and humans, that while unfamiliar, were recognizable. The term "Age of Discovery" has fallen out of favor in recent years because it has so often been used to describe a world divided between active Europeans who bravely explored the world and the "others" who passively waited to be discovered. However, even with the flaws in this traditional use of this phrase, the idea of an "age of discovery" still has usefulness -- if we reject the simplistic active/passive dichotomy and imagine a period in which everyone was engaged in discovery, in which new encounters were forcing people everywhere to confront and reimagine their old assumptions about the world. The world that exploration discovered was one that grew increasingly smaller, increasingly more connected, and increasingly less diverse.

Conquest

While exploration had an enormous long-term impact on the story of world history, it was conquest that had the larger impact on people's lives. From 1400-1700, imperial expansion consolidated an enormous percentage of the world's people into just a few large states. We can conservatively estimate that by 1600 just three empires -- the Ming Empire in China, the Mughal Empire of South Asia, and the global Spanish Empire -- controlled 53 percent of global population. Early modern empires certainly did not influence their subjects as intensively as modern nations do their citizens, but they nevertheless did promote common systems of law, religion, language, currency, and bureaucracy, to name a few examples. In addition, the presence of roads, canals, and heavily frequented sea lanes would encourage movement and interaction within the empire. allowing for more informal exchange of influences amongst imperial subjects. Imperial expansion, therefore, led to tens of millions of people across the globe becoming integrated into fewer political formations while exposing them to a narrower set of influences and, thus, contributing to a more globalized world.

Trade

Silver, spices, sugar, slaves --as a truly global economy emerged in this era, these were among the commodities that drove it. Long distance trade networks already existed by 1400, but largely to supply luxury goods to a small number of wealthy elites. The vast majority of people were still dependent on local production and local exchange. This had not changed for most people by 1700, but nevertheless there had come into being a system of global exchange which transformed patterns of production and consumption.

Specific regions came to fulfill particular roles within this system of increasing economic interdependence:

- Southeast Asia was the source of spices like nutmeg, cinnamon, cloves, and pepper that were so desired from East Asia to Western Europe and even in the still developing European colonies in the Americas.
- India also provided spices but became even more significant for its production of the finest cotton textiles in the world whose lightness, breathability and beautiful colors, patterns and designs made them the more practical alternative to silk among the global elite.

- The islands and coastal regions of the Caribbean Basin emerged as key producers of subtropical plantation crops like sugar and tobacco for the emerging markets of Europe.
- The plantation agriculture of the Americas could not have developed as it did without the labor markets of West Africa through which increasingly large numbers of enslaved people would be shipped across the Atlantic under brutal conditions.
- The mainland Spanish colonies of Mexico and Peru became the largest sources of silver from which the ore then flowed around the world as a kind of global currency.
- Europe itself produced nothing of value to this emergent economy, but Spanish, Portuguese, Dutch, English, and French ships were the dominant carriers of goods among the continents.
- Lastly, at the center of all this was China, the most populous, sophisticated, and productive state in the world. Perhaps more than any other single factor, it was Chinese demand for silver and the world's demand for Chinese products that drove the global economy.

This global economy was still in its infancy by 1700, but had already begun to have transformative effects on local economies, on modes of production and on patterns of consumption across the world.

Exploring the history of the world from 1400-1700 through the lens of emergent globalization reveals a complex, but traceable story. The story begins in a world still very much defined by isolation and ends with a world marked by increasing interconnectedness. Or, to return to the language we began with, this was a story of the seas of isolation being drained, of those bubbles that restricted interaction being popped, and of the innumerable sets of distinct traditions that had once prevailed increasingly being forged into the beginnings of a single world society. In these first two units, then, we will see the manner in which exploration, conquest, and trade would drive the process of globalization and transform the lives of individuals, societies, and environments across the entire world.

Unit 9: The East, 1300-1700
Kenneth J. Hammond, New Mexico State University

Reading: China
In the 1340s central China was struck by the same plague, known as the Black Death, which was devastating Europe. It had apparently spread along the trade routes across Central Asia, reaching both ends of the Eurasian landmass. Millions of people died, and local economic, social, and political systems were dramatically disrupted. The Yuan dynasty, through which the Mongols had ruled China since their conquest of the ancient empire in the middle of the 13th century, proved incapable of effectively responding to the crisis. This was due to the factionalism and infighting among the ruling elite at the capital Dadu, modern day Beijing, and because of corruption and incompetence on the part of local administrators.

Emergence of the Ming Dynasty
The dynasty lost control of much of the country, and local rebellions by desperate people soon coalesced into armies, challenging the power of the Mongol state. Through the 1350s and early 1360s rival military strongmen competed for control, and by 1368 one such leader, Zhu Yuanzhang, succeeded in defeating his rivals and then driving the Mongols out of China. He proclaimed the establishment of a new dynasty, the Ming, and created the foundations for a government which would last for nearly 270 years.

Zhu Yuanzhang had risen from near the bottom of society to become the emperor of China. He had developed a visceral distrust of the old *literati* elite and of merchants and others who he had seen seeking to profit from the suffering of others during the hardships of the plague years. He had a vision of a well-ordered society based on small farmers, and set out to create such a system through limiting both commercial activity and the size of landholdings. But he was also somewhat paranoid about his own power, fearing that his officials were plotting against him, and wanted to know as much as he could about the affairs of his empire.

He oversaw the establishment of a network of roadways over which imperial couriers could carry information from across the empire to the capital, and could relay his edicts and instructions to local officials. This post road system proved effective in government administration, but it also gave rise to unintended consequences. The secure and efficient road system helped facilitate the revival of long distance trade across China, contributing to the renewed growth of the commercial economy which flourished under the Song dynasty (960-1279) but receded under the Mongols. By the middle of the 15th century China's economy was growing steadily, and in the 16th and early 17th century it continued to expand significantly.

Zhu Yuanzhang ruled as the Hongwu emperor until his death in 1398. He was succeeded by his grandson, the Jianwen emperor, but that ruler was soon overthrown by his uncle, who resented being passed over for the throne. Zhu Di became the Yongle emperor in 1402, and is seen as a second founder of the dynasty. He softened some of the harsh elements of his father's rule, and forged a new working relationship with the literati elite, the men who through education and success in the imperial examination system provided the corps of officials to staff the state bureaucracy. The literati were formally recognized through their achievements in cultural life, most notably success in the civil examinations, which tested knowledge of the Confucian ethical doctrines that were the official orthodoxy of the imperial state.

The Literary Elite
But their power was also based in their control over land, the main source of wealth in China's economy. To acquire the education needed for success on the examinations a young man had to study an average of 18 years, and this meant that only families with sufficient wealth to forgo the labor of a young man in the fields could have a chance at producing a successful examination

candidate. The examinations were in theory open to most Chinese men, but the economic barriers to success screened out all but those from wealthy land owning families. Merchants and their sons were barred by law from sitting for the exams, as their wealth was considered morally tainted in classical Confucian thought.

The literati elite was the ruling class of Ming China, and the imperial state served to maintain and protect their interests. The emperor wielded ultimate power, but he relied on the scholar-officials to actually conduct the business of governing. The state was centered on the capital, which from 1420 on was located in Beijing. At the top were Grand Secretaries, who worked directly with the emperor to formulate policy and oversee administration. Six ministries, of Revenue, Personnel, Justice, Public Works, War, and Ritual (which included education and the examination system) ran the day-to-day affairs of state. Outside the capital a hierarchy of provincial and local administration was staffed by officials who served three year terms and were subject to regular performance evaluations. A Censorate existed alongside the regular bureaucracy to monitor the activities of officials at all levels, with the power to denounce corrupt officials directly to the emperor. This system had evolved over the previous millennium and a half, and had become very effective and efficient.

China's Commercial Economy

The rapid growth of China's commercial economy gave rise to the emergence of new elite elements, without access to the examination system, but still eager to compete for status and, when possible, access to power. Merchants became influential through collaboration with established landed elites, as gentry families (another name for the large landowning lineages) began to invest quietly in commercial ventures. But merchants also began to compete with the literati for cultural influence, fostering the growth of an art market, and engaging in forms of patronage such as restoring temples or publishing elegant editions of classical texts. Especially in the market towns and cities of the Jiangnan region, where the Yangzi River flows to the sea, between modern Shanghai and Nanjing, traditional landed elites came to share the cultural arena with men they sometimes saw as commercial upstarts, but whose wealth facilitated their access to, and sometimes control of, cultural resources.

The Ming dynasty enjoyed relative peace and stability through the 15th century and much of the 16th. There were occasional local uprisings, and the Mongols returned as a security concern along the northern border in the 1450s and again in the 1550s, when charismatic leaders managed to assemble cohorts of followers large enough to launch campaigns into Ming territory. Coastal piracy was a serious concern in the middle years of the 16th century as well. But for the most part the dynasty was able to meet the challenges it faced, and to maintain the kind of security and stability which allowed the people to pursue their livelihoods, and the population to increase, reaching perhaps 150 million by the later part of the 16th century.

New Confucian Ideas

The growth of the commercial economy not only produced competition among old and new elites, but also put stress on established hierarchies and ways of thinking. As more and more people lived their daily lives in an environment shaped by market forces, and in which individuals increasingly pursued their economic interests in competition with others, the stage was set for the emergence of new ideas about how the world works. Confucian thought was the broad stream of intellectual culture in China, supplemented by Buddhist and Daoist ideas. Confucianism was not a monolithic system, but encompassed a wide range of schools of thought and interpretation. There was an official state orthodoxy based on the ideas of the Song dynasty philosopher Zhu Xi (1130-1200), but many other versions of Confucian thought persisted as well.

Around the turn of the 16th century a scholar official named Wang Shouren, also known as Wang Yangming, developed new interpretations of Confucian ideas which gained great traction in the dynamic cultural context of commercializing China. Wang emphasized individual moral responsibility and agency, arguing that all people have within them an innate knowledge of the good, and that everyone has an obligation to act on the basis of that knowledge.

In some ways Wang's thought can be seen as analogous to the Reformation ideas of Martin Luther and others in Europe, advocating individual religious conscience and the empowerment of moral individuals through their own access to knowledge, as in reading the Bible in the vernacular, or language of the common people. Some of Wang's followers, known as the Taizhou School, promoted a view of society which emphasized individualism and egalitarianism. This is one of the features of Ming China which makes the use of the label "early modern" appropriate, along with the development of the commercial economy which welcomed the emergence of these new ideas.

Wang Yangming died in 1528. His ideas became widely influential throughout the remaining decades of the Ming. The 16th and early 17th centuries saw the development of China's commercial economy reach its peak before it was disrupted by the transition to the next dynasty, the Qing, ruled by the non-Chinese Manchus. Much of the dynamism of the Ming economy during this period was driven by the influx into China of silver. In the 15th century silver came into China largely from Japan, where new mining operations expanded the available supply. But after the establishment of Spanish colonial rule in the New World in the first half of the 16th century silver began to flow across the Pacific in the "Manila Galleons" ships which sailed from Acapulco in Mexico to Manila in the Philippines, a Spanish possession in East Asia. Silver facilitated commercial activity, and drove other changes in China as well.

Most importantly, the Ming state reformed its taxation system in the third quarter of the 16th century to require payment of taxes in silver rather than in grain or cloth. This had a very positive impact on the commercial economy, and benefited those parts of China where markets were most fully developed. But in other areas, especially the arid northwest, silver remained scarce, and the new policies led to deepening poverty and distress among many poor households. By the early 17th century local unrest began to spread in rural areas, and by the 1630s serious rebellions began to weaken the dynasty. The imperial court was increasingly dysfunctional due to factionalism and corruption, and by the 1640s the Ming state began to collapse. Peasant rebels seized the capital in April 1644, and the last Ming emperor committed suicide.

Emergence of the Qing Dynasty
While the Ming had been weakening, a new force had been rising in what is now northeast China, known as Manchuria. The Manchus were a new tribal alliance of non-Chinese peoples which had grown more powerful and ambitious in the early 17th century. They had been fighting Ming armies outside the Great Wall for more than 20 years when the rebels overthrew the Ming in April 1644. The Manchus were able to enter China proper through the pass in the Great Wall where it reaches the sea east of Beijing, in collaboration with the Ming general in command of the garrison there, Wu Sangui. Together the Manchu forces and Wu's army marched to Beijing and drove the rebels out. The Manchus then announced their intention to stay, and they launched the overall conquest of China and the founding of the Qing dynasty, which was to last until 1912.

It took the Manchus nearly 20 years to fully bring China under their control. But the Qing dynasty was fortunate to have three very competent and diligent rulers come to the throne in the first century and a half of their rule. The Kangxi emperor (r. 1660-1720), the Yongzheng emperor (r. 1721-35), and the Qianlong emperor (r. 1736-95) presided over an age of peace and prosperity in China proper, and of dramatic expansion of the borders of the empire into Central Asia. The modern extent of the People's Republic of China is a legacy of the Manchu conquests. These three emperors oversaw the revival of the Chinese economy, forged an effective diarchy with the literati elite, and managed the affairs of state with confidence and care, becoming model rulers in the Confucian tradition despite their non-Chinese ethnicity.

By the latter years of the 18th century China and the Qing empire began to face new challenges, both domestic and foreign. The productive capacity of the agricultural economy reached a plateau which saw living standards stagnate and then begin to decline. And the rising tide of the Industrial Revolution was about to radically transform the nature of global economic and political relations. But China under the Qianlong emperor remained the wealthiest country in the world, with the most desired products and the longest lasting political order anywhere on the planet.

Reading: New Visions of the City in Early Modern China (Topical Essay)
New Visions of the City in Early Modern China

Kenneth Hammond specializes in the study of China in a comparative and global perspective. He has written widely on the subject of Ming Dynasty China, but his recent work has focused on the urbanization and the rise of cities from the Song through the Ming Dynasties. In this essay, he presents his research on how the Chinese presented cities in maps and cartography. He presents the various genres of cartography in the Ming period and explains the map making process. While early map making in China, as everywhere, had no standard mode of presentation (as it does today), nevertheless, Chinese maps were very detailed and quite accurate. They particularly served well the purposes of traveling merchants.

The painting, Along the River During the Qingming Festival, by the Song dynasty artist Zhang Zeduan (1085–1145) captures the daily life of people and the landscape of the capital, Bianjing, today's Kaifeng, from the Northern Song period. Zhang Zeduan includes the lifestyles of all people of the time from rich to poor, engaging in different economic activities in both the countryside and the city. The painting is renowned and is often called "China's Mona Lisa," because of its great beauty.

When historians divide the past into distinct periods it is often based on specific features which are seen as characteristic of a particular era. The Ancient World is seen as a time of great agrarian empires, while the European Middle Ages are defined by the system of feudalism. In recent scholarly discourse, the idea of the Early Modern period has been widely used to talk about societies in which various developments such as secularism, economic commercialization, increased long-distance trade and communication, or the emergence of "scientific" ways of thinking are found together.

The early modern model was first developed to explain the course of European history from about the 15th through the 18th century. However, it has been expanded and further elaborated upon to make it applicable to other parts of the world, and in this process the chronological parameters of the concept have also been extended.

One of the features often associated with early modernity is the rise of cities, especially cities as marketplaces. Markets and urban centers have existed for millennia in human history, but in the early modern period, commercial cities are much more numerous and occupy a more central place in social and economic life. They form nodes within larger systems of capital accumulation and exchange.

In looking at the history of China, scholars have long recognized that there was a major transformation of economic activity during the Song dynasty (960-1279), which had many manifestations in social and intellectual life. This transformation is often referred to as the Song commercial revolution. One prominent characteristic of this development is the proliferation of market towns and major changes in the organization and functioning of cities, especially in the Jiangnan region of eastern China, where the Yangzi River reaches the sea. This area became the wealthiest, most sophisticated, and most urbanized part of the empire.

As cities became more important and as urban life changed in various ways, cities came to be represented visually in different ways as well. Maps and other views of cities began to appear in increasing numbers and varying formats. In China this process can be seen beginning in the Song dynasty. After a downturn in urban growth during the century and a half of Mongol conquest and alien rule (1230s-1360s), and further decline during the early Ming (1368-1500), the commercial economy revived and spread throughout the empire during the later Ming (1500-1644), and cities were ever more important centers of economic and social life.

My recent research has focused on how cities were represented graphically, especially in maps, in early modern China. Urban cartography is a process of cultural construction. Maps are not simple, direct reflections of the shape and arrangement of urban space. Mapmakers necessarily select particular things for inclusion in the images they produce, and exclude many things as well. This process of selection is shaped by a variety of factors in each instance of cartographic production. How a city is portrayed, how the buildings, walls, roads and waterways, or the way a city is situated with regard to its surrounding geography, all are decisions made by cartographers or those who commission their work.

Chinese cartographers were capable of making maps which depicted urban space with the kind of precision and accuracy we associate with modern, scientific surveying. In 1229 a map of the city of Pingjiang, now known as Suzhou, was inscribed on a large stone stele, almost nine feet tall, to commemorate the completion of a program of urban renewal carried out under the local magistrate Li Shoupeng.

This map (fig. 1) shows the streets and canals of the city in great detail and with exact precision. The map survives in a museum in Suzhou, and even today it can be seen to represent the layout of the old city with reasonable accuracy. The Suzhou stele demonstrates that Chinese mapmakers were able to produce this kind of accurate image by the 13th century. And yet when we examine maps and other graphic images of cities produced over the next few centuries, we often find that they do not embody this kind of technical accuracy, but rather represent urban space in ways which often diverge significantly from the physical reality of place.

Cartographers made choices of what they included and excluded from images of cities, and about how the things which were included were represented. These choices were shaped by the interests or agendas of the people or institutions which were having the maps made. These could vary widely, and early modern city maps in China reveal the range of such interests in specific ways. Here are just a few examples that highlight this phenomenon.

One of the most significant genres in which maps of Chinese cities appeared was the local gazetteer. Gazetteers were produced in great numbers from the Song dynasty on down through later Chinese history. They were local histories and included a wealth of information about the geography, economy, social life, and famous people or events of a particular place. Gazetteers could be produced for a county, a prefecture, a province, or even sometimes for the empire as a whole. Local gazetteers survive in large numbers and have been a great source of information for historians. Gazetteers usually included maps of the locality where they were produced, and these often included cities, such as the county seat or the prefectural capital.

A gazetteer of Suzhou which was produced during the Hongwu era of the Ming dynasty (1368-98) includes a map of the city (fig. 2). This map is clearly much different from the 1229 stele map. The city is shown as a basically square rather than rectangular, space, longer from north to south than east to west in comparison to the map portrayed on the stele. Within the walls of the city the representation of features is much more minimal, and the complex interrelationship of canals and streets is not indicated.

The gazetteer map concentrates on the depiction of buildings of public significance. These include government offices, of note, the county seats of Changzhou and Wu counties, located to the east and west of Suzhou, and the prefectural government headquarters in the central-south part of this city. The government granaries and storehouses are included as well. Government schools and private academies are also shown, reflecting the importance of education in Chinese elite culture. Religious sites, such as temples and monasteries, are clearly indicated. The walls and gates of the city are shown in graphic form, with the crenellations of the wall and the gate towers carefully drawn. Labels on the map show administrative districts. The moat and the waterways connecting Suzhou to the surrounding Jiangnan region are shown, situating the city within the regional social and economic landscape.

The map is rich in some kinds of information, and yet it is not a truly accurate image of the city. It could not be used to determine the distance between places within the walls, though it does suggest the basic spatial relationships between important sites. This is not a navigational aid, but rather a portrayal of a political and social space. Public structures were emphasized while private or residential spaces were neglected. Gazetteers were the products of administrative initiatives, often sponsored by local magistrates or prefects, and this map clearly reflects their concerns with good government and proper social order, basic elements of Confucian political culture.

A very different kind of image of a great city can be seen in a guidebook to Beijing written in 1560 at the height of the Ming dynasty. This short book, about 20 pages of text, includes a map of the city which is grossly distorted in terms of its representation of the shape of the capital (fig. 3). The guidebook was written by a retired government official, Zhang Jue, who had lived in Beijing for more than 20 years, and wanted, as he wrote in a preface to the text, to provide a way for people to visualize the city while holding the book in their hands and without having to leave the comforts of their homes. The book describes the city based on its division into wards, going street by street, in great detail, including accounts of shops, temples, government buildings, markets and workshops, as well as the "eight great sights" of the capital and the surrounding region. It is the earliest such city guide to survive.

The map which accompanies the text is remarkable for its disregard for the actual shape of the city. Beijing is a city built in accordance to the classical Chinese design principles for an imperial capital. As it stood in the middle of the 16th century, the city was comprised of two sections, a basically square area in the north, and a more rectangular southern extension (fig. 4). The overall shape of the city was longer from north to south than it was east to west. Yet the map in Zhang's book shows a space which is much wider east to west than north to south.

Within the walls of the city the visual representation is again very minimal. The great lakes in the northwest part of the city are shown, and there are drawings of a handful of structures, including the Bell Tower and Drum Tower, a simplified image of the Imperial Palace, and four sets of pai-lou, commemorative gateway structures that mark the location of important market areas. Otherwise, the map is dominated by text, specifically the names of the 33 wards into which the city was divided. The names of the wards are given on the map in their approximate location within the city, though there is no indication of the delineation of boundaries between them.

Zhang Jue's book is meant to be a guide to the streets and lanes of the capital, and the richness of its textual detail does indeed provide a very precise account of the layout and dense urban fabric of the city. The map, by contrast, is highly abstract, and would be of little use to anyone trying to find a specific route from one place to another across town.

It does, however, serve as a kind of basic orientation framework, showing the relationship between the location of the wards, and providing a bare minimum of specific information about some of the most basic landmark features of the urban scene. The map would give the reader of the text enough information to locate a particular place discussed in the body of the work within the city, and to see the city in the context of the surrounding region. A handful of important scenic spots, such as the Zhurong Pass, the Lugou Bridge, or the Dongyue Daoist Monastery outside the walls of the city provide a larger geographic context for the capital.

These three maps — the stele map of Suzhou from 1229, the Hongwu gazetteer map of Suzhou, and the 1560 guidebook map of Beijing — illustrate some of the range of cartographic practice in early modern China. As cities became increasingly important as centers of the commercial economy, as well as in their traditional roles as seats of governmental administration, images of urban places proliferated. Chinese cartographers were technically capable of the accurate representation of city spaces, as the Suzhou stele clearly shows.

Yet maps of cities often diverge significantly from the actual physical form of the place being depicted, and cartographers made major choices in what they included and excluded from their maps. The production of cartographic images was always a matter of cultural construction, of creating an image to assert certain interests or agendas. These could be public and administrative, as in the gazetteer map of Suzhou, or private, indeed personal, as with Zhang Jue's guidebook. Many other maps of cities were produced in the early modern period, and these examples offer only the most basic indication of the range and complexity of the choices made by cartographers and their patrons and employers.

Reading: Japan

Between 1350 and 1750 Japan first endured a long period of internal fragmentation and military conflict. Then it embarked on the final phase of its era of warrior rule under the Tokugawa shogunate. This saw the restoration of unity and stability, and also the emergence and flourishing of an urban commercial society within the confines of the samurai regime.

Shogun and Samurai

The mounted warriors known as the samurai, literally meaning 'those who serve,' became the dominant class in Japan in the 12th century, establishing their power over the old imperial elite and creating a military government which effectively ruled the country in the emperor's name. The first period of samurai rule, known as the Kamakura shogunate, ended in 1333, and a second era began by the end of the 1330s, known as the Ashikaga. The Shogun was the top military leader, and he presided over a hierarchy of lords, known as *daimyo*, and their retainers, who in turn were served by ordinary mounted warriors. Each local lord had his own castle, and the samurai lived off the wealth produced by the farming population, which they extracted in the form of taxes and other assessments.

By the middle of the 15th century, though, the power of the Ashikaga shoguns was waning. Disputes over the succession to the shogunal title led to major factional divisions among coalitions of daimyo. In the 1460s a war broke out which engulfed the country for more than a decade. When the Onin War was over, Japan was fragmented politically. The Ashikaga Shogun continued to exercise power in the immediate vicinity of the capital at Kyoto, but the rest of the country was divided into local domains, each under the rule of a daimyo.

Warfare amongst the daimyo was chronic for the next century, a period which became known as the Warring States, or Sengoku in Japanese. This was a time of hardship for many ordinary farming families, and the shifting fortunes of conflict and the insecurity of daily life gave rise in some parts of the country to local self-defense associations. Groups of villages came together, often with the assistance of Buddhist monks, to form pacts pledging mutual aid in times of difficulty and collective responses to threats from outside forces, mainly meaning marauding samurai armies.

The turmoil of the Sengoku period continued into the middle of the 16th century. No individual daimyo was able to establish dominance, and alliances between groups of local leaders generally proved short lived, so that the fragmentation of the country persisted. But in the 1540s new factors entered into the situation which would soon lead to the emergence of forces which could put the country back into a more coherent form. The arrival of the Portuguese in 1542 introduced foreign weapons and ideas. These would become increasingly powerful in the coming decades before being rejected and suppressed, once the country was reunified at the beginning of the 17th century.

Portuguese Traders

Portuguese merchants and soldiers were on a Korean ship which was blown off course and wound up off the island of Tanegashima, off the south coast of Kyushu, the southernmost of the main islands of Japan. The local daimyo sent representatives to report on the foreigners, and the Portuguese were glad to show off their gunpowder weapons. This made a great impression on the samurai. Before long the Japanese began to reproduce, and then refine, the design of European guns. Not all daimyo saw the value of firearms, since the samurai were traditionally warriors of the bow and the sword. And not all domains had the resources to develop a weapons production capacity. But some did, and among these emerged the leaders who would reassemble political unity in the last decades of the 16th century.

In addition to firearms, the Portuguese also introduced Christianity. Soon missionaries were coming to Japan in growing numbers, especially members of the Dominican and Franciscan orders. They found in Japan a social landscape not completely dissimilar to that which they knew in Europe: a fragmented political order dominated by mounted warriors in armor, castles scattered across the land, and a religious system centered on large monasteries filled with robe-wearing monks with tonsured heads. Catholic missionaries began to have great success reaching out to Japanese people who were weary of the chronic warfare and the insecurity of their land. They saw in the Christian message of salvation a source of comfort in their sufferings. Christianity spread quickly, especially in southern Japan.

Hideyoshi

From 1560 through the end of the century a series of three leaders arose who successively put the broken pieces of Japan back into a single order, although it was one which retained significant local autonomy. First Oda Nobunaga began campaigns in central Honshu, defeating neighboring lords and creating the largest area of control in over a century. Nobunaga was assassinated in 1582, and was succeeded by Toyotomi Hideyoshi, one of his subordinate commanders. Hideyoshi pursued the goal of unification further, building on the gains Nobunaga had made, but following some new policies which advanced his goals. Where Nobunaga had often been harsh towards his defeated opponents, Hideyoshi sought to incorporate former foes into his emerging political system. By the end of the 1580s he had effectively reunited the country under his leadership. The line of emperors continued unbroken in the capital at Kyoto, but real power remained in the hands of the samurai elite.

Having defeated his rivals in Japan, Hideyoshi found himself leading a massive military establishment with no one to fight. He conceived the ambition of conquering China, and in the 1590s launched a series of campaigns in Korea meant to take his force into the Ming empire. The Koreans fought fiercely, and Chinese forces came to their support, so the Japanese never reached Chinese territory. But the Imjin Wars, as they are known in Korea, were devastating to the peninsula, as we will discuss later. When Hideyoshi died in 1598, the Japanese forces immediately withdrew.

In the wake of Hideyoshi's death a struggle for dominance ensued. Daimyo, loyal to Hideyoshi's young son, formed one alliance, while followers of Tokugawa Ieyasu, one of Hideyoshi's leading retainers, sought to claim the dominant position for him. In September 1600 a great battle took place at Sekigahara, in which the Tokugawa army decisively defeated the rival coalition, giving Ieyasu the preeminence he had pursued. Three years later he was given the title of Shogun by the emperor, and the Tokugawa shogunate which he created would last until 1867.

The Tokugawa Shogunate

The leaders of the new government faced several challenges. Ieyasu gathered a team of advisors around him, and they crafted a plan for shaping a new order in Japan. They saw four main areas of concern. First, they wanted to suppress the use of firearms. These had played a decisive role in the fighting for reunification and for the establishment of Tokugawa power, but the new leaders saw firearms as dangerous and as inconsistent with the honor of the samurai. Any ordinary farmer could be trained to fire a gun in short order, while the skills of the samurai needed to be refined over a lifetime. The shogunate banned the possession of firearms and conducted a countrywide search for guns. They were confiscated and then stored in warehouses. These weapons were often excellently made, and some were brought out more than 200 years later for use by the Japanese army in the 19th century. But for the time being they were locked away, and the way of the sword once again prevailed.

A second major concern was Christianity. The foreign religion was seen as subversive, and the loyalty of Catholics to the Pope in Rome was unacceptable. A series of measures were taken to restrict and then suppress the practice of Christianity. This led to a massive rebellion in the late 1630s, which was harshly repressed. The Church was driven underground, where secret groups maintained their activities over the next couple of hundred years. The anti-Christian measures went in tandem with the third area of concern, which was the disruptive presence of foreigners. By the 1630s all foreigners were banned from Japan, with the exception of a small community of Dutch traders who lived on a tiny man-made island in the harbor at Nagasaki, far from the imperial and shogunal capitals at Kyoto and Edo (Tokyo). Dutch ships were the only Western vessels allowed to enter Japanese waters, and even this trade was highly restricted. Japan isolated itself from the outside world in order to maintain a stable and secure life for its people.

Within Japan the fourth focus of the Tokugawa founders was the re-establishment of a stable social hierarchy. The chaos of the Sengoku period, and the upheavals of the wars of reunification, had loosened the bonds which held traditional society together. The Tokugawa leaders wanted to restore their idea of a proper order, and especially to reinforce the dominant power of the samurai class. They ordered all people to register as members of one of four classes; samurai, farmers, artisans, or merchants. Some people fell outside these classes, like monks or actors, and they were in a separate group with very low status. These class statuses were hereditary. Social mobility was not the goal.

By the end of the 1630s the new Tokugawa order was firmly in place, and it proved to be in many ways a very effective system. The Shogun presided over a loose network of local lords, who were bound in oaths of loyalty, but who retained significant control over affairs in their own domains. They were obliged to spend every other year in residence at the Shogun's capital in Edo, a system known as alternate attendance.

The country was at peace through most of the Tokugawa years, and the population grew steadily. For the most part the social order envisioned by the founders remained in place. Many samurai had to adjust to a life in which they maintained their status and practiced their martial skills, but in which there were no longer actual wars to fight. Some became professionals of one type or another — doctors, legal experts, or teachers. Others fell on hard times, and samurai debt became a serious problem. But overall the social order remained stable and life generally improved for many Japanese.

Japanese Economy

In one area, though, the 17th and early 18th centuries proved to be quite dynamic. This was the emergence of an urban commercial economy and society. As in China, traditional Confucian thought looked down on merchants. In Japan this meant that commercial profits were not regularly taxed, though samurai lords often exacted various forms of revenue from their commercial subjects. The stable and secure environment of the Tokugawa realm allowed for the flourishing of businesses, and over time major cities like Edo and Osaka grew into early modern metropoli. Production of consumer commodities expanded, and along with a rising class of prosperous merchants and traders a consumer society began to develop. Entertainment quarters became famous for theaters and geisha, and publishers fed an eager market for dramas and stories. By the middle of the 18th century Japan was a prosperous country, with a large and stable core of farmers, and an unintended but very lively urban commercial sector. The warrior elite remained securely dominant, and the country remained secluded from the disruptive influences of the outside world. As the 19th century got underway all that would soon begin to change. But Tokugawa Japan as an early modern society had a long and successful run, setting the stage for the major transformations of the post-samurai age to come.

Reading: Korea and Vietnam

While China and Japan were coping with the effects of their rapidly developing commercial economies and the challenges of administering complex political societies, Korea and Vietnam largely continued to adapt within more traditional social and political frameworks. In Korea a new dynasty was established late in the 14th century which would endure, with ongoing modifications to meet new challenges, until the early 20th. Vietnam, during the period under consideration here, struggled to maintain its independence from China, while also seeking to enhance its capacity for effective governance by appropriating and modifying certain aspects of its large neighbor's imperial system.

Korea

Korea had managed to navigate the difficult years of Mongol dominance in the 13th and early 14th centuries through a combination of overt collaboration and covert, though largely passive, resistance. Some elements within Korean society cooperated more actively with the Mongols, who did not directly administer Korea but rather worked through the existing Korean monarchy to control the peninsula. But much of the political and social elite merely endured Mongol domination, while awaiting the day when they could reassert Korea's independence. With the collapse of Mongol power in China during the 1360s that day arrived.

In the decades immediately following the withdrawal of Mongol influence in Korea the political system struggled to find a new stability, but there were deep conflicts within the state, and between the state and the aristocratic elite. Long simmering tensions between Confucian civil officials and the leaders of the military revived and threatened to plunge the country into internal disorder. By the early 1390s the existing government faced deep challenges. At that point a military strongman named Yi Song-gye seized power and established himself, in 1392, as the ruler of a new dynasty, sometimes known by his family name as the Yi Dynasty, but also referred to as the Joseon Dynasty.

Joseon Dynasty

Yi Song-gye and his immediate successors into the mid-15th century sought to resolve some of the fundamental problems of the Korean political system, and were largely successful in their efforts. Perhaps most importantly, they sought to defuse the tensions between civil and military officials by eliding the distinction between them. The Joseon state promoted the idea of the *yangban*, which means "two groups," civil and military officials, as a single ruling elite. They adapted the Confucian examination system from China, and formally considered officials from both categories to be equal in status. In some ways this can be seen as a sort of compromise or hybridization of the political elite systems of China and Japan, Korea's larger and more powerful neighbors. While in China the civil officials clearly dominated the military, and in Japan the warrior samurai elite controlled both military affairs and civil administration, in Korea the yangban were defined as a blended class which combined the functions of both groups.

The Joseon state flourished through the 15th and 16th centuries. Korea benefited from the growth of the economies of China and Japan, but did not develop the kind of significant commercial sector which was becoming so important for its neighbors. While the royal government recruited officials through its version of the Confucian examination system, the power of the landholding aristocracy remained pre-eminent across the peninsula. The major challenge to Joseon survival came not from domestic issues, but arose as a result of the reunification of Japan. By the last decade of the 16th century, Hideyoshi Toyotomi had largely completed that task and was seeking new arenas in which to deploy the military forces under his leadership. His plan to attack Ming China was based on using the Korean peninsula as the gateway to China. In 1592 samurai armies crossed into Korea.

The ensuing Imjin War lasted from 1592-98 and caused great damage to Korea. Japanese forces never reached China, and Ming armies came across the Yalu River to back up the Korean soldiers who were fighting the samurai. It was only with Hideyoshi's death in 1598 that the war came to an end. The fighting left a devastated economy for Korean rulers to deal with, and the antagonism between Japan and Korea generated by this invasion lingered throughout subsequent centuries. In the wake of this conflict the Joseon state became increasingly concerned with stability and security, and Korea sought to insulate itself from the political affairs of surrounding states.

In the 17th and early 18th centuries, as the Ming dynasty collapsed and the power of the Manchus arose next door, Korea largely shunned involvement in these events while seeking to maintain profitable trade and tribute relations with the vast empire next door. Korean political culture remained closely linked to China. Korean officials often traveled to Beijing to take part in the Qing Confucian examinations in order to enhance their prestige at home. Daughters of prominent Korean families sometimes became consorts of Chinese or Manchu emperors, fostering close ties between the elites of the two countries. Intellectual and cultural influences from China were important in Korea as well. But the Korean kings did not seek to engage in political or military activities outside the peninsula, and were principally concerned with peace and effective governance in their own domain.

Vietnam

While the period from 1350 to 1750 saw only one change in the ruling family in Korea, and that at the very beginning of the era, Vietnam went through a series of changes in rulers. It also faced a renewed effort by China to incorporate the country into the Ming empire. Vietnam had been part of successive Chinese dynasties from the Han through the Tang, but had been successful since the 10th century in creating an independent state, combining elements of Confucian political culture with influences from adjacent Southeast Asian societies such as the Champa kingdom and Khmer empire. After the end of Chinese attempts to reassert control in the early 15th century a series of Vietnamese rulers oversaw the development of new political institutions, with significant influence from Chinese administrative models. By the end of our period Vietnamese territorial expansion south into former Champa and Khmer regions greatly extended the size of the country, and set the stage for internal power struggles which would lead to a new era of rule by the Nguyen family from the late 18th century through the mid-20th.

Like other parts of Eurasia, Vietnam had felt the effects of Mongol power in the 13th and 14th centuries. As the Mongols retreated in the final third of the 14th century, the existing Tran dynasty, which had ruled Vietnam during the previous century and a half, began to falter. A struggle for control of the royal court in Hanoi and the succession to the throne created the opportunity for Chinese intervention at the beginning of the 1400s. Rival factions in Vietnam appealed to the Yongle emperor to legitimize their claims to the monarchy. The Chinese saw this as a chance to bring Vietnam under Ming rule and send a military force to invade the country. From 1407-27 the Ming occupied Vietnam, but local resistance was intense, and once the Yongle emperor died in 1425 the will to persist evaporated and Ming forces withdrew.

Le Dynasty

A new dynasty, founded by a man named Le Loi, the resistance leader against Chinese rule, would remain in place until 1788. During this period the Le rulers styled themselves as emperors and built an administrative system modeled on the Chinese. Confucian officials in Vietnam blamed the weakness and fragmentation of the country, which had undermined the Tran and opened the door for Chinese invasion, on the influence of Buddhism and Buddhist monks at the Tran court. They sought to create a more fully Confucian-dominated state. Government institutions were set up in the same ways as the Ming state, and a Chinese-style legal code was established. Recruitment for government service was done through an examination system, with the Confucian orthodoxy of the Zhu Xi school as the norm, exactly as in Ming China.

The stability brought by the new Le dynasty created conditions which facilitated both economic and territorial expansion. Vietnam's population grew steadily, cultivation of new strains of rice expanded agricultural productivity, and the resulting rise in economic fortunes translated into enhanced revenues for the state through taxation. This in turn gave the Le rulers the power to support Vietnamese settlers who were moving steadily southward, displacing the existing populations of the former Champa kingdom and the Khmer villages of the Mekong River delta.

The successes of the Le state did not mean the Le family enjoyed complete control over the country. Two great families came to wield military power in the northern and southern parts of the empire. In the north the Trinh became the dominant group, providing military support to the Le rulers and in effect, rather as the samurai did in Japan, exercising real power in the emperor's name. In the south the Nguyen family dominated the new territories, also invoking the Le rulers as their legitimate lords, but defying the power of the Trinh. The rivalry between these two families would eventually lead to civil war in the late 18th century, with the Nguyen emerging victorious and presiding over the last Vietnamese dynasty.

The expansion of Vietnam into the Mekong Delta created new social conditions in this part of the country. Maritime trade with other Southeast Asian states gave rise to a commercial sector in the Vietnamese economy which came to provide a significant proportion of state revenues. Migration from southern China and the absorption of the Cham and Khmer populations created a complex ethnic society, within which a community of Japanese emigrants also developed, in part due to the closing of Japan in the early Tokugawa years. While the Le state remained dominated by Confucian officials, Mahayana Buddhism became powerful in southern Vietnamese society. These economic and cultural divergences also contributed to the political fragmentation which would erupt into civil war in the 18th century.

By the middle of the 18th century East Asia was on the brink of a new era of change and transformation. The Manchu Qing dynasty in China presided over perhaps the wealthiest economy in the world, and one of the largest territorial empires. China's commercial economy was linked to the global system through trade at the port of Guangzhou in southern China, and the influx of Spanish silver from the 16th century on had contributed to the dynamic growth of Chinese fortunes. Tokugawa Japan had isolated itself from the disruptive influences of the West, but was also undergoing rapid commercial development which would set the stage for its encounter with the global capitalist economy in the middle of the 19th century.

Korea and Vietnam, by contrast, were maintaining Confucian political orders which ruled over agrarian societies that featured significant Buddhism elements. Each had faced the threat of invasion and domination by their powerful neighbors. However, both had successfully repelled these, the Koreans surviving the Japanese invasions of the 1590s, and the Vietnamese maintaining their independence in the face of Ming forces in the years between 1407-27. Great changes lay ahead for all four of these countries, but in the mid-18th century these would still have been hard to envision. Soon the rising power of the West, driven by the Industrial Revolution, would launch major reconfigurations in global affairs. But that is a story yet to unfold.

Unit 10: The Early Modern West, 1500-1700

Paula Findlen, Stanford University

Reading: The Maritime Expansion of Early Modern Europe

The year 1453 was also the year when the Ottoman Turks captured Constantinople, bringing an end to Byzantium, the eastern half of the ancient Roman Empire. Subsequent efforts to expand Ottoman territory westward diminished the great Venetian trading empire in the Eastern Mediterranean that inspired Marco Polo to travel all the way to China, and brought Turkish ships and armies as far as the shores of southern Italy when they occupied Otranto in 1480-81. The Spanish reconquest of the kingdom of Granada by King Ferdinand and Queen Isabella in 1492 became all the more important in light of these external pressures. Defeating the last Muslim stronghold in Western Europe signaled the strength of Christianity as a potential unifying force. The Spanish reinforced this message by expelling the Jews that same year and eventually expelling the Moriscos (Muslims converted to Christianity) in 1609.

Neither the pope nor the Spanish monarchs who celebrated this victory could anticipate what a nine-year-old Saxon schoolboy named Martin Luther (1483-1546) would unleash when he grew up. Luther, who became an intense, probing Augustinian monk nailed the Ninety-five Theses, enumerating all the problems and abuses of the institutional Church, on the door of the cathedral in Wittenberg in 1517. This first salvo of the Protestant Reformation tore apart a barely reunified Church and held important political, religious, and human consequences for the next centuries.

The Rise of the Portuguese Empire

In 1500, Western Europeans were also in the process of exploring new ways to engage and profit from the world around them. During the late 14th and 15th centuries, the Portuguese used their prowess in shipbuilding and navigation to explore the West African coast in search of lucrative opportunities. They hoped to find the legendary kingdom of Prester John and form an alliance with this Christian monarch. Starting with the capture of the Muslim stronghold of Ceuta on the Moroccan coast in 1415, followed by the conquest of the Madeira, Azores, and Canary Islands, they established fortified trading outposts, known as factories, at strategic intervals. The one built at São Jorge da Mina (now Elmina, Ghana) in 1482 to secure Portuguese commerce in ivory, gold, and slaves still exists today as a reminder of the ways Europe began to transform Africa. Afro-Portuguese ivories and other artifacts that still exist today in many museums are another talisman of how European markets inspired the creation of hybrid artifacts that belonged to both worlds.

By 1483, the Portuguese were in the Kongo, returning to Lisbon with Kongolese emissaries. In 1488, one year after sending an expedition to Ethiopia, Portuguese navigators rounded the Cape of Good Hope. Within a few years, they established a trading partnership with King Nzinga, a Nkuwu of the Kongo, who converted to Christianity in 1491 and took the name of João I to signal his kinship with the Portuguese monarch. Tapping into preexisting Kongolese slave markets and taking advantage of the Kongo's proximity to the island of São Tomé, which became a colonial sugar plantation, the Portuguese became the dominant European presence in Africa until the mid-17th century. King Manuel I proudly informed the pope that the kingdom of Prester John existed, claiming that the Portuguese had found it in Ethiopia in 1521. The rise of Portuguese Asia began with the fusion of commercial acumen and evangelical mission that led the Portuguese to circumnavigate Africa.

When Vasco da Gama made his famous voyage to Calicut in 1497-98, he was surprised to encounter two North Africans on the Malabar Coast who spoke some Genoese and Castilian. European merchants had traveled in this direction for a number of centuries, yet none of the medieval European trading empires established a permanent colony in Asia. Da Gama's return to Lisbon in September 1499 laid the groundwork for the Portuguese monopoly of the spice trade for the next century. King Manuel I grandiosely proclaimed himself "Lord of the Conquest, Navigation, and Commerce of Ethiopia, Arabia, Persia, and India." The Venetian embassy to Lisbon in 1500 ruefully declared that Portuguese commerce had "joined two different worlds," recognizing immediately the threat it posed to their own prosperity. The rapid establishment of Portuguese colonies in Goa (1510), Malacca (1511), and Hormuz (1515) anchored the empire firmly in the East.

The 1517 Portuguese embassy to Canton indicated a desire to extend their reach even further, though the Ming emperors initially had no interest in doing business with these barbarians from the West. By the 1520s, almost half of the Portuguese Crown's revenue came from trade with Africa and Asia. The subsequent creation of a Portuguese colony in Macao (1557) ultimately anchored trade with China and new opportunities in Japan. These were buttressed by the early successes of Jesuit and Franciscan missionaries who converted as many as several hundred thousand Japanese to Christianity by the end of the 16th century. From this point onward, Europeans envisioned a world in which trading islands and fortified ports created a fragile web of connections between Europe and the rest of the world.

Challenging the Portuguese, Negotiating with the Ottomans
Beginning with the Spanish monarchs Ferdinand and Isabella, who employed Christopher Columbus in 1492 to sail west in search of a different route to the East, virtually every European state aspiring to commerce in Africa, Asia, and the Middle East challenged Portuguese claims. They purloined Portuguese maps, debated the legitimacy of their territorial acquisitions, redrew the boundaries, or simply ignored them. They eagerly consumed travelers' accounts of this emerging empire, hungry for any information that might give them the advantage. This was why the Venetian Giovan Battista Ramusio devoted the first volume of his popular *Navigations and Travels* (1550-59) to Portuguese accounts of Africa and the Indian Ocean. When the Mughal emperor Akbar (r. 1556-1605) conquered Surat in 1573, he quickly understood the importance of making inquiries about "the wonders of Portugal and the manners and customs of Europe" and sent an embassy to Goa to find out more about the dominant European power in Asia. They were the *farangi*. This was the Persian term for "Franks" and common throughout Asia as a legacy of the medieval Crusades. These were the people Akbar felt he most needed to know.

During this period, European states also found themselves alternating between war and diplomacy to secure the shifting boundaries between their own territories and the Ottoman Empire. In 1529, Suleiman the Magnificent's troops reached Vienna after defeating the King of Hungary. The Habsburgs responded to the Ottoman challenge on multiple fronts. In the early 16th century, the Spanish began to fortify strategic locations along the North African coast, including Tripoli in 1510. Charles V launched a massive naval campaign to take Tunis from the Ottomans in 1535, and his son, Philip II, took the Strait of Gibraltar in 1564. One year later, the Spanish arrived in the Philippines. With the conquest of Manila in 1571, they established an Asian base from which to threaten Portuguese commerce in Asia. A Spanish embassy to China departed from Manila in 1575. The Americas were not their only prize, and the priorities elsewhere evolved and changed between the 16th and 17th centuries. The Spanish learned from long experience that it was better to negotiate with the Ottoman sultans than make war on them. This was especially important as they faced internal unrest in the European part of the Empire, in the Kingdom of Naples, and especially the Spanish Netherlands.

Throughout the late 16th century, the Spanish continued to dream of ways to conquer China by using their ports in Acapulco and Lima. Surely, however, their experience of waging war against the Ottomans, who gained control of Tripoli, Algiers, and Tunis prior to the Spanish-Ottoman peace of 1580, was a reminder of the perils of venturing too far afield against a powerful foe. The rash young Portuguese king, Sebastian I, died in the battle of Alcácer Quibir on August 4, 1578, attempting to restore the deposed Moroccan sultan Abu Abdallah Mohammed to his throne. Philip II became his heir, leading to a long period in which Spain and Portugal shared the same monarch (1580-1640) but nonetheless kept their empires apart. The more he heard about the size, scale, and complexity of the Ming empire, the less he listened to foolhardy advisors with fantasies of conquering Asia with a handful of ships and soldiers. Instead, Philip II saw the hybrid community that emerged in Manila – Spanish colonists and missionaries, indigenous and Chinese converts to Christianity, mestizos, and a large community of Chinese merchants in Parian – to be a much better way to do business in this part of the world.

Investing in Companies

Northern Europeans witnessed the rise of Iberian empires with envy and strove to find a place for themselves in this new world. Privateers made illicit forays along the African coast and sailed the Indian Ocean. Pilots, sailors, and ambitious men with the kind of expertise that long-distance trade required found employment with the Portuguese and the Spanish, becoming valuable sources of information for their compatriots eager to compete and profit. Increasingly, European states understood that the ability of a state to reach beyond Europe mattered to its political and economic standing within Western Europe.

The English played an especially interesting role in the development of a new approach to collective investment in long-distance trade known as the joint-stock company. Previously, medieval merchants had formed partnerships by drawing up contracts. Joint-stock companies sold shares to many investors to finance long-distance trade with state sponsorship. The Company of Merchant Adventurers to New Lands, formed in London in 1551 with around 240 investors, sought a northeastern route to Marco Polo's fabled Cathay and from there to the Spice Islands. Only one of the three ships attempting the initial voyage in 1553 returned the following year, carrying a letter from Tsar Ivan IV addressed to Queen Elizabeth I that welcomed trade between the two nations. Thus, the Muscovy Company was born in 1555, the first of many joint-stock companies throughout Europe founded between the 16th and 18th centuries. This approach to investing in long-distance enterprise was a distinctly early modern phenomenon.

While some companies made the Americas the object of their interest, many others focused on Africa, the Middle East, and especially Asia. Towards the end of the 16th century, the number of companies proliferated, first in England – the Venice Company, the Barbary Company, the Turkey Merchants, the Spanish Company, and the Levant Company – and then in the Netherlands. The English East India Company, which emerged in 1600, and the Dutch East India Company, founded in 1602, became the most influential and long-lasting. They claimed the right to trade anywhere, declaring themselves exempt from the treaties of Tordesillas (1494) and Zaragoza (1529), agreements made between two Catholic nations with the assistance of the pope. More importantly, they ignited a debate about whether any nation could possess the sea. The Dutch jurist Hugo Grotius's *The Freedom of the Seas or the Right Which Belongs to the Dutch to Take Part in the East India Trade* (1609) subverted this as a legal principle.

When we look at a map, both England and the Netherlands are among the smallest regions of Western Europe. Like Portugal, they were seafaring nations that aspired to more than they naturally possessed. The rise of the English East India Company occurred after the defeat of the Spanish Armada in 1588 during an era in which the English willingly sought alliances with Morocco, Persia, and even the Ottomans. Not only were they seeking to expand the spheres in which they did business, but they held the goal of explicitly allying with Spain's enemies. The Dutch East India Company arose in the midst of the Dutch revolt against Spanish rule, which led to their independence in 1648, but focused more of their energy on transforming Portuguese Asia into the Dutch Batavia. Historians have described the Portuguese-Dutch wars of the 1630s as the "first world war" because they took place on four continents and the open waters between them. The Portuguese retained Goa, but little else remained of their once-thriving commercial empire.

The Dutch Commercial Empire

By the mid-17th century, the Dutch were indisputably the most profitable of the European trading nations. The Dutch trading post established in Bantam, Java in 1603 became the nucleus of Dutch Batavia in 1619. The Dutch took advantage of anti-Portuguese sentiment in Japan that had been accentuated by the violent suppression of Christianity in the early 17th century. They became the only European nation to enjoy trading rights with Japan after the failure of the English factory at Hirado (1613-23) and the expulsion of the Portuguese in 1639. In 1624 they occupied Taiwan, and in 1641 they gained control of Malacca, wresting the spice trade away from the Portuguese while systematically taking over most of the Portuguese trading outposts in Africa, including the Cape of Good Hope in 1652. There they laid the foundation for the rise of a new society known as

Afrikaners (South-African born whites of European descent), a term first used in 1707 to describe a colonial society with its own language. Many leagues to the east, the Chinese and Japanese concluded that the Northern Europeans known throughout East Asia as the "Red Hairs" – to distinguish them from the largely dark-haired Iberians known as "Southern Barbarians" – were here to stay. Almost one million Europeans traveled to Asia on Dutch ships in the 17th and 18th centuries.

In the 17th century, both England and the Netherlands promoted an aggressive strategy of long-distance commerce and warfare at the expense of the Iberian empires that preceded them, at times partners and at times fierce competitors in the pursuit of empire. Both societies shared a sophisticated understanding of the relationship between capitalism, commerce, and empire. The Amsterdam Stock Exchange, founded in the same year as the Dutch East India Company, became a place to buy and sell shares in this new venture, invest in commodities, and assess profit and risk. Most importantly, it encouraged individuals to invest their personal wealth in the growth of a commercial empire.

During the greatest period of Dutch prosperity, England found itself in the midst of a Civil War, followed by an interregnum after the execution of Charles I in 1649. Internal political problems diverted their attention from enticing external possibilities. The restoration of the English monarchy in 1660 renewed investment in the empire, including the building up of the British navy which allowed them to increasingly challenge the Dutch, at home and abroad. A new company focused on Africa emerged in 1660 to become the Royal Africa Company by 1672. Charles II's marriage to Catherine of Braganza produced the ill-fated acquisition of Tangier from Portugal in 1661, over vocal opposition by the Spanish and the Dutch. Despite costly investment in its harbor and defense, English Tangier's greatest threat proved to be the Moroccan sultan and Barbary pirates, leading to a complete withdrawal by 1684, recognizing that the establishment of the East India Company in Madras (1639), Bombay (1661), and Calcutta (1690) was a much sounder investment. The British did not have a direct foothold in the Mediterranean until the Treaty of Utrecht ceded Gibraltar to them in 1713. This strategic outpost played an essential role in naval security and transshipment for the modern British Empire, and its sovereignty is still contested by Spain.

Observing the Dutch and the English successfully subverting the Iberian empire, other European nations renewed their efforts to establish a commercial presence in Asia. The Danish Crown chartered its East India Company in 1616, followed by the French (1664), Swedish (1731), and the Austrians (1775). None enjoyed the success of Great Britain as an 18th-century empire. While the Dutch remained the sole European nation to trade with Japan until 1854, the British parlayed their East India Company into the control of the Indian subcontinent. In 1717 they began to trade directly with China. With the conquest of Bengal from the Mughals in 1757, the defeat of the French during the Seven Years War (1757-63), and the exploration of the Pacific in the next decade, Great Britain took an important step towards becoming a global empire.

In the late 18th century, as the number of Dutch ships sailing to the East Indies declined, London ballooned into a sprawling, cosmopolitan metropolis, becoming a city of one million by the end of the century. The world population had almost doubled since 1500 but even in light of this growth, the transformation of London from a city of around 60,000 in 1500 to one of the largest cities in the world was notable. Its thriving Royal Exchange surpassed Amsterdam's stream of capital. India cotton, Chinese tea and porcelain, and African slaves fueled this spectacular growth. The Dutch East India Company dissolved itself in 1795. The British had only recently ceded parts of North America to a new nation, but their presence in other parts of the world was greater than ever.

Reading: The Political Economy of Early Modern Europe

The traditional perception of the medieval feudal order was never unilaterally in force across Europe. This view held that the common people worked the land and served the needs of powerful landed nobles and bishops. In turn, the nobles and bishops provided armed forces and spiritual guidance. One of the goals of a very stable system was to secure obedience to a powerful prince.

Conversely, ambitious men and women — entrepreneurial merchants, sailing captains, talented artisans and artists, adventurous soldiers, and politically savvy priests — could always find a pathway from the lower rungs of society into the higher circles of power. In fact, the most dynamic and wealthy area in late medieval Europe was northern Italy, where the merchant class formed republics that exceeded the influence and power of most royal courts. But the several crises of the late medieval period, from the Black Death (1347-1348) to the Protestant Reformation (1517), frayed the fabric of the feudal robe of authority and morality even where it was most pervasive. Under these conditions, princes proved to be the most nimble in capturing the loyalty of entrepreneurial or ambitious citizens and adapting to changing circumstances.

Population Growth

After losing between a third and half of the European population to the Black Death, or plague, of 1347-1348 and the many epidemics that followed in the next 100 years, Europe managed by 1500 to recover to its 1340 population level. Population growth continued with a strong upward trend, reaching 61.6 million in 1500, 70.2 million in 1550, and 78 million in 1600. The distribution of population across the continent was also shifting. Northwestern Europe (especially the Low Countries and the British Isles) witnessed the most vigorous expansion. The population of cities also grew more rapidly than the countryside. In 1500, only 5.6 percent of the total population were city dwellers. This number grew to 7.6 percent by 1600. As kings placed their courts in larger cities — -Naples, Rome, Madrid, Paris, Vienna, and later London and Moscow — and marshaled the resources of society in their favor, these cities exploded in size. Commercial ports, which might also have been capitals, formed a second tier of large cities — Venice, Livorno, Seville, Lisbon, Antwerp, Amsterdam, Bremen, and Hamburg.

Population dipped slightly in the 17th century. Part of the cause was a series of religious wars lasting from 1550 to 1650. For a variety of reasons, both confessional and political, kings were divided. Some allied on one side with Catholicism and the Church, and others allied with the Protestants inspired by the priest Martin Luther to challenge the spiritual and political authority of the Church. These struggles culminated in the bloody Thirty Years' War (1618-48) that had drawn in most of the monarchs of Europe to wage war at one time or another, almost all on German soil. Six million are estimated to have died in the process.

But nature, in the form of the Little Ice Age, also contributed to a pause in mid-17th century growth. Around 1645, astronomers noted with their new invention — the telescope — that there were no sunspots, and northerners reported that the *aurora borealis*, or Northern Lights, bright lights which occur in the sky near the Arctic, had seemed to disappear. There was clearly a decline in solar energy for several decades, and the earth cooled as a result. Winters became harsher and summers wetter, and the amount of arable land shrunk, much of it covered with snow or flooded and turned into swamps by too much rain. The growing season was shortened by approximately a month. With most of the European population living near subsistence levels, the Little Ice Age had a devastating effect, especially on Europeans living in the northern reaches of the continent.

World of Capital

Natural disasters like the plague or the Little Ice Age, as well as man-made catastrophes, however, only seemed to alter the balance of the factors of production — labor, land, and capital — away from feudalism. The new system — capitalism — would allow a free market to determine the allocation of resources. Money, or capital, became increasingly important, especially in relationship to land. In the 16th century, capital flowed toward technology. Investments in agricultural tools increased labor productivity. The new technologies made food more available, and prices dropped. Throughout the 16th and 17th centuries, the falling food prices devastated land owning aristocrats, but lower prices helped common men and women. They increasingly had room in the budget to buy merchants' manufactures.

Technology brought great changes. It dramatically improved industries such as shipbuilding or firearms and munitions, both of which became very important to these centuries. It could also create industry in the manner the movable type printing press created the book industry. Peasants moved from country to urban settings with the goal of becoming artisans or merchants. The 16th century became known as the "bourgeois century." Europeans were gaining something they never had before — a technological edge over all other civilizations.

Most historians pinpoint the beginning, or at least the maturation, of Western capitalism in the 16th century. Over the next 200 years, two broad trends can be discerned. The first was the shift of capital from the Mediterranean to the Atlantic seaboard — a movement from Venice, Florence, and Milan to Amsterdam and London. Even more important was the gap between Eastern Europe, where capital remained largely locked up in estates, and Western Europe, where conditions were more favorable to enterprise. In the East, the landowning class managed to achieve political independence from their monarchs, weakening them. The towns declined and the propertied class, though divided by many rivalries, were still successful in reversing the fate of workers — reducing the peasantry everywhere to servitude.

Workers in the West also served, but they could more readily become merchants. Western entrepreneurs began to employ management practices that increasingly required workers to adhere to a clock and not merely a season, their labor quantified and paid accordingly. Ultimately, workers would be prepared psychologically for the factories of the 18th and 19th centuries. Long supply lines for industries were developed and maintained across Europe. For example, the shipbuilding supply line extended back to lumbermen in forests and sailcloth weavers, rope makers, and blacksmiths in towns. Each delivered goods according to specifications in quality, quantity, and time dictated by the shipbuilders.

Merchants became more efficient and broader in their thinking about how to link markets. Insurance, brokerage, and credit-trading facilitated international dealing and amassing of capital. Medieval fairs had long counteracted the isolation of regional economies. Now in Lyon, Hamburg, and Danzig merchants could encounter price lists, auctions, and specialization in certain commodities. Merchants also needed information which they acquired through the burgeoning business of newspapers; by 1753 the sale of newspapers exceeded seven million.

The more powerful monarchs of France, England, Spain, Burgundy, Sweden, and Portugal and forward-looking city governments assisted trade and commerce by building roads, harbors and docks, market plazas, lighthouses, navigation charts, and canals that linked rivers. Strong monarchs, particularly in the 18th century, broke down the medieval customs of tolls on roads and special tariffs or taxes on particular goods which promoted local and regional monopolies which had been detrimental to long-distance trade.

Across Western Europe, merchants adopted the existing Italian practices of bills of exchange and double-entry bookkeeping. In 1660, banking facilities had been severely harmed by princes who borrowed money readily and then reneged on their debts. The largest banking family in Europe, the Fuggers, were ruined by their princely debtors. Later, German, Dutch, and English bankers managed to bring order and regulation to the industry to prevent such failures. Joint-stock companies formed to spread the risk in the dangerous business of shipping goods by sea.

The Atlantic Revolution
At the same time that Europeans were reorganizing the continent for a dramatic cycle in the growth of wealth, they also navigated to the Americas, Africa, and Asia, introducing even more complex opportunities and challenges for their political economy. Arguably the encounter with the Americas was the most profound phenomenon. The important difference was that Africa and the Far East were trading zones, where Europeans obtained slaves, raw goods, and manufactured goods, negotiating with local and regional traders. In the Americas, they were colonists first and traders second. While the Natives of the Americas did engage in substantial trade with Europeans

in some raw goods that were difficult to acquire such as beaver pelts, Europeans generally took over or developed the systems of extraction of raw goods from the American continents using the Native labor. By colonizing the labor, they had to relocate some Europeans into the Americas, who in the course of the 16th and 17th century learned how to colonize and develop these zones, and then link up their trade into the existing markets and networks of Europe. By the 18th century, the Atlantic had become a critical component of European economies.

When the Portuguese in 1498 opened direct maritime links with India and the East Indies, and by the late 16th century China and Japan, the Italian merchants who had managed the old Silk Road trade from the East, in Venice and Genoa, faced for the first time competition from the Atlantic ports, first Lisbon and Antwerp, and later London. The Italians were quick to recognize the possibilities of the new western routes to the Far East and jumped into the early navigational enterprises. They provided sailors like Christopher Columbus and funding to the Spanish and Portuguese expeditions. But it was London, Lisbon, and Amsterdam that became the ports of both American and Asian trade. This did not happen right away. The 16th century was still governed by the powerful late-medieval trade networks that made a city like Venice a jewel of beauty and wealth. But in the mid 17th-century crisis, the old merchant networks that flowed through Venice and the Hanseatic League faltered.

There was one thing that the Americas provided for Europe that was essential from the very beginning — silver. By mid-16th century, the Spanish had figured out how to efficiently apply mercury to silver deposits and turned the small mountain of Potosi in their new colony of Peru into the largest silver lode the world had ever seen. The Spanish minted the silver into a 25 gram piece called a peso, or sometimes called "pieces of eight." From about 1550 to 1850, the Spanish treasure fleet transported the equivalent — in today's prices — of a half trillion US dollars, 66 percent of which went directly into the European economy. The rest went to Asia, where Europeans had to pay for goods manufactured there (superior in quality to those from Europe) with silver. Spanish silver created a beneficial gradual price inflation over the centuries. It helped the everyday merchant, though not necessarily the Spanish Crown. It also obviated the need for paper currency, which had been attempted several times in parts of Europe — only to fail.

The Rise of the Sovereign

In the 15th century, the political life of Europeans generally revolved around the gentry, a privileged minority. Common people saw themselves less as citizens than as the clients of a great lord or local interests that were definitely, but distantly, tied to a king. But medieval corporative bonds had already begun to fray by 1500. When the interests of their king, lord, and bishop diverged, it left common people in a dilemma about where to place their loyalty. As the aristocracy lost economic power and the Church was challenged by the Protestant revolt, the monarchs of Western Europe were left in a commanding position. And they began to provide the common people with new theories of citizenship in a nation-state embodied by a sovereign.

Not surprisingly, war was the means by which this new national identity was forged. From the Italian Wars starting in 1494 to the Treaty of Westphalia in 1648 which ended the Thirty Years' War, Europe, in one region or another, was almost constantly in a state of war. Often, the war aims of kings were rather traditional, such as when Henry VIII kept provoking the French over his useless claims to lands in France, or Charles V traveling all over Europe trying to hold together a Holy Roman Empire that was breaking apart from confessional politics. Yet another example was Philip II of Spain spending unheard of amounts of money to send armies to the north of Europe in a losing effort to hold onto his old Burgundian inheritance. But the processes of war and statecraft that they employed to reach goals helped to create a sense of nationality in the courts of kings and opportunities for ambitious young men.

Kings developed permanent embassies in each others' courts and diplomatic networks, which allowed them to not only represent nations but also to spy on each other in order to learn how to maintain their own national security as well as forward the goals of kings. When banking families stopped loaning money to kings in the 16th century, a rising class of professional administrators, unconnected to aristocracy, stepped in to fill the role of the king's executive. Most famously, Henry VIII relied upon Thomas Cromwell, the son of a blacksmith, to centralize fiscal administration and bureaucracy in England.

Then there was the military revolution, led by enterprising princes and their generals. They employed new gunpowder technology and new tactics of war. They organized units of men with newer and cheaper guns, created specialized methods for the use of cavalry and artillery, and learned to coordinate efficiently large armies. The Spanish called the Dutch Republic the "plaza of war," because it was the place where many of these experiments in the military revolution were first attempted. The Spanish themselves innovated the strategies necessary to organize long supply lines to support massive armies, in their case, from Spain to Italy, and north to the Low Countries of northern Europe.

Increasingly, monarchs found that recruiting soldiers from their own citizenry was more effective and reliable than paying mercenaries or depending on their impoverished nobles to raise armies and pay soldiers out of their own pockets. The patriotic French citizen soldiers of Napoleon's powerful armies in the late 18th century proved the value of this long-term development. As nations came under attack by sea, the Dutch and the English began to regularize early sea-going merchants and adventurers into ships-of-the-line, and then navies, to protect the homeland, as happened in 1588, when the Spanish Armada was met and destroyed by a talented English fleet. By the end of the 18th century, the British had a powerful navy that controlled not only the English Channel but the Atlantic Ocean.

During the 16th and 17th centuries, there was only one great external threat to the European rulers, Suleiman the Magnificent (1494-1566). As Sultan of the Ottoman Empire, he attempted to invade Eastern Europe and made a bid to control the Mediterranean Sea from his imperial base in modern-day Turkey. His land venture was partly successful, and his armies reached the gates of Vienna. However, after the 1560s, European ships of the alliance of Charles V, and later his son Philip II, and the doge of Venice, kept the Turks at bay. After that, the Europeans had the great fortune of forging nation-states, sorting out the powerful from the less powerful, and practicing the art of war on one another without external threat or interference for the rest of the early modern period.

Reading: The African Slave Trade

Slavery, or the forced labor of humans by humans, has been common in all parts of the world since the Neolithic revolution in agriculture about 11,000 years ago. Written records dating back to 4,000 BCE refer to slavery as a well-established institution. There were actually various forms of slavery in ancient and medieval times. The most familiar to us is what is called chattel slavery, where the human being is considered a piece of property.

As in all other parts of the ancient world, in Africa, these forms of slavery were common practices. However, systematic capture and removal of slaves to other continents was not common. The one exception was in the ancient Roman world. North African Romans purchased African slaves in the Trans-Saharan trade, but this trade was relatively small compared to the European slaves of the Roman Empire. The exploitation of African chattel slavery on a large scale began after the 7th century — first through the Arab slave trade, and then later and more massively, in the Atlantic slave trade. During approximately 10 centuries, Africa became a human commodity zone for global trade.

The Arab Slave Trade

The process of integrating the African slave trade into the Arab trading network from the 7th century onward was gradual. Arab slave traders had a dilemma. The Qu'ran allowed slavery; it simply did not allow a Muslim to turn a fellow Muslim into a slave. Therefore, as slave traders in the Middle East converted to Islam in the 8th and 9th centuries, they had to seek a supply of slaves from just beyond the frontier of Islam. Arab traders had been trading, including minor slave trading, with the coast of East Africa for centuries. The slave trade consisted of Africans bringing Bantu-speaking people from the interiors of modern-day Kenya, Tanzania, and Mozambique to the Swahili coast, where Arab traders bought and shipped them to the Middle East. The other route was African slaves brought from Central and West Africa north to slave markets on the edge of the Sahara Desert and then shipped by Arab traders in caravans across North Africa to Egypt and the Middle East. These slaves were used mostly for domestic slavery as servants but also as eunuchs to guard the harems, where wealthy Arabs kept their wives and concubines, or as soldiers in special army units. Some chattel slaves were used in mines and to perform other dangerous labor.

Larger slave market opportunities, however, presented themselves as Arab traders began to dominate ports and shipping routes in the Indian Ocean in the 9th-11th centuries. Increased market access meant increased demand for slaves and, therefore, increased enslavement of Africans. We do not have numbers about the medieval slave trade in Africa that served these Arab ports and markets, but estimates for the entire trade are 17 million for more than a millennium, or thousand years, of trade. Trade for the period 1500-1900 CE equaled as many as five million. Clearly the trade began to diminish about the same time as the Atlantic slave trade in the latter half of the 19th century. The main Arab slave outpost in the 19th century was Zanzibar, and it is estimated to have sold 25-50,000 slaves in that century. As Europeans began to colonize Africa in 1870-1900, they shut down the coastal markets and major centers for slave trading in the cities, relegating trading to smuggling operations. While the Arab slave trade was not as intense or large as the Atlantic slave trade, it lasted much longer — from about the 7th century until the 1960s — in one form or another.

The Atlantic Slave Trade

The next phase of Africans being sold as commodities into a global market is the Atlantic slave trade, which began in the 15th century and lasted until the late 19th century. This was almost wholly a chattel slave market. The slaves were owned as property. Some performed domestic duties, but they generally lacked legal rights and their masters could do with them as they pleased, including holding them as sex slaves. The primary use of the slaves, however, was as field labor to man plantations and factories that produced extremely lucrative, globally traded products — silver and gold, sugar, tobacco, indigo, rice, and cotton — with particularly brutal consequences. At least 12 million Africans were transported across the Atlantic to the Americas in the approximate four centuries of this trade.

Portugal and Plantation Slavery

The Portuguese were the first Europeans to enter Africa in a direct trade. Portugal's initial interest in Africa was gold and cutting out the Saharan traders who had managed the gold trade of interior Africa for centuries. The rich gold fields of Bure and Bambuk in West Africa could only be reached by the Sahara. But by the mid-15th century, the Portuguese had learned to sail along the African coast and set up trading in gold at Senegambia, near the gold region. They also began to include small numbers of African slaves in the holds of their ships, mostly for domestic servitude in European households. By the close of the 15th century, 10 percent of the population of Lisbon, Portugal, then one of the largest cities in Europe, was of African origin. The Portuguese continued exploration down the coast of Africa and began to develop commercial and political relations with Benin (present-day Nigeria) and the Congo, putting them in touch with other domestic slave markets.

The accessibility of these slave markets, however, would not have been useful if confined to selling domestic slaves into Europe, which had sufficient labor to meet needs. But the Portuguese soon began to develop sugar plantations on islands off the coast of Africa that they had settled as part of their African expedition — the Madeiras, the Cape Verdes, and the island of São Tomé. This was a perfect climate for growing sugar cane, but it required a lot of labor. Not only did the islands not have the indigenous labor, it was backbreaking and dangerous labor that made for short lives. Nevertheless, sugar was a highly desirable commodity in Europe and made extremely good profits for the Portuguese. Some economists regard sugar, after gold and silver, as the first great global commodity. The Portuguese brought in a steady and replenishing supply of slaves to these islands and organized the process of "factories" for sugar production on a large plantation scale.

By the middle of the 17th century, the slave trade entered its second and most intense phase. The creation of ever-larger sugar plantations and the introduction of other crops such as indigo, rice, tobacco, coffee, cocoa, and cotton would lead to the displacement of an estimated seven million Africans between 1650 and 1807.

African Enslavement

While European and Arab traders purchased slaves at entrepots on the coasts and in the desert, they did not capture the slaves. Enslavement was an African occupation. Who could become a slave? Potentially anybody. Alleged criminals and witches and social misfits could find themselves sent to the international slave trade, along with rebels and debt peons whose family members could not protect them. Though kidnapping was a crime in many African communities, the lure of profits in the slave trade led to gangs of kidnappers and widespread abductions and raids on villages. But the pretext for most African enslavement was war. And some historians argue that the slave trade itself encouraged more of these struggles, especially among African kingdoms in and near the major slave zones.

By 1650, the kingdom of Oyo had become a consolidated imperial power in the interior of the Bight of Benin by defeating the Bariba and Nupe in the north and other Yoruba states to the south. The wars between various Gbe groups resulted in the rise of Dahomey and its victory over Allada in 1724. These wars accounted for the deportation of over a million Africans along the Bight of Benin coast. The Akan wars of the late 17th century and the first half of the 18th century were a struggle for power among states in the Gold Coast hinterland. Akwamu, Akyem, Denkyira, Fante, and Asante groups battled for more than half a century for control of the region. By the mid-18th century, Asante emerged as the dominant force.

The 60-year period of the Congo civil wars, ending in 1740, was responsible for the capture and enslavement of many. The spread of militant Islam across West Africa began in Senegambia during the late 17th century. The jihad, or holy war, led to two major political transformations: the emergence in the late 18th century of the Muslim states of Futa Jallon in the Guinea highlands and Futa Toro on the Senegal River. The jihad movement continued into the 19th century, especially with the outbreak of war in 1804 in the Hausa states (northern Nigeria). After 1700, the importation of European firearms heightened the intensity of many of the wars and resulted in a great increase in the numbers of enslaved peoples.

But at a higher level, the political fragmentation — many small centralized states and federations — made it virtually impossible to develop methods of government that could effectively resist the impact of the slave trade. Even the largest states, such as Asante and Oyo, were small by modern standards. Personal gain and the interests of the small commercial elites who dominated trade routes and ports worked against the freeing of captives, offenders, and displaced children, who could easily end up in the slave trade.

Traders and Trade

Western European countries established distinct national trades. The European port cities most involved in this growth industry were Bristol, Liverpool, and London in England; Amsterdam in Holland; Lisbon, the Portuguese capital; and Nantes, located on the western French coast. On the African side most captives were traded from several ports: Luanda (Angola), Whydah (Bight of Benin), Bonny (Bight of Biafra); and the adjacent "castles" at Koromantin and Winneba on the Gold Coast accounted for at least a third of the Africans transported to the Americas. Other major ports included Old Calabar (Bight of Biafra), Benguela (Southern Angola), Cabinda (north of the Congo River), and Lagos in the Bight of Benin. Altogether, these nine ports accounted for at least half of all the Africans deported to the Americas.

Europeans competed with one another for these ports, building fortified slave "castles," or factories. The trade was propelled by credit flowing outward from Europe and used by merchants to purchase men, women, and children in West Africa. They advanced goods on credit in lieu of payment in captives, including cowry shells, strips of cloth (often imported from India), iron bars, copper bracelets (manillas), silver coins, and gold. But firearms were the most valued exchange commodity in the Gold Coast wars of the 18th century. Interestingly, the slave castles had their guns fixed to face the ocean, as their greatest danger was from other European nations not the Africans.

The Middle Passage

The slave trade was a high-risk enterprise. The commodity was people; they could escape, be murdered, commit suicide, or fall victim to epidemics or natural disasters. The European insurance industry was built up in the 17th century to cover the risk of ocean-going shipping, but most particularly slave shipping. On the first leg of their three-part journey, often called the Triangular Trade, European ships brought manufactured goods to Africa; on the second, they transported African men, women, and children to the Americas; and on the third leg, they exported to Europe the sugar, rum, cotton, and tobacco produced by the enslaved labor force. There was also a direct trade between Brazil and Angola that did not include the European leg. Traders referred to the Africa-Americas part of the voyage as the "Middle Passage" and the term has survived to denote the Africans' ordeal.

Well over 30,000 voyages from Africa to the Americas have been documented. The dreadful Middle Passage could last from one to three months and epitomized the role of violence in the trade. Based on regulations, ships could transport only about 350 people, but some carried more than 800 men, women, and children. Branded, stripped naked for the duration of the voyage, lying down amidst filth, enduring almost unbearable heat, compelled by the lash to dance on deck to straighten their limbs, all captives went through a frightening, incredibly brutal and dehumanizing experience.

Mortality brought about by malnutrition, dysentery, smallpox, and other diseases was very high. Depending on the times, upwards of 20 percent died from various epidemics or committed suicide. Venture Smith, describing his ordeal, wrote: "After an ordinary passage, except great mortality by the small pox, which broke out on board, we arrived at the island of Barbadoes: but when we reached it, there were found out of the two hundred and sixty that sailed from Africa, not more than two hundred alive." It was not unusual for captains and crew to toss the sick overboard; and some even disposed of an entire cargo to collect the insurance rather than try to sell a small cargo of sickly slaves.

Africans in the Americas

About 80 percent of all African slaves ended up in the Caribbean and Brazil. While there were many industries in these areas, sugar was the most prominent product of the Caribbean and Brazil; thus, the close association between sugar and slavery. The slaves came primarily from Senegal and Gambia on the west coast of Africa, Ghana along the slave coast, and the Congo and Angola.

In the past, American historians regarded slavery in the South of the US as more of a traditional institution than an economic one. In other words, slavery was an inefficient institution that slaveholders hung onto for cultural reasons. But recent economic histories have demonstrated that the slaves were quite valuable and made up a good portion of the wealth of slaveowners. In 1860, just before the Civil War, the purchase of a "prime" or young adult male slave would have cost $150,000 in 2016 dollars. And that was double the price the slave owner would have had to pay 14 years earlier. Purchasing a slave was an enormous investment, and it is hard to imagine that it was done strictly for tradition. In fact, the total wealth value of all slaves living in the South was 13 trillion dollars in 2016 dollars. In the 1850s, that total wealth value had grown 40 percent, compared to about 25 percent for non-slave wealth growth in the US economy. Slaves represented about 50 percent of total wealth in the South in 1860. Though it is difficult to think of human beings as objects or machines, in fact, slaves were the most valuable single commodity in the US economy. Their collective human labor was responsible for the building of the American economy in several regions of the country. In other slave zones, like Brazil and the Caribbean, they were almost wholly responsible for the building of modern economies.

The Suppression of the Atlantic Slave Trade

The third and final period of the transatlantic slave trade began with the ban on the importation of captives imposed by Britain and the United States in 1807, which lasted until the 1860s. Brazil, Cuba, and Puerto Rico were the principal destinations for Africans, since they could no longer legally be brought into North America, the British or French colonies in the Caribbean, or the independent countries of Spanish America. Despite this restricted market, the numbers of deported Africans did not decline until the late 1840s. Many were smuggled into the United States. In the early 19th century, the British navy was given standing orders to board and remove the slave cargoes of all slave ships they encountered in the Atlantic. Tens of thousands of Africans rescued from the slave ships were forcibly settled in Sierra Leone, Liberia, and several islands of the Caribbean. Nevertheless, more than 3.3 million African slaves were successfully transported to the Americas between 1801 and 1867, the vast majority to Brazil and Cuba.

Reading: The Rise of Muscovy
The Initial Rise of Muscovy

Most people do not know that the cultural heart of modern-day Russia, its origins, do not lie in Moscow. Rather, the Slavic peoples who lived in a region around the city of Kiev called Kievan Rus" formed the first distinctive Russian civilization. From the 9th through the 11th century, Kievan Rus" flourished as an important trade and cultural satellite of the Byzantine Empire. In fact, the people of Kievan Rus' were converted to Christianity through the Byzantines. But in 1237-40, Kievan Rus" was conquered by the Golden Horde, the westernmost khanate of the Mongol Empire. The horde killed half the population of Kievan Rus' and dominated their society for nearly two centuries. However, the Horde did not choose to range north and a couple of relatively independent former states of Kievan Rus' — Novgorod and Vladimir Suzdal — managed to remain independent. In the 13th century Moscow in the small state of Muscovy was little more than an eastern trading post of Vladimir Suzdal and most definitely on the periphery of Kievan Rus'. Muscovy's remote, forested location offered some security from Mongol attack and occupation, though the Muscovites were careful to form periodic alliances with the leaders of the Horde. A number of rivers gave the Muscovites trading access to the Baltic Sea to the west, the White Sea to the north, the Caspian Sea to the south and Siberia to the east.

More important to Moscow's development was its rule by a series of princes who were ambitious, determined and fortunate. The first ruler of the principality of Muscovy, Daniil Aleksandrovich (d. 1303), secured the principality for his branch of the Rurik Dynasty. His son, Ivan I (r. 1325-40), known as Ivan Kalita ("Money Bags"), obtained the title "Grand Prince of Vladimir" from his Mongol overlords. He cooperated closely with the Mongols and collected tribute from other Russian principalities on their behalf. This relationship enabled Ivan to gain regional ascendancy, particularly over Muscovy's chief rival, the northern city of Tver'. In 1327 the Orthodox metropolitan bishop transferred his residency from Vladimir to Moscow, further enhancing the prestige of the new principality.

Ivan the Great, 1462-1505

In the 14th century, the grand princes of Muscovy began gathering Russian lands to increase the population and wealth under their rule. The most successful practitioner of this process was Ivan III, also known as the Great. In 1478, he conquered the state of Novgorod and later the city of Tver' in 1485. When the Mongols gave up overlordship of Russian territories around 1480, Muscovy gained full sovereignty over the ethnic Russians and united all of them by the beginning of the 16th century. Ivan competed with his powerful northwestern rival Lithuania for control over some of the semi-independent former principalities of Kievan Rus' in the upper Dniepr and Donets river basins. Through the defections of some princes, border skirmishes, and a long, inconclusive war with Lithuania that ended only in 1503, Ivan III was able to push westward, and Muscovy tripled in size under his rule. Through inheritance, Ivan obtained part of the province of Ryazan', and the princes of Rostov and Yaroslavl' voluntarily subordinated themselves to him. The northwestern city of Pskov remained independent in this period, but Ivan's son, Vasily III, who ruled from 1505 to 1533, later conquered it.

Ivan III was the first Muscovite ruler to use the titles of tsar and "Ruler of all Rus'," which all Russian rulers used after his time. By assuming the title of tzar, a Russian interpretation of the word Caesar, the Muscovite prince underscored that he was a major ruler or emperor on a par with the emperor of the Byzantine Empire or the Mongol khan. Indeed, after Ivan III's marriage to Sophia Paleologue, the niece of the last Byzantine emperor, the Muscovite court adopted Byzantine terms, rituals, titles, and emblems such as the double-headed eagle. They styled themselves "autocrats." At first, the term "autocrat" connoted only the literal meaning of an independent ruler, but subsequently it came to mean unlimited rule on a par with the unlimited style of rule of the Byzantine emperors. In fact, when the Byzantine Empire fell to the Muslims in 1453, the Muscovites regarded themselves as the heirs apparent of that leadership tradition, which had an enduring legacy in the centuries to come.

Ivan the Terrible, 1533-1584

The development of the tsar's autocratic powers reached a peak during the reign of Ivan IV, known as the Terrible. Although intelligent and energetic, Ivan suffered from bouts of paranoia and depression, and his rule was punctuated by acts of extreme violence. No doubt, his paranoia was enhanced by the fact that he became grand prince of Muscovy in 1533 at the age of three. Various factions of the Russian aristocracy, the boyars, competed for control of the regency throughout his childhood, which created a good deal of chaos. When he came of age to rule in 1547, he attempted to assert control beginning with his coronation as tsar, an elaborate ritual modeled after those of the Byzantine emperors. With the advice of a group of trusted boyars, he began well with a series of reforms — a new law code, reorganization of the military and better coordination with local government.

But a few years later, Ivan developed a hostility toward his advisers. In 1565 he divided Muscovy into two parts: his private domain and the public realm. For his private domain, Ivan chose some of the most prosperous and important districts of Muscovy. In these areas, Ivan's agents attacked boyars, merchants, and even common people, summarily executing some and confiscating land and possessions. Thus began a decade of terror in Muscovy. As a result of this policy, called the oprichnina, Ivan broke the economic and political power of the leading boyar families, thereby destroying precisely those persons who had built up Muscovy and were the most capable of administering it. Trade diminished, and peasants, faced with mounting taxes and threats of violence, began to leave Muscovy. Efforts to curtail the mobility of the peasants by tying them to their land brought Muscovy closer to legal serfdom. In 1572 Ivan finally abandoned the practices of the oprichnina .

Despite the domestic turmoil of Ivan's later rule, he continued to expand Muscovy, annexing the Kazan' Khanate on the middle Volga in 1552 and later the Astrakhan' Khanate, where the Volga meets the Caspian Sea. These victories gave Muscovy access to the entire Volga River and Central Asia. Muscovy's eastward expansion encountered relatively little resistance. In 1581 the Stroganov merchant family, interested in fur trade, hired a Cossack leader, Yermak, to lead an expedition into western Siberia. Yermak defeated the Siberian Khanate and claimed the territories west of the Ob' and Irtysh rivers for Muscovy. Expanding to the northwest toward the Baltic Sea proved to be much more difficult. In 1558 Ivan invaded Livonia, eventually embroiling him in a 25-year war against Poland, Lithuania, Sweden, and Denmark. Despite occasional successes, Ivan's army was pushed back, and Muscovy failed to secure a coveted position on the Baltic Sea. Ivan's domestic and foreign policies had a devastating effect on Muscovy, and they led to a period of social struggle and civil war, the so-called Time of Troubles.

The Time of Troubles, 1598-1613

In 1584, Ivan was succeeded by his son Fedor, who was mentally deficient. Actual power went to Fedor's brother-in-law, the boyar Boris Godunov. Perhaps the most important event of Fedor's reign was the proclamation of the patriarchate of Moscow in 1589. The creation of the patriarchate climaxed the evolution of a separate and totally independent Russian Orthodox Church. In 1598 Fedor died without an heir. Boris Godunov then convened a zemsky sobor, a national assembly of boyars, church officials, and commoners, which proclaimed him tsar, but Godunov only lived a few more years. For the next 15 years, prominent boyar families took control of government, then were overthrown by pretenders, claiming to be lost sons of Ivan the Terrible, who mounted the throne only to be cast aside, followed by boyar rule. Various factions invited foreign powers to enter Russia and periodic famines worsened the situation. Finally, in 1613, a new zemsky sobor proclaimed the powerful boyar Mikhail Romanov as tsar, beginning the 300-year reign of the Romanov family.

The Romanovs

The immediate task of the new dynasty was to restore order. Fortunately for Muscovy, its major enemies, Poland and Sweden, were engaged in a bitter conflict with each other, which provided Muscovy the opportunity to make short-lived truces with Sweden and Poland. After an unsuccessful attempt to regain the city of Smolensk from Poland in 1632, Muscovy made peace with Poland in 1634. Polish king Wladyslaw IV, whose father and predecessor Sigismund III had helped Mikhail Romanov to become tsar of Muscovy during the Time of Troubles, renounced all claims to the title as a condition of the peace treaty.

The early Romanovs were not particularly strong rulers. Under Mikhail, state affairs were in the hands of the tsar's father, Filaret, who in 1619 became patriarch of the Orthodox Church. Later, Mikhail's son Aleksey (1645-76) relied on a boyar, Boris Morozov, to run his government. Morozov abused his position by exploiting the populace, and in 1648 Aleksey dismissed him in the wake of a popular uprising in Moscow. The autocracy survived the Time of Troubles and the rule of weak or corrupt tsars because of the strength of the government's central bureaucracy. Government functionaries continued to serve, regardless of the ruler's legitimacy or the boyar faction controlling the throne. In the 17th century, the bureaucracy expanded dramatically. The number of government departments increased from 22 in 1613 to 80 by mid-century. Although the departments often had overlapping and conflicting jurisdictions, the central government, through provincial governors, was able to control and regulate all social groups, as well as trade, manufacturing, and even the Orthodox Church.

The Legal Code of 1649

The comprehensive legal code introduced in 1649 illustrates the extent of state control over Russian society. By that time, the boyars had largely merged with the elite bureaucracy, who were obligatory servitors of the state, to form a new nobility, the dvoryanstvo. The state required service from both the old and the new nobility, primarily in the military. In return, they received land and peasants. In the preceding century, the state had gradually curtailed peasants' rights to move from one landlord to another; the 1649 code officially attached peasants to their domicile. The state fully sanctioned serfdom, and runaway peasants became state fugitives. Landlords had complete power over their peasants and bought, sold, traded, and mortgaged them. Peasants living on state-owned land, however, were not considered serfs. They were organized into communes, which were responsible for taxes and other obligations. Like serfs, however, state peasants were attached to the land they farmed. Middle-class urban tradesmen and craftsmen were assessed taxes, and, like the serfs, they were forbidden to change residence. All segments of the population were subject to military levy and to special taxes. By chaining much of Muscovite society to specific domiciles, the legal code of 1649 curtailed movement and subordinated the people to the interests of the state. Under this code, increased state taxes and regulations exacerbated the social discontent that had been simmering since the Time of Troubles.

Kiev and Westernization

Muscovy continued its territorial growth through the 17th century, but it was generally confined to the eastern and northern parts of modern Russia. But expansion into the southwest around Kiev opened up in the 1650s when the Polish Empire began to deteriorate. This region of Poland had actually been under the control of Ukrainian Cossacks, warriors organized in military formations who lived in the frontier areas bordering Poland, the Tatar lands and Muscovy. Although the Cossacks had served in the Polish army as mercenaries, they remained fiercely independent and staged a number of uprisings against the Poles. In 1648 most of Ukrainian society joined the Cossacks in a revolt because of the oppression they had suffered under Polish rule. Once the Ukrainians threw off Polish rule, they needed military help to maintain their independence and they offered to place Ukraine under the protection of the Muscovite tsar, Aleksey I. Poland made war against Russia until 1667, when the peace between the two countries split Ukraine along the Dniepr River, reuniting the western sector with Poland and leaving the eastern sector self-governing under the suzerainty of the tsar.

Muscovy's southwestern expansion, particularly its incorporation of eastern Ukraine, led to the introduction of western ideas into the heart of the traditional and backward Muscovy culture. Most Ukrainians were Orthodox in their faith, but their close contact with the Roman Catholic Polish church also brought them western intellectual currents. Through Kiev, Muscovy gained links to Polish and Central European influences and to the wider Orthodox world. Although the Ukrainian link stimulated creativity in many areas, it also undermined traditional Russian religious practices and culture. The tsar's court also felt the impact of Ukraine and the West. Kiev was a major transmitter of new ideas and insight through the famed scholarly academy that Metropolitan Mogila (Mohyla) founded there in 1631. Among the results of this infusion of ideas into Muscovy were baroque architecture, literature, and icon painting. Other more direct channels to the West opened as international trade increased and more foreigners came to Muscovy. The tsar's court was interested in the West's more advanced technology, particularly when military applications were involved. By the end of the 17th century, Ukrainian, Polish, and West European penetration had undermined the Muscovite cultural synthesis — at least among the elite — and had prepared the way for an even more radical transformation.

Peter the Great, 1682-1725, and His Reforms

Peter I, known as Peter the Great, reigned jointly with his half-brother Ivan V (1682–96) and alone thereafter. Unlike his half-brothers, Peter was a robust and energetic man, who had an intense curiosity about the West. He obtained this interest early in life from his mother, Natalya Kirillovna Naryshkina, whose guardian had raised her in an atmosphere open to progressive influences from the West. At the beginning of Peter's reign, Russia was backward by comparison with the countries of western Europe. This backwardness inhibited foreign policy and even put Russia's national independence in danger. Peter's aim, therefore, was to overtake the developed countries of western Europe as soon as possible, in order both to promote the national economy and to ensure victory in his wars for access to the seas.

Peter's Grand Embassy, 1697-98. As soon as his half-brother died and he exercised sole power, Peter sent a Grand Embassy of his leading diplomats and advisers for a tour of western Europe, lasting from March 1697 to August 1698. Interestingly, Peter traveled in the embassy incognito, which was difficult since he was 6 feet 8 inches tall. Nevertheless, one day he would negotiate with monarchs and diplomats to strengthen his alliances with the West against the Turks, whom he was battling for access to the Black Sea. The next day he would work secretly on the Dutch docks as a shipbuilder to gain a greater understanding of how to build ships. Then another day he would buy the latest in military weapons for his armies. And finally, he would stroll the straight streets and wide boulevards of the great western cities — Paris, Vienna, Berlin — and take notes. Later in the early 18th century, the audacious Peter founded and built from nothing his new capital of St. Petersburg on the Baltic Sea, exactly in imitation of what he had seen in the West. Peter returned to Russia determined to break the resistance of the boyars and the clergy and severely punish any opponents to his grand projects. In the next 25 years, he initiated a series of reforms that affected every field of the national life — administration, industry, commerce, technology, and culture. Historians consider him perhaps Russia's greatest statesman, reformer and leader.

Centralization of government. Early on, Peter tackled the administrative reform of cities and towns, linking them to his royal administration and delinking them from local provincial boyars and powers. By a decree of 1699, townspeople (artisans and tradesmen) were released from subjection to the military governors of the provinces and were authorized to elect municipalities of their own, which would be subordinated to the Moscow municipality, or ratusha. This reform was carried further in 1720, with the establishment of a chief magistracy in St. Petersburg, to which the local town magistracies and the elected municipal officers of the towns were subordinated. All townspeople, meanwhile, were divided between "regulars" and "commons" (inferiors). The regulars were wealthy merchants, professionals, artisans and tradesmen. The commons were hired labourers. Thanks to the reforms, the economic activity and the population of the towns increased. Anyone engaged in trade was legally permitted to settle in a town and to register himself in the appropriate category, and there was a right of "free commerce for people of every rank."

In order to create a more flexible system of control by the central power, in 1719, Russia was divided into 50 provinces, which in turn were subdivided into districts. After conducting a census in 1722, Peter attempted to collect a poll tax in place of the traditional hearth tax and provoked a rebellion. Therefore, he decided to create a layer of army regiments attached to each province to make sure that in the future his reforms were obeyed. In the course of Peter's reign, medieval and obsolescent forms of government gave place to effective autocracy. In 1711 he abolished the boyarskaya duma, or boyar council, and established by decree a Senate as the supreme organ of state — to coordinate central and local government, to collect revenue, make expenditures and draft legislation, but all of this according to his edicts. He was especially jealous of any sign of corruption on the part of the members of the Senate. Such crimes were brought directly to the tsar's attention and were punished brutally.

Industry. Under Peter, large capital investments were made, and numerous privileges were accorded to businessmen and industrialists who could deliver results. The initial impetus was support for armaments. Wars with his neighbors, particularly Sweden, made industrial development an urgent matter. In order to provide armaments and to build his navy (Russia had virtually no warships at all), metallurgical and manufacturing industries on a grand scale had to be created. Peter allowed the businessmen who joined his reforms to buy peasant serfs for labour in workshops, with the result that a class of "enlisted" serfs came into existence, living in specified areas and bound to the factories. Peter also relied on foreign military experts to give guidance to his reforms. Interestingly, the Russian metallurgical industry was so far advanced under Peter that by the middle of the 18th century Russia led Europe in this field. Peter also increased foreign trade seven times over during his reign.

The military. Before Peter, tzars were reliant upon the nobility to raise armies to support the crown. Peter established a standing, regular army on completely modern lines. While he drew his officers from the nobility, he conscripted peasants and townspeople into the other ranks. Service was for life, and he made sure his soldiers were well equipped. For the artillery, obsolete cannons were replaced with new mortars and guns designed by Russian specialists. The Army Regulations of 1716 were particularly important; they required officers to "show initiative" in the face of the enemy, rather than blindly following orders. For the navy, Peter's reign saw the construction, within a few years, of 52 battleships and hundreds of galleys and other craft; thus, a powerful Baltic fleet was brought into being. Several special schools prepared their pupils for military or naval service and finally enabled Peter to dispense with foreign experts.

Cultural and educational measures. At the start of the new century, January 1, 1700, Peter introduced a new Russian calendar that conformed to European usage with regard to the year. Prior to Peter, the Russian year began on September 1. In 1710 the Old Church Slavonic alphabet was modernized into a secular script. Peter also became the first ruler of Russia to sponsor education along secular lines and to bring an element of state control into that field. Various secular schools were opened. In many cases, compulsory service to the state was preceded by compulsory education for it. Russians were also permitted to go abroad for their education and indeed were often compelled to do so (at the state's expense). The translation of books from western European languages was actively promoted. The first Russian newspaper, Vedomosti ("Records"), appeared in 1703. The Russian Academy of Sciences was instituted in 1724. At times, Peter enforced superficial Europeanization and rather brutally. For example, he decreed that the nobility and merchants had to shave their beards and wear western dress, but he did not extend the edict to the very conservative peasantry.

The church. In 1721, in order to subject the Orthodox Church of Russia to the state, Peter abolished the Patriarchate of Moscow. Thenceforward, the patriarch's place as head of the church was taken by a spiritual college, namely the Holy Synod, consisting of representatives of the hierarchy obedient to the tsar's will. A secular official — the ober-prokuror, or chief procurator — was appointed by the tsar to supervise the Holy Synod's activities. The Holy Synod ferociously persecuted all dissenters and conducted a censorship of all publications. Priests officiating in churches were obliged by Peter to deliver sermons and exhortations that were intended to make the peasantry "listen to reason" and to teach such prayers to children that everyone would grow up "in fear of God" and in awe of the tsar. The church was thus transformed into a pillar of the absolutist regime. Partly in the interests of the nobility, the extent of land owned by the church was restricted.

The nobility. Despite Peter's hostility toward the boyars as a political class, his reign was actually quite good for large landowners. Almost 100,000 acres of land and 175,000 serfs were allotted to the wealthy landowning class in the first half of the reign alone. Moreover, a decree of 1714 instituted succession by primogeniture and prevented the breaking up of large properties. The nobility, in turn, had to accept Peter's Table of Ranks (1722), which required that promotion in the state services depended on services actually rendered instead of ancestry. They also had to accept factory owners into the ranks of the nobility, providing new blood. Thus, Peter reduced the power of the meddlesome boyars by expanding and diluting their ranks.

When Peter died early in 1725, he left an empire that stretched from Arkhangelsk (Archangel) on the White Sea to Mazanderan on the Caspian and from the Baltic Sea to the Pacific Ocean. Though he had in 1722 issued a decree reserving to himself the right to nominate his successor, he did not in fact nominate anyone. His widow Catherine, whom he had crowned as empress in 1724, succeeded him to the temporary exclusion of his grandson, the future Peter II.

Reading: Columbus and Vespucci: A Tale of Two Discoveries
Columbus, the Experienced Navigator
Why was "America" not named after the Genoese explorer Christopher Columbus (c. 1451-1506) but instead after his far more obscure contemporary Amerigo Vespucci (1451-1512), a Florentine agent, financier, and relentless self-promoter?

There is no known portrait of Columbus during his life. On the left is one of the three earliest portraits of Columbus after life; it hangs in the Naval Museum of Madrid. There is only one certain painting of Vespucci during life. On the right is a portion of a fresco of the whole Vespucci family in the Madonna della Misericordia by Domenico Ghirlandaio in Florence, c. 1472. Vespucci was about 20 at the time of this fresco.

The intertwined careers of the Genoese weaver's son and navigator Columbus and the better educated Florentine procurement agent turned explorer Vespucci illustrate well how different skills provided unique opportunities for the first and second generations of men who crossed the Atlantic. It is not a coincidence that both of them were Italian. The Italian mercantile and banking culture of medieval and Renaissance Europe was an international enterprise that thrived in the heyday of Mediterranean trade and travel.

The Genoese were a commercial seafaring nation like the Venetians who produced great navigators. Columbus was decisively cut from this cloth and acquired virtually all the skills that brought him fame at sea, as a navigator proficient at dead reckoning which required a sailor's know-how of distance, speed, and location. He sailed as far north as England, perhaps even Iceland, as far south as the African coast, and west to the Azores before venturing across the Atlantic.

Largely self-educated, Columbus was ambitious in acquiring the knowledge he needed to fuel his desire to pilot ships on new ventures for any monarch who would finance him and his brothers. He read the ancient and medieval classics—Ptolemy's Geography, Pliny the Elder's Natural History, John Mandeville's fantastically imaginative Travels, Pierre d'Ailly's medieval cosmography, and Marco Polo's account of his commercial voyage in Central Asia and China—but also consulted the Florentine mathematician Paolo Toscanelli who assured Columbus that the Atlantic was smaller than the ancients thought.

This emboldened his plan to sail west to reach the fabled East. During the 1480s Columbus approached the Portuguese king twice with his proposal but did not receive his support. The Spanish monarchs saw Columbus's proposal as an opportunity to compete with the Portuguese who had been exploring and trading along the West African coast since around 1450 and were their principal rivals in the conquest and colonization of the Azores, Canaries, and Madeiras. They hoped to strengthen Spain's position as an Iberian trading nation.

Columbus's and Vespucci's Voyages

After a decade of attempting to gain patronage, Columbus finally received the financing he needed to provision three ships containing approximately 90 men to venture across the Atlantic. In August 1492 he traveled with letters of introduction addressed to the Great Khan and other Eastern rulers, fully expecting to see "Cipangu" (Japan) before he reached the Asian mainland. When Columbus arrived in the Caribbean, he encountered the Tainos and began to assess the economic value of the natural commodities of this unknown island and the nature of its people.

Columbus returned to Spain, his first voyage widely celebrated. His first letter of 1493 was printed nine times in this first year and went into 20 editions by 1500. The Spanish monarchs were well satisfied with this promising start to a new venture and the Pope rewarded them in May 1493 by granting Castile the right to possess "lands and islands both distant and undiscovered" for the glory and extension of Christendom.

Columbus proclaimed himself "Admiral of the Ocean Sea, Viceroy and Governor of the islands newly discovered in the Indies." His prospects seemed bright and endless. Columbus now had the attention of financial backers in Seville, where there was a large Genoese community and a smaller Florentine one that included Giannotto Berardi who had recently become the Medici agent in Seville.

It was through Berardi that Amerigo Vespucci met the great explorer Columbus. Vespucci had first encountered Berardi in the late 1480s when he was asked to go to Seville to interview him for the job. He returned there by 1492, no doubt enticed by the lure of profits in an emerging economy, and began to work for Berardi. As a result, Vespucci was an eyewitness to Columbus's first voyage and a minor actor in the second.

When Berardi agreed to become one of Columbus's principal partners—investing heavily in 12 of the 17 ships, carrying 1200 men, livestock, and sugarcane plants with the goal of colonizing the new territories during the second voyage (1493-96?)—Vespucci became another partner. This costly and ill-fated venture to the Lesser Antilles and Cuba, where Columbus first encountered the warlike Caribs and experienced rebellion from the Taino who were now suffering the devastations of disease, greed, and forced labor at the hands of Columbus and his men, left Berardi with a mountain of debt that Columbus could not repay.

Despite profits made from the sale of the natives whom Columbus enslaved when nothing else yielded the income he needed, the costs far exceeded the returns. Berardi died in December 1495, leaving his agent Vespucci to deal with his debts. The Spanish monarchs began to inspect their admiral's behavior more critically, and Columbus's third and equally disastrous voyage (1498-

1500) led to his imprisonment for poor governorship. When Ferdinand and Isabella revoked Columbus's exclusive right to explore the territory they now claimed, Vespucci was on the first Spanish ship commanded by someone other than Columbus to make the trans-Atlantic crossing.

In his famous Utopia (1516), the imagined voyage to nowhere, Sir Thomas More described his fictional traveler Raphael Hythloday (hith'-lo-day) accompanying Vespucci on three of his four voyages. More wrote that he had chosen Vespucci because accounts of his travels were "common reading everywhere." Vespucci's fame primarily derived from two books created by others from the letters Vespucci had written to his benefactors about his real and his imagined voyages. We have certain evidence of only two voyages—one in 1499 with the Spanish commander, Alonso de Ojeda and one in 1501 with the Portuguese commander Gonçalo Coelho.

After his second voyage, he assured his Florentine patron, Pierfrancesco di Lorenzo de' Medici that "those new regions which we searched for and discovered with the fleet, at the expense and orders of His Most Serene Highness, the King of Portugal … can be called a new world," meaning not a part of Asia as Columbus had asserted. "I have discovered a continent in those southern regions that is inhabited by more numerous peoples and animals than in our Europe, or Asia or Africa," he proudly declared, repudiating ancient wisdom that no living being could inhabit the Torrid Zone. Vespucci filled his report with lush descriptions of tropic nature accompanied by lurid accounts of every manner of cannibalism, moral ambiguity, and sexual depravity he attributed to the Tupinamba tribe he encountered for a brief 27 days.

The Naming of the New World
Translated into Latin by the Vicenza humanist Fra Giovanni del Giocondo to reach a European-wide audience, the Mundus Novus (New World) was published in Florence towards the end of 1502 or beginning of 1503. It instantly became a bestseller with numerous reprintings and translations in a matter of a few years. Vespucci's growing reputation as the great Florentine chronicler of the New World encouraged him to circulate additional letters he had written to Pierfrancesco de' Medici about his Spanish voyage of 1499-1500 and the subsequent Portuguese journey of 1501-1502 that made his reputation.

In 1504 Vespucci and his supporters created a new book, this time in Italian, entitled the Letter of Amerigo Vespucci Concerning the Newly Found Islands in His Four Voyages. Also published in Florence, it bore a dedication to Vespucci's schoolboy friend Piero Soderini, who became head of the Florentine Republic that ousted the Medici from power in 1494. This second publication presented Vespucci not as a traveler in the wake of Columbus but as a seasoned explorer whose discoveries surpassed those proudly announced by the Genoese admiral in his account of his own four voyages.

Vespucci now presented himself as arriving in Venezuela in 1497, a year before Columbus. His imagined exploration of the Yucatán Peninsula, Gulf of Mexico, and perhaps even Florida, where no European landed until Juan Ponce de Léon in 1513, completed the fantasy of discovery. And yet without the dream how could the reality move forward? The same year that Ponce de Léon arrived in the southeastern part of North America, the Spanish explorer Vasco Núñez de Balboa first saw the Pacific that some felt Vespucci was the first to imagine. In his Letter Vespucci further embellished the details of his actual voyage down the Brazilian coast, advertising a subsequent trip to the same region that he claimed to have taken with the Portuguese in 1503-04. Anyone familiar with the actual details of Vespucci's movements knew that he was back in Spain by October 1502. But this did not exactly matter to eager readers of his voyages. Who was to distinguish between voyages real and imagined, except those on board? The reality of the Americas was a kind of thrilling fiction for most Renaissance readers who never took this voyage themselves but heard and read about it.

Interestingly enough, Columbus took no offense. He continued to see Vespucci as a trustworthy and knowledgeable agent in their mutual enterprise of discovery, recommending him warmly to his son Diego and supporting his decision to return to Spain to become a Spanish citizen in return for sharing what he knew from his Portuguese adventures. Vespucci lived with Columbus, taking advantage of the books and manuscripts in his impressive library, and acted as a witness to the Genoese explorer's draft testament before he died in May 1506.

Arguing that Vespucci deserved this honor for discovering the "fourth part" of the globe, Waldseemüller declared, "I see no reason why anyone could properly disapprove of a name derived from that of Amerigo, the discoverer, a man of sagacious genius." Others did not agree and were outraged at the omission of Columbus's name from the world map. In 1513 Waldseemüller revised his map, crediting Columbus as the most important discoverer of this fourth continent. Yet he did not rename America "Columbia." Instead he took the safer path of neutrality by relabeling it terra incognita, or unknown land.

In March 1508 the Spanish crown appointed Vespucci piloto mayor (chief navigator) in the Casa de Contratación, the Spanish House of Trade founded in 1502 in support of their commercial ventures. They expected Vespucci to instruct and examine pilots in proper techniques of celestial and cartographic navigation, using instruments such as the quadrant and the astrolabe in which he claimed great expertise in all his published letters. They also requested that he create a new Padrón Real, the official state map of Spanish discoveries incorporating information from every voyage. Vespucci never made a new map and died in 1512. In 1525 his nephew Giovanni, who succeeded him as piloto mayor, was accused by the Spaniards of being a Medici spy, as the age of Italians who sailed the Atlantic came to a close. Thus ended the era in which a man like Vespucci could persuade his readers that he knew and discovered more than those with hard-earned experience like Columbus.

Waldseemüller's initial judgment of Vespucci, based on his self-aggrandizing letters, continued to influence others who filled in the portrait of America first sketched at the beginning of the 16th century. Vespucci's name migrated to other maps and globes. In time, people forgot why anyone had ever questioned the decision to name this continent after a glib, silver-tongued Renaissance dealer in fine wines, jewels, and just about anything else that could turn a profit. Vespucci attached himself to Columbus's coattails, purloined his reputation, and shook off Columbus's doubts about what he had seen by insisting that it was absolutely new. From Seville, this crafty Florentine must have smiled almost as knowingly as his contemporary Machiavelli when he heard how a Swiss mapmaker assured his fame by placing his name on the map.

Reading: The Wars of Religion and the Thirty Years' War

Before 1650, Europeans regarded religion as the glue that held together society; it was not just a matter of conscience but also a matter of state. The traditional saying was: "One faith, one law, one king," and without the three together, there would be chaos. Religious heresy, therefore, was also treason against the king and the state. Thus, when Martin Luther and the Protestant faith challenged the Catholic faith in 1517, every European knew that both the church and the government would be in disarray, and it frightened them.

Luther himself understood this and discouraged his followers from rebelling against their kings. If facing persecution at the hands of an overzealous Catholic monarch, his solution was to move to the territories of a Protestant ruler. In the years 1517 to 1560, kings also attempted to keep the peace between Protestants and Catholics, none more than the Holy Roman Emperor Charles V. But by the 1560s, disputes between Catholic and Protestant monarchs finally became open conflict. The worst of the religious wars were in 1562-1598. Open hostilities ceased with the Edict of Nantes in 1598. Some aspects of prior religious conflicts were revived in the 30 Years' War (1618-48), but these were finally settled with the Peace of Westphalia (1648), which finally codified religious tolerance in western Europe.

Royal Conflicts in France

The greatest danger for Europe was always conflict among the principle crowns — France, Spain, Austria and England. Under Charles V, his kingdom of Spain had remained staunchly loyal to the Catholic faith, though he was more conciliatory and tolerant in his Austrian, German and Flemish kingdoms. The amiable Charles died in 1568, but even before then he was abdicating power to his brother Ferdinand I in the Holy Roman Empire and his son Philip II in Spain and the Low Countries. While Ferdinand continued Charles's peacemaking policies in Germany and Austria, Philip was less conciliatory and saw himself as the tip of the spear for the Catholic faith in his domains and Europe generally. Meanwhile, in the 1530s, Henry VIII of England divorced his Spanish wife, Catherine of Aragon (Philip's great aunt), and married Anne Boleyn, in the process converting England from the Catholic to the Anglican faith. Anglicanism was Protestant doctrine, but most importantly was a state-dominated religion; the king, not the Pope, was the head of the Anglican faith. Henry's son Edward and later his daughter Elizabeth maintained the Anglican order.

Like parts of central Europe, France had Protestant and Catholic strongholds among its subjects. But it also had a powerful nobility that confessed to both faiths and often tried to use religious politics, sometimes called "confessional politics," to further family interests. In the first half of the century, France had two relatively strong kings, Francis I and Henry II, but Henry died unexpectedly in 1559, leaving his 15-year-old son Francis II in charge. Powerful noble families began to take advantage of a weak French monarchy and muscle their way into power, using confessional politics.

The House of Guise was the most powerful of these. Francis II was already married to the Duke of Guise's niece, called Mary Queen of Scots because she was also heir to the Scottish throne. The Guise were well connected to royalty and had exceptional leaders — Francis, Duke of Guise, was a military hero and his brother, the Cardinal of Lorraine, was a great scholar and statesman. Their rivals were the Montmorency, an ancient noble family that also had royal ties and claimed the right to tutor and raise up the young Francis II. Although the French crown had been supporters of the Pope and the Catholic faith and the Guise were also strong adherents, the Montmorency were divided into several camps. Most particularly, the Bourbon branch, including Antoine de Bourbon, King of Navarre, and Louis de Bourbon, Prince de Condé, were faithful Protestants, along with Admiral of France, Gaspard de Coligny.

Francis II's mother, Catherine de' Medici, tried to steer her son and his advisors to take a middle path of religious toleration. She sponsored an "Edict of Toleration" in January 1562, which made the practice of Protestantism not a crime, although it was restricted to preaching in open fields outside the towns and to the private estates of Huguenot (Protestant) nobles. This was not well-received by many Catholics and was completely ignored by the contending royal houses.

Conflict soon broke out when the Catholic Duke of Guise's men fired on and killed some Huguenots (Protestants) at a church service in Vassay. Appalled by the "Massacre at Vassay," Huguenots appealed to the Protestant Prince de Condé to become the "Protector of the Churches." He formed a noble coalition to protect the Protestant faithful, and from this point the leadership of the Huguenots moved from pastors to noble "protectors." Condé took a string of towns along the Loire River and made his headquarters at the city of Orléans, appealing to Protestant leaders of Germany for troops and money. The Guise organized the Catholic cause and struck back. In the process several key leaders on both sides were killed and chaos was beginning to rule the day in France. With the Huguenot heartland in the south virtually untouched and the royal treasury hemorrhaging, the crown's position was weak and Catherine bent her efforts towards a settlement, which proved unsatisfactory to all sides. The wars of religion would plague France for another 40 years.

The St. Bartholomew's Day Massacre (1572) and the Aftermath

In the next 18 years, the same standoff in power raged across France. The weak king, Francis II died, and his equally weak brother Charles IX came to power; their mother Catherine continued to rule and pursued a peace-at-all-costs strategy. But her every move was subject to scrutiny for favoritism by the Catholic or Protestant causes. The Guise were determined to destroy the Huguenots, but Huguenot protectors — the Prince de Condé and the Admiral de Coligny — managed to keep the south of France in Protestant hands. The new threat to the peace of France, however, came when these noble houses began to appeal for outside help — the Catholics to the King of Spain and the Protestants to Germany, the Netherlands and England. The French people, mostly in the south, suffered tremendously from these wandering Catholic and Protestant noble armies, many filled with mercenaries, who pillage the countryside and destroyed crops, villages, churches, even cities; the crown simply did not have the political strength to control the will of the powerful nobles.

The tensions took their toll. Protestant rhetoric had become increasingly revolutionary in the late 1560s, with leading thinkers advocating that Christians did not have the obligation to obey leaders who themselves defied God. The Protestant leader John Calvin himself came to the conclusion, after advocating for many years that obedience to the civil authorities was a Christian duty, that a prince that persecuted the Protestant church had forfeited his right to be obeyed. There were also economic differences between the two camps. Protestants were often more greatly represented in the newer and more lucrative trades, such as printing. The Protestant emphasis on literacy as the basis for understanding the Bible made for a generally better-educated group. Protestantism was more an urban than a rural phenomenon (except in the Southwest), one well-suited to capitalists and merchants. The years of persecution had created a cell-like structure of congregations, consistories and synods where people in the group stuck together and helped each other, both in matters of religion and everyday business. On the other side, Catholics felt that the toleration of heresy in their midst was a disease in the body of Christ and in the body politic. There was increasing rhetoric among the popular priests to purge this infection and restore God's favor and social stability.

These social problems formed the backdrop to the most important event of the Wars of Religion — the feast of St. Bartholomew on August 23, 1572. The occasion was Catherine's successful negotiation of the marriage of her daughter Margaret of Valois to the Protestant leader, Henry of Navarre, which was held on August 10. The entire Huguenot leadership was in Paris to celebrate the wedding and stayed on for the later religious feast. On August 22, an assassin shot the Protestant Admiral de Coligny, breaking his arm but not killing him. Huguenots were outraged, threatening riot and murder and advising Coligny to leave the city; he refused. The next day, the decision was taken on the Catholic side to attempt another assassination and this time, for reasons that are not entirely understood even today, they received the tacit assent of the Queen Mother Catherine.

That night Coligny was pulled from his sick bed, stabbed to death and thrown into the street. When the news spread throughout Paris, Catholics went into the homes of known Huguenots and massacred them, continuing for three days. Henry of Navarre was dragged from his bridal suite in the royal palace and threatened with death if he did not convert to the Catholic faith, which he did. Henry was a prisoner of the court for the next four years, living in constant fear of his life.

The St. Bartholomew's Day Massacre, as it came to be known, destroyed an entire generation of Huguenot leadership and precipitated the decline of the Protestant church in France, but that would not be apparent for some years. Nevertheless, the Protestants hung on tenaciously to the end of the century. In fact, many surviving Protestant communities became more radicalized, speaking a rhetoric of resistance to tyranny. They periodically refused to pay taxes to the king, citing the rumor of the crown's role in the Massacre.

King Charles died and the crown passed to the third of Catherine de' Medici's sons, Henry III, who also proved not strong enough to get control of the country. Meanwhile, Condé and other Protestant leaders were abroad seeking money and armies in Germany and appealing to southern French noble families to come to the Protestant cause. The Protestant cause was buoyed when Henry of Navarre escaped the court in February 1576. The Catholics made an effort to form a League in opposition to the growing threat, but the Protestants maintained their control in the south. War and chaos raged on, but finally a solution to the Wars of Religion began to emerge in 1584. It was not by force that the end would come but rather by dynasty. King Henry III was childless and seemingly unable to produce an heir. His younger brother who would have been his heir died in 1584. The next in line to the throne and the heir presumptive was the Protestant leader, Henry of Navarre, who was married to Henry III's sister, Margaret of Valois.

The War of the Three Henries and the League (1584-1598). The prospect of a Protestant prince was deeply disturbing to Catholics. Henry III tried to convince his brother-in-law and heir Henry of Navarre to convert to Catholicism and remove the specter of a Protestant prince. While Navarre was not a particularly religious man and coveted the crown, he logically feared that such a renunciation of his faith would lose him his Protestant support. Catholics began to think that it was necessary to overthrow the monarchy to save it and rallied around the Duke of Guise, another Henry, who now claimed the crown for himself. Guise revived the Catholic League and made a pact with Philip II of Spain, who poured money into the Guise cause for the next decade. Thus began the bloodiest phase of the Wars of Religion — the War of the Three Henries.

Another stalemate had formed — Henry of Guise and the Catholic League in good control of the north and the east; Henry of Navarre and his cousin Condé entrenched in the south and west; and Henry III stuck in Paris, with a radical Catholic city population who had nothing but contempt for him. In the summer of 1588, the city went into revolt, setting up barricades (for the first time in what would become a venerable Parisian protest tradition), forcing King Henry to flee and inviting Guise to take over the city. But King Henry III soon got his revenge for Henry de Guise's betrayal; he had him assassinated. King Henry then tried to make an alliance with his brother-in-law, Navarre. But in July 1589, a radical Catholic monk managed to get access to King Henry III, killing him with a long knife.

Henry of Navarre was now the only Henry left and he acted quickly, taking his southern army north and sweeping through the northern strongholds of the Guise. He then laid siege to Paris in the spring and summer of 1590. Although he reduced it to severe hunger, the Spanish helped the Guise to bring food in and relieve the city. Navarre withdrew. But, in July 1593 he struck a masterful political stroke — he converted to the Catholic faith. Though some of his Protestant supporters left him, he gained even more moderate Catholics who had become weary of war. He had himself crowned as the first Bourbon monarch of France and then, in the spring of 1594, he entered Paris without firing a shot.

Henry had proved himself to be an astute political survivor in the wars of religion, and now was proving himself a very clever politician. He began a vigorous program of winning over the support of moderate Catholics with a combination of charm, force, money and promises. A great deal of money was spent guaranteeing various nobles pensions and positions in exchange for their support, and a great deal of money was given to the towns to discourage rebellion.

In 1594-98, some of the hard core forces of the Catholic League remained in the field, with the help of Philip II. But finally in 1598, Philip signed the Treaty of Vervins with the new King Henry IV and the other Catholic nobles gave up. That same year Henry IV published the Edict of Nantes, which granted Huguenots freedom of worship and civil rights. But the Protestant cause was much diminished by the conversion of Henry. Henry's Bourbon heirs gradually reduced the influence of Protestantism in French realms and eventually took away the terms of the Edict of Nantes. France would become a staunchly Catholic country.

The 30 Years' War and the Treaty of Westphalia, 1618-1648

The Wars of Religion, mostly in France, demonstrated that wars in one part of Europe, that is, France, could readily metastasize and draw in the rest of the powers of Europe. Nevertheless, the violence of those religious wars was mostly confined to France. The Edict of Nantes kept the peace in France and generally in Europe for about two decades. But it did not finish the struggles between confessional powers. Religious conflict raised its head this time in Germany. More than 60 years before, the Habsburg emperor Charles V had abdicated the emperorship of the Holy Roman Empire to his younger brother Ferdinand I. Both Charles and his brother managed confessional affairs in such a way as to keep the peace relatively well in the empire. But their deft touch was lost on some of their heirs. In 1618 Ferdinand II, the new emperor came to the throne and immediately attempted to enforce the observation of Catholicism across the empire. Bohemian Protestants soon rebelled against the crown in what was called the Prague Defenestration.

On the Protestant side, the Bohemians had the support of Protestant kings in Denmark and Sweden. Ferdinand had the support of the revived Catholic League, which included Spain, France, Flanders (modern-day Belgium) and parts of Germany. Though Catholic forces had the upper hand in the first ten years, the Protestants rallied under the brilliant military leader and new young Swedish king, Gustavus Adolphus. But soon the initial confessional lines of conflict were blurred by the political rivalries between France and the Habsburg coalition of Spain and Austria. France soon pulled away from the Catholic League; the Portuguese rebelled against their Spanish overlords; and Denmark switched sides from the Protestants to the Catholic League. There was even more turmoil when in 1643, the French king Louis XIII died, leaving his five-year-old son Louis XIV in charge. As in the religious wars of the previous century, noble factions rivaled to exercise power for the child-king.

During the 30 years of war that lasted from 1618 to 1648, the central part of Europe experienced the worst violence and destruction that it would know until the 20th century. Germany's population decreased by 30 percent on average; in a few areas as many as two-thirds of the people lost their lives. For decades, armies mostly filled with mercenaries roamed Germany, slaughtering the population and destroying tens of thousands of monasteries, castles, towns and villages. Famine and disease were widespread. The Holy Roman imperial power retreated to Austria, as the Holy Roman Empire began to break down and pull away from the emperor. The Netherlands and Switzerland were confirmed independent.

The Dutch Republic alone managed to emerge from the conflict a little better than before. The republic had been part of the Low Countries inheritance from Charles V to his son Philip II. But seven of the Low Country counties rebelled in 1580. Despite Philip II's best efforts, marching Spanish armies north to the Low Countries for decades, the rebelling counties formed an independent republic — the Dutch Republic. They successfully fought off all efforts to reconquer their territories, and Spain finally accepted that independence in 1648. The Dutch were superb tradesmen and merchants and flourished in the 17th century, which was called the Dutch Golden Age.

Peace of Westphalia, 1648

Exhausted by decades of war, the warring powers (the Holy Roman Empire, France, and Sweden) sat down to peace talks at Osnabrück and Münster in Westphalia over the course of four years. Not one treaty but several from these meetings ended the massive war, including the Treaty of Hamburg, the Peace of Münster, followed by the Treaties of Münster and Osnabrück. Together these treaties are known as the Peace of Westphalia.

But the peace was more than just a cessation of hostilities. The 30 Years' War rearranged the European power structure. The greatest power, Spain, had clearly declined in the 1640s, losing Portugal and then half the Low Countries to Dutch independence. When Louis XIV came of age in the 1660s, he reorganized the country and brought French power to its height. The Austrian Habsburgs lost power over much of Germany. The war resulted in the increased autonomy of the many constituent states of the Holy Roman Empire, limiting the power of the emperor and decentralizing authority in German-speaking central Europe. But the Habsburgs did manage to consolidate their power in their historic homeland of Austria and continued to be an able rival of France and the Ottoman Empire.

Furthermore, in the Peace of Westphalia, we see the legal foundations of the modern nation-state. Previously, many people had borne overlapping, sometimes conflicting political and religious allegiances. Henceforth, the inhabitants of a given state were understood to be subject first and foremost to the laws and edicts of that state authority, not to the claims of any other entity, be it religious or secular. It became easier to levy national armies, loyal to their state and its leader, so as to reduce the need to employ the hated mercenaries who had become the scourge of Europe. Moreover, the 30 Years' War was the last religious war of mainland Europe. While there were a few minor religious conflicts, the Peace of Westphalia seems to mark the point in time when Europeans finally accepted religious toleration as a fundamental tenet of society and state.

Reading: The West Looks East, Again

In 1506, after several years of exploring the Levant and parts of Asia before returning to Lisbon in 1508, the Bolognese traveler Ludovico de Varthema (ca 1470-1517) was surprised to discover two Milanese gunners living in Calicut, India. Their delight in meeting a fellow Italian was matched only by their sadness and desperation at being stuck halfway around the world. If they returned to Goa, they feared punishment from the Portuguese on whose ships they had sailed. Any attempt to leave Calicut risked the wrath of the local ruler, who closely guarded them in order to benefit from their ability to cast European weapons to fortify his city, presumably to avoid further onslaughts from the Portuguese during the first decade in which they established their presence in India.

After returning to Goa, Varthema was distressed to discover that the Portuguese pardon he obtained failed to save them from the surveillance and suspicion surrounding the movements of Europeans in Calicut, perhaps especially those employed for their expertise by the king. A household slave warned of their imminent departure, precipitating a riot in which they were killed. Varthema later purchased the freedom of the half-Indian son of one of the men and had him baptized. Young Ludovico died the following year. Such was the tenuous nature of the hybrid, partly European society forming in Asia after the arrival of Vasco da Gama in Calicut on May 20, 1498.

Varthema published his bestselling Itinerary in Florence in 1510, barely a decade after the Portuguese crossed the Indian Ocean. His remarkable voyage of 1504-08 emerged from the desire to see places "the least frequented by Venetians" and write about the experience of travel upon his return. The novelties he wished to see for himself did not belong to the New World, however. Varthema arrived in India shortly after the appointment of the first Portuguese viceroy in 1505. He left before the Portuguese completed their fort in Goa in 1510 to establish this important base of operations. He was an eyewitness to the birth of the Portuguese Empire, and a free agent who traveled with the Portuguese, but he was not beholden to them, making him one of the most interesting kinds of global travelers.

Sailing to the Indies

When the German gunner Hans Staden found employment on Portuguese ships in order "to see India," he did not especially care whether this meant going east or west since this distinction was largely without a difference until well into the 16th century. Columbus sailed southwest from Seville in search of an alternate route to the Indies for his Spanish patrons, Ferdinand of Aragon and Isabella of Castile, largely because Portuguese navigators were systematically making their way along the West African coast, establishing trading forts to secure their investments in this part of the world.

By 1481, Bartolomeu Dias arrived at the Cape, making the prospect of circumnavigating Africa a reality. News of Columbus's discoveries did not reorient their desire to find an eastern route to Asia. Pedro Álvares Cabral, who commanded the first Portuguese fleet to set sail after da Gama returned to Lisbon in 1499, only touched down briefly in Brazil because his primary objective was India. Once the Portuguese mastered the Indian Ocean, they continued to expand their base of operations in this region with varying degrees of success. In 1514, King Manuel I magnanimously sent an Indian elephant from Lisbon as a tangible demonstration to the pope of just how far the Portuguese empire extended. The Rhinoceros that followed a year later died in a shipwreck in 1516 before reaching Rome but lived on in artist Albrecht Dürer's famous image of an exotic animal he had never seen but drew from a description.

Despite the great publicity proclaiming the discovery of a "New World" in the Americas, many early modern Europeans continued to see Africa, the Middle East, and Asia as more important to their vision of the world. Between 1480 and 1609, Europeans published about four times as many books on the Ottoman Empire and Asia as they did on the New World. Varthema's Itinerary was among them. Well into the 17th century, the French and the English continued to dream of a Northwest Passage. Samuel Champlain hoped that further exploration of the St. Lawrence River would lead him from New France to China, while a 1634 French map indicated a potential passage to Japan via the Great Lakes. Geography was as much about desire as reality, especially when dealing with the unknown.

During the 16th century, the number of Europeans traveling east increased dramatically. Varthema is a precocious example of a European eager to see Asia. The Portuguese ennobled Varthema for his service as a factor, the agent in charge of a commercial trading outpost. He belonged to the first generation of Europeans who no longer assumed that the primary conduit to the East was a Venetian ship headed to Cairo, Alexandria, Aleppo, or Constantinople. At the beginning of the 16th century, the Genoese had largely departed from the Eastern Mediterranean. The Venetians navigating these waters engaged in a delicate ballet with the Ottomans whose piratical incursions threatened many Italian coastal towns as their empire expanded further west. Portuguese caravels became the primary transportation for successive generations of Europeans to develop a far greater knowledge of and presence in the East, transforming it and themselves in the process.

As Varthema made his way back to Italy, a Portuguese adventurer named Duarte Barbosa (1480-1521) decided to write a careful account of his travels along a similar route. Tellingly, he began his journal as he rounded Cape of Good Hope since he understood that the Guinea Coast was already familiar territory after a half-century of military and economic incursions by the Portuguese in Africa. Instead, the eastern coast of Africa – and fundamentally everything between there and Marco Polo's legendary Cathay – remained largely unknown. Barbosa carefully described a region of the world undergoing great transformations.

As his ship left Mozambique behind, island hopping until it reached the mouth of the Red Sea, he reflected on how the Portuguese left a wake of devastation and destruction behind them. Barbosa described well the Portuguese technique of fortifying strategic locations to establish a permanent presence, discouraging competition and resistance by military force, and making strategic alliances with local rulers eager to do business with the Europeans at the expense of the Muslim merchants and rulers who preceded them. By the time he reached the island of Hormuz, initially conquered by the Portuguese in 1507 to control trade routes through the Persian Gulf, Barbosa had established the pattern by which the Portuguese advanced from East Africa to the Indian Ocean.

Barbosa served as factor in Cochin and Cannanore and learned Malabari. He described Goa as a polyglot colonial city in the making, filled with "Portuguese, Moors, and Gentiles." Fascinated by the Brahmins as well as the "Christians of India," he looked for traces of European merchants and missionaries who had preceded him. At the Cape of Cormory he noticed an Armenian church, containing tombs with Latin inscriptions, now become a place of worship for passing sailors. The cosmopolitanism of the world he found enthralled him; only one remote island struck Barbosa as so uncivilized that it brought to mind "the people of the Canary Islands." He mistook African yams for American maize, yet ultimately, it was Asia that most interested him. Barbosa's *Book of What I Saw and Heard in the Orient* circulated for approximately 40 years in manuscript form among the Portuguese, Genoese, and Spanish.

The Venetian editor Giovan Battista Ramusio finally printed a version in 1554, encouraging the next generation of readers to believe what Barbosa said but certainly had not observed of the Chinese – that they were tall, beardless small-eyed men who dressed and spoke like Germans. Of the Formosans (Taiwanese), he had even less to say because "they have not come to India since the King of Portugal possesses it." Such was the unreliable but not easily contested nature of global information in an age of contingent, long-distance encounters.

Captivity and Conversion

Ramusio published some of the most informative accounts of the regions of the world that greatly mattered to European ambitions in his *Navigations and Voyages* (1550-59), with each volume focusing on travel accounts of different parts of the non-European world. Tellingly, he began with Asia and Africa before collecting some of the most interesting reports of the Americas. In 1550, he printed a *Description of Africa* written around 1526 by al-Hasan al-Wazzan (ca 1492-ca 1550). Raised in Fez, he was the learned agent of the sultan of Fez, Muhammad II, and born in the final days of Muslim Granada before its reconquest by the Spanish. In 1518, he was captured by a Spanish pirate while returning from Arabia after he had witnessed the Ottoman conquest of Egypt. Al-Wazzan spent nine years in Italy where he converted to Christianity in 1520. The Medici pope, Leo X (who received the gift of Hanno the elephant,) baptized him with the Christian name of Joannes Leo de Medici, though he would call himself "Leo the African."

While improving a prior Latin translation of the Qur'an and writing about Africa, al-Wazzan heard the Portuguese describe their discovery of the kingdom of the legendary Christian ruler Prester John in Ethiopia. Before returning to North Africa and renouncing Christianity, al-Wazzan witnessed the 1527 sack of Rome by imperial troops; he probably experienced Charles V's conquest of Tunis in 1535, perhaps involving some of the same soldiers. Although al-Wazzan never managed to write about his experience of Europe and parts of Asia, his *Description of Africa* remained the most important and comprehensive account of Africa read by Europeans for the next two centuries, written by a European-born Muslim who, for a period of his life, was a Christian serving the pope.

By the mid-16th century, entrepreneurial Europeans ventured beyond the edges of empire. Take the case of the notoriously unreliable Fernão Mendes Pinto (ca 1510-83) who spent two decades in Asia after leaving from Lisbon in 1537. Whether he ever touched ground in Ethiopia or went beyond Canton in his alleged excursions to China is uncertain. His four voyages to Japan did indeed take place – he proudly claimed to be the first European to set foot in Japan when his ship was blown off course to the island of Tanegashima around 1543.

By the time Mendes Pinto's *Travels* appeared in print in 1614, he seemed the very embodiment of the kind of opportunistic European whose chameleon-like identity allowed him to assume many guises. Was he captured and enslaved by the Ottomans somewhere between Eastern Africa and the Red Sea? Did he become a pirate between the Gulf of Tongking and the South China Sea who allegedly (and rather improbable) served a year of hard labor working on the Great Wall? Did he fight against the Portuguese viceroy in Burma yet represent him as a quasi-ambassador to the daimyo of Bungo on his final trip to Japan?

His admiration for St. Francis Xavier (1506-52), who pioneered the Jesuit mission to Japan, was quite sincere. Xavier inspired him to support Jesuit efforts to convert the Japanese to Christianity, including funding to build the first Christian church, but whether Mendes Pinto actually entered the Society of Jesus in Goa in 1554 for two years is open to doubt. Amerigo Vespucci, the smooth-talking Florentine who transformed his real and imagined voyages to the Americas into a bestselling book that earned him a continent, was not the only early modern traveler to tell a tall tale – or be celebrated and mythologized by others simply for having gone the distance.

Writing to the East

In 1561, Queen Elizabeth I wrote the first of multiple letters to rulers in the East, requesting that the Russian tsar and Persian shah offer her emissary, Anthony Jenkins, safe-conduct as he sought to gain trading privileges for the English. The shah knew a few things about the Spanish and the Portuguese but nothing of the English. Instead, in the 1570s the Moroccan and Ottoman sultans both wrote to the English queen, seeking an alliance. The Moroccan sultan Ahmad al-Mansur's efforts to court "sultana Isabel" was far more serious, as an independent North African nation vulnerable to both European and Ottoman ambitions. In 1589 a Moroccan embassy to London charged with encouraging the English to join a campaign to take Portugal from the Spanish floundered. A second embassy in 1600, the year al-Wazzan's *Description of Africa* appeared in English, yielded no further commitments on the part of the English.

In 1583, William Harborne traveled through Persia with more royal letters, now addressed to the Mughal emperor Akbar and an unnamed "King of China." However, Elizabeth I did not count on only one route for her message to reach her counterparts in Asia. In 1602 she wrote a new letter to the "great, mighty, and invincible Emperor of Cathay." It was a description possibly inspired by the recent English translation of Marco Polo and reports about Matteo Ricci (1552-1610), invited to Beijing by the Wanli emperor in 1601 after years of working to develop the Jesuit mission in China.

The newly formed East India Company entrusted the queen's second letter to George Weymouth (1585-1612), a captain employed to seek out the Northwest Passage. The letter was written in English but translated into Latin, Spanish, and Italian in the hope that a Jesuit such as Ricci might translate the contents for the emperor. It made it almost to Hudson's Bay before Weymouth prudently decided he should go no further. Finally, in 1984, a British archivist delivered a copy of the letter to China. Hoping that this voyage would succeed where earlier ones failed, Elizabeth I warmly predicted, "By this means our countries can exchange commodities for our mutual benefit and as a result, friendship may grow." It took another century for this desire to become a reality.

In the next decades two Ethiopian monarchs, Za Dengel (r. 1603-04) and Susenyos (r. 1606-32), wrote letters to the pope and King Philip III of Spain declaring their decision to embrace Roman Catholicism in lieu of Ethiopian Orthodox Christianity and asking for military support against their enemies. Paul V responded with the promise to send Amharic and Ge'ez type to print the Catholic version of the word of God in Ethiopia. In 1613, Susenyos attempted to send an embassy with the Jesuits to Madrid and Rome. It failed because of internal hostility from Ethiopian Christians and external pressures from the Ottoman Empire. Undeterred, he converted to Roman Catholicism and declared it the religion of his empire in 1624. This led to a succession of revolts that ultimately brought him to rescind this decision in 1632 while retaining his own religious conviction. His successors expelled and persecuted the Jesuits, and with them the Portuguese who traded in this region. By 1640 they neither wrote nor received letters from Catholic popes and kings.

In the 1670s, a young Venetian named Ambrosio Bembo (1652-1705) traveled through the Levant and India to see how much this part of the world had changed. He observed the decline of the Portuguese Empire and thwarted Spanish ambitions in light of the growing presence of the Dutch, French, and the English. Each merchant flew the flag of his country on the top of his palace in Surat, and a seemingly infinite array of goods flowed in and out of the port cities. In Mumbai he ate an Anglo-Italian meal on Chinese porcelain with the half-Venetian Enrico Gay and his Indian Christian wife; he drank wine from the Canary Islands with the head of the English East India Company. While Bembo found "European things" costly in India, he was nonetheless able to purchase an elegant French suit. The world that Elizabeth I and her contemporaries hoped to encounter was now within their grasp.

Bembo marveled at the speed and variety of European news he was able to receive in Persia and India. It came from many different sources – Catholic missionaries, Protestant merchants and soldiers, and a wide variety of people making a living in this interconnected world who were in regular communication despite the distance. He jokingly observed that wherever he went, people asked if he was a physician. He did not mention meeting another Venetian, Nicolò Manuzzi (1638-ca 1720), who lived most of his life between Madras and Pondicherry and seems to have been a self-taught surgeon. Certainly, Manuzzi was an excellent example of why Italians were considered healers, and not only by resident Europeans.

Manuzzi is best remembered today for his *History of the Mughal*, a manuscript he sent to Venice in the early 18th century written in an eclectic mixture of Italian, French, and Portuguese. Manuzzi explicitly addressed his history to "the Europeans" – a category that became more meaningful to him after many decades in the melting pot of late 17th-century India where he could not see himself as exclusively Venetian. He was a European living in an East that was no longer mythical or vague because it had come into focus over the past two centuries. Sending and receiving letters, sharing news, living, intermarrying, and doing business in a complex world reshaped by European ambitions, he epitomized the European who wrote from the East and, unlike Marco Polo, chose not to return home.

Reading: The Early Modern Global Travelers

Travel was an opportunity to observe, learn, and reflect, and early modern Europeans did all of these things in ever greater numbers. Through travel one could view personal experiences of the world in a broader, comparative context. The Europeans who traveled east understood all too well that they entered a world whose political and economic systems were rapidly changing and whose religious beliefs were equally under scrutiny, especially by those who hoped to convert people of one faith to another. They began to pay greater attention to the many differences among peoples that they observed, in some instances approaching the nature of cultural difference as a project of ethnographic imagination. Differences in food, clothing, jewelry, hair, bathing, and sexual customs, the presence of tattoos and piercings, the use of chopsticks, the variety of weapons, ships, different kinds of writing systems, and paper all captured their attention. The most fundamental distinction concerned the nature of the European presence in each region. Societies subdued or colonized by Europeans interacted with travelers in an entirely different way than societies under local rule, or those that posed a real threat to Christian Europe's borders, as in the case of the Ottomans.

By the time the Portuguese explorer Vasco da Gama reached India, Constantinople had been in Ottoman hands for almost half a century. Ottoman ships routinely threatened the coastal towns and ships of the Adriatic and Mediterranean, making slavery and the prospect of forced conversion one of endemic fears of the voyage that no one wanted to take. As a result, thousands of Europeans found themselves captive in North Africa, the Barbary Coast, or the Ottoman Empire for anywhere from a year to a lifetime, awaiting redemption. In the Eastern Mediterranean and Eastern Europe, people who had previously been Byzantine, Venetian, Genoese, or Habsburg subjects, or who enjoyed some degree of political autonomy from these empires, now became Ottoman subjects. After making major incursions into Venetian territory in the Eastern Mediterranean in the late 15th century, the Ottomans turned their attention to Eastern Europe. In 1521 they captured Belgrave, followed by Buda in 1526. Then, in 1529, they alarmed all of Europe with the first siege of Vienna. Next, they challenged the Portuguese for control of the Indian Ocean. The shifting boundaries between various European states and the Ottoman Empire transformed the lives and identities of those caught in the fray. Some indeed remade their lives around these circumstances, recognizing the growing importance of go-betweens whose skill with languages and knowledge of other cultures made them valuable agents in an interconnected world.

Diplomats and Missionaries

One of the most important kinds of travelers to emerge in this context was the diplomat. While viceroys ruled Portuguese and Spanish colonial territories, and factors tended to the profit of empire, consuls instead represented their state to foreign powers. The Venetian *bailo*, or diplomat, in Constantinople, for example, represented Venetian political and commercial interests in this part of the world. At the same time, he worked to redeem Venetian captives, acting as an informed observer for his state through a network of informants, translators, and friends. By 1535, the French had an embassy after making peace with the Ottomans, and eventually, with much greater unease, so did the Habsburg emperors. The growth of diplomacy ensured the regular presence of a diverse community of resident Europeans who also began to write about their travels. The apothecary Pierre Belon (1517-64) accompanied the French ambassador in 1546-49 as part of his entourage and found himself admiring many aspects of Ottoman society, including its modesty, sobriety, cleanliness, charity, and social openness, in comparison with his own. As a Protestant, Belon especially appreciated the religious plurality of Ottoman society where "each man is permitted to live according to his own faith." He wrote these words during the French Wars of Religion, recognizing that his society was far less accommodating than the one he encountered.

Portuguese Goa became a point of departure for merchants, embassies, and growing numbers of missionaries sent to evangelize in the East. The Japan mission inaugurated by Xavier resulted in a highly publicized Japanese embassy to Rome orchestrated by the Jesuits. Four young male converts sailed from Nagasaki in February 1582 with their Jesuit companion Diego de Mesquita and a Japanese Jesuit rebaptised George Loyola for Macao before traversing southern India to Goa and Cochin. There they studied Latin and Portuguese in preparation for their arrival in Lisbon, where they landed in August 1584. They were greeted by young Portuguese who were wearing Japanese kimonos. The Japanese Christians subsequently enjoyed audiences with Philip II of Spain and pope Gregory XIII in Rome. They left Lisbon in April 1586, laden with European gifts for the shogun. They completed further studies in the Jesuit colleges of Goa and Macao and installed a European printing press in Goa. Following the inevitable delays brought on by the monsoon season, the Japanese party and their Jesuit advisors returned to Nagasaki in July 1590. Faith inspired long-distance travel as much as commerce, politics, and curiosity. The number of European missionaries traveling to every part of the world continued to grow.

During this same period, a Catalan Jesuit, Antoni Montserrat (1536-1600) left Goa for the Mughal court, traveling through a part of India not under Portuguese control. On the road between Surat and Rander, Montserrat was the recipient of the antagonism shown to Europeans when natives attacked his party yelling, "Franks, Franks!" Only reassurances that he was neither Portuguese nor had an interest in war nor profit mollified the angry crowd. While the Portuguese strove to appear Japanese when they greeted the four boys who disembarked in Lisbon, the Mughal emperor Akbar (r. 1556-1605) and his sons honored Montserrat by putting on "Portuguese dress." Later, the Jesuit discovered that the Mughal emperor had an equal passion for Spanish clothes and loved European swords as well. At the emperor's request, Montserrat tutored his second son, Murad. Meanwhile, he learned Persian from a Christian convert from Hormuz so that he could better participate in the conversations of this sophisticated, urbane court. Montserrat hoped that Akbar would convert to Christianity since Akbar exhibited a strong interest in other faiths and seemed critical of Islam. In the end, Montserrat realized that the emperor's interest in Christianity emanated from a pragmatic openness to what he might learn from the world, much the same as the way he studied European maps while asking the Jesuits how they gained their knowledge of Asia, rather any strong conviction. Permitting a few Europeans to join his court allowed the Mughal emperor to expand his mental horizons, but he had no intention of being subjected to their faith.

Sailors, Pirates and Renegades

Travel was not only about obtaining local knowledge of the language, customs, and culture of a region where Europeans hoped to establish a presence, it was also about grasping the world as a whole. The first Europeans to circumnavigate the globe were the 18 survivors of the 1519-22 voyage commanded by Ferdinand Magellan – murdered in the Philippines the year before a single ship limped home to Cadiz. Magellan's shipmate, Antonio Pigafetta, kept a meticulous journal which became his *Report on the First Voyage around the World*, originally published in 1524-25 and republished by Ramusio in 1550. He named the vastness of the "Pacific Ocean" though not the Philippines. Those islands were named in honor of King Philip II as a result of a later Spanish expedition in 1542. The next European to circumnavigate the globe would do so a half-century later. It was then the flamboyant Elizabethan pirate Sir Francis Drake (ca 1540-96) sailed into Plymouth on the *Golden Hind*, his ship laden with Spanish booty, to greet his queen in 1580.

Drake's success inspired others to replicate his voyage. The Franciscan, Martín Ignatius de Loyola, great-nephew of St. Ignatius, managed this feat twice in the 1580s while trying to establish a mission in China. Loyola became famous for his report on the region; the Spanish had been aspiring to colonize it from their base in Manila since 1571. They had limited understanding of the scale and complexity of the Ming empire, and envisioned a conquest like those they conducted in Mexico and Peru. Both the English and the Dutch increasingly challenged Spanish global ambitions, and looked for vulnerabilities in their system of long-distance trade. Sir Thomas Cavendish captured the Manila Galleon off the Baja Peninsula in 1587, the year before the Spanish Armada attempted to invade England; he returned with a ship laden with Chinese silk and other Asian commodities. Cavendish failed to return from his second attempted circumnavigation. Global travel was a high-risk endeavor despite the potential for great rewards.

Carletti left Japan too early to witness the meteoric career of the English captain William Adams (1564-1620) who joined one of the earliest Dutch expeditions to Asia. He arrived in Japan in 1600, with a handful of other survivors on a ruined ship that barely managed to reach shore. Adams successfully thwarted Portuguese and Jesuit hostility to the unexpected presence of northern European Protestants. He persuaded Tokugawa Ieyasu, who became shogun in 1603 but ruled unofficially by 1600, that the Dutch and English saw Japan as a natural ally in their incursions into

Spanish and Portuguese Asia, and they hoped to establish favorable commercial relations with him. He shared "a chart of the whole world" with the shogun to show him the different routes by which Europeans traveled to Asia.

Adams spent the rest of his life in Japan. He brokered the establishment of Dutch (1609) and English (1613-23) factories in Hirado. While supporting his English wife and children, he also married a Japanese woman, having two children with her and another with a concubine. The shogun made him a samurai, and honored him with offices and an estate. Commonly known today as Miura Anjin (The Pilot of Miura), he sailed throughout Southeast Asia on behalf of the Japanese and the English East India Company. The English captain John Saris called Adams a "naturalized Jappaner." Observing how fluidly the son of a Kentish shipbuilder integrated into Japanese society, Saris did not necessarily mean this as a compliment, since the English samurai's loyalties seemed suspect. Yet he recognized that without Adams's fluency in language and customs, it would have been impossible to negotiate such a favorable trade agreement with the Japanese.

The early modern go-between was indeed a compelling, if unnerving, figure. Take the flamboyant Sir Anthony Sherley (1565-1635). This mercenary fought in European wars for whoever would employ him before finally joining piratical expeditions to West Africa and the Caribbean. He claimed to have "opened up the Indies" to the English. After traveling from Venice to Persia (modern-day Iran), he also boasted that he could create a secure trading route through Persia and Muscovy that would give the English an advantage over the Portuguese. Sherley also promised access to Mughal India and many other extravagant claims that no one in London could verify from a distance. Yet there was no doubt that he acted as one of Shah Abbas I's ambassadors during his return to Europe in 1599. He subsequently represented the pope to the Portuguese viceroy in Goa, and the English, Spanish, and Holy Roman Emperor Rudolph II during a trip to Morocco to negotiate an anti-Ottoman alliance. Sherley died in Granada, trying to convince the Spanish that his vast experience of the world would assist them in preventing the Dutch and the English from overtaking Iberia's role in the East.

Matrimonial bonds sometimes served as useful avenues to diplomatic and trade alliances. The Roman nobleman Pietro della Valle (1586-1652) became one of the most famous Europeans to find a spouse during his travels. Prior to arriving at the Safavid court in Isfahan in January 1617, he married the Syrian Christian Ma'anī Jowayrī (d. 1622), in Baghdad. Her native language was Arabic, and probably she spoke Armenian as well. They spoke Turkish, which was also the language della Valle used in conversation with the Persian shah regarding the pope. During his 12 years away from Europe, della Valle had his portrait painted first in Syrian, and then Persian dress. He altered his hair, beard, and mustache to conform to local customs. He witnessed the Anglo-Persian conquest of Hormuz by the Portuguese in 1622 – a tangible outcome of Shah Abbas I's interactions with the English. Della Valle then traveled with the English to the East India Company factory in Surat. When he reached Goa in 1623, della Valle decided to resume wearing "our European garb" because he recognized that he was now in a European-dominated city.

Becoming European Abroad

Increasingly, questions of identity and belonging fascinated the most observant Europeans who traveled and lived beyond the boundaries of Western Europe. They commented on the creolization of many European colonies and trading outposts. Landing on St. Helena in 1691, an island located between Africa and Brazil that had been under English, Dutch, and Portuguese influence at various times, the swashbuckling William Dampier (1651-1715) – who thrice circumnavigated the globe, going as far south as Australia where he described the aboriginal tribes – declared that the young women of the island were "but one remove from the English." What did it mean to be almost English? Or for that matter, how could one tell the difference between someone who arrived in Europe from another continent and someone who simply pretended to be foreign and exotic? Take the fascinating example of George Psalmanazar (1679-1763). This Frenchman pretended to be Irish, then Japanese, and most infamously Formosan. He allegedly escaped the dual subjugation of Japanese rule and Catholic missionary zeal to find liberty in Anglican Protestant England. This suggests how being a European in a globalizing world might inspire new kinds of experiments in assuming identities.

One year before Psalmanazar's *Memoirs* appeared in print, Lady Mary Wortley Montagu's (1689-1762) letters, written in 1717 during her husband's brief appointment as the English ambassador in Constantinople, were finally published. The flamboyant Wortley Montagu dressed in Turkish clothes after returning to England and presented herself as a cosmopolitan woman, arguing for the authenticity of her own experience of the Ottoman Empire. She shared what she had learned as a woman--privileged access to spaces where only women could enter like the Turkish baths. Nonetheless, Wortley Montagu could not resist enhancing her experience of travel. She recalled conversations with learned Muslims, who thought she knew Persian because she had read European novels about Persia, and told her readers that after a year in Pera (the neighborhood near Galata, the old Genoese colony of Constantinople north of the Golden Horn, where the European embassies were housed), "I am in great danger of losing my English." Wortley Montagu presumably acquired some Turkish but mostly spoke a variety of European languages with other Europeans in a city where she elegantly compared the variety of people to the tulips famously cultivated in Turkish gardens. This was her brief but powerfully formative experience abroad.

Wortley Montagu's sophisticated sense of cosmopolitan identity did not acknowledge the kind of forced immersion in global geopolitics that younger contemporaries, Elizabeth Marsh (1735-85) experienced. Marsh was a Portsmouth shipbuilder's daughter who endured captivity in Morocco, returning from her father's posting in Gibraltar, and subsequently divided the remainder of her life between England and India, writing about her experiences of the Maghreb in *The Female Captive* (1769). She highlighted her pointed refusal of Moroccan dress inside the palace of sultan Sidi Mohammed, understanding this gesture as a prelude to forced conversion and entry into his harem. Marsh's son Burrish would become fluent in Persian because of his apprenticeship at a young age to a Persian merchant, making him a valuable agent in the growth of British India. Her experiences and attitudes towards travel reflected the growth of the British Empire in many different parts of the world.

"Did I consider myself an European, I might say my sufferings were great," Equiano wrote with bitter irony in the opening of his book. Equiano was no Psalmanazar, superficially playing with new identities in an interconnected world. Instead, he is an important example of the kinds of new identities that became possible under changing circumstances, a man of African origin unwilling to live in America, unable to find a permanent home in Africa, but seeing England as the place "where my heart had already been." He died in London a reasonably prosperous man with two Anglo-African daughters born from his marriage to Susanna Cullen. Equiano was indeed a voice that the Europeans who created the Middle Passage needed to hear and learn from, but he was also a new kind of European.

Reading: The Intellectual Revolutions and Technology Transfer

In July 1687, Thomas Hyde (1636-1704), the learned Bodleian librarian who later became a Laudian professor of Arabic at Oxford, wrote a letter to Robert Boyle (1627-91), introducing a young Chinese Christian, Michael Shen Fuzong (ca 1658-91). Fuzong hoped to meet the renowned experimental philosopher in London. Boyle was a founding member of the Royal Society (1660), England's first scientific society. He was known throughout Europe for his innovative approach in the laboratory for testing the nature of the elements through alchemical analysis in the laboratory and the use of new instruments such as the air-pump in his experiments. He embodied the kind of broad, probing, and disciplined curiosity about the nature of knowledge that was the essence of the age of Copernicus, Galileo, Descartes, and Newton, an era commonly known as the Scientific Revolution. Boyle's reputation as a man of science captured the attention of one of the few Asians to travel to Western Europe in this period. He was also eager to meet the young Chinese scholar.

Eastern and Western Bodies

Shen Fuzong was a physician's son from Nanjing, a second-generation Christian educated by the Jesuits, making him that rare Chinese scholar proficient in Latin as well as classical Chinese. In 1681, he left China in the company of the Flemish Jesuit Philippe Couplet (1623-93), the learned procurator of the China mission. Couplet oversaw the publication of *Confucius, Philosopher of the Chinese* (1687) with Shen Fuzong's assistance. The reason for the translation of the majority of the Confucian canon by Jesuit missionaries was to demonstrate the elegance, sophistication, and reasonableness of Chinese philosophy and its compatibility with Christianity. In Paris, Shen Fuzong catalogued Chinese manuscripts in the royal library, showed Louis XIV how to use chopsticks, and left behind a specimen of his calligraphy. Wherever he went, he answered questions about the Chinese language and learning.

Hyde was renowned for his knowledge of Eastern languages, though it is not clear how much Chinese he actually knew when compared to his proficiency in Hebrew, Arabic, Persian, and Syriac. He was especially interested in comparing ancient weights and measures and preserving the great tradition of astronomy in Samarkand that was cultivated by the Timurid ruler and astronomer Ulugh Beg (1394-1449). Hyde had annotated and published Beg's 1437 star catalogue in 1665 for a European audience. Hyde was eager to show Shen Fuzong the Bodleian Chinese manuscripts, many of them dealing with medicine, meanwhile disparaging the Chinese as "a people wholly ignorant of anatomy."

Hyde was nonetheless curious about how they were diagnosed and cured. Boyle more ecumenically observed, "probably their writings and their practice may teach us something new." The Dutch East India Company physician, Willem ten Rhijne, had only recently published *On Acupuncture* (1683). It was based on his experience of Japanese medicine while working on the island of Dejima where the Japanese confined Dutch traders in Nagasaki Harbor. His book raised many interesting questions about East Asian medicine as a science of the surface, rather than an empirical investigation of the internal workings of the human body, increasing European curiosity about other medical traditions.

Shen Fuzong promised that he would try to send samples from the Chinese pharmacopoeia to Oxford during his return voyage. He did not live to see the first work of European anatomy produced in China – *Ge ti ciowan lu bithe (Complete Record of Anatomy*, 1723). The eight-volume Manchu translation was created for the Kangxi emperor by the French Jesuit Dominique Parrenin, who joined the Society of Jesus when Couplet and Shen Fuzong were in Paris. Thus, by the early 18th century, the imperial court in Beijing knew of William Harvey's discovery of the circulation of the blood and other important insights emerging from the European revival of anatomy. This renewed interest had been inaugurated by Andreas Vesalius's *On the Fabric of the Human Body* (1543) which complemented growing European awareness of some of the most distinctive features of Chinese medicine.

In Japan, a practical appreciation for the most successful aspects of "redhead" surgery, botany, and pharmacy – the term for Dutch medicine used to distinguish it from the Portuguese – eventually blossomed into a genuine intellectual curiosity about Western science and medicine. This was especially so after Japanese prohibitions against importing European books were lifted in the 1720s. The emergence of *Rangaku* (Dutch Studies) in the 1770s included the *Kaitai Yakuzu (A New Anatomical Atlas*, 1774). It was the work of two Edo physicians, Sugita Genpaku (1733-1817) and Maeno Ryotaku (1723-1803), so deeply invested in the introduction of Western learning to Japan that they learned Dutch to complete this translation of a European anatomy.

All this was still in the future when Hyde and Boyle contemplated what they might learn from Shen Fuzong, while he considered what he might discover in conversation with British scholars who did

53

not even share his Catholic faith. European scholars were aware that China had rich alchemical and metallurgical traditions, ancient traditions of printing and papermaking, and the ability to transform nature into lucrative commodities such as silk and porcelain. There was much to know, especially from someone fully versed in Chinese science who could converse with them in Latin.

Looking Beyond The Map

Together Shen Fuzong and Hyde annotated some of the most interesting Oxford treasures, including the Selden map, a Chinese merchant map of East Asia that entered the collection in 1659. Maps were both repositories of valuable knowledge and a kind of paper technology that allowed people to move throughout the world and locate themselves within it. Like the compasses, astrolabes, quadrants, and sextants – used by multiple cultures to navigate but not by all – maps made a powerful impression during any first encounter. Francesco Carletti was struck by the absence of maps on Japanese ships in the late 1590s. When William Adams arrived in Japan in 1600, the Japanese confiscated his sea charts and instruments though he seems to have retained "a chart of the whole world" to show the future shogun Tokugawa Ieyasu how Europeans reached Japan, thus earning his goodwill.

Two decades earlier, in 1580, Father Antonio Montserrat brought a European atlas as a gift for the Mughal emperor Akbar who used it to locate Portugal and his own empire while inquiring how Europeans "knew the names of the provinces and cities of India." Geography manifested Francis Bacon's well-known aphorism that knowledge is power. This is precisely why Akbar's son, Jahangir, had himself depicted in about 1615 embracing Shah Abbas I of Persia atop a European-inspired globe. It is also why generations of Jesuits in China offered their cartographic skills to the emperor, as well as their fellow Europeans. Hyde knew very well why it was important to ask someone fluent in Chinese to help him decode the Selden map during the period in which the British began to expand their presence in Asia. Science was indeed a handmaiden to empire.

After leaving Oxford, Shen Fuzong continued to answer Hyde's questions on a wide variety of other subjects, including the Chinese game of Go, for a book Hyde was preparing titled, *On Oriental Games* (1694) until he embarked on his return voyage. Communication was never easy. He alluded to his difficulty using a European-style pen to write in Latin, knowing that Hyde could not read an entire letter in Chinese. Shen Fuzong hoped to answer the Oxford scholar's questions more fully from Lisbon, where he could consult greater numbers of Chinese works, and ultimately from China. In return, Shen Fuzong thanked Hyde for the gift of European mathematical instruments to take back to China, though he also hoped that he might obtain "curious glasses such as microscopes or optic tubes, and the like, things both most pleasing to the Chinese, and also to me."

In the 1680s, Shen Fuzong surely knew that some of the more technically inclined Jesuits earned the Kangxi emperor's favor by teaching him how to cast European ordinance and assisting Chinese scholars in writing manuals explaining how to use firearms. He may even have heard how readily the Japanese adapted European firearms for their own purposes, after three Portuguese adventurers on a Chinese junk — one of them Mendes Pinto — shipwrecked on the island of Tanegashima in 1543. They showed the local daimyo how to shoot, selling him their two arquebuses at a handsome profit. Lord Tokitaka's request that his swordsmith replicate the weapons marked the beginning of the integration of European-style firearms into the thriving Japanese armaments industry for the next century.

The Japanese increasingly took guns into battle. Their invasion of Korea in 1592 exemplified the many different routes by which firearms arrived in East Asia as Japanese used a combination of Japanese and European guns to combat Koreans bearing weapons made or acquired with Chinese assistance. However, all this was a distant memory by the 1680s, in contrast to the growing presence and production of firearms in the regions of India with a regular European presence. The cessation of internal wars in the struggle for power in Japan, changing sensibilities about the uses of these European-inspired weapons, and the expulsion of the Portuguese with the suppression of

Christianity greatly diminished the demand for guns. The Dutch found the Japanese curiously uninterested in the weapons they brought to Dejima.

What Can Strange Devices Do?

By contrast, during the 17th and 18th centuries, European scientific instruments – what the Japanese called kiki (strange devices) – became prized commodities in many parts of the world. Galileo's discoveries with the telescope, beginning in 1609, were known to Chinese astronomers, especially after the German Jesuit Johann Adam Schall von Bell (1592-1666) published *Yuanjing Shuo (On the Telescope*, 1626), to explain an instrument that arrived in China with him and his confreres in 1619. A Dutch captain brought a telescope to Japan in 1613; the English ambassador Thomas Roe presented one to the Mughal emperor, Jahangir, two years later. By the mid-17th century, the English factors representing the East India Company routinely requested telescopes as presents designed to smooth relations with local rulers. The telescope had become one of the icons of the European arrival in Asia.

Looking through the telescope confirmed something Chinese scholars had already confronted when they gazed at Ricci's Chinese map of the world created with Mercator's techniques of projection – new technologies allowed people to see things differently. To what degree did they also convey new knowledge? Enthusiastic advocates of European science proclaimed the telescope the most useful of all the "marvelous devices of the Far West," but critics felt that the love affair with Western knowledge had gone too far. This was the fundamental tension at work in virtually every society where Europeans established a significant and sustained presence that had longstanding intellectual traditions of great antiquity and sophistication.

In 1644, Schall controversially became the first Jesuit to head the Bureau of Astronomy in Beijing. His assistant and successor, Ferdinand Verbiest (1623-88), worked with Chinese artisans in the early 1670s to construct large bronze astronomical instruments. They were modeled on engravings of the 16th-century Danish astronomer Tycho Brahe's instruments at his fabled observatory at Hven, and they still exist today atop the Beijing Observatory. Couplet and Shen Fuzong brought a copy of Verbiest's Manchu grammar with them to introduce Europeans to the language of the Kangxi emperor, who seemed potentially open to a dialogue with the West. He was their modern Confucius who expressed a desire not only to learn from others but to establish a mathematical academy in Beijing in imitation of the scientific societies he heard about in Europe. Shen Fuzong's ability to act as a go-between was a reflection of these larger forces at work between Europe and Asia.

The microscope that Shen Fuzong requested was a much more recent invention. Galileo's experiments with a "little eyeglass" to complement his telescope evolved into the compound microscope created by Boyle's contemporary, Robert Hooke (1635-1703), curator of the Royal Society's experiments. Hooke's *Micrographia* (1665), the earliest book devoted to microscopic observation, inspired a Dutch artisan, Anton van Leeuwenhoek (1632-1723), to perfect a handheld microscope with a finely ground lens which allowed him to observe nature's most minute details. In 1673, the Royal Society published Leeuwenhoek's account of his earliest discoveries. Two years later, a microscope arrived in Suzhou. It took much longer to reach Japan, but by the mid-18th century, the Japanese marveled at how much a *mikorosukopyūma* – their transliteration of "microscope" – changed the way they saw the world.

The concept of "detailed viewing" became a cultural obsession. European insects, inspired by the engravings in Dutch books inspired by Hooke's and Leeuwenhoek's pioneering work, haunted Japanese dreams and fantasies. Experiments with magic lanterns, electrical generators, and copperplate engraving accompanied these developments. A Japanese student of the evolution of European prints — woodblocks to copperplate engraving and etching — observed, "Even though we often cannot read the inscriptions written in the Dutch language, we still can get a thorough understanding of many of the things described merely by studying the pictures carefully." The Chinese painters and mathematicians interested in optics in Shen Fuzong's day also understood that seeing was indeed a kind of technology, often mediated by strange devices.

In the late 1680s, Shen Fuzong was in a unique position to assess both Chinese interest in Europe and European knowledge about China. As his comments on writing as a culturally specific technology suggest, he was an astute observer of the different means of transmission. In China, he had seen the use of Asian woodblock printing to create books and images with European content. He also was familiar with another hybrid artifact – books and images filled with Chinese characters produced by European printing presses. These were shipped halfway around the world by artisans capable of running the machines and teaching others how to cast and set type. Fuzong witnessed the Paris publication of *Confucius, Philosopher of the Chinese*. This book was made in Europe using a combination of Western and Chinese type and was the culmination of his understanding of the role of technology in communicating knowledge between cultures.

The challenge of creating a European type for languages that looked, in the words of a Jesuit in Goa, "impossible to cast" was an ongoing challenge to scholars like Hyde who understood languages to be the key to unlocking the universality of knowledge. In July 1674, the Venetian traveler Ambrosio Bembo commented on an abandoned ruin of a printing press in the Carmelite monastery in Isfahan. It had been installed in 1629 to print books in Arabic and Persian at the request, years before, of the deceased Shah Abbas I, after he had seen an Arabic book printed by the Medici Oriental Press (1584-1614) in Rome. Ultimately, it was never used. Not every European technology found an eager audience, just as not every Asian commodity inspired generations of Europeans to learn how to imitate its techniques of production as Europeans did with papermaking, gunpowder, silk, lacquerware, and especially porcelain.

Nonetheless, in the early modern period the printing press became one of the most global European artifacts. It traveled with Jewish scholars from Lisbon to Fez in 1516 to supply this exiled community with Hebrew books. A polyglot printing press intended for Ethiopia found an accidental home in the Jesuit college in Goa in 1556 when the Catholic mission in Africa faltered and the Portuguese community in India began to thrive. Macao had a printing press by 1588. It was brought by the Japanese embassy returning from Europe and operated by two of the Japanese Christians who learned the art of printing and type casting in Lisbon. In 1590, it accompanied them to Japan, inaugurating a decades-long tradition of printing there until the suppression of Christianity led to the sale of the press to missionaries in Manila around 1620. The Dutch East India Company established a printing press in Batavia in 1669, followed by one in Ceylon in 1743, and eventually Cape Town in 1795. The European press arrived in Calcutta with the British in 1777 and Cairo with the French in 1793.

What would Shen Fuzong have made of these uneven and often ad hoc developments? Unfortunately, his contributions remain limited to the decade in which he traveled to and from Europe, since he died on a ship off the coast of Mozambique in 1691 while attempting to bring all that he had learned home to China. Neither European nor Chinese medicine could save the man Hyde memorialized as his "informant on all matters Chinese" from the African tropical fever to which he succumbed. The brutal realities of how disease traveled were all too often no match for the more leisurely progress of scientific knowledge.

Reading: The Reformation

The late medieval Roman Catholic Church was not only a spiritual institution but an organization very involved in the politics of Italy and Europe. The pope had become a major player in the game of Western European politics. As the Church became wealthier and more powerful on the European stage, it was increasingly perceived as more bankrupt as a spiritual force. The costs of building magnificent architecture in Rome, such as St. Peter's Basilica and the Sistine Chapel, led the Church to policies that were easily abused, such as selling of indulgences (or spiritual privileges) and the exploitation of pilgrimages to Rome. Princes and common people were not only disturbed about abuses in Rome but also in their local ecclesiastical communities. Increasingly, the local bishop lived like an aristocrat and very often away from his post. Convents and monasteries had gathered great wealth through the centuries, none of which could be taxed by princes and kings.

Periodic scandals erupted about the conduct of nuns and priests who hardly concealed the fact that they were violating their vows of chastity, even openly promoting their illegitimate children.

Though most Western Europeans in the 15th and 16th centuries revered the Church as they had before and believed in the spiritual solace it had to offer, the clear evidence of corruption in the Church rankled enough to cause many to question its legitimacy. Yet, the place where the Church was coming into conflict was not necessarily among the common people; rather it was with the Western European princes and nobility. By the late 15th century, political authorities across Europe were attempting to curtail the public role and considerable power of the Church. Princes found some justification for their efforts to restrict the Church in the heightened criticism of the Church by late medieval reformers, and there were many.

Already in the 13th century, reformers emerged to try to restore Christian spirituality to the institutional Church, including St. Francis of Assisi and Peter Waldo. In the 15th century, Jan Hus of Bohemia and John Wycliffe of England critiqued the Church more directly, not only for its abuses but also for restricting the texts and ceremonies of the Church to the privileged class of priests. The Church hardly helped its reputation with the Papal Schism, a split within the Catholic Church lasting from 1378 to 1417 in which three men simultaneously claimed to be the true pope. At one point there were two Papal offices, one in France and one in Rome. Driven by politics rather than any theological disagreement, the schism was finally ended by the Council of Constance (1414–1418). But the damage to the Church's reputation was lasting. In the early 16th century, Erasmus of Rotterdam, the great humanist scholar, urged the Church toward liberal reforms that would get at the root of its difficulties, but the popes of the Renaissance in the late 15th and early 16th centuries acted like princes more than priests.

The most effective reform leader was, without doubt, Martin Luther, a German Augustinian monk and later professor of theology at the University of Wittenberg in Germany. Like many doubting clergy and laypeople, he had clandestinely read the forbidden works of Jan Hus and at the same time publicly supported the reforms suggested by Erasmus. But in 1517, he became outraged when a Dominican monk and indulgence seller, Johann Tetzel, came to Wittenberg on a mission to raise money for the building of St. Peter's Basilica in Rome. In effect, the indulgence was forgiveness of sin and a guarantee of salvation in the afterlife if the sinner would give money to the Church. Indulgence sellers would actually provide a certificate to the sinner, as if he were signing a contract for his soul. The incident inspired Luther to come out publicly with his criticisms of both the practice and the Church generally. He listed his criticisms in his famous *Ninety-five Theses*, written in October 1517 and later widely circulated in Germany

Martin Luther and Protestantism

There is little to no evidence in 1517 that Luther intended to inspire the massive socio-political movement that became the Reformation. Writing and distributing the *Ninety-five Theses* was a typical strategy for invoking a debate within the Church about its practices. But the *Ninety-five Theses* was very sharply critical of the Papacy. In the 86th thesis, for example, Luther wrote: Why does not the pope, whose wealth today is greater than the wealth of the richest Crassus [Croesus, a wealthy ancient Greek king], build the basilica of St. Peter with his own money rather than with the money of poor believers?

In addition, while he did not lay out an alternative interpretation of Christian doctrine in the *Ninety-five Theses*, in his writings of the next 12 months, he began to do so.

Luther always claimed that what distinguished him from previous reformers was that he not only attacked corruption in the Church, he also critiqued what he perceived to be the theological root of the abuses -- the perversion of Church doctrine regarding redemption and grace. Luther deplored the way the Church entangled God's free gift of grace in a complex system of indulgences and good works. He declared that the pope had no authority over whether a person went to Purgatory and therefore could not exempt someone from suffering in the afterlife if they gave money to the Church. He even argued that there was no foundation for the saints in the gospels. Worship of saints was very well engrained in European life, and gifts to saintly sites, churches, and icons were a very lucrative source of revenue for the Church. Luther boiled down his new doctrine to a couple of phrases: *"Sola scriptura"* (only Scripture is authoritative, not the Church doctrine) and *"Sola fide"* (there is only justification by faith, not by works).

The effect of his doctrine was spiritually and politically devastating to the Church. The Church's position on the grace-works question was the idea that salvation is jointly affected by humans and by God — by humans through marshaling their will to do good works and thereby to please God and by God through his offer of forgiving grace. Luther broke dramatically with this tradition by asserting that humans can contribute nothing to their salvation: salvation is, fully and completely, a work of divine grace. This interpretation took away from the Church its role as intermediary between God and man. In effect, Luther was demanding that each believer become his own intermediary. He reinforced this doctrine by translating the Bible from Latin into German, which allowed the faithful to see for themselves what God had to say without consulting the Church. In addition, if the Church had no role to play in public life, that was good news for the western princes who were chafing at the political interventions of Rome in their affairs. Luther was suggesting that the Church remove itself entirely from public affairs and confine itself to assisting the faithful.

In less than a year, by the summer of 1518, Luther's works were circulating and his ideas bubbling up all over Europe. The causa *Lutheri* ("the case of Luther") had progressed far enough to require that he present himself in Rome to be examined on his teachings. Reminded of how Jan Hus had been lured to a church council, only to be arrested and eventually burned at the stake, Luther demurred. This time, however, he had intervening on his side his territorial ruler, the elector Frederick III of Saxony. In a compromise, the Church agreed to examine Luther in the southern German city of Augsburg, where an imperial Diet, or meeting of the crown princes and lead clergy of Germany, was in session. Frederick was not necessarily a follower of Luther's ideas but was willing to defy Rome sufficiently to make sure Luther was treated fairly. It was a sign of more widespread princely dissatisfaction with Rome. At his interrogation, Luther refused to repudiate his writings and criticisms. The Church excommunicated him in January 1521. At another church council, the Diet of Worms in January to May 1521, Frederick again gave safe conduct and again Luther refused to repudiate his work. A warrant for Luther's arrest was issued. Frederick, however, spirited Luther away to Wartburg Castle in Germany and there Luther stayed, safely writing an entire corpus of works that further defined fundamental doctrines of Protestantism.

Reformation and Politics

Luther emerged from Wartburg Castle in March 1522 and returned to Wittenberg to begin preaching from the pulpit again. This time he was no longer a breaker of doctrines; he set himself up as a conservative force within the Protestant movement. He decried more radical doctrines and spoke against the many small fractured movements and reform leaders who, though inspired by Luther, wanted to go to a more radical fringe of the movement. He began to organize the Lutheran Church among his followers in northern Germany. In the mid-1520s, this more conservative approach was sorely tested when peasants in southwest Germany were inspired by radical Protestant ministers to revolt against their feudal overlords in what was called the German Peasant War.

For centuries, western princes had had to contend with periodic uprisings of peasants against oppressive taxes, unfair feudal practices, and abusive nobles. Most rebellions were readily put down. All recognized, however, that these revolts could become particularly energized and dangerous if they became linked to spiritual defiance in the form of Protestantism. If a peasant believed that his soul was in danger, he could become a more tenacious foe than one who was only fighting for mere economic or political rights or advantages.

Luther was not unsympathetic to the demands of the German peasants in 1524-25, but he encouraged them to obey the civil authorities. Luther's view was that man was fallen and too sinful to survive without aid. In the political realm, this aid took the form of civil government. The authority of the Church for Luther was limited to spiritual matters only and should have no influence in the governance of the people. As a pragmatic matter he understood the problems of trying to govern by Christian principles alone, and acknowledged that civil powers had a role to play.

A man who would venture to govern an entire community or the world with the gospel would be like a shepherd who should place in one fold wolves, lions, eagles, and sheep. The sheep would keep the peace, but they would not last long.

But the German Peasant War was complicated. Certain leaders of the revolt, most importantly Thomas Müntzer, had once been followers of Luther but had turned against him because they believed he had not gone far enough. Luther could be very hard on those he felt had betrayed him. Luther also paid a price for the hot rhetoric of his pamphlets and harsh language for authorities. Many peasants did not see the nuances of his positions and instead read his work as a prompt to revolt against the corrupt higher nobility. Revolts broke out in Franconia, Swabia, and Thuringia in 1524, even drawing support from disaffected nobles, many of whom were in debt. Gaining momentum under the leadership of radicals such as Müntzer, the revolts soon turned into all-out war in 1525. During a tour of Thuringia, Luther became enraged at the widespread burning of convents, monasteries, bishops' palaces, and libraries. On his return to Wittenberg, he wrote a strongly worded pamphlet, *Against the Murderous, Thieving Hordes of Peasants*, that called for the nobles to put down the rebels like "mad dogs:" In 1525, the nobles managed to suppress the revolt and Müntzer was tortured and executed, along with many of the leaders.

Despite the peasant war, in terms of politics, the real political impact of the Reformation was not a class-based struggle. Rather, if anything, it hastened the emerging power of the princes over their old medieval allies — the leaders of the Church. Even the term "Protestant" has roots that evoke the princes. When the Holy Roman Emperor put pressure on the rulers of the German states to turn against Luther, a number of princes issued a protest, saying that their duty to God was higher than their duty to the emperor. Because of this stand, their opponents labeled them "Protestants," a term that eventually spread from politics to religion.

Luther, in fact, initially had high hopes for the secular authorities. He urged the lay princes, as Christians in authority, to serve as emergency bishops in reforming the Church:

Let every person be subject to the governing authorities ….In our day the secular powers are carrying on their duties more successfully and better than the ecclesiastical rulers are doing. For they are strict in their punishment of thefts and murders…. But the ecclesiastical rulers,… actually nourish pride, ambitions, prodigality, and contentions rather than punish them (so much so that perhaps it would be safer if the temporal affairs of the clergy were placed under secular power).

Against Rome's century-long attempt to make the Church dominant over the state, Luther wanted to show how church and state could work together under God's rule. He argued that God works in the spiritual realm through the gospel and in the temporal realm through secular authority.

A positive experience between church and state, however, was rarely realized in the next century. In fact, what emerged was a phenomenon called "confessional politics." Princes and rulers would confess either to Roman Catholicism or one of the emergent churches of Protestantism, and then would attempt to enforce civilly the standards of that faith, often persecuting adherents of other faiths. It led to nearly 130 years of religious wars in Europe. The last few decades in the Thirty Years' War was one of the worst periods of war and violence in European history. Only in 1648 with the Treaty of Westphalia, did European princes negotiate a peace that ended the demands for confessional loyalty of subjects. It eventually led toward a wider philosophical acceptance in Europe of the separation of church and state.

Varied Reformation Movements
Luther was the most influential leader of the Reformation, but not the only one. Almost immediately after he left the Diet of Worms, other leaders both more radical and more conservative emerged to lead various movements within the Reformation movement. After 1526, Luther was no longer a dynamic Reformation leader and became something of a bitter man. Various other reform leaders came forward with interpretations of Christian doctrines he could not

abide, and they founded rival churches on the basis of those differences. Today, the differences seem rather inconsequential. But, once the Reformation challenged the dominant Roman Catholic Church, men grappled with what could take its place and were inclined to highly contentious views. One thing that these movements had in common with Luther's experience was that every religious interpretation seemed to have a highly political consequence.

German Reformation

The Reformation movement within Germany diversified almost immediately from Luther's initial acts, and other reform impulses arose independently of Luther. In Zurich, Switzerland, the reform leader Huldrych Zwingli built a Christian theocracy, blending church and state in the service of God. While Zwingli agreed with Luther about the centrality of the doctrine of justification by faith, he differed with Luther on the issue of holy communion. Luther had rejected the Roman Catholic teaching of "transubstantiation," where bread and wine in communion became the body and blood of Christ. Zwingli took a more moderate position, saying that it obviously was not a physical transformation but was spiritual and an acceptable declaration of faith by the recipients.

Another group of reformers called the Anabaptists argued that baptism should not be performed on infants. The Catholic Church wanted to cleanse the child of sin with the baptism ceremony as soon as possible after birth, so that he or she could become a part of the Church. But the Anabaptists argued that only adults who had professed their faith in God could understand the significance of the ceremony and, therefore, receive baptism. Strangely, every other reform church and leader seemed to condemn the Anabaptists, and they were persecuted severely. Because of the persecution, they were forced into a marginal position in the Reformation. Nevertheless, they survive as Mennonites and Hutterites to this day. There were also less well-known sects that opposed the teaching of the Trinity, where God is the father, the son (Jesus Christ) and the Holy Spirit. These were known as Socinians, and they established congregations mostly in Poland.

French and Swiss Reformation

John Calvin, a French lawyer who fled France after his conversion to the Protestant cause, founded a church In Geneva, Switzerland. Calvinism was an intricate, rather legalistic interpretation of Protestantism, much inspired by Calvin's great work, the *Institutes of the Christian Religion* in 1536. It was the first systematic, theological treatise of the new reform movement. Calvin also agreed with Luther's teaching on justification by faith. However, he found a more positive place for law within the Christian community than did Luther. In Geneva, Calvin was able to experiment with his ideal of a disciplined community of the elect. Calvin also stressed the very strict doctrine of predestination, that even before birth God had selected those who would be saved and those who would not. Like Zwingli he believed that communion was a spiritual partaking of the body and blood of Christ. And in fact the two churches under Calvin and Zwingli eventually merged into a Reformed church in mid-century.

English and Scotch Reformation

In England the Reformation's roots were even more political. Henry VIII struggled to have a legitimate male child and worried that the lack of a male heir would send the country into a long succession struggle, as happened in the 15th century with the War of the Roses. Henry's father Henry VII was a low-level noble who nevertheless triumphed because internecine war killed off all of the princely and noble rivals. When Henry VIII was unable to have a male heir by his Spanish wife Katherine of Aragon, the daughter of the powerful monarchs Ferdinand and Isabella of Spain, he asked the Pope to annul the marriage. Pope Clement VII naturally refused rather than upset his Spanish allies. Henry repudiated papal authority, divorced his wife, married his pregnant English mistress Anne Boleyn, and in 1534 established the Anglican Church. The new church was unique in that the king was its supreme head — a clear politicization of the church.

Henry immediately acquired all of the monasteries, lands, and churches of the former Catholic order in England, becoming very rich in the process. But he also gave generously to his new church, whose ministers developed a comprehensive liturgy that advanced Protestant thinking and culminated in the English-language translation of the Bible, eventually called the King James Bible.

Meanwhile in Scotland, the reformer John Knox, who spent time in Geneva and was greatly influenced by John Calvin, led the establishment of Presbyterianism. Presbyterians strongly advocated the notion that a church was no institutional structure, it was an organized community of believers who were essentially equals.

Catholic Reformation

To the credit of Rome, the Church did not sit idle while large swaths of Europe were lost to Protestantism. Led by popes in the 16th and 17th centuries, the Church struggled against Protestantism and also made internal reforms. It acknowledged that its Renaissance popes were too political and reinforced the spiritual roles of Church leaders. New religious orders and other groups were founded to effect a religious renewal, including the Theatines, the Capuchins, the Ursulines, and especially the Jesuits. Later in the century, John of the Cross and Teresa of Avila promoted the reform of the Carmelite order and influenced the development of the mystical tradition. Francis of Sales had a similar influence on the devotional life of the laity.

Pope Paul III (r 1534–49) is considered to be the first pope of the Catholic Reformation. He ordered the meeting of another Council of Trent, three meetings in fact, at which the church responded emphatically to the issues at hand. It attacked Luther's interpretation on the role of faith and God's grace and against Protestant teaching on the number and nature of the sacraments. Disciplinary reforms attacked the corruption of the clergy. There was an attempt to regulate the training of candidates for the priesthood; measures were taken against luxurious living on the part of the clergy, the appointment of relatives to Church office, and the absence of bishops from their dioceses. Prescriptions were given about pastoral care and the administration of the sacraments.

The Vatican founded the Roman Inquisition in 1542 in an effort to combat heresy. It was more successful in controlling doctrine and practice than similar bodies in those countries where Protestant princes had more power than the Roman Catholic Church. The Spanish Inquisition had been empowered since the 1480s. In fact, in both Italy and Spain, Roman Catholicism remained strong. Where political and military power needed to be exercised against rebellious princes, the Church could count on powerful Roman Catholic princes like Emperor Charles V and his son Philip II.

A major emphasis of the Catholic Reformation was an ongoing missionary endeavour in parts of the world that had been colonized by predominantly Roman Catholic countries. The work of such men as Francis Xavier and others in Asia and of missionaries in the New World was rewarded with millions of baptisms, if not true conversions. There were also attempts to reconvert areas of the world that had once been Roman Catholic, such as England and Sweden.

Reading: The Renaissance

The Renaissance was an intellectual movement in the 15th and early 16th centuries, one of the most influential and dynamic periods of the people of Western Europe. The historians Jules Michelet and Jacob Burckhardt first used this title, which means "rebirth" in French, in the 19th century. The people who lived through these momentous events did not give a title to their times. Nevertheless, they regarded their intellectual and cultural efforts as remarkably innovative. And they credited the new ideas to their project of reviving or giving a new birth to ancient Greek and Roman ideas and rejecting Medieval ones. In fact, it was Renaissance writers who first began to talk of the centuries between themselves and the ancients as the Middle (or medieval) Ages and sometimes the "Dark Ages," as though these centuries were of little importance compared to what came before and after. As historians have acknowledged today, the Renaissance actually owes much to the Middle Ages. Even so, Renaissance men and women were successful in their critique of the twin institutions that held together society in the Medieval period — the Catholic Church and the feudalism of the landed aristocracy — and effectively accomplished the reform and diminishment of both.

Northern Italy

The epicenter of this rebirth was undoubtedly northern Italy. And it is quite logical that this part of Europe would become the center of innovation, for northern Italy was quite different than the many principalities and kingdoms of the rest of Europe. Italy had no king but was broken into a large number of small states, many of which were organized around prominent cities. Moreover, these urban Italians did not live under a feudal structure where their labor was attached to the land belonging to a feudal noble. In the 12th century, the German bishop Otto von Freising returned from a visit to northern Italy and remarked that the northern Italian city-states had a widespread new form of political and social organization and that they seemed to have exited from feudalism in a way that elevated merchants, commerce, and even the common man. A century later, as if to confirm Freising's views, the painter Ambrogio Lorenzetti painted a fresco in the city-state of Siena called the *Allegory of Good and Bad Government* (ca 1338-40). It glorified the virtues of fairness, justice, good administration, and most important, republicanism, or rule by the people.

Not all of the city-states of northern Italy were exactly like Siena, however. Venice was a commercial oligarchy, led by an elected doge, or duke, who held dictatorial powers for life, so long as he pleased the rather large and wealthy merchant class. The duchies of Ferrara, Milan, and Modena were generally run by ancestral aristocratic families, but like the Venetians, they were answerable to other powerful factions in their cities. Other city-states openly argued that they were republics governed by the popular majority — Florence, Lucca, Genoa, and Siena. They went through cycles of semi-democratic governance followed by crises when they often drifted toward their most powerful merchant families to provide temporary dictatorial leadership and stability. The most famous of these families was the Medici of Florence. The first two Medici leaders of Florence — Cosimo and Lorenzo — were brilliant at providing one-man rule without seeming to dictate. They cleverly used their family fortunes to cultivate the arts and promote civic pride in Florence, keeping the favor of the *populo*, the common people, if not always their rivals among the other wealthy families.

But one thing that all the city-states of northern Italy had in common, as Freising noted, was extraordinary commercial wealth. The Medici were the wealthiest family in Florence — and most of Italy as well. However, just five or six generations before they were nothing more than merchants in the cloth trade. They transitioned from the manufacture of cloth to banking, amassing greater wealth as bankers to the kings of Western Europe. Commerce brought great fluctuations in the fortunes of men, their wealth growing exponentially compared to the landed wealth of the old feudal aristocracy elsewhere. Great wealth led to more leisure for study and intellectual pursuits for their children and grandchildren. They could also patronize the arts and architecture, bringing prestige to their families. City ports in northern Italy were the *entrepôt*, the entry point, to all of Europe for the trade and commerce of the Silk Road of the Far East and the Levant on the eastern shore of the Mediterranean. The Italians held a key position. They were the first to receive and then introduce into Europe new ideas and new styles from cultures all over the world. In fact, the Venetians decorated their Church of San Marcos with artifacts from their travels and trade across Eurasia.

Crisis

The rest of Europe was also changing, albeit more gradually. Crisis forced their hands. The Black Death of the mid-14th century was very bad in the short run for northern Italy but good in the long run. Since the ships carrying plague from central Asia landed in northern Italian ports first and their cities were more densely packed with potential victims, the northern Italians experienced higher death rates. But the demographic collapse that took 30-40 percent of the population of Europe was far more devastating for the feudal system that propped up the elite in the rest of Europe. With fewer people, there was a decreased demand for food. Therefore, the value of the vast holdings of aristocratic land dropped precipitously. Without laborers to work the fields, feudal lands lay fallow everywhere, and there was a higher premium placed on the labor of common men and women. In addition, the wealth of common men increased because the families that survived the plague inherited the property from their many deceased relatives. Everywhere, common people had greater control, and the ideas of Renaissance Italy appealed to them, while feudalism slipped away.

Moreover, the prestige of the two great institutions of the medieval order — the Church and the feudal nobles — suffered because of their failure to provide answers to the suffering and devastation wrought by the plague. The Catholic Church compounded their problems in the Papal Schism. From 1378 to 1417, the College of Cardinals split in half and elected two separate popes. The one who had the support of the Italians remained in Rome, and the one with the support of the French king ruled from Avignon, a city in southern France. Not surprisingly, the common people surmised that the Church had become less a spiritual institution and more of a political one in addition to becoming, in some cases, the puppet of powerful kings.

Finally, those rising and powerful western kings in Spain, Portugal, France, and England increasingly dominated the weakened feudal aristocracy. In the 16th century, they took greater control of taxes, legal jurisdictions, armies, and even the lives of the nobles. They kept close control over the aristocrats by bringing them to the court, holding them there, and managing the details of their lives. This included who they married, what their children would do, and most important, how they spent their money — which mostly went to the service and prestige of the kings. At the royal courts, kings created a glittering society and new centralized administrations, attracting the nobility and gaining the loyalty of the common people who turned away from their feudal nobles. Often, at court, they imitated the cultural standards and styles of the Renaissance Italians in dress and food and became patrons of art, architecture, and music. The rise of this court society, which was the genesis of great centralized national governments, reached its summit in the 17th century.

Humanism

Humanism was the principle innovative idea which drove the Renaissance. Humanism is an ideology which elevates the value and agency of human beings, both as individuals and in groups, and generally promotes rationalism over the acceptance of tradition, dogma, or superstition. This may not seem like much today, as these tend to be modern values, but it was a radical shift from Medieval thinking. Right away one can see that humanism would challenge traditional institutions like the Church and feudalism. If the value of human beings was elevated, then common men could rid themselves of the social and economic shackles of their birth. If rationalism overcame superstition, then learning, science, and innovation, as opposed to the dictates and dogma of the Church, were the important tools of the new human agency.

We can say that in northern Italy there was already a great deal of human agency, even in the Medieval period. But Renaissance writers put these ideals into words — consulting the Greek and Roman texts of antiquity. Most historians date the popular embrace of these writings to the late 14th century, just a couple of decades after the Black Death. The three literary figures who initiated the trend were Francesco Petrarca, or simply Petrarch, Dante Alighieri, or simply Dante, and Giovanni Boccaccio. They were followed over the next hundred years by many other great Italian writers — Poggio Bracciolini, Leonardo Bruni, Marsilio Ficino, Giovanni Pico della Mirandola, Lorenzo Valla, and Coluccio Salutati.

Renaissance authors were aided by the numerous discoveries made during the period of ancient classical texts. For example, Petrarch, who can generally be regarded as the first humanist, discovered and published the letters of Cicero, a great ancient Roman intellectual, writer, and politician. In fact, the main argument of the literary humanists was for people to use these sources as guides for how to live in "modern" times. And there was just as much dispute among the Renaissance literary humanists as there was among Cicero and his contemporaries regarding life and living. For instance, should one follow an active life, involved in the politics of the day, or a contemplative life, among one's books in the countryside?

There was no single answer to these questions. The humanists' point was that a person should have the freedom, as they presumed the ancients did, to consider all the alternatives. One should not simply accept the dictates assigned by Medieval institutions. In fact, one should critique those institutions because one should be skeptical and critical of everything. It is a common mistake to assume that humanists rejected the Church. While some were vociferous critics of the Catholic Church, virtually all were Christians, and many were actually priests and religious devotees. Rather, Renaissance literary humanists believed that human agency and the mind was a gift from God and that God would want humans to exercise their minds and wills. It would not be until the 18th century that intellectual leaders began to openly question the existence of God.

Literary humanists provided the first steps, helping men break free from the medieval mental strictures to embrace free inquiry and criticism and apply it to other fields, such as art, politics, science, medicine, geography, and technology. From Italy, their ideas spread to northern Europe. They were aided by the invention of printing in the mid-15th century. Foremost among these northern humanists was Desiderius Erasmus from the Low Countries (modern-day Netherlands), writing in the early 16th century. Erasmus is most noted for his efforts to bring humanist inquiry and skepticism into the dogma of the Catholic Church; not to destroy it but to reform it. However, the consequences of his literary efforts were great. By demonstrating repeatedly that Church dogma deviated significantly with accurate translations of early Church documents, Erasmus created doubt regarding the Church's authority, even in its own founding documents. Eventually, this climate of doubt would lead to Martin Luther and the Reformation, with whom Erasmus at first sympathized but eventually rejected.

Renaissance Art
The common view of the Renaissance is that it was an art movement. But the art of the Renaissance is more accurately a superb visual chronicle of the intellectual foment of the time — particularly the idea of human agency. Renaissance art, unlike its medieval predecessor, had more realistic presentations of human beings often confronting human concerns. For example, in the medieval period, we would have seen numerous placid and staid images of the Virgin and child, a popular topic of art at the time, much like this one by Berlinghiero Berlinghieri in the 13th century.

By the height of the Renaissance, two centuries later, one of its greatest artists, Leonardo da Vinci, created his own version of the Virgin and child genre. He portrayed a very womanly Virgin Mary with her own mother Anne, playfully caressing the baby Jesus, as any human mother at any time would do. His depiction of Virgin and child celebrates the human delights of motherhood just as much as it respects the holy figures in the painting.

Moreover, Renaissance art exhibited qualities of the classical age. Artists turned to the three-dimensional form and placed a premium on movement in their art. What survived from the Greeks and Romans were statues of people who actually looked and moved like living people, unlike the two-dimensional, flat medieval portraits. So, as they imitated classical art, innovations in Renaissance sculpture preceded the innovations in painting by nearly a half century. When the late 15th-century artists took their brushes to the fresco wall or to the canvas, they endeavored to give a three-dimensional, sculptural quality to their paintings. To achieve these qualities, artists turned to mathematics and science and even developed mathematical formulas for the aesthetics of harmony, balance, symmetry, and perspective that were so indicative of the new art. (See Renaissance Art for a more detailed account of the evolution of art in the period.)

Renaissance Politics
As with so many other things, northern Italy was both a cradle and a cauldron when it came to politics. This was due to three innate characteristics of the political culture of Italy at the time. First, there was the presence of the Vatican, the seat of the Catholic Church, which had a constant need of diplomats to manage its affairs in Italy and with the crowns of Europe. Second, northern Italy had many city-state governments in which ambitious young men might find an administrative or even a leadership calling. And, finally, there was a great deal of militant competitiveness among these many small states, both with one another and within themselves. Leaders required constant political vigilance and observation to make sure that no one state or clan took advantage of another. Modern tourists marvel at northern Italy's beautiful, tall towers in its small towns built atop its hills. What they do not realize is that these locations had political significance. Their

positioning was defensive in nature and designed to protect against the armies of other small states. The tall towers were actually watchtowers from which wealthy Italian clans could spot approaching rival clans intent upon attacking them.

Truly, trouble spurred political innovation in Italy. Things were tense but balanced for much of the late medieval and early Renaissance periods. In 1494, however, they fell quickly into disarray due to external events. Initially, Charles VIII of France claimed the kingdoms of Naples and Sicily in southern Italy as his own and sent a large army south through Italy. The Spanish king, Ferdinand, soon saw an opportunity to claim southern Italy for himself and sent an army north through Italy under his general, Gonzalo de Córdoba. With these two powerful armies ravaging the countryside and the French and Spanish kings demanding alliances from each of the states they passed through, Italy became a massive battleground for nearly two years. Ultimately, the Spanish won and the French retreated, but each continued to interfere in the politics of Italy for decades.

In the aftermath of these tumultuous events, one of the many ambitious young Italian men, Niccolò Machiavelli of Florence, took his first steps into public life. In the wake of the French assault, the Medici had been deposed. After the French army left, the Florentines attempted to reestablish a true republic and hired Machiavelli as a diplomat. His office gave him the opportunity to travel Italy and observe closely powerful men and battling states. Unfortunately, by 1512, the Florentine Republic fell to the Medici. Machiavelli was exiled and spent much of the rest of his life writing literature, histories, and one extraordinary book that he described to his friends as a mere "whimsy" — *The Prince*. His whimsy became one of the most famous books ever written.

The Prince was written in a style called the "Mirror for Princes" that was common even in ancient times. Effectively, it was an advice book for kings and leaders. Traditionally, such books admonished leaders to adopt the practices of the best prince as their model, most often the most moral prince, or the one that would be most admired by a Christian. Machiavelli had seen many leaders in the previous two decades who either fit or did not fit this model and concluded that their goodness was irrelevant to effective leadership. Afterall, what use was it for a prince to be moral and good, if the prince lost power and saw his state fall into the hands of immoral or, even worse, incompetent leaders. Therefore, Machiavelli's standard for success was for the prince to do whatever helped him and his state to survive and prosper. According to Machiavelli, the prince should look for what he called "effectual truth." In other words, he should analyze whatever has kept leaders, from antiquity to the present, in power.

Machiavelli never established universal laws for policy or political behavior even though he is often called the father of modern political science. Rather, *The Prince* is a series of observations about "effective truth" in politics. For example, liberality might work for a hereditary prince because he has the weight of history and reverence on his side, and even the popular expectation of liberality. But it may backfire on a new prince, a military leader or astute politician, who comes to power and is warily watched by the people. Liberality may lead to greater taxation and then criticism; therefore, a reputation for stinginess might be better for him.

Through the centuries, many proclaimed Machiavelli to be an evil advisor, and the term "Machiavellian" means someone who lacks a moral compass. But we must remember that Machiavelli was steeped in the skepticism of the Renaissance. He wanted proof of what was working in reality and treated politics as just another subject of study. In his personal views, however, he sometimes revealed a desire to reach some greater good. In fact, he ends *The Prince* with a passionate exhortation to his fellow Italians to answer the calls for more effective leadership that would free Italy from the powerful grasp of its French and Spanish interlopers.

Renaissance Science and Technology
In the 16th century, during the latter part of the Renaissance period, great strides were made in the sciences, particularly astronomy, chemistry, mathematics, and anatomy, as well as technology. Some historians argue that the early Renaissance may have delayed these scientific discoveries for a century because of its preference for human-centered subjects like politics and history. But without question, the 16th century was an age of brilliant scientific breakthroughs and investigations that continued for another 150 years in what we call the Scientific Revolution.

To a certain extent, curiosity about the natural world was partly spurred on by the Age of Discoveries, which began in earnest in the 1490s. Within a few decades, Europeans circumnavigated the globe. In fact, some historians have persuasively argued that the movement toward science, and particularly scientific classification, began when Europeans started collecting unusual natural objects and brought them back from their travels around the world. Collecting became an important activity of the wealthy, not only to show one's worldly sophistication but also to demonstrate one's interest in the scientific study of natural things. The Italians called it the *studiolo*, and elsewhere it was called the cabinet. The fall of Constantinople to the Muslims in 1453 brought hundreds of scholars carrying in their packs ancient scientific texts. The early 16th century of nascent collecting and reading and discerning the natural knowledge of the ancients soon led to the beginnings of systematic analysis in the later part of the century.

While the tendency toward scientific inquiry and method was evident everywhere, perhaps the field that was the greatest triumph of Renaissance science was astronomy. The discoveries of the 16th-century astronomers and their new technology of the telescope was a profound innovation. One day men looked up and saw stars, planets, and the sun moving across the sky as if in a movie. This was the geocentric, or Earth-centered, view held by the medieval astronomers who followed the teachings of the ancient Greek Egyptian Ptolemy. The next, they came to understand that the Earth was not the center but simply a minor actor in the great solar system and that planets revolved around the sun, and possibly the sun revolved around something else yet to be determined. It was called the heliocentric, or sun-centered, theory of the movement of the solar system. This was the view of the great three Renaissance astronomers of the 16th century — the Polish Nicolaus Copernicus (1473-1543), the German Johannes Kepler, and the Italian Galileo Galilei.

In the true Renaissance spirit, Copernicus, steeped in Ptolemy's ideas, found much to critique. He turned to another ancient, Aristarchus, who had long ago proposed the heliocentric hypothesis but was ignored. By 1514, Copernicus was convinced that heliocentrism was correct and spent the next three decades writing mathematical proofs for the system. It was dangerous to provide alternatives to the Earth-centered universe, as Ptolemy's ideas were wholly endorsed by the Catholic Church. A system that made the Earth the center of the universe seemed most congruent with Biblical dogma. Therefore, it is not surprising that Copernicus published his famous book *De Revolutionibus Orbium Coelestium* in 1543, the last year of his life.

At first, Copernicus's heliocentric theory was rejected. Even in the last decade of the 16th century, both theories were taught to students, such as the young Johannes Kepler (1571-1630). As a teacher in Graz, Germany, however, Kepler wrote a vigorous defense of Copernican theory. However, the problem for Kepler, the mathematician, was that Copernicus was not precise enough. Copernicus had proposed that the planets have perfectly circular orbits around the sun. But other astronomers, such as the Czech Tycho Brahe, had demonstrated mathematically that the orbit of Mars would not follow Copernicus's circular model. Kepler spent years inductively proving a series of hypotheses that eventually led him to conclude that Mars, and therefore all of the planets, had an elliptical, or oval, orbit not a circular one, around the sun. Moreover, the planets' orbits were influenced by their proximity to the gravity of the sun both in their position relative to the sun and in their orbits. He published his mathematical formulas in several works, including *The New Astronomy*. The work of Kepler elevated the question of gravity as a primary mover of the planets, setting the stage for Isaac Newton's theories of gravity in the mid-17th century.

The contemporary of Kepler was the Italian scientist, Galileo Galilei (1564–1642). Known simply by his first name, Galileo was neither just an astronomer nor mathematician, but a polymath, a person who worked in various scientific fields. He is most well known as a physicist because he studied the principles of speed and velocity, gravity, relativity, inertia, and projectile motion. He was extremely fond of the new technologies of science and worked to improve instruments like the pendulum and the hydrostatic balance, and perfected the telescope. With his telescopes, he was the first to observe sunspots, the phases of Venus, and several of the moons of Jupiter. He also popularized science among the nobility by staging astronomy viewings with his telescope.

Much revered in Italy, Galileo was initially supported by the Church, particularly the Jesuits. Eventually, however, after the Church denounced heliocentrism, Galileo was brought before the Inquisition, condemned, and put under house arrest for the rest of his life. It was a great blow to Italian science and is partly responsible for the shift of scientific creativity to the northern capitals of Europe in the 17th century. In fact, much of the energy of innovation of the Renaissance in art, science, engineering, and commerce had shifted to Northern Europe by the beginning of the 17th century.

Reading: Renaissance Art
Proto-Renaissance (1280-1400)
As noted previously, it is a mistake to believe that the Renaissance, for all of its innovation, was a completely radical departure from the Medieval period that preceded it. In fact, there were many aspects of the Renaissance that can be dated back to the late 13th century. One of these was inspired by St. Francis of Assisi (ca 1181-1226), who rejected the formal Scholasticism of prevailing Christian theology, which had presented a fairly dour and dogmatic face to the world. St. Francis praised the beauties and spiritual values of nature and took joy in the works of men. His example not only influenced Renaissance writers, it also inspired Italian artists.

Thus, we can see some of the coming revolution in art of the Renaissance in the work of a few artists before 1400 — a period sometimes called the proto-Renaissance. The most famous of these was the Italian artist, Giotto di Bondone (ca 1266–1337). Working a hundred years before the Renaissance, Giotto's paintings lack the accuracy of symmetry and perspective of those after 1400; however, he was the first to attempt three-dimensional qualities in his painting. As is seen in this painting called *Lamentation (Mourning of Christ)*, his subjects have some three-dimensional depth and seem to be moving in natural ways. The picture has a true narrative quality. For example, the figures look at Christ with their backs to the observer as if to draw the person into the painting. This aspect is very unlike Medieval paintings which appear more like staged sets. Giotto's characters still look a bit cartoonish, but they are clearly emotional, weeping and distressed, unlike the passive style of most Medieval depictions.

Giotto was clearly beginning to break away from the flat, linear decorativeness and hierarchical compositions of his predecessors and contemporaries. Unfortunately, he was the exception rather than the rule. The public loved Giotto and gave him outstanding commissions, but they did not see the revolutionary character of his art as yet. It would not be until the early 15th century that Italian artists actually changed the rigid rules of composition that had dominated the Middle Ages.

Early Renaissance (1400-90)
An example of the public's hesitancy was an art competition in Florence in 1401 to win the commission to design bronze doors for the baptistry of San Giovanni. Two men who would become giants in the Renaissance, Filippo Brunelleschi (1377-1446) and Donato di Niccolò di Betto Bardi, known as Donatello (ca 1386-1466) lost the commission to a more traditional artist, Lorenzo Ghiberti. Brunelleschi immediately left Florence to travel to Rome, and there is some evidence that Donatello also went to Rome in the next years. There, they immersed themselves in the observation and study of ancient architecture and sculpture.

When Brunelleschi returned to Florence, he accepted several commissions to build public buildings and most had features very reminiscent of the classical style of ancient Rome. But in 1418, another art competition was held in Florence that became a seminal moment in Renaissance art. Florence had built the foundations and walls of their great church, Santa Maria del Fiore. Construction had begun in 1296, but the building remained without a roof for most of the next century because no one could figure out how to build a dome large enough to cover its rather ambitious interior expanse. No freestanding dome of this size had been built since antiquity, and the Florentine city council had prohibited the large buttresses that would have made it possible within the constraints of Medieval engineering. However, while Brunelleschi was in Rome more than a decade earlier, he had spent a good deal of time studying, measuring, and taking notes on the mathematical and engineering methods of the largest surviving domed building from ancient Rome — the Pantheon.

Brunelleschi entered the dome competition against Ghiberti again, suggesting solutions he had derived from his study of the Pantheon. This time it was Brunelleschi who won. He spent most of the rest of his life until 1446 building the dome for the church, which came to be known as "Il Duomo." It was the landmark of Florence and a visible sign of the humanists' argument — the way forward was to look far into the past.

Upon his return to Florence, Donatello as well began to create sculptures that echoed some of the ancient statuary of Rome, including an early marble statue called *David*. The subject was the central character in the Biblical story of the young Jewish David who killed the giant soldier, Goliath, using a sling to hurl a rock which fatally struck Goliath in the head. Goliath died instantly, allowing David to walk right up to him and sever his head. The marble statue showed David at this moment, standing in triumph over Goliath with one foot on the giant's head. Some historians note that the theme of David was popular in Florence because it was an allusion to the upstart Florentines and their new-found influence and power on the world stage.

While this early statue, *David*, showed many of the classical influences Donatello found in Rome, it was not the sculpture that would amaze the art world. Cosimo, the patriarch of the Medici and leader of Florence, commissioned a bronze statue of David from Donatello around the 1440s. Donatello's new *David* was the first freestanding statue since antiquity that could be observed in the round, and it was also the first fully nude statue of the male figure. This *David* had movement and beautiful symmetry. It also had personality, with a triumphant smirk on *David*'s face, as he gazes down at the head of Goliath. Moreover, the male figure was anatomically realistic and classical in its idealistic portrayal of the body. Most importantly, *David* was both controversial and sensational in the world of art.

Brunelleschi and Donatello led the way in reviving antiquity through architecture and sculpture. In turn, their work inspired Renaissance painting in its presentation of the new humanist style. When painters took up the brush, they sought to transform the three-dimensional qualities of sculpture onto the two-dimensional canvas. In doing so, they followed Brunelleschi's mathematical precision in creating new rules of perspective and Donatello's earlier and later imitations of the classical traditions of the nude.

The first painter to capture these elements was a Florentine artist who lived an unfortunately short life. Simply known as Masaccio (1401-28), he was a good friend of both Brunelleschi and Donatello, and there is much evidence that he was an ardent follower of Brunelleschi's experiments with perspective. Masaccio's paintings eventually helped create many of the major conceptual and stylistic foundations of Western painting — compositions with sophisticated intellectual content, extraordinary human emotions, and a high degree of naturalism.

Amazingly, most of his new art was realized in the six years when he had the commission to complete frescos on the walls of the Brancacci Chapel of the Church of Santa Maria del Carmine. The striking feature of the Brancacci frescoes, as shown here in *The Expulsion of Adam and Eve from the Garden of Eden*, was Masaccio's new freedom in the expression of emotion. The bodies of the naked Adam and Eve, driven from Paradise, are almost distorted in the intensity of their shame, as seen in the agonized upturned face of Eve. When word about the extraordinary Brancacci paintings got out, artists from all over Italy came to see them and this tradition — paying homage at the Brancacci — inspired some of the most famous artists of the Renaissance.

In the late 14th century, architects, sculptors, and painters followed the lead of these three great artists and further perfected the fundamental techniques of perspective, encouraged the revival of antiquity, and continued the emphasis on humanism. Several individuals deserve mention, including Fra Angelico, Piero della Francesca, and Sandro Botticelli. The first two concentrated on religious art, but Botticelli was an enthusiast for the revival of classical mythology. He produced two of the signature paintings of the Early Renaissance for his patron, Lorenzo di Pierfrancesco de' Medici, a cousin of the Florentine family leader, Lorenzo the Magnificent, the son of Cosimo. The first painting was an allegory, the *Birth of Venus* (1482), which has become an icon of the Renaissance.

A much-loved painting, also iconic of the Renaissance, was *Primavera* (ca 1478), which shows the three Graces dancing while Flora scatters flowers on the ground. These beautiful paintings represent well the rarefied atmosphere of the Florentine court in the late 15th century, before it was brutally interrupted by the Italian wars of 1494-95.

High Renaissance(1490-1597)

Florence had been the center of art for nearly a century, but now the center shifted toward Rome. This 35-year period is called the High Renaissance. To be sure, the masters who epitomized this period — Leonardo da Vinci (1452-1519), Michelangelo di Buonarroti (1475–1564), and Raphael Sanzio (1483–1520), all trained at an early age in Florence — particularly under the patronage of the Medici family. But as the Medici were driven from Florence in 1494,the mantle of patronage was inherited by other ducal families along with the Vatican popes. In fact, one of the Medici family was elevated to that office, Pope Leo X, and became a great patron of the arts during his papacy (1513-21). In fact, a series of popes (Julius II, Leo, Adrian VI, and finally Clement VII) were to one extent or another major patrons of Renaissance art. Ironically, while the three major painters of the High Renaissance created some of the finest painting masterpieces of the High Renaissance and advanced this medium in many ways, two of the three artistic giants were actually not that interested in the art of painting.

Leonardo

In reality, Leonardo was a polymath, a man capable of the sophisticated study of numerous fields including physics, anatomy, engineering, military technology, natural science, and art. His range of talents left him with little time to paint, and he seemed rather indifferent to it. In 1482, when he was just coming into his own as a painter in Florence, Leonardo sent a letter to Ludovico Sforza, the duke of Milan. In it he offered to serve the duke and listed ten skills. The first nine touted his military engineering capabilities and listed projects from portable bridges to a Renaissance version of the tank. In the tenth item, he mentioned that he also had skills as an architect, a sculptor, and finally, a painter. Perhaps the most celebrated painter in the history of Western Europe mentions offhandedly — oh yes, he also does a little painting!

In fact, Leonardo had many unfinished paintings because he became easily bored with it. But of the small portfolio of his work, we have three of the greatest paintings ever created — *Mona Lisa* (ca 1503), *The Virgin of the Rocks* (ca 1485), and the sadly deteriorated fresco *The Last Supper* (1495–98). And there about a dozen other paintings, any one of which would have made the reputation of any other painter. The keys to all of Leonardo's paintings were exquisite symmetry, balance, perspective, naturalism, and use of light. These brought to the apex the characteristics of the preceding century of Renaissance advancement in the painting medium. But he also seemed to have painting skills that exceeded his fellows and perhaps have not been duplicated since. No one seemed able to bring the subject of the painting right out of the background the way he did. He called his technique *sfumato*, smoky, or the blurring of colors in such a way as to avoid hard lines. Sfumato is evident in perhaps the most famous painting of all time, his portrait of the wife of a patron — *Mona Lisa*.

Michelangelo

Where Leonardo was rather dismissive of his art, Michelangelo regarded himself as a sculptor, first and foremost, and only as a painter and architect when forced by his patrons. Yet, he is remembered for all three and for a prodigious artistic output over his long life. His earliest sculpture includes one of the great masterpieces, the *Pieta* (1499), which depicts the dead Jesus in the arms of his mother. He then sculpted his own giant version of *David* for the city of Florence in 1501-04. His fame in Florence already established, Pope Julius II summoned him to Rome and then assigned him the task, which Michelangelo dreaded, of painting the Sistine Chapel. This is one of his few paintings, but it is perhaps his most memorable work. He labored for four years, from 1508 to 1512, to complete it. The entire Biblical story is told in a series of scenes starting with Genesis in the center and then radiating out to cover the entire ceiling. A devout man, Michelangelo conveys his personal vision of the Bible through the lens of a man infused with the humanism of his times. After 1520, Michelangelo is,undisputedly, the greatest artist of the late Renaissance. He was commissioned to do a number of architectural projects, first in Florence and then in Rome. In the 1530s, he designed the buildings on the Capitoline Hill and placed the famed antique statue of Marcus Aurelius in the Piazza del Campidoglio in front. The final architectural commission of Michelangelo's long life came in 1546. Against his will, he was put in charge of the new St. Peter's Basilica and designed the building much as it looks today. Before he died in 1564, he saw the construction of the great drum supporting the dome of the basilica. After Il Duomo in Florence, it was the second great dome of the Renaissance. It was completed after Michelangelo's death in 1564 but in accordance with his design.

Raphael

The third great artist of the High Renaissance, Raphael, was thoroughly devoted to painting and painting alone. At the start of the 16th century, he came to Florence and became famous for a series of beautiful Madonna and Holy Family portraits. In 1508, Julius II summoned him to Rome to complete several masterpieces. These are the painted frescoes on the walls of the Pope's meeting rooms, or *stanze*, in the Vatican. The most famous of these is Raphael's greatest work called the *School of Athens* (1508–11). In this large fresco Raphael brought together representatives of the Aristotelian and Platonic schools of thought. Instead of the densely packed, turbulent surface of Michelangelo's Sistine Chapel, Raphael placed his groups of calmly conversing philosophers and artists in a vast court which had vaults that receded into the distance. The *School of Athens* is often regarded as a symbol of Renaissance art because of its perfection in perspective, as well as its use of color and composition.

Raphael had a relatively short life, dying in 1520, but he accomplished mastery of one more genre which would become even more popular in the late 16th century — the male portrait. His subjects included both his papal patrons, Julius II and Leo X, and his friend, the writer Baldassare Castiglione. The paintings have neutral backgrounds which brings attention to the drama which surrounded these powerful men. Compared to earlier examples of Renaissance painting, there is a more limited range of color with an emphasis on blacks and browns. The exquisite clothing and medals of office, however, shimmer against the darker backgrounds. The subjects are also posed in an informal manner, often looking or positioned away from the observer. In effect, Raphael was inventing a new style of male portraiture that would be followed by artists in the 16th century, particularly those who painted royal portraits.

The Northern Renaissance and Venetian Painting

Most Renaissance painting of high quality was in Florence and Rome before 1520, however, Flanders (modern-day Belgium) in northern Europe, had a brief flourish of Renaissance artists in the 15th century with Jan van Eyck (1390-1441), Robert Campin (ca 1375-1444), and Rogier van der Weyden (1400-1464). Jan van Eyck's *Altarpiece* at St. Bavo's Cathedral in Ghent (1432) was perhaps the most significant work. But, we can see most readily the new style of portraiture and the commercial connections of Flanders with northern Italy in another piece. This is Eyck's portrait of a married couple — an Italian merchant in Bruges, Giovanni Arnolfini, and his wife Giovanna — now known as *The Arnolfini Marriage* (1434).

Dürer

But perhaps the northern painter who is most associated with the spread of the Renaissance is a young German artist named Albrecht Dürer (1471-1528). Dürer's was trained by his father as a goldsmith in Nuremberg, Germany. In 1494, and again in 1505, he traveled to northern Italy to meet and learn from leading Renaissance artists. It is evident the Dürer's skills as an artist reach far beyond goldsmithing. An early self-portrait demonstrates the extent to which he absorbs the Renaissance artistic style, as well as the lifestyle. It is the first example in history of an artist presenting himself as an eye-catching figure of dramatic interest, and a self-portrait genre that would be followed by artists down to modern times.

In Italy, he also began to perfect his talent for watercolor — sketching trees by a lake, a castle on a hill, or mountain valleys. These watercolors are not preparatory work for oil paintings; they are done, it seems, purely for pleasure. Dürer breaks new ground yet again, travelling to Antwerp in 1520, when he keeps a journal illustrated with sketches. These early experiences lead him on to a lucrative and pioneering business in printmaking, using techniques of woodcut, engraving, and etching. Since the invention of the printing press in the mid-15th century, small books and broadsheets create a new market for this medium of illustration in the 16th century.

Titian

In the 15th century, Venice was not a center of Renaissance art. But the doges and leading commercial families dabbled in patronage. Some home-grown artists emerged, but the master, by far, was Tiziano Vecelli (1488-1576), known as Titian. By 1520, he had accepted and executed several commissions for Church altarpieces and secular paintings for the wealthy of Venice and soon princes across Italy, such as the Duke of Ferrara. But Titian also painted portraits of the rich, famous, and princely, and it was here that he gained a reputation and following. By the 1530s, he painted Charles V, the Holy Roman Emperor, Charles's son Philip II of Spain, and Francis I of France, as well as more minor royalty across Europe. He was so much in demand that he managed to convince these clients that he could do their portraits without traveling to them, but staying in Venice and merely restyling previous portraits that had been painted by other artists.

In these portraits, Titian perfected the informal style of portraiture first introduced by Raphael earlier in the century and made it a signature of the royal portrait. Kings and princes are pictured on horseback and with their dogs. They are posed standing, looking away from the observer and in both jovial and somber moods. In a manner similar to Raphael, the paintings tended to have dark or neutral backgrounds, in contrast to early Renaissance painting practice, so that the royal subjects, their rich and elaborate clothing, and their medals and marks of state could stand out.

The death of Michelangelo in 1564 generally marks the end of Renaissance art. Even Michelangelo himself, in a few later works, begins to show elements of the Baroque, the next great era in art. By the time the great Renaissance epoch closed in the mid-16th century, the standard work of artists had been transformed and was of better aesthetic quality than almost any painting completed before 1400. Renaissance art was indeed revolutionary.

Reading: The Idea of Absolutism

The term 'absolutism' entered the language of politics — in French — during the decade after the French Revolution in 1789. Its first appearance in English came, more than a generation later, in the radical and liberal literature of the years around 1830. The system or concept to which the term referred was of course much older — generally referring to the monarchies of the 16th and 17th centuries. It was against absolute monarchy that the revolutionary and radical writers of the late 18th and the early 19th centuries contended, seeing it as the most stubborn obstacle to their goal of establishing republics, or governments ruled by the people.

What is Absolutism?

Absolutism is a political theory and form of government where unlimited, complete power is held by a centralized sovereign individual, with no checks or balances from any other part of the nation or government. In effect, the ruling individual has 'absolute' power, with no legal or electoral challenges to that power. In practice, historians argue about whether Europe saw any true absolutist governments, or whether certain governments were absolute. But the term has been applied — rightly or wrongly — to various leaders, from Julius Caesar to Adolf Hitler, but most commonly to the monarch Louis XIV, who ruled France in 1661-1715.

The most common theory used to underpin the early modern absolutist monarchs was "the divine right of kings," which derived from medieval ideas of kingship. This theory claimed that monarchs held their authority directly from God, that the king in his kingdom was as God in his creation. The theory enabled the absolutist monarchs to challenge the power of the church, effectively removing them as a rival to the sovereigns and making the kings' power more absolute. Sometimes against its better judgement, the church came to heel and supported absolute monarchs. French Bishop Bossuet held that kings were God's representatives in the political affairs on earth. Royal power was absolute but not arbitrary: not arbitrary because it must be reasonable and just, like the will of God which it reflected. It was absolute in that it was free from dictation by parliaments, estates, or other subordinate elements within the country. Law, therefore, was the will of the sovereign king, as long as it conformed to the higher law which was the will of God.

While many political philosophers struggled against absolute monarchy, not all were against absolutism. For the English political philosopher Thomas Hobbes, absolute power was seen as an antidote to the craven nature of men. He argued that men may have the natural right to govern themselves, but he gives up these natural rights to a single individual, or a king, for his own self-preservation and protection from other powers and forces that might harm him. By putting power in the hands of the absolute ruler (or even a ruler who is not absolute), men can choose to safeguard order and give themselves security. The alternative, according to Hobbes, might be a violent, haphazard solely driven by basic forces like greed.

The Spread of Absolutism

In continental Europe in the 17th century, however, absolutism was practiced with varying degrees of success. First, absolutism seemed very desirable to many people in Europe in the 17th century. Before absolute monarchs established their authority, Europe had been in endless chaos, full of wars and social instability. The 30 Years War that ravaged Europe in 1618-48 devastated much of the Germanic states. Even France, a supposedly united country, was divided by classes, regions and religions. There was in fact no means of consolidating the powers of the French state until a single man, Louis XIV, took his position as the absolute ruler, monopolizing administration of justice and the use of force and establishing a system for collecting taxes and a huge administrative bureaucracy. Before Louis XIV, local nobles and even some bishops would pass legal judgements on the common people. Soldiers formed private armies, selling their services as mercenaries and sometimes looting and raping local villages at will. Local entities forced arbitrary tax collection on commoners at will. Louis XIV made war, tax collection and legal administration the occupation of the state and under his control. There was indeed more order and more peace.

Second, seeing the success of the "sun king." Louis XIV, monarchs across Europe, especially militaristic kingdoms such as Prussia and Russia, followed the example. The requirements of absolutism brought into play many modern developments. Providing for the standing armies of absolute monarchs often had a beneficial economic growth effect on the countries. Absolute monarchs began to pursue sound financial policies and financed various industries. The culture of obedience to the monarch engendered a more organized, legal and peaceful citizenry. The czar Peter the Great is a classic example of an absolutist monarch who tried to change his kingdom socially. In his case, he attempted to eliminate the influence of the East and engaged in a process of westernization, in which new western ideas and technology have been brought within the Russian border. He even moved his capital from Moscow to a more western location near the Baltic Sea and built the new capital of St. Petersburg according to western architectural standards.

The Spanish kings attempted to mimic the French example. But the great monarch of Spain was in the 16th century — Philip II. And he had established the example of a Christian king who saw himself as the tip of the spear for the Catholic Church and did not claim divine right. Also, the Spanish kings had long since turned their attention to the New World and their vast colonies there. They centralized government effectively but in the service of a mother country who saw her future as a colonial power. In England, the Stuart kings James I and Charles I also believed in absolutism. But the government, which was mainly made up of devout religious leaders, such as Oliver Cromwell, refused to hand over the authority. As a result, civil war occurred, the king was defeated and Parliament triumphed for good.

Indeed, the exception to the spread of absolutism in Europe was England. In medieval times, the parliament of the people had gained some traction with a document called the *Magna Carta*, which strengthened alternative sources of power. Both the Tudor and Stuart monarchs attempted to increase their powers in the 16th and 17th century. But in the mid 17th century, Parliament executed Charles I and ruled for a brief time in the period of the Long Parliament and Oliver Cromwell. The Stuarts returned to power in the latter part of the century but with much reduced power. By the end of the 18th century, England was well on the way to the constitutional monarchy that has passed down to the present — symbolic rather than powerful.

The Nature of the Absolute State
Absolute power was never quite as absolute as the kings and their detractors claimed. What we now generally believe is that Europe's absolute monarchs still recognized — still had to recognize — lower laws and offices, but maintained the ability to overrule them if it was to benefit the kingdom. Absolutism was a way the central government could cut across the different laws and structures of territories which had been acquired piecemeal through war and inheritance, a way of trying to maximize the revenue and control of these sometimes disparate holdings. The absolutist monarchs had seen this power centralize and expand as they became rulers of modern nation-states, which had emerged from more medieval forms of government, where nobles, councils/parliaments, and the church had held powers and acted as checks, if not outright rivals.

It developed into a new style of state that had been aided by new tax laws and centralized bureaucracy, allowing standing armies reliant on the king, not nobles, and with concepts of the sovereign nation. Indeed, the demands of an evolving military are now one of the more popular explanations for why absolutism developed. Nobles weren't exactly pushed aside by absolutism and the loss of their autonomy, as they could benefit greatly from jobs, honors and income within the system.

However, there is often a conflation of absolutism with despotism, which is politically unpleasant to modern ears. This was something absolutist era theorists tried to differentiate, and modern historian John Miller takes issue with it too, arguing how we might better understand the thinkers and kings of the early modern era: "Absolute monarchies helped to bring a sense of nationhood to disparate territories, to establish a measure of public order and to promote prosperity…. We need, therefore, to jettison the liberal and democratic preconceptions of the twentieth century and instead think in terms of an impoverished and precarious existence, of low expectations and of submission to the will of God and to the king …."

The End of Absolute Monarchy
During the Enlightenment, several 'absolute' monarchs — such as Frederick I of Prussia, Catherine the Great of Russia, and the Habsburg Austrian leaders — attempted to introduce Enlightenment-inspired reforms while still strictly controlling their nations. Serfdom was abolished or reduced, more equality among subjects (but not with the monarch) was introduced and some free speech allowed. The idea was to justify the absolutist government by using that power to create a better life for the subjects. This style of rule became known as "enlightened absolutism," sometimes "enlightened despotism." Some leading Enlightenment thinkers, believing that republics were a bridge too far, advocated this interim effort at enlightened despotism as the best hope for the common people at that time.

Nevertheless, the age of absolute monarchy was swiftly coming to an end in the late 18th and early 19th centuries, as popular agitation for more democracy and accountability grew. Many former absolutists (or partly absolutist states) had to issue constitutions, but the absolutist kings of France fell the hardest, the great grandson of the sun king Louis XIV, that is Louis XVI, was removed from power and executed during the French Revolution. If Enlightenment thinkers had helped the early absolute monarchs, the Enlightenment thinking they developed helped destroy their descendents.

Reading: Scientific Revolution

The Scientific Revolution was a series of events over approximately two centuries. 1550-1750, that transformed and developed the scientific fields of mathematics, physics, astronomy, biology, anatomy and chemistry. It was the foundation of modern science and also gave rise to and greatly influenced the intellectual movement known as the Enlightenment. Men moved from a less mystical view of their environment and the received wisdom of the ancients to an objective search for the patterns and consistencies in nature, so that they could more readily predict and control their reality.

Previously, the Scientific Revolution was historically treated as a 17th- and 18th-century phenomenon. Today, however, historians have pushed the very beginnings of the Scientific Revolution to the mid 16th century and the end of the Renaissance, when a number of scientific discoveries were emerging, most importantly the heliocentric universe proposed by Nicolaus Copernicus in his important work *On the Revolutions of the Heavenly Spheres* (1543). We speak of the Scientific Revolution taking place in two phases. The first phase focused on the recovery of the knowledge of the ancients and the dramatic efforts to systematize the collection of knowledge. This phase ended in about 1632 with the publication of Galileo's *Dialogue Concerning the Two Chief World Systems*. The second phase was dominated by the "grand synthesis" of Isaac Newton's *Principia* (1687), formulating the laws of motion with universal gravitation in a new cosmology. Both Galileo and Newton were the great figures striding across a growing and powerful landscape of scientific discoveries from the mid 17th> to the mid 18th centuries.

Several historical events coincided with the first phase of the Scientific Revolution. First, the Renaissance encouraged men and women to think logically and systematically reason about the world around them. Even Renaissance artists were not satisfied with simple images of the human body. Many actually did dissections of cadavers to develop a more perfect representation of their human figures. Second, exploration of the rest of the world, which began in the late 16th century and brought Europeans into regular encounters with Africans, Amerindians and Asians, forced them to think about the diversity of nature and the diversity of human culture in ways they had not known before. Explorers opened up new trade routes and brought to Europe strange new creatures like iguanas, rhinoceri, flesh-eating plants and scantily-clad Native Americans. Europeans responded by collecting the menagerie of global objects, but soon followed with scientific classification systems and soon after methods of systematically experimenting in the brave New World.

Scientific Method

Fundamental to the emerging science was not only this vast body of new information coming from the four corners of the world, but a way of determining what is knowledge. There were two key standards developed in the first phase of the revolution -— scientific method and empiricism. Today, we take for granted scientific method, a procedure of systematic observation, measurement and experiment, and the formulation, testing, and modification of hypotheses and theories, or conclusions. But prior to the 17th century, most scientific behavior was actually trial and error or haphazard observations. Little could be concluded but a good deal of data was collected and some observations were very valuable. Perhaps it is not surprising that the best progress was made in cosmography, or what we call today astronomy. The movement of the solar system was observable every night and, of course, changed hardly at all. Thus, the patterns of movement were more noticeable, if the scientist was prepared to rely upon his observations rather than received knowledge, as was the case of Copernicus, the first great scientist of the Scientific Age.

Such received knowledge of the ancients, like Ptolemy, was appreciated and used but eventually set aside, as a research tradition of systematic experimentation was slowly accepted by the European scientific community. The inductive approach — the search for patterns from observation and the development of explanations, or theories, for those patterns through a series of hypotheses — became increasingly predominant through the two centuries of the Scientific Revolution. It contrasted with the earlier, Aristotelian approach of deduction, where a system of knowledge was laid out and observations of the universe were checked against it. In practice, many scientists and philosophers believed that a healthy mix of both was needed — the willingness to question assumptions, yet also to interpret observations assumed to have some degree of validity. By the end of the Scientific Revolution the world of book-reading philosophers had been replaced with men who regarded themselves as "scientists," investigating a mechanical, mathematical world that could be known through experimental research.

Empiricism

In reality, both inductive and deductive philosophers advocated empiricism, that is that all knowledge is gained via a sensory experience, through the eyes, ears, taste, feel and smell. The emerging scientific method depended on empiricism. But not all scientists agreed about how absolute a role empiricism should play. Two contenders in the great debate about the basis for knowledge of the early 17th century were Sir Francis Bacon, the great advocate of empiricism, and Rene Descartes, who was the champion of rationalism. Rationalists had claimed that there are significant ways in which our concepts and knowledge are gained independently of sense experience.

In the long-run, empiricism triumphed. The great Enlightenment philosophers — Thomas Hobbes, George Berkeley and David Hume — were the primary exponents of empiricism and developed a sophisticated empirical tradition as the basis of human knowledge. Another influential formulation of empiricism was John Locke's *An Essay Concerning Human Understanding* (1689), in which he maintained that the only true knowledge that could be accessible to the human mind was that which was based on experience. He wrote that the human mind was created as a *tabula rasa*, a "blank tablet," upon which sensory impressions were recorded and built up knowledge through a process of reflection. While scientists today do not agree that the brain is a blank tablet (there being many biological precursors to sense experience), the important factor was that sense experience was the most reliable and objective observation of phenomena for scientific purposes.

Baconian Science

But it was Francis Bacon who was the first philosopher to really lay out the underpinnings of empiricism. In fact, Bacon is known as the father of empiricism. His works established and popularized inductive methodologies for scientific inquiry, often called the Baconian method, which is now called the scientific method. Most importantly, his demand for a planned procedure of investigating all things natural marked a new turn in the rhetorical and theoretical framework for science, much of which still surrounds conceptions of proper methodology today.

Bacon proposed a great reformation of all processes of knowledge for the advancement of learning, divine and human, which he called *Instauratio Magna* (The Great Instauration). For Bacon, this reformation would lead to a great advancement in science and a progeny of new inventions that would relieve mankind's miseries and needs. His *Novum Organum* was published in 1620. He argued that man is "the minister and interpreter of nature," and that "knowledge and human power are synonymous." Moreover, the great transformations in man's existence "are produced by the means of instruments" — a kind of belief and confidence in technology that we mostly accept today but was rather unusual in his time.

Bacon was an optimist. He argued that by the knowledge of nature and the use of instruments, man can govern or direct the natural work of nature to produce definite results. Therefore, man, by seeking knowledge of nature, can reach power over it – and thus reestablish the "Empire of Man over creation," which had been lost by the Fall of Adam and Eve. In this way, he believed, would mankind be raised above conditions of helplessness, poverty and misery, while coming into a condition of peace, prosperity and security.

For the purpose of obtaining knowledge of and power over nature, Bacon outlined in this work a new system of logic he believed to be superior to the methods of the ancients and the medievals. Bacon believed that the scientist should proceed with inductive reasoning from fact to axiom (well-founded conclusion or theory) to physical law. Before beginning this induction, though, the enquirer must free his or her mind from certain false notions or tendencies which distort the truth. In particular, he found that philosophy was too preoccupied with words, particularly discourse and debate, rather than actually observing the material world: "For while men believe their reason governs words, in fact, words turn back and reflect their power upon the understanding, and so render philosophy and science sophistical and inactive."

Bacon considered that it is of greatest importance to science not to keep doing intellectual discussions or seeking merely contemplative aims, but that it should work for the bettering of mankind's life by bringing forth new inventions, having even stated that "inventions are also, as it were, new creations and imitations of divine works." He touted the far-reaching and world-changing character of inventions, such as the printing press, gunpowder and the compass.

William Gilbert, the father of electricity and magnetism, was also an early advocate of inductive method, even before Bacon. His book *De Magnete* was written in 1600. describing many of his experiments. From these experiments, he concluded that the earth was itself magnetic and that this was the reason compasses point north. Gilbert's book was influential not only because of the inherent interest of its subject matter, but even more for the rigorous way in which Gilbert described his experiments and his rejection of ancient theories of magnetism. In many ways, he was one of the first scientists not only to reason about scientific knowledge, but to demonstrate the way a scientist should work and write.

Galilean Science

After the triumph of the scientific method and empiricism, two major figures of the new science who made immeasurable contributions were Galileo Galilei of Italy and Isaac Newton of England. Galileo Galilei has been called the father of modern observational astronomy, the father of modern physics and even the father of modern science. His original contributions to the science of motion were made through an innovative combination of experiment and mathematics. Galileo was one of the first modern thinkers to clearly state that the laws of nature are mathematical. In *The Assayer*, he wrote "Philosophy is written in this grand book, the universe ... It is written in the language of mathematics, and its characters are triangles, circles, and other geometric figures."

In broader terms, his work marked another step towards the eventual separation of science from both philosophy and religion &$8212; a major development in human thought. He was often willing to change his views in accordance with observation. In order to perform his experiments, Galileo had to set up standards of length and time, so that measurements made on different days and in different laboratories could be compared in a reproducible fashion. This provided a reliable foundation on which to confirm mathematical laws using inductive reasoning.

Newtonian Science

Sir Isaac Newton (1642-1726) was an English mathematician, astronomer and physicist. In his own time, he was called a "natural philosopher" and was widely recognised as one of the most influential scientists of all time, and a key figure in the Scientific Revolution. His book, popularly called *Principia* (1687), laid the foundations of classical mechanics or physics. Newton also made pathbreaking contributions to optics, the study of sight and light, and shares credit with Gottfried Wilhelm Leibniz for developing the infinitesimal calculus.

In *Principia*, Newton formulated the laws of motion and universal gravitation that formed the dominant scientific viewpoint until being superseded by the theory of relativity. Newton used his mathematical description of gravity to prove Johannes Kepler's laws of planetary motion, accounting for the trajectories of comets, tides, the precession of the equinoxes and other phenomena. He further demonstrated most of Copernicus's theory of heliocentricity. He demonstrated that the motion of objects on earth and celestial bodies could be accounted for by the same principles.

Newton also built the first practical reflecting telescope and developed a sophisticated theory of colour based on the observation that a prism separates white light into the colors of the visible spectrum. His work on light was collected in his highly influential book *Opticks*, published in 1704. He also formulated an empirical law of cooling and made the first theoretical calculation of the speed of sound. Beyond his work on the mathematical sciences, Newton dedicated much of his time to the study of alchemy, but most of his work in those areas remained unpublished until long after his death.

After the death of Newton, we can say that the Scientific Revolution was over, but the work of science was central to European thinking and life. The two great revolutions of the 19th century — the Industrial Revolution and the rise of nation-states and republics — owed much to the way that the demands for reason and objective analysis of the Scientific Revolution become such a part of the European mind.

Overview of Era VI: Change Becomes a Regular Experience, 1700-1800

Joshua Weiner, American River College

Imagine growing up in a world without choices. From birth your destiny would be set -- where you lived, what you did, who you lived among -- would all be subject to very little variation and mostly the result of chance rather than agency. Your life would still be subject to circumstances of nature and random chance, but in most other ways you would go through life with little hope or expectation of change. It is important to imagine such a world because for most of human history that was the experience of the vast majority of people. Even if we narrow our scope to the last few thousand years, we would find that most people lived in agricultural societies within which it would be common for children to grow up alongside their parents on the same plot of land that their grandparents, great-grandparents, and even more distant ancestors had occupied.

In addition, across those generations that plot of land would be worked with basically the same technologies, under similar economic conditions, by individuals whose spiritual and cultural ideas remained relatively consistent. When I asked you to imagine a world without choices, therefore, I did not simply mean a world of people trapped in circumstances not of their own making. But it was one in which few have any sense that a realistic alternative even existed or that conditions did or should change over time. To a large extent, birth continues to be destiny even in our own world. The difference is that even those born into desperate conditions today are at least aware of the potential for social mobility, if they could just get into the right school or have the perfect jump shot or win the lottery.

One byproduct of a life with very few choices and very little sense of opportunity is that there is little space for the kind of angst that comes from unrealized ambition. If people have no expectations for a life different from the one they lead, then they cannot be disappointed when those expectations go unmet. This is not to say that everyone simply accepted their circumstances no matter how dire. Peasant rebellions, for instance, did occur historically, but in most cases only when the level of misery slipped below acceptable levels.

As an example of this, it took a mixture of government cruelty, misrule, the widespread outbreak of plague, and poor climate conditions to ignite the peasant rebellions against Mongol rule in late-14th century China, which led to the creation of the Ming Dynasty. Peasant rebellions of this sort in China and elsewhere, however, were most often framed in religious terms, as movements in preparation for some sort of divine intervention. Most humans simply did not feel as if they had the ability to alter the basic nature of their existence through their own actions. As we enter the period from 1600-1850, however, even as people still may not have expected real change to occur during their own lifetimes, the world was beginning to change around them.

The impact of the early period of globalization discussed in World History Era 5 was being increasingly felt around the globe through the increased movement of people, goods, crops, and ideas from place to place. The result was that more people in more places around the world became aware of opportunities through which they could transform their lives. Even as most would not pursue these new opportunities, the very fact that they existed meant that staying on the land and doing the things that had always been done could be seen as a choice instead of an inevitability. For those who did seek to take control of their destiny, on the other hand, many did not find the success they envisioned. Those who did could only understand their own success relative to those who had achieved even more.

Generally, improved material conditions and standards of living across the world did not, therefore, always result in populations who were satisfied with things as they were. Rather, those who were disenchanted felt that things were not better. In turn, as humans became more accustomed to the idea of change, they increasingly came to understand that, rather than simply wait for conditions to change around them, they could themselves become agents of change. In turn, this realization further sped up the rate by which change occurred and the end results were significant revolutions in demographics, human thought, politics, and the global economy. World Era 6 will address these revolutions.

Demographic Revolution

The revolution in demographics leading up to 1850 was defined by three trends -- unprecedented population growth, increasingly long-distance migration, and urbanization. These trends were certainly not as pronounced as they would become by the end of the 19th century, but still mark a break with earlier human eras. The spread and adoption of crops like corn, potatoes, sweet potatoes, and rice to new environments both increased the global food supply and increased the amount of land that could be exploited by human settlers. Advances in mapmaking, navigation, and shipbuilding technology, alongside improved transportation networks, made it easier to move people across distances while providing needed resources to growing cities. The result was a global population that was larger, more mobile, and more concentrated in cities than ever before.

The vast bulk of migrants during this era came from West Africa -- from where they were carried across the Atlantic Ocean as enslaved people -- or from southeastern China -- from where they filled in newly conquered or newly developed territories of the Qing Empire or migrated outside the empire into Southeast Asia. Population growth was a much more widespread phenomenon. The intensity of the transatlantic slave trade meant that population in Africa may have stagnated or even dropped during this time, but every other continent saw significant and unprecedented population increases. Urbanization was a similarly global trend with new urban centers emerging in some areas and older cities exploding in population in others.

Intellectual and Political Revolution

The major revolution in human thought in the era relates to an 18th-century European intellectual movement known both to history and to its contributors as the Enlightenment. It is important to understand the Enlightenment as a European phenomenon that had global dimensions, since it was partially the result of global influences while also having significant influence on the globe. It played out specifically in Europe even as the factors that encouraged it could be found in other societies. In a broad sense, a significant contributor to the emergence of new ideas was the overall increase in available knowledge. In the 15th century, little of what Europeans (or any other people for that matter) had known about the world was based on direct experience and instead came from a mix of rumors, legends, ancient sources, and scriptural and church traditions. As European ships dispersed to all corners of the globe, however, they brought back with them not only spices, textiles, and other goods, but vast new quantities of knowledge based on direct experience. With more information available from larger parts of the globe, old assumptions became harder to sustain and new questions needed to be asked.

Those who have been deemed Enlightenment philosophers generally came from the ranks of the lower nobility, the merchant class, or the professional class. They had usually received some formal education and had read widely in both the classics and in newer works emerging from the growing European publishing industry. The societies they lived in were increasingly more prosperous, orderly, and efficient, even as they largely continued to be constructed around traditional political and social structures. In the context of this increased order and prosperity European intellectuals had the luxury to ask whether the machinery that made these things possible was still necessary. Maybe, they began to realize, the social and political order was not as fixed and eternal as the ruling class suggested.

It must be noted that although Enlightenment scholars often used universal language, their arguments about freedom, liberty, and rights were often understood to apply to people like themselves. It was the rare individual who assumed that such high-minded principles should apply to others -- women as well as men, peasants as well as the educated middle class, the variety of mixed race and indigenous people in Spanish America as well as to rich *criollos* born in the western hemisphere, the millions of enslaved people on the plantations of the Americas as well as to those who profited from their toil. Despite these limitations, Enlightenment ideas and the revolutions they inspired would help reshape the political and social order on both sides of the Atlantic and create new sets of assumptions about the state and society that would eventually spread throughout the world.

Economic Revolution

For the vast majority of human history, we have had access to only limited supplies of energy with which to engage in useful work. Until the advent of agriculture, our ancestors could rely only on energy that they had captured though gathering plants and hunting animals. The Agricultural Revolution was so significant because domesticated plants and animals made available huge new quantities of energy. Agriculturalists could now plant and harvest large fields filled with cereal crops,exploit domestic animals for their meat, milk, hides, and furs, and bring in enslaved or hired men and women to perform the labor. As important as this was, however, energy supplies were still limited by available land and by the annual flows of solar energy that came to Earth.

In the 18th century, English engineers seeking to solve a specific set of problems related to mining produced the first workable steam engines. When paired with fossil fuels like coal, these engines were able to unlock vast new quantities of energy and thus unleash human productivity from the factors that had bounded it for so long. The result was a series of global changes as revolutionary as any that humanity had ever experienced. The Industrial Revolution redefined so much about human life and did more than any other single process to shape the modern world. Industrialization helped

- Shift ideas of labor, gender roles, childhood, family life, and identity.
- Make once valuable skills obsolete while promoting formerly useless ones to being indispensable.
- Reshape the notion of the workday while helping to construct the modern concept of time.
- Elevate a new middle class into prominence to serve as managers, accountants, and clerks.
- Bring what Timothy Blanning called, "a new kind of poverty," more permanent and less cyclical than what farmers had once experienced.
- And, perhaps most significantly, completely reshape global economic and political relations.

Where for so long the most powerful states and richest economies had been in Asia, now the new industrial societies rose to unprecedented heights of productivity, wealth, technological brilliance, and military power. By 1850, this process was still playing out, but the trend lines were clear. Those countries that successfully embraced the technology and organizing principles of industrialization were launched into a frenzy of change that transformed virtually everything around them, while those that did not or could not embrace industrialization increasingly faced a future marked by stagnation and political domination. With industrialization, one of the greatest engines of change in human history had arrived.

By the middle of the 19th century, the world looked significantly different than it had 100 years earlier. Populations who originated on different continents were now mixed together in ways that would have seemed impossible in earlier eras. A political and social order that had once seemed unchangeable now seemed to be in flux. Economic conditions which had prevailed for thousands of years were in the midst of a revolution. By 1850 the modern world had been born and change would now become an unavoidable element in human life.

Unit 11: The Middle East and South Asia,1500-1900

James D. Clark, American Institute of Iranian Studies

Reading: The Three Empires at their Apex
Resumed Ottoman Expansion after 1500

The Ottomans had been expanding their small principality in northwestern Anatolia since the 14th century. By 1499 they were engaged in eastern Anatolia and northwestern Iran where the new Shiite Safavid dynasty presented a challenge. Sultan Selim (r. 1512-20) defeated the Iranians at the decisive battle of Chaldiran (1514), thereby halting Safavid advances into Anatolia and allowing him to focus on the eastern Arab lands. In 1517 the Ottomans seized Egypt, Greater Syria, and Mesopotamia from the Mamluks, and over the following decades they advanced across North Africa and southwards to Mecca and Medina in Arabia. That acquisition of the Arab Middle East altered the composition of the empire by increasing the Muslim portion to rough equality with that of the Christian. It also gave the Ottomans dominance of the eastern Mediterranean.

The height of the empire came under Suleiman (1522-66), usually called "the Magnificent" in the West, but "the Lawgiver" (*Kanuni*) in Turkish. The Ottoman sultans assumed the title of "caliph" after the conquest of Egypt when it was transferred from the last Abbasid caliph to them. Possession of the title was not emphasized, however, until the 19th century when it was used to garner universal Muslim support against European penetration and dominance.

Several institutions accounted for Ottoman success through the 17th century. One was the Janissary corps, which was composed of slave infantry devoted to the sultan. Another was the *sepahi* or cavalry, which composed the bulk of the military. The *devshirme* system whereby Christian boys were taken from their families, converted to Islam, and trained for positions with complete loyalty to the sultan was the manner by which they supplied many of the officials for the empire's bureaucracy. Another was the *millet* system whereby each major religious community (*millet*) — especially those of the Greek Orthodox, Armenians, and Jews — was recognized and given autonomy in its own affairs.

After conquering the Middle East, the Ottomans resumed their advances beyond the Balkans and into Eastern Europe. Hungary became a tributary following an Ottoman victory at the Battle of Mohacs in 1526. Three years later the Ottomans besieged Vienna, the capital of the Hapsburgs, for the first time. They also continued to consolidate their hold over the eastern Mediterranean by taking the islands of Rhodes (1520), Cyprus (1570), and Crete (1664). They were still strong enough in the late 17th century to besiege Vienna a second time in 1683, though they once again failed to take it.

Like nomadic conquerors before them, the Ottomans adopted many aspects of the more advanced cultures that they conquered. Byzantine civilization strongly influenced many aspects of Ottoman culture, the most apparent being in architecture. The most renowned builder was Sinan (d. 1578), who designed a large number of outstanding structures across the empire, including the Sulemaniye Mosque in Istanbul and the Selimiye Mosque in Edirne. The Hagia Sophia and other structures in Istanbul and throughout former Byzantine lands provided models for Ottoman architects.

In literature the Ottomans represented a continuation of eastern Islamic tradition. By the 14th century Persian was well established as the language of literature in most eastern Islamic lands. One of the outstanding Ottoman poets, Fuzuli (d. 1556), wrote in the Persian divan style. The poet Baqi (d. 1600) was imitated by subsequent Ottoman poets. Naf'i (d. 1635) was representative of the Indo-Persian (Hindi) style also current in Iran and India in the 17th century. That style was more elaborate than the preceding Khorasani and Eraqi styles, and, primarily using the genre of the *ghazal*, it employed more abstract and realistic imagery.

The Safavids and Shiism in Iran

The Safavids had their origins in both a Sufi order from the Caucasus and in the Shiism of Turkish tribes in eastern Anatolia. From 1501 to 1524 the founder, Shah Ismail, carved out a Turco-Persian Shiite empire in Iran, the Caucasus, and western Afghanistan. With his capital at Tabriz, Tahmasp I (r. 1524-76) strengthened Shiite dominance in the new realm.

Most Muslim Iranians were Sunni in 1500, as they had been since the 7th century. Because of a dearth of Shiite theologians in Iran, the Safavids brought scholars from other Shiite communities, especially Mt. Lebanon, to teach the tenets of the sect. Zealous in their adherence to Shiism, the Safavids often persecuted Sunnis and suppressed Sufi orders. Once it became ensconced, Shiism served to distinguish Iran from other Muslim lands. Being Shiite became one of the elements of Iranian identity thereafter.

The dynasty reached its height under Shah Abbas I (r. 1587-1629). He enlarged the empire by driving the Uzbeks from Khorasan and the Ottomans from Azerbaijan and by occupying Ottoman Mesopotamia. (Mesopotamia went back and forth between the Safavids and Ottomans from 1508 to 1638.) Abbas also started a corps of slave soldiers resembling the Ottoman Janissaries. They were called *glolams* and were mainly Georgians. They complemented the *qizilbash* tribesmen, the traditional Safavid supporters. None of the shahs who followed Abbas matched the earlier ones in ability. Harem politics dominated the years from 1629 to 1694, although the empire remained relatively prosperous and peaceful.

That prosperity engendered a cultural flowering. In the arts, miniature painting stood out. Behzad (d. 1535-6) was the most renowned miniature painters of his era, and Reza Abbasi (1565-1635) became the outstanding exponent of the Isfahani school of painting. Shah Abbas transformed his capital of Isfahan into a remarkable city with the Maydan-e Shah (shah square), the Royal Mosque, the Shaykh Lotfullah mosque, and the *Si-o-seh* (33) and Khwaju bridges over the Zayanderud River. There were some outstanding scholars during the period such as Shaykh Baha'i (d. 1620-1), a Sufi poet, Shiite theologian, and mathematician, the philosopher and Shiite theologian Mir Damad (d. 1630), and the prolific Shiite theologian Muhammad Baqer Majlisi (d. 1700).

In contrast with painting — and somewhat ironically given that Iran was the principle Persian-speaking country — literature was little patronized by the Safavid shahs, even though were some notable exponents of classical Persian poetry such as Vahshi (d. 1583). Nonetheless, during the Safavid era many Iranian poets emigrated to the more receptive Moghul court.

Another Turkish Muslim Dynasty in South Asia

The history of South Asia was always one of political consolidation followed by disintegration as successions of conquerors built empires that subsequently broke up into local and regional kingdoms. Another of those periods of consolidation began soon after 1500 when the Mughals came out of Central Asia to unify northern India.

From 1526 to 1530, Babur (1483-1530), who had been ousted from his state in the Ferghana Valley in Central Asia and ruled Kabul, seized northern India following the battle of Panipat (1526) where the last ruler of the Delhi sultanate was defeated. By the time of his death Babur's empire ranged from Kabul to Bihar. Akbar (r. 1556-1605) regained Afghanistan, the Punjab, Rajput, and Bengal after they were lost under his father, Humayun (1530-56), and extended the empire to Gujarat and invaded the Deccan. He became what the Europeans called the "Great Mughal." The Mughal system of administration established under him was continued even under the British Raj. It was also with Akbar that the first direct contacts with Europeans occurred, and visits continued to increase thereafter.

Along with expansion of the Mughal realm, Akbar's greatest accomplishment was a fostering of Hindu-Muslim cultural and religious rapprochement. He married a Rajput princess, allowed Hindus into the harem, and abolished the poll-tax on non-Muslims. He was curious about other religions, including the Christianity Europeans brought, and he organized debates among their representatives. He went so far as to attempt the creation of a new religion combining Zoroastrianism, Islam, and Hindu beliefs.

One of the Muslim opponents of Akbar's universalist tendencies was Ahmad Sirhindi (d. 1625), a reformer who had a classical Sufi orientation. Shah Valiullah (d. 1762), another Sufi reformer, tried to harmonize the various Muslim traditions based upon the shariat and supported many of Sirhindi's ideas.

Akbars' two immediate successors, Jahangir (1605-27) and Shah Jahan (1627-57), continued Akbar's policies. During their reigns, portraiture and architecture attained a notable height of refinement.

The Mughals valued literature and the arts even though the greatest emperor, Akbar, was illiterate. Babur was the most prominent (Chaqatai) Turkish writer of his time, and his memoir, the *Bāburnāma*, is a classic. Persian was the language of high Islamic culture and the Mughal court. Muhammad Urfi (d. 1590-1) was one of the Persian poets of the ornate style known as "Indian" (*Hindi*). Another was the Indian Fayzi (d. 1595). The Mughal court attracted and patronized many Iranian poets such as Sa'eb (d. 1669-70). Those Iranian emigrant poets numbered as many as 150 and received greater appreciation in India than in Safavid Iran. That poetry of the Mughal court influenced Ottoman poets. Another notable man of learning was the brother of Fayzi, Abdulfazl Allami, who was a scholar, a courtier, and a historian of Akbar, whom he portrayed as a philosopher king and a "perfect man" (*insāne-e kāmel*).

Over time, and in addition to the official language of Persian, the new language of Urdu (meaning "army camp") came to be used by Muslims. It was Hindi, but written in the Arabic script and with a larger Persian and Arabic vocabulary. Around 1700, the form of Urdu spoken in the Moghul court combined with the literary Urdu used in the Deccan among Muslims and led to the rise of Urdu literature in later centuries.

The last of the major Moghul emperors, Awrangzeb (1658-1707), reversed the policy of cooperation with Hindus and attempted to Islamize all of the Indian subcontinent. After 1681 he concentrated on the Deccan where he subdued the remaining Muslim powers. He also aroused an enduring Hindu revolt by the Marathas, a yeoman and warrior caste, founded by Shivaji (d. 1680).

Reading: A Reversal of Fortune in the 18th Century

The 18th century saw a depression in Middle Eastern and South Asian social and cultural life. It was the least notable of all Islamic centuries in achievements of high cultural excellence and less prosperous than previous centuries. The Ottoman and Moghul states were often losing lands to the European powers and fighting domestic opponents. The Safavids vanished altogether early on, and the Europeans avoided the subsequent chaos.

The Ottomans go on the Defensive

Earlier historians tended to see Ottoman history in terms of its rise and fall, with decline setting in after the reign of Sulayman the Magnificent because of military defeats and economic problems, especially inflation. More contemporary scholars see the period from the 17th to 20th centuries as one of transformation wherein the Ottomans struggled to find a new imperial synthesis within a changing environment. In any case, the Ottoman state lasted until 1922, a testament to the durability and effectiveness of its institutions.

After three centuries of conquests the Ottomans experienced their first setbacks in the late 17th century in wars with Austria and Poland between 1682 and 1699. They were defeated a second time at Vienna (1683) and subsequently lost Serbia. The Treaty of Karlowitz (1699) gave Austria most of Hungary and constituted the first surrender of territory. A second major defeat at the hands of the Hapsburgs culminated in the Peace of Passarowitz (1718). That setback was followed by a period of westernizing reform known as the "Tulip Age" (1718-30) under the Sultan Ahmet III

(1673-1736) and his vizier Ibrahim Pasha (1666-1730). (The cultivation of tulips whence the period derived its name was one display of exotic luxury among the wealthy.) One sign of progress then was the importation of the first printing press in 1726. The period was ended, however, by the reactionary Patrona Revolt by Janissaries and the people of Istanbul.

Military setbacks resumed later in the century. In 1768 the Ottomans started a war with Russia wherein the Ottoman fleet was destroyed and Russia occupied Rumania and the Crimea. Defeat at the hands of the more advanced European powers continued with the total defeat of the Ottomans at the hands of the Russians by 1773. The Treaty of Küchük Kaynarji (1774) the following year humiliated the Ottomans by not only ceding the Crimea to the Russians, but recognizing the Czar as the protector of Orthodox Christians on Ottoman territory. Another setback during the 18th century was the renegotiation of capitulations with Europeans. Additional privileges were given to them, including the right to grant certificates of protection to non-Muslim Ottoman subjects.

Iran's Century of Turmoil
The Safavids suffered a quick demise partly because of the over centralization of the administration. They failed to develop an effective imperial bureaucracy as the Ottomans had. The last Safavid monarch, Husayn (r. 1694-1722), was particularly intolerant with respect to religion, and his and the dynasty's rule ended with an Afghan revolt in 1722 and the capture of Isfahan. As so often occurred following the collapse of the imperial center, fragmentation ensued and chaos engulfed Iran for much of the 18th century.

The absence of a strong authority ended when Nader Qoli, a Turkoman of the Afshar tribe in Khorasan, declared himself shah in 1736. He restored the empire of the Safavids in a remarkably short time and took Afghanistan (1729), invaded Mesopotamia (1733), and advanced as far as the Moghul capital of Delhi, which he sacked (1739). Nader Shah was an Asian conqueror in the mold of Tamerlane. Though the Safavids were the standard, he did not recreate their cultural brilliance. The one non-military issue of note was his fruitless attempt to bridge the Sunni-Shiite divide by promoting a non-sectarian form of Islam.

Nader Shah's unexpected death in 1749 reignited the tribal contests for control of Iran. Eventually, Karim Khan Zand (1750-79), a Lor chieftain from the southern city of Shiraz, established sovereignty over the south of the country. His reign, unlike that of Nader Shah, was characterized by stability, relative calm, and moderation.

Iran descended into intertribal conflict a third time when Karim Khan died in 1779. The heirs of Nader Shah (the Afshars) and Karim Khan (the Zands) battled, but it was Aqa Muhammad Khan (d. 1795) of the Turkish Qajar tribe who eventually succeeded in extending his rule across the entire plateau and into the Caucasus. He was crowned shah in 1795 on the Moghan Plain, as Nader Shah had done 60 years before.

Despite the recurrent political turmoil, an important development occurred in religion during the 18th century. Two schools of Shiite theology, the Akbaris and Osulis, competed for dominance. By the end of the century the Osuli school had become preeminent. Although the Akhbaris endured, especially in Iraq, the Osuli school, with its tenet that believers had to imitate a mujtahid or senior cleric, became dominant in Iran and has remained so to the present. That gave rise to a clerical hierarchy using titles such as *hojjatolislam* and *ayatollah*.

Moghul Decline and Ascendancy of the British
Much as Iran, South Asia broke up after Awrangzeb's death in 1707. The emperor Bahador (1707-12), in spite of some successes, failed to reverse that decline. The Mughals lost direct control of their provinces in the south and east, though they etained their allegiance. Autonomous states filled the vacuum caused by the absence of a strong central authority. The empire was weakened further by the defeats it suffered from the Hindu Maratha confederation. With their center at Poona, the Marathas conquered the Deccan and around 1740 invaded the north in an attempt to displace the Mughals. In the northwest, the militant Sikhs established an autonomous state in the Punjab. Many of the provincial governors, or *nawābs*, such as those of Bengal and Oudh, also

gained independence, and the Afghans launched invasions from the north. Reversing the unifying effects the empire had had, communities withdrew into themselves. Nader Shah's sack of Delhi effectively ended imperial Moghul power in India. The Iranian conqueror also carried away the Peacock Throne, which thereafter adorned Iranian courts.

That disintegration of the Mughal Empire benefited the European powers and allowed them to penetrate the subcontinent. Europeans had been on the peripheries of India since the 16th century and had been free to trade mainly in spices and textiles. In the 17th century that changed to more commercial crops for export. Portuguese, Dutch, British, and French trading companies sought opportunities and competed with one another.

The British East India Company was initially only interested in conducting business, not in establishing colonies. Despite disagreements with Awrangzeb, it had established stations at Bombay and Calcutta by 1700. It drove the Portuguese out of India, but the French became rivals in the mid-17th century, especially under the governorship of Joseph Dupleix (1697-1763), who operated against the British from his stronghold at Pondicherry. In 1757, as part of the global conflict between Britain and France known as The Great War for Empire (1756-63), the British won the Battle of Plassey. That eliminated the French in India and led to British control over Bengal and further acquisitions. Following the global defeat of France in 1763 the East India Company, using private armies composed of British as well as Indian troops, greatly expanded its control over the disunited Indian states. Company policy was to pit the princes and regional leaders against one another. In 1764, it defeated the Mughal army and gained the right to tax. Bengal became its base, and from there it conquered first Nepal and then the Punjab by the mid-19th century. The company then controlled all of the subcontinent.

Reading: An Intensification of Challenges

The defeats that began in the 17th century and continued through the 18th compelled Ottoman leaders to consider remedies. By the end of the 18th century, they were aware that change was needed to halt European encroachment. The empire was forfeiting territory after losing on the battlefield because of superior European weaponry and tactics. Those losses to European armies that were better trained and equipped led the Ottomans to seek remedies from those same enemies.

The next attempt at reform in the empire came at the end of the 18th century when Sultan Selim III (r. 1789-1807) tried to establish a new military and bureaucratic structure (a "new order" [nezam-i jadid]) in the empire alongside the traditional institutions. In a typical pattern, he was overthrown by reactionary elements consisting of Janissaries and provincial officials who felt threatened by the proposed changes.

Despite that setback, Sultan Mahmud II (1808-39) carried on with his predecessor's policies and proved more successful. He centralized political control by means of modernizing the military and the administration. He also destroyed the Janissary corps and suppressed the provincial officials who had stymied Selim III's efforts. Finally, he subordinated the conservative ulema to the Ottoman state. In that way, he was able to more freely implement the needed reforms.

At the same time, the new ideology of nationalism began to influence the communities of the empire, especially the Christians in the Balkans. A Serb revolt occurred from 1815 to 1817. The first major rebellion was that of the Greeks, which ended in 1839 with independence.

In the middle of the century Czar Nicholas I of Russia famously referred to the Ottoman Empire as "the sick man of Europe" (1853). In an attempt to allay European concerns about the empire's health, another period of reforms was initiated across the middle of the 19th century (1839-61) with the overtly westernizing Tanzimat (restructuring) under Sultan Abdulmejid (r. 1839-61), Reshid Pasha (1800-58), and Fuad Pasha (1815-69). Those were continued under Sultan Abdulaziz (1861-76). The cost of the reforms, however, drove the Ottomans to seek loans from the

Europeans. Proving insufficient, Istanbul declared bankruptcy, and as a result, the Ottoman National Public Debt Administration was established, and it effectively gave European governments and bankers control of Ottoman finances. The Ottomans had gone from being the dominant power in the Middle East and the rival of European powers to being supervised by them.

The years 1876 and 1877 were momentous. The sultan Abdulmecid was deposed and his successor quickly suffered the same fate. The third sultan that year, the young Abdulhamid II (r. 1876-1909), was persuaded by Midhat Pasha (1822-83), a prominent official and reformist, to create the first Ottoman constitution. The novel reforms lasted a very short time. The following year (1877), Abdulhamid suspended the constitution, forced his opponents underground, and ruled as an autocrat until the end of his reign in 1909. Thus began and ended the first and only Ottoman experiment in constitutional government in the 19th century. Major reforms in the fields of education, transportation, and communications did occur, however, under the Hamidian autocracy.

Over the last quarter of the 19th century nationalism continued to spread among Christian communities in the empire. That led to uprisings that were often brutally put down. In 1894 a revolt suppressed by Kurdish irregulars resulted in the killing of 10-20,000 Armenians. An insurrection also occurred in Crete (1897), and another war with Greece (1896-7) took place. Events such as those against the empire's Christians, and the manner of their depiction in the European press, revived the image of the "ugly Turk."

In a development of the Young Ottoman movement, military students in Istanbul founded the first "Young Turk" revolutionary organization called the Society of Union and Progress (1889). That movement came to fruition in 1908 when the Young Turk officers mounted a coup that overthrew the sultan and established a republic, though one dominated by them.

The Ottoman Empire's Christians were not the only subjects gaining autonomy or independence from Istanbul in the 19th century. The predominantly Muslim provinces of Morocco, Algeria, Tunis, Egypt, and Syria all became autonomous early in the century. (Algeria was later invaded by France in 1832 and became the first part of French North Africa.)

Egypt's Rise as a Separate Power

The French invasion of Egypt in 1798 initiated the modern era in the Middle East and created an interest in European culture among the Egyptians. In the power struggles after the French withdrawal, the Albanian Muhammad Ali (1805-48) took sole control of the country in 1811 when he massacred the Mamluks, the traditional rulers. He intended to turn Egypt into a modern industrial and military power independent of the Ottomans. To do that, he created industrial monopolies and confiscated landed property and religious endowments (*waqfs*). Educational missions were sent to Europe to acquire the necessary new skills and techniques. Using his new army, he suppressed the Wahhabis in the Arabian Peninsula to aid Istanbul. In 1822 he sent his army into the Sudan in search of slaves for his army. Syria was invaded in 1831. The advance continued the next year into Anatolia toward Istanbul until European intervention halted it. The Treaty of London (1841) forced an Egyptian withdrawal from all territories save the Sudan. That was followed by the dismantling of the military and industrial complex Muhammad Ali had created.

A progressive agenda was resumed under Khediv (a Persian title first used by Muhammad Ali but not recognized by Istanbul until 1867) Ismail (1863-79), who sought to transform Egypt into a part of Europe. There were several initial successes. The boom in the cotton market during the American Civil War improved the economy. The Suez Canal was opened in 1869 and brought some trade back to the Middle East that Europe had gradually deprived it of by circumventing the region 400 years before.

The costs of modernization proved too much, however. The government declared bankruptcy because of the excessive loans and their interest payments. Consequently, it sold its shares in the Suez Canal to the British in 1875, and a European control organization — the Caisse de la Dette — was set up to oversee Egypt's finances the following year.

Affairs came to a head soon after Tewfiq Pasha (1879-92) replaced the deposed Ismail. In 1881, native Egyptian officers under Colonel Ahmed Urabi mutinied in protest against the privileges accorded the Turkish-Circassian elite in Egyptian society. The officers joined with pro-constitutionalists and followers of Jamal od-Din Afghani, the leading advocate of Pan-Islamism and anti-imperialism, and succeeded in temporarily imposing their will on Tewfiq. But that popular uprising frightened the British because of the threat it posed to the canal, the key to their communications with India. Thus, they defeated Urabi's army and occupied Egypt in 1882.

Although London originally had no intention of staying in Egypt, it needed to establish an administration for it. Lord Cromer (1882-1905) became the first proconsul of the new possession, and he succeeded in improving conditions in several areas. His actions led to the expansion of the economy and its stabilization. He improved irrigation, and the market production of cotton increased. He also carried out reforms such as the abolishment of the use of *corveé* labor. Ominously, the resultant improved living conditions led to a rapid rise in population that would continue to the present and create intractable problems for later governments.

The outstanding pupil of Afghani in Egypt was Muhammad Abduh (1849-1905), a theologian, prominent Islamic thinker, and exponent of Islamic modernism. He abandoned Afghani's strong anti-imperialist stance in favor of collaboration with the British and gradual change in lieu of revolution. As head of the Islamic college of al-Azhar in Cairo and the grand mufti of Egypt, he attempted educational and legal reforms.

Several movements emerged in the 18th and 19th centuries that looked to Islam for inspiration. In the Arabian Peninsula, the preacher Muhammad ibn Abd al-Wahhab allied with the tribal chief Muhammad bin Sa'ud thereby converting the latter's tribal raids into Islamic crusades aimed at enforcing an austere interpretation of Islam. Also in the 18th century the Senussi tribe, inspired by their Sufi roots, emerged from the North African desert to preach Islamic renewal in Cyrenaica. And toward the end of the 19th century, a man claiming to be the Islamic "Mahdi" (renewer of the faith) appeared in the Sudan and led a movement that challenged the British in Egypt until its eventual defeat in the 1890s.

Such movements were not new phenomena in Islamic civilization. It was the same cyclical pattern that the famous philosopher ibn Khaldun — the "father of sociology" — had described in his seminal book *The Introduction* (al-Muqaddimah). Therein he described a process whereby tribes emerged from the desert, conquered the cities, ruled for a time, and were then overcome in turn by another tribe from the desert.

A Century of Weakness and Limitations in Iran

Historical periods frequently fall to correspond neatly with standard dating patterns. Thus, the beginning and end of centuries do not always correspond with what we would consider a historical period. Such is the case with early modern Iran. It is convenient to refer to it as a "long" century (a period of time greater than one century but considerably less than two) for several reasons. It corresponds with the rule of the Qajar dynasty (1795-1925). Aqa Muhammad Khan's conquest of all Iran ended the turmoil of the 18th century. During the period's duration political, economic, and social conditions did not change appreciably, and significant modernization only began after the founding of the Pahlavi dynasty in 1925. Iran remained fundamentally traditional, though changes had begun.

The ascendency of the Qajar dynasty at the beginning of the 19th century also coincided with both increased Russian aggression and interaction with Europeans. During the reign of Fath Ali Shah (1796-1834), two wars were fought with Russia (1805-12 and 1826-7) after which Iran lost all of the Caucasus. Russia continued its push east of the Caspian Sea and into Central Asia, a region formerly within the Iranian sphere. Moscow also received capitulatory concessions in trade from Iran in the Turkomanchai Treaty of 1828.

Iran suffered setbacks at the hands of the British as well. Iran had considered Herat and what is now western Afghanistan part of Iran since Safavid times. To press their claim, Iranian forces seized Herat in 1857. The British, however, wishing to maintain the region as a buffer against

Russia, quickly forced Tehran to withdraw its forces and sue for peace, which came with the Treaty of Paris (1856). The Iranians were therein forced to recognize the independence of Afghanistan.

There was an awareness among some Iranians that changes had to be made if Iran was to confront the Europeans and prosper economically. Abbas Mirza (1789-1833), the governor of Azerbaijan, made the first reforms in the military during the wars with Russia. Reforms waned following his sudden death in 1833, yet others, especially those who traveled abroad, realized their urgency. Over the second half of the 19th century, the prime ministers Mirza Taqi Khan Amir Kabir (1848-51), Mirza Hosayn Khan Sepahsalar (1871-3), and Mirza Ali Khan Amin od-Dowleh (1897-8) all tried to institute reform in the government, but their actions were adamantly opposed by the conservative forces that dominated Iranian society.

Tehran became ever more in need of funds from the 1860s. In an effort to raise those funds the government sold concessions to Europeans. Those were intended to bring in revenues and allow Europeans to develop areas of the economy the Iranians could not. The largest and most renowned of those was that given to Baron Julius de Reuters in 1872. It allowed him to build railroads, mine for minerals, and create a bank. The concession was soon canceled because of Russian opposition. Another major concession came two decades later when a monopoly over the production, sale, and export of tobacco was granted to the Englishman Major Gerald Talbot in 1890. The shah was forced to cancel that concession in 1892 because of strong domestic opposition from the ulema, bazaaris, and even his own family. With concessions being either thwarted or inadequate, the Iranian government turned to foreign loans. The first was obtained to pay for the cancellation of the tobacco concession. Several more were taken during the reign of Mozaffar od-Din Shah (1896-1907) as Iran's financial problems worsened. Though Iran thus became indebted to Europeans in the last decade of the century, that occurred later than for the Ottomans and Egyptians, and not to the same degree.

Despite being in the midst of a great power rivalry, a few developments did take place in Iran during the 19th century. A telegraph system was established in the 1860s and a postal system in the 1870s. The Russians trained and led a new military unit called the Cossack Brigade (1878). Steamer ships began plying the Persian Gulf from the 1870s and the Karun River after 1888. The only railroad, six miles in length outside Tehran, was finished the same year.

Indians under Englishmen

While the 19th century brought ever-greater European penetration of the Ottoman Empire and Iran, South Asia went from British dominance to becoming a British possession. The British succeeded in establishing their hegemony, either by conquest or treaty, over almost all of the subcontinent between 1798 and 1818. Only the Punjab, which was controlled by the Sikhs, held out until 1849.

A major turning point came with the Indian Mutiny (Sepoy Rebellion) of 1857-8. A revolt began in the army and spread across the north and then to other parts of India. The rebels expressed their loyalty to the last Mughal. It took several months to suppress and engendered fear and hatred in both rulers and ruled. It shocked the British and caused an anti-Muslim reaction. Thereafter, many in the administration distrusted the "natives," cantonments were built for British residents, and equality between colonizers and colonized was discouraged. The Mughal dynasty was terminated, as was the rule of the East India Company. The British Parliament assumed control of the subcontinent and the governor-general became the viceroy of the queen, reporting to a minister. India hence became the "jewel in the crown" among British colonial possessions.

The Indians responded to the mutiny and the British reaction to it in various ways. A sense of nationalism began to overtake traditional regionalism. (Ironically, perhaps, British unification of the subcontinent had created the environment for nationalism's development.) The Indian National Congress was founded by moderates in 1885. Dominated by Hindus, it reflected liberal democratic ideals. Muslim Indians who rejected accommodation with the British created the rival Muslim League. Hence, in spite of greater national awareness, ethnic and religious identities hindered unified political action. Nationalism would gain momentum in the 20th century and culminate in independence in 1947.

There were also divisions within the Muslim community. In the 1830s Sayyid Ahmad of Rae Bareli popularized Wahhabism in India. He opposed Sufism and the inroads Hindus had made into Islam, and he declared jihad against the British and the Sikhs. Some Muslims such as Sir Sayyid Ahmad Khan advocated collaboration with the British, the adoption of British culture, and suggested that Islam conform to natural law. To promote his views he established Aligarh College in 1875. He was attacked by Afghani and the orthodox ulema. The latter founded a rival school at Deoband (1867), which advocated an anti-imperialist ideology. Yet, even in the 19th century, India, the land of religions, produced new ones. The Ahmadi sect appeared advocating a mixture of Islam, Hindu, and Christian beliefs. (Like Sikhism, it represented the eclectic tendency in Indian culture.)

While nascent Indian nationalism criticized British rule, the British had many accomplishments other than uniting the subcontinent for the first time. They instituted some social reforms such as outlawing the practices of *suttee*, the practice of a widow immolating herself on her dead husband's funeral pyre, and *thugee*, criminal gang practices. They carried out land reform, improved the tax collection system, and created a civil service system for South Asia. They built one of the largest railroad systems in Asia. They created telegraph and postal systems, and expanded the irrigation systems that were so important to Indian agriculture. Their language, English, also became the *lingua franca*, the official language of commerce, for all of their vast domains. The British eventually passed as had all conquerors of India. The difference was that they were never assimilated into Indian society as others had been.

The picture of the Middle East and South Asia by 1900 was far different from that of 400 years previous. The Ottomans endured, but their realm had shrunk considerably from its height three centuries before. The Young Turks, who took power in 1908, searched for a way to hold the empire together. But the most enduring Muslim empire would meet its demise after World War I. With the occupation of 1882, Egypt had become a protectorate of Britain. As in India, Egyptian nationalism would continue to grow until 1922 when the country gained independence. The economic situation of Qajar Iran continued to worsen until protests broke out in December of 1905. That marked the beginning of the Constitutional Revolution (1905-11), which would produce the country's first constitution and parliament, a vicious civil war between pro-constitutionalists and pro-monarchists, and finally end with the Russians occupying the north of the country. Of the three, only South Asia became a colony and an integral part of the British Empire. British development of the country would continue into the 20th century, as would Indian nationalism.

Reading: Iran's Encounter with Modernity in the 19th Century (Topical Essay)

James D. Clark is an expert in Iranian and Arabic studies of the modern period. He has taught in Tehran, Central Asia, and in the United States. In particular, he has researched and written about Iranian-Azerbaijan relations in the 19th century. And his research interest includes Russian relations with its Middle Eastern neighbors to the south. Professor Clark has also translated several classic pieces of Persian literature into English.

The photo is of the Kiani crown, considered the most opulent crown of an monarchy perhaps in world history. It was the crown of the Qajar Dynasty, 1779-1925, This opulent and splendid crown was worn for coronations, The Kiani crown is a physical manifestation of the belief in the divine royal glory. Made from red velvet and encrusted with thousand of gems, It is testimony to the excesses of the Qajar Shahs who were always inclined towards pompous behavior.

Historians of Iran differ as to when the modern period in the country's history began. Some maintain that it was after 1500 with the coming of the Safavid dynasty (1501-1722). That rests on two developments that occurred during their reign: the reunification of the country under a single state and the restoration of the traditional borders that it still has today, and the conversion of the majority of Iranians to the Shiite sect of Islam. Despite those important events, however, there were no corresponding changes in Iranian society, culture, or economics. Other historians argue that those only began to change after the Qajar dynasty (1795-1925) came to power. It was during their reign that changes became perceptible in many areas of society as a result of increasing contacts with Europe and the world.

When Aqa Mohammad Khan in 1779 finally won in the struggles that followed the downfall of the Safavids in 1722, Iran was still very much the same society it had been for the previous thousand years. Its population was overwhelmingly illiterate, at least half of the people belonged to nomadic tribes, and most of the remainder lived in small villages. There were only a few larger towns or cities.

The coming to power of the Qajars coincided closely with the modern era in the Middle East, which began with the Napoleonic invasion of Egypt in 1798. However, Iran encountered modernity later and adopted it markedly slower than either the Ottomans or the Egyptians. Change took place, but it did not define the period. Traditionalism continued to characterize the country, its society, culture, economy, and politics.

Attempts to Reform from the Top

Interaction between Iran and the rest of the world increased steadily over the century as more and more Europeans went to Iran and more Iranians traveled abroad to the Ottoman Empire, Egypt, and India, as well as Europe. A few foreign embassies were established in Tehran and consulates were opened in some provincial capitals. The first Iranian embassies were also opened in a few major European capitals and Istanbul. Iranian merchant communities existed in major foreign cities such as Istanbul, Cairo, Bombay, and Baku.

The first impetus for change inside the country was the same that the Ottomans had experienced — defeats at the hands of Europeans on battlefields. Iran and imperial Russia warred twice over the Caucasus (1805-13; 1826-8), and Abbas Mirza (d. 1833), the Qajar heir apparent and governor of the province of Azerbaijan, bore most of the responsibility for fighting those. Repeated setbacks compelled him to seek assistance from other European powers. First the French and then the British sent advisors to improve Iranian tactics and strategy. With their help, an arsenal and foundry were also built in Tabriz to produce cannons and ammunition. Those initial reforms in the military dissipated, however, following Abbas Mirza's early death in 1832.

Abbas Mirza, the first of three reform ministers, exemplified how initial modernization in Iran tended to be pursued by individuals at the pinnacle of government. At mid-century, Mirza Taqi Khan (1807-52), known as "Amir Kabir" (the great commander) had observed different systems during stays in Ottoman Anatolia and in Russia. He became the chief advisor to the young Naser od-Din Shah (1831-96; r. 1848-96) in 1848 and quickly began reforming the government. Some involved reorganizing the military, as Abbas Mirza had done. Others made changes to the budget and tax collection in order to increase receipts and decrease expenditures. Amir Kabir also engaged in public works, city planning, and factory building. He encouraged mining, sent Iranians abroad to learn new skills, and brought foreigners to Iran to teach them. He established the first school along European lines, the *Dar ol-fonun* polytechnical school, which employed Austrian instructors.

A second experiment in reform came in the 1870s with Mirza Hosayn Khan, who was prime minister (1870-3) and minister of war (1873-80). Like Amir Kabir, he attempted to reorganize the army and sought to better regulate governmental affairs by creating a cabinet system, establishing provincial councils, and convening a consultative council in Tehran to advise the shah. In 1873 he took Naser od-Din Shah on his first of three trips to Europe — the first for an Iranian monarch — to see Europe, the fount of modernity, firsthand.

A final attempt at governmental reorganization came when Mozaffar od-Din Shah (1853-1907) installed Mirza Ali Khan Amin od-Dowleh (1844-1904) as prime minister in 1897. A long-time reformist, Amin od-Dowleh had earlier pioneered a progressive curriculum in education by supporting the Roshdiyyeh school in Tabriz. As prime minister, he quickly addressed the pressing problems of state finances, court extravagance, and tax collection. He proposed changes to the customs administration, the mint, and the financial system and advocated the securing of a foreign loan to cover expenses. Although he resigned before his plan could be implemented, two of his goals were attained: the operation of Iranian customs by Belgians and the acquisition of a loan from the Imperial Bank of Persia.

All of the above reformers faced strong opposition from conservative forces and vested interests in Iran. The conservatives united to pressure a young Naser od-Din Shah to remove Amir Kabir and they forced Amir Kabir to commit suicide in 1852. Similarly, provincial governors, the official class, and the *ulema*, learned class, forced the shah to dismiss Mirza Hosayn Khan in 1873 and again in 1880. Few of his reforms survived, though his house, somewhat symbolically, became the country's parliament building in 1907. And Amin od-Dowleh was compelled to leave office by the same forces after only 18 months in office.

Aspects of Modernity in the 19th Century

Despite the attempts by those three ministers to reform the Iranian government, over the century Iran adopted limited aspects of modernity in some areas and became somewhat integrated into the developing world economic system. Overall, a twelve-fold increase in trade occurred between 1800 and 1913. The balance of trade was probably even until 1860, while a deficit existed thereafter. The composition of trade also changed. Typically, machine-manufactured textiles from Europe became the leading imports and drove out the domestic handicraft industry.

The importation of so-called "colonial" products such as sugar and tea increased sharply. Iran went from being a net exporter to a net importer of cereal grains, and whereas silk had been the most important export until mid-century, the export of cash crops such as cotton and rice increased greatly thereafter. The direction of trade changed as well. Afghanistan, Central Asia, the Ottoman Empire, and India had been Iran's traditional trading partners. Britain became more important in the 1850s and 1860s, and at the end of the century a sharp increase in trade with Russia occurred.

Some improvements occurred in transportation that facilitated travel. In 1889, there were only two carriage roads in the entire country, one linking Tehran with Qazvin and another connecting the capital with the religious center of Qom. A few minor roads such as that to Doshan Tepe (1874), another from Tehran to the shrine of Shah Abd ol-Azim (1875), and one north to the British Legation at its summer quarters in Qolhak were built around Tehran.

A carriage road was built from Tabriz to Jolfa in the northwest of the country. European engineers constructed new streets in Tehran, replacing the usual narrow and winding alleys. The Russians built roads across the north of the country between 1890 and 1910 that connected various cities and ports. Overall, however, as in other areas, road construction in Iran was far less than that in Ottoman realms or India.

The postal system benefited from those road improvements that did take place. The traditional post rider (*chapar*) system used caravan routes that consisted mainly of ruts. An Austrian organized a system along European lines beginning in 1874. Beginning in Tehran, it was gradually expanded to Jolfa via Tabriz and to Rasht via Qazvin. Three years later Iran was admitted to the International Postal Union.

In communications, the horse was superseded by the electric telegraph, which arrived in Iran in 1859. That occurred by chance when the British wanted telegraphic lines to India following the Mutiny of 1857. The trunk line was extended for the Iranians to various provincial cities, and a line was soon built to Tabriz and extended northwards to Jolfa and southwards to the Persian Gulf city of Bushehr. By 1890, Iran had 3,000 miles of line, staffed by Iranians and linking every important Iranian city. Naser od-Din Shah was so taken with the new device that he had one installed in his palace residence so as to promptly receive and send messages.

The first printing press appeared as early as 1816 in Tabriz and then Tehran. Others then began working in other major cities. They published mainly small numbers of scientific, religious, and historical works. Abbas Mirza sent one Mirza Ja'far to Moscow in 1824-5 to learn lithography while another student was sent to St. Petersburg to learn printing. (Following its introduction, printing vanished from Iran for approximately 50 years. During that time only lithography was used.)

The first newspaper, *Vaqāyeh-e ettefāqiyeh* (current events), appeared in 1850 headed by a British editor and publishing extracts from European journals. By 1890, four additional publications were available: the official newspaper Iran, the semi-official *Ettelāh* (information), *Sharaf* (honor), and the *Isfahan* cultural publication *Farhang*. The popular newspaper Akhtar, however, published in Istanbul, was banned in Iran because of its criticism of the Iranian government.

A modern mint was established in the north of Tehran in 1877, and it employed a German overseer and used French dies in its machinery. By 1890 it was the only mint in the country, all of the provincial mints having ceased operations. Modern banking began when Baron Julius de Reuter founded the Imperial Bank of Persia in 1889. It was granted a monopoly over the issuance of currency and had branches in several major cities.

The only major reform in the military during the 19th century was the creation of the Iranian Cossack Brigade by the Russians in the 1870s. It became the best-trained and best-led unit in the country. Reza Khan, the founder of the Pahlavi dynasty, was a Cossack officer. Except for that, by the end of the period the Iranian army existed almost only on paper.

The Road to a Constitutional Revolution

After Mirza Hosayn Khan fell from favor in 1880, Naser od-Din Shah did not support any reformist measures until his assassination in 1896, perhaps for fear of disrupting the traditional order. He also ceased sending students to Europe and increased censorship of the press. His last two prime ministers thereafter aimed only to maintain the status quo.

A chronic shortage of revenues always plagued the Iranian government and hindered any efforts associated with modernization. That led to granting the European powers concessions, which offered the prospect of revenues as well as development. The most extensive was the Reuter Concession of 1872 that gave the British subject Baron Julius de Reuter the right to exploit much of the country's resources for 70 years. It was cancelled, however, due to Russian opposition.

The subsequent Falkenhagen concession (1874) to the Russians, which allowed the building of a railway from Jolfa to Tabriz, was blocked by the British. Because of an 1890 Russian veto of railroad construction, the only railroad in Iran until well into the 20th century was six miles of track that linked Tehran to a shrine. It was finished by Belgians in 1888. (Iran's financial straits would not be alleviated until oil was discovered and exploited — again by a concession given to a British subject — after 1908.)

Another important concession was granted to a British subject in 1890 for a monopoly over the purchase, sale, and export of tobacco in Iran. It was cancelled two years later because of widespread popular opposition that was, at least in part, instigated by Russia. The shah had to take out a loan from the Imperial Bank of Persia to pay the penalty for cancelling the concession. That became the Iranian government's first loan. The one Amin od-Dowleh acquired for Mozaffar od-Din Shah in 1898 became the second. Other loans to the Russians came later. Though that indebtedness to Europeans came later than it had to the Ottomans or Egyptians and it was for a smaller amount, it nevertheless indicated the government's failure to address pressing financial and economic problems.

The Iranians adopted aspects of modernity considerably more slowly than their Ottoman and Egyptian contemporaries. A weak central government and entrenched traditional interests that resisted changes to the status quo were two prominent reasons. Economic and political conditions worsened over the decade-long rule of Mozaffar od-Din Shah (1896-1907). At the same time, more and more Iranians were becoming aware of their relative backwardness. That was especially true of the growing number of Iranians who traveled or lived abroad.

Their writings and actions prepared the ground for the Constitutional Revolution (1906-11), which was the first popular rebellion to occur in the Middle East. Although some change did occur as a result of that — such as a constitution and parliament — Iran remained a fundamentally traditional society until the late 1920s when increasing oil revenues provided the funds needed to transform the country.

Overview of Era VII: The Birth of Modernity, 1800-1900

Joshua Weiner, American River College

In World History Era 7, we will see the way in which the 19th century built on, accelerated, and even twisted many of the processes and ideas discussed in the previous era. The technological and organizational revolutions associated with industrialization created conditions in which

- A few powerful states could dominate the rest of the world directly as well as indirectly.
- The pace of migration would continue to grow, shifting and mixing populations all over the globe and creating entirely new types of societies.
- The transatlantic slave trade slowly died out even as slave societies continued to grow and intensify for much of the century.
- The horrors of the French Revolution led many in Europe to retreat into a reactionary conservatism while others around the world began to embrace the notions of national pride and popular sovereignty engendered by that revolution.
- And, broadly speaking, the realities of slavery and imperial rule helped establish a sense of human difference much starker and more unchangeable than ever seen before.

The late 19th century was, therefore, a period that saw the development of many of the ideas and structures that continue to connect and divide us to this day. It was a period defined by unmatched imperialism, the first stirrings of nationalism, and a racial ideology that co-opted science in order to justify the exploitation, disenfranchisement, and dehumanization of human groups who were said to stand in the way of civilization and progress. While imperialism, nationalism and racism can each be examined on their own, it is equally important to understand the way these ideologies existed in dialogue and as a result strengthened and reinforced each other. The spread of European imperialism was used by ideologues as evidence of racial superiority while contributing to feelings of national greatness. The emergence of racial ideas suggested the inevitability of empire and could serve as the basis for the national idea. Nationalist feelings in turn contributed to racial identities while spurring the quest for imperial expansion which could serve as evidence of national greatness.

Imperialism

Over the course of the 19th century, imperialism grew to reach new and unprecedented heights. Unlike the previous era when the greatest imperial formations spread across Asia, imperial power in this century projected outward from Europe. Two of the largest imperial powers of the era were Great Britain and France, both of whom had established formal and informal rule in territories that stretched across the world. At the beginning of the century, the Russian Empire already reached from the Baltic Sea to the Pacific Ocean and continued expansion would push the empire's borders increasingly to the south. The Spanish, Portuguese, and Dutch were not the powers they had been in the 16th and 17th centuries, but they continued to hold onto extensive territories of their own.

These traditional European imperial powers were joined by the new powers of Germany, Japan, and the United States, who had all graduated to Great Power status by the beginning of the 20th century. Whether old or new, the empires of the modern era were markedly different from those that came before. While all empires are founded on some degree of technological, economic and military supremacy, the people of modern empires additionally believed that their superiority was somehow inevitable due to ideas of race and nationalism. Where earlier forms of imperialism allowed for some blurring of the line between rulers and ruled, modern imperialism, based as it was on the idea of natural superiority, attempted to create and maintain clear boundaries between those two categories of people. The colonizers and the colonized were fundamentally different from each other according to modern imperial ideology. This difference was not simply something that existed in the minds of the colonizers, but something that could be observed in the physical geography of colonial society. One's status would never be in doubt since the entire structure of the society served to remind the individual of where he or she stood; there could be no mistaking the colonizer from the colonized.

Nations and Nationalism

Two things to understand about humans are, first, we are social animals and, second, we are storytelling animals. These may seem to be unrelated to each other, but, in fact, they are inextricably connected. Our ability to create large and relatively durable societies is tied to our ability to craft stories that make those societies and the hierarchies that bind them seem logical and eternal. Those stories we tell about ourselves are vehicles that carry sets of values, traditions, rituals, rules, and taboos, or, in other words, culture. Our stories do such a good job of imparting these elements of culture that we often forget that they are stories and instead believe that they represent something natural or innate. Prior to the 19th century, humans had often been organized into large scale political units but had mostly constructed their identities on more small-scale local connections. During that century, however, new stories emerged that, with the aid of technology, were able to connect more people in more convincing ways than ever before. These stories were able to help construct powerful ideas like those of race and nation. The nation was made up of millions of individuals, increasingly citizens, who were bound together by culture, by history, by principles, or by blood.

Nationalism was one of the most powerful ideological forces to emerge in the 19th century. As entire populations began to dedicate themselves to national service while also being instilled with national pride, the nation itself became the beneficiary. For states, the ability to appeal to and, at times, manipulate the nationalism of their citizens made them incredibly powerful. Those states that successfully paired nationalism with industrialization were lauded as "Great Powers" and gained the ability to exercise greater authority over a bigger portion of the Earth's territory than was ever possible before. Most societies, however, did not reside in this lofty atmosphere. The reality for hundreds of millions of people in the late 19th century was one of social, political, and economic domination at the hands of one of the major industrial nations. This experience of imperialism would ultimately become a major inspiration for national movements throughout the world. Such movements sought to, at least, improve the standing of colonized people within the imperial context and, at most, to achieve complete liberation from imperial rule.

Race and Racism

While scholars still debate the age and origins of the idea of race, it is indisputable that understandings of race evolved over the course of the 19th century. As that century began, the prevalence of racial slavery across the Americas had already helped stoke feelings of superiority amongst the slaveowning class and those who aspired to become part of that class or, at the very least, were sympathetic to the institution of slavery. As independence movements swept through the Americas in the late-18th and early 19th centuries, a contradiction emerged. How could men who, with one hand, hold others in bondage, fight for principles of natural rights, liberty, and freedom with the other? If certain people were undeserving <i>by nature</i> of those rights, then it became easier to morally justify slavery and in the process solve this contradiction. A similar dynamic emerged within the expansionist powers of Europe that needed to square the expanding rights of their own citizens with the increasingly autocratic rule over their colonies. One way to understand race in the 19th century is, therefore, as a defense of the indefensible -- the brutality of the plantation system, the theft of land from indigenous people, the savage exploitation of the imperial system.

If such people represented distinct and inferior races then they were not capable of receiving rights that could now be justly monopolized by those deserving of the title of free men. To those who sought to make such arguments, "science" proved to be their greatest ally. In the 19th century, a new racial scholarship emerged that used the language of science to make unscientific claims. This scientific racism is more aptly referred to as a pseudoscience given its tendency to begin with a conclusion and work backward. Despite this shoddiness, by the beginning of the 20th century, race science had become one of the dominant intellectual trends of the era.

As a new century began, a new set of ideas and a new power structure were increasingly dominant. Global empires centered on Europe were the most powerful states in the world, having added nearly nine million square miles of territory in the 44 years leading up to World War I. Within those imperialist states, citizens increasingly embraced a sense of identity based around the idea of the nation, and empire itself came to be seen as a symbol of national greatness. Within the empires, colonized people came to see nationalism as a means of unifying people towards the goal of national liberation. Both imperialism and nationalism were reinforced by ideas of race that had emerged in tandem with the two ideas.

For many people, the pseudoscience of race was the defining attribute of all human relations. It explained and justified imperialism, determined the potential for both individuals and societies to achieve civilization and progress, and was one of the bases of national identity. The fact that its claims were ultimately unscientific and based on pre-existing prejudices was less important than the fact that it used the language and authoritativeness of science to justify the prevailing power structure. For those who benefited most from that power structure in the years leading up to World War I, it was possible to see the world as more stable and orderly than it had ever been. Those who held to this view were soon to be proven definitively, disastrously wrong. Within the illusion of order, fissures had been forming. These fissures grew into cracks, and with the year 1914, the whole structure would collapse.

Unit 12: Europe and the World
J.P. Daughton, Stanford University

Reading: The Promises of Enlightenment

The Europe that Cook set sail from was a continent in flux and poised for momentous change. While Cook and his shipmates possessed many ideas and sensibilities that can be identified as "modern," much of Europe remained a place almost unrecognizable today. Huge swaths of uninhabitable land covered the continent. Most rivers had no set route, regularly flooding their banks, cutting new paths from year to year. Much of central Europe was marshland, swamps, and floodplains, as well as dense, forbidding forests. This was the land of legends and fairy tales: "Little Red Riding Hood," with its dark woods and predatory wolf, was a popular folk story in the 18th century, no doubt because it represented a world familiar to listeners. The countryside was full of mystery and dangers. In forests, one could encounter vicious animals, including wild boars, wolves, and bears, as well as threatening people. The late 18th century witnessed efforts across Europe to tame and conquer nature. Forests were cleared. Unwanted animals were systematically hunted, often to near-extinction. Advances in engineering enabled rivers to be straightened and swamps to be drained. Science and technology began to bring order and discipline to the land.

Europeans lived remarkably varied lives. The vast majority of 18th-century Europeans were peasants, agricultural workers whose lives were defined by poverty, hunger, and uncertainty. They tended to live in very simple houses, often with earthen walls and mud or stone floors, sharing their living space in cold months with farm animals. Socially and politically, the peasantry was dispossessed. They usually had few legal rights, paid heavy taxes, and worked land owned by the gentry, usually for their landlords' benefit.

Middle Class

It was the landed aristocracy that held power. As had been the case for centuries, European states were still ruled by monarchs and the nobility, which represented about three percent of the population across the continent. Not all nobles were wealthy. While some owned spectacular homes and vast tracts of land, others, especially in parts of Eastern and Southern Europe, were nearly destitute. But all noblemen enjoyed certain privileges that gave them a variety of legal rights over the peasantry, which represented the bulk of the population. As the 18th century progressed, however, this hierarchy started to weaken. As Europe's wealth was increasingly linked to international trade, especially to the slave economies of the New World, a new class of urban professionals trained for work in finance, law, and bureaucracy began to grow.

Gaining economic strength, this emerging middle class developed a social identity of its own that challenged the existing political order. To distinguish themselves from both the landed gentry and the urban and rural poor, middle-class men and women devised new forms of leisure and sociability, built in large part around reading, knowledge, and the sharing of ideas. The 18th century witnessed a veritable revolution in publishing, which, thanks to rising literacy, became a lucrative business. The century saw the spread of the daily newspaper, the first of which was launched in London in 1702. Eighty years later, there were nearly 40 daily papers in provincial towns across Britain, reporting everything from local politics to international news. A variety of other kinds of publications, including political pamphlets, philosophical and scientific treatises, and a new genre of fiction, the novel, also found broad new readerships. The information, arguments, and emotions contained in such publications filled the minds and hearts of readers across Europe, and fuelled discussions and debates in the favorite gathering places of the educated elite: salons, coffee houses, and scholarly academies. This was the milieu of the Enlightenment.

What is Enlightenment?

There was no single intellectual perspective that defined the Enlightenment; instead, the term elicited a spirit of the age. While worldviews differed widely, there was a common belief that knowledge should be useful, shared, and drawn upon to improve society. In his famous 1784 essay, "What is Enlightenment?," the German philosopher Immanuel Kant (1724-1804) urged his reader, *"Sapere Aude!* (Dare to know!) Have the courage to use your own intelligence!" The Enlightenment was in large part defined by criticism, by the questioning of established traditions, morals, and commonly held beliefs (including religious ones). It was *epistemological* – that is, many scientists, philosophers, and critics reflected not simply on new ideas, but also on how to think, especially about the natural world and society. This interest in knowledge was not purely scientific; people of the age did not simply ask *why* things happened.

A group of influential thinkers, called the *philosophes*, were particularly committed to changing the world around them. The *philosophes* were a cosmopolitan group, primarily men, from across Europe and even North America, united in a "Republic of Letters." While their intellectual perspectives differed, they all shared a belief in Progress. For most, human progress was largely about the improvement of society through the ability to manipulate the natural world through technology, to overcome ignorance bred of superstitions and religion, and to eradicate cruelty and violence through reform. Many Enlightenment thinkers considered themselves "intellectual activists" who could use their knowledge to make society better, to improve life, and to increase happiness.

Engagement with Knowledge

Perhaps one of the clearest examples of how Enlightenment figures imagined putting knowledge to work was the production of a massive *Encyclopedia* under the direction of Denis Diderot (1713-84) and Jean Le Rond d'Alembert (1717-83). This French encyclopedia, billed as a "Systematic Dictionary of Sciences, Arts, and Crafts," was begun in 1751 and took nearly 30 years to complete. It ran to nearly 30 volumes with over 70,000 entries written by many leading thinkers of the day, including many philosophes. Entries reflected the values of their authors, focusing on science, technology, philosophy, and the natural world; religion, by contrast, played a minimal role. Tellingly, the entry for "encyclopedia" itself stated that the aim was to make all the knowledge of the world "useful" and widely disseminated so that future generations could become "more virtuous and happier" through consultation. The *Encyclopedia* was a publishing sensation, striking fear into conservative elements of European society with its innovative method of examining the world. Efforts by government and religious authorities to censor it failed to stop volumes from being smuggled and sold secretly to an avid reading public.

The Enlightenment fascination with learning coincided with a new level of engagement with societies around the world previously unknown to Europeans. Exploration – in the Pacific via expeditions like James Cook's, and in the New World – as well as expanding trade networks in hitherto unknown parts of Africa and Asia pushed Europeans to reimagine human society. While most philosophes never stepped outside of Europe, reports of new peoples and cultures led many to speculate on the causes of variation in human societies. Many writers agreed that human beings, regardless of where they lived, shared fundamental characteristics. Then how to explain the myriad differences of economic wealth and social practices?

A range of answers attracted adherents. Some writers pointed to differences in natural resources and climatic conditions to explain why certain societies seemed more peaceful, wealthy, or complex than others. Others suggested that non-Europeans lived as "savages" because their societies had simply not enjoyed the progress that Europe had. By this theory, Europeans had once been "primitive" like Africans, Native Americans, or Pacific Islanders, but through innovation and knowledge, Europe had progressed to achieve a level of "civilization" far removed from the state of nature. Many in Europe, however, simply believed non-white people to be inherently inferior to Europeans. Such a view justified, in many minds, the continued enslavement of Africans and indigenous populations, as well as the violent acquisition of land around the world by European explorers and traders.

Although many in Europe were convinced of the benefits of their own "civilization," the Enlightenment produced a host of new ideas aimed at creating a more just and equitable society. The explosion in publishing, which allowed political critics of all stripes to circulate pamphlets and books, challenged the political status quo in Europe and the New World. Educated elites increasingly questioned established morals, traditions, and commonly held beliefs, including religious ones. Such critique did not stop with the most powerful institutions in European societies, including monarchies, the aristocracy, and the Catholic Church. By the late 18th century, philosophers and political figures questioned the legitimacy of what was considered corrupt and tyrannical institutions. Reason and a belief in virtue, it was argued, legitimized a call for greater participation in national politics. This was the birth of ideology: ideas about society were turned into plans for political change.

For many philosophers like Kant, using knowledge to challenge existing hierarchies was something limited to educated, white, and relatively affluent men. This was equally true of François-Marie Arouet, better known as Voltaire (1694-1778), one of the most influential political critics of the era. Born to a bourgeois family and armed with a vicious wit that got him repeatedly imprisoned, Voltaire argued that man was essentially good, but that bad institutions caused misery. A Deist, he insisted that the Church and nobility, with their morals and laws, held back man's potential. Without such interference, knowledge and work, hallmarks of civilization, would have a liberating effect. As he asserted in his famous novel *Candide* (1759), "All men must cultivate their own garden." But, again, while Voltaire used universal language – "all men" – he really had in mind men of his own ilk. Women, slaves, and even poorer, less educated men were excluded from direct participations in many visions of a reformed society.

A notable exception, however, was Jean-Jacques Rousseau (1712-78), a prominent Swiss writer, who believed that all humans were born in a similar state of nature; it was civilization that corrupted them. Man is born free, he argued, but society made it so that everywhere he lived in chains. Rousseau broke with the philosophes in his belief that society and "civilization" could corrupt as much as liberate. Rousseau, then, offered a different conception of society, one that was at once contractual and built on the participation of "citizens." Sovereignty, he argued, was to be found not in a monarch or other leader, but in the citizens. The "general will" of the people was to inform how a leader acted. Should the general will be ignored, citizens had the right to demand new leaders.

The Enlightenment and the Ruling Class

Ideas generated by the likes of Voltaire and Rousseau were cause for concern in the hereditary monarchies of Europe. Nowhere was this truer than in France, where, by 1789, years of poor planning and economic stagnation had pushed the country to bankruptcy. Strapped for cash, King Louis XVI (1754-93) had no choice but to call for the meeting of the Estates General, representatives from the Three Estates – namely, the clergy, aristocracy, and commoners – who were assembled in cases of state emergency. The King's aim was to ask the Estates General to solve the current financial crisis by raising taxes. But Louis XVI got more than he bargained for. First, the aristocracy refused to raise taxes significantly on themselves, instead opting to pass taxes disproportionately hard on peasants and the urban poor, two groups already suffering from years of bad crops and rising prices. And, second, the representatives of the Third Estate, most of whom came from the educated, urban elite, took the opportunity to use their own values to call for far more sweeping reforms than Louis XVI had demanded.

As discussions at Louis XVI's palace at Versailles broke down, the Third Estate adjourned to a nearby tennis court and, on June 20, 1789, took an oath to found a National Assembly. The King did his best to ignore this newly created legislative body. But the summer produced further disturbances. First, women marched on Versailles, demanding the King's attention. And, then, in the face of continued shortages and stalemate, the urban poor in Paris grew impatient at the mounting price of bread. On July 14, 1789, a group of Parisians stormed the Bastille, a prison in the middle of city that, while largely empty, nonetheless stood as a symbol of monarchical power.

The crowd freed a handful of prisoners and claimed a cache of weapons. It is said that Louis XVI, upon hearing news of the Bastille, asked an aide, "Is this a revolt?" "No, Sire," came the answer, "It is a revolution."

The French Revolution is significant in European history in that it posed, for the first time, fundamental questions about how to define a modern nation. Drawing on Enlightenment ideas about social and political reform, the National Assembly gathered to define a new kind of government. The clearest statement of their vision was the *Declaration of Rights of Man and the Citizen*. Its language was universal as it outlined the "natural, inalienable, and sacred rights of man." It drew heavily on natural law, asserting that, "All men are born and remain free and equal in rights." And it used Rousseau's concepts of sovereignty and the citizen. Unlike under the Old Regime, which was founded on privilege and the will of God, the new government insisted that "the source of sovereignty resides in the nation." The Revolution of 1789 embodied many of the central tenets of Enlightenment thought about society, liberty, and sovereignty.

But there were limits on liberty and on who would have a real stake in the new nation. Citizenship, which included the right to vote, was greatly expanded from what it had been under the Old Regime but was nonetheless limited to about 200,000 white men of certain wealth and education. More radical elements, including the *sans-culottes*, working people in Paris so named because they wore pants instead of the knee-britches of the wealthy, grew impatient with continued economic malaise and fearful of the mounting threat of invasion by the crowns of Europe. By 1792, a more virulently anti-aristocratic climate had set in, precipitated in part by Louis XVI's attempt to flee the country in the dead of night, apparently to seek refuge with the Austrian monarchy. What followed were two years of civil bloodshed, known as the Terror, in which tens of thousands of aristocrats and priests were tried and executed for allegedly being enemies of the revolution. With the First French Republic declared in 1792, Louis XVI and his wife, Marie-Antoinette, were sent to the guillotine in early 1793.

By the mid-1790s, the Radical Revolution, with its experiments in universal manhood suffrage, had burned itself out. Revolutionary politics continued, though in a more conservative key. Then, in 1799, a young Corsican general in the French army, Napoleon Bonaparte (1769-1821), came to power by *coup d'état*. Napoleon had become known a year earlier when he led his men, as well as a team of historians, archaeologists, and artists, on a conquest of Egypt. Like Captain Cook, Napoleon's foray into the land of pharaohs combined an Enlightenment desire for knowledge with modern Europe's hunger for global power.

Napoleon was certainly a product of the Enlightenment: his rise through the ranks of the army was made possible by liberalization brought by the revolution. And, once in power, his conquests through Europe were driven in part by the desire to spread the ideals of the French Revolution. His Napoleonic Code rationalized many of the laws inspired by the Enlightenment and remains the basis of many of Europe's current legal systems. But he also represented many of the failures of the Enlightenment. He quashed democratic dreams in 1804 when he crowned himself emperor. Abroad, he tried to defeat a slave-led revolution in the Caribbean colony of Saint Domingue that had been inspired by the events of 1789. At home, he cracked down on labor organizations, undermined women's legal status, strengthened the police, and essentially abolished elected bodies.

Napoleon's final defeat in 1815 put an end to the revolutionary experiment that had begun in 1789. What followed was a period of repressive Restoration, with a new king on the throne in France, and monarchy back in firm control in Europe. The ideas that had been formulated in the late-18th century spread well beyond the borders of France and, indeed, Europe. But the promises of the Enlightenment were left unfulfilled and unresolved. The hope for liberty and, increasingly, equality would inspire further debates, conflicts, and even revolutions. And, paradoxically, the "civilization" so admired by many Enlightenment thinkers would justify the oppression of millions of subjects in Europe's colonial empires throughout the 19th century.

Reading: The French Revolution, 1789-1799

The French Revolution was a period of ideological, political, and social upheaval, during which the French polity, previously an absolute monarchy with feudal privileges for the aristocracy and Catholic clergy, underwent radical change to forms based on Enlightenment principles of republicanism, citizenship, and rights. The changes were accompanied by violent turmoil, including executions, repression, and warfare involving the entire continent of Europe. The Revolution, however, was unable to establish a durable system of governance, and in the following century, France would be governed variously as a republic, a dictatorship, a constitutional monarchy, and two different empires, under a dozen different constitutions.

Causes of the French Revolution

Historians disagree about the political and socio-economic nature of the Revolution. The first, what we would consider, "modern" interpreter was the French historical sociologist Alexis de Tocqueville (1805-1859). In *The Old Regime and the French Revolution*, De Tocqueville argued that the French Revolution made a positive contribution to the modernization of the French state, which he believed actually began under the French Bourbon monarchs. The reason that the Revolution ultimately failed, however, was because the deputies and politicians of the Revolution were inexperienced in the practical running of a democratic republic and relied too much on abstract concepts of democracy and republicanism in the Enlightenment to guide their efforts.

On the other hand, during much of the 20th century, the interpretations of social historians and philosophers, especially those following Karl Marx, attributed the causes of the French Revolution (and most other historical events) to a class struggle. They suggested that the old aristocratic order, or the *ancien régime*, succumbed to an alliance of lower classes — the middle class, or bourgeoisie, aggrieved peasants, and urban wage-earners. However, in the 1980s, French Revolution historians, many influenced by Francois Furet, moved away from an explanation based on social classes and returned to the view of De Tocqueville. They have argued that not only inexperience of self-governance was a problem, but a furor of revolutionary rhetoric about liberty and equality spun out of control and coincided with traditional populist movements of the peasants and working classes.

There are more interpretations of the French Revolution than these. In fact, it has been one of the most studied events in human history — a very complex event, not easily explained. But there were many economic and social factors that contributed:

- Economic and psychological burdens of the many wars of the 18th-century, especially with Great Britain and Austria.
- Unmanageable national debt, part of which was incurred when the French supported the American side in the American Revolution.
- An unequal tax burden on the working poor that periodically provoked rebellion.
- The landowning Roman Catholic Church, with its tax on crops known as the *dime*.
- The conspicuous consumption of the royal household and the noble classes.
- High unemployment and widespread famine.
- Enlightenment influence on the professional and mercantile classes, especially its criticisms of the privileges of aristocracy and royal absolutism.
- Resentment of aristocratic and clerical privilege.
- Inability of Louis XVI and his advisors to deal with any and all of these problems, partly due to the lack of an effective parliament to help the King respond to various crises.

Again, according to De Tocqueville-inspired interpretations, the only available answers to these dilemmas in the late 18th century came from the energetic and vibrant rationalist philosophies of the Enlightenment. Philosophers argued that it was not only possible but right to overthrow quickly the existing political order, by force if necessary, on the grounds of abstract principles rather than existing laws. There was little tradition and custom of national French assemblies and legislative bodies. In that respect, it was quite different from the English and American rebellions which sought to make government respect the law, especially the common laws that had emerged from medieval times and were reinforced by British parliaments who had historically and more effectively asserted shared rule with their kings. In French society, all power was perceived to be localized in the kings. As the most powerful of the French monarchs, Louis XIV, said, "L'etat, c'est moi." — I am the state.

The Outbreak of Revolution, 1789

The immediate trigger for the Revolution was the reemergence of the Estates General — the moribund parliament of France. Faced with unfathomable financial strain, Louis XVI, turned to his finance minister, Loménie de Brienne, to raise funds. Loménie de Brienne convened an Assembly of Notables, a group of nobles, clergy, bourgeoisie, and bureaucrats, selected in order to bypass the parlements, the provincial courts that traditionally managed the tax collection. The crown wanted the group to approve a new land tax that would, for the first time, include a tax on the property of nobles and clergy. The Assembly of Notables pushed back and instead demanded that Louis XVI call the Estates General. The King agreed and convened the French parliament in May of 1789, the first time it had met since 1614.

The historic act of calling the parliament generated an expectation of reform of some kind. The Estates General was made up of the First Estate (the clergy), the Second Estate (the nobility), and the Third Estate (the middle class and peasants), each receiving one vote. Immediately, the Parisians began to agitate to change the vote by headcount and double the number of votes for the Third Estate. These disputes were not settled before the Estates met at Versailles and resentments grew. At the convocation of the parliament, the Third Estate continued to rail for vote by head, while the other two estates dug in their heels for an equal vote of all three estates.

In June, the Third Estate broke from parliament and declared themselves the National Assembly of "the People." They invited the other orders to join them, but made it clear they intended to conduct the nation's affairs with or without them. Louis XVI ordered the closure of the hall in which the National Assembly met, so they reconvened at a nearby indoor tennis court, where they proceeded to swear the Tennis Court Oath (June 20, 1789), under which they agreed not to separate until they had given France a constitution. A majority of the representatives of the clergy, the First Estate, soon joined them, as did 47 members of the nobility, the Second Estate. On July 9 the National Assembly reconstituted itself as the National Constituent Assembly.

Conservative members of the royal court, including Queen Marie Antoinette, encouraged Louis XVI to resist the Assembly, and on July 11, he fired his finance minister, Jacques Necker, who had encouraged the king to work with the Assembly. Many Parisians presumed Louis's actions to be the start of a royal coup by the conservatives and began an open rebellion. Paris was soon consumed with riots, anarchy and widespread looting. The mobs had the support of much of the French Guard, including arms and trained soldiers, because the King had essentially abandoned the city. On July 14, the crowds stormed a jail fortress called the Bastille near the middle of the city, capturing a large number of weapons and ammunition. The Bastille served as a potent symbol of everything hated under the old regime.

The King and his military supporters backed down, at least for the time being. Nobles were not assured by this apparent reconciliation of King and people. They began to flee the country as émigrés, agitating for a European coalition against France, and some began plotting civil war within the kingdom. By late July, the countryside began to rise up in an insurrection known as "la Grande Peur" (the Great Fear).

On August 4, 1789, the National Constituent Assembly convened and proceeded to abolish feudalism, seigneurial rights of the aristocrats, and the tithes, forced contributions to the Catholic Church. In a few hours, the ancien régime was close to being demolished. Looking to the American Declaration of Independence, the assembly published the *Declaration of the Rights of Man and of the Citizen*, on August 26, 1789. The National Constituent Assembly functioned not only as a legislature, but also as a body to draft a new constitution. Ignoring aristocratic sympathizers who argued for the creation of a Senate of the Second Estate, the Assembly decided instead on a single, unicameral assembly. The King retained only a "suspensive veto" — the ability to delay the implementation of a law but not block it. On October 5, 1789, a group of mostly working women marched on Versailles, demanding an end to bread shortages and the return of the king and the royal family to Paris. Under a guard of 20,000 men, the royal family was returned to Paris.

King, Constitution, and Legislative Assembly, 1790-1791

This period saw the rise of the political "clubs" in French politics, foremost among these was the Jacobin Club; over 100 clubs had affiliated with the Jacobins by August 10, 1790. Royalists also attempted to form clubs but were much less successful. The National Constituent Assembly continued to diminish the standing of aristocrats, adding more and more nobles to the *émigré* community abroad. There were several small counter-revolutionary uprisings but they uniformly failed. The crucial French army was on neither side, the officer corps severely divided between revolutionaries and counter-revolutionaries. Under the circumstances, the royal family, which was unable to leave, decided to practice cooperation with the new legislators.

At this moment, most of the Assembly favored a constitutional monarchy rather than a republic. Though the monarch would be little more than a figurehead; at least he and his family would be safe. But the royal family soon came under tremendous suspicion. Louis made the mistake of taking the advice of the conservative General Bouillé, who while he condemned both the nobility abroad and the Assembly, promised the King and his family refuge and support in his camp at Montmédy. On the night of June 20, 1791, the royal family fled the Palace of the Tuileries in Paris, wearing the clothes of servants while their servants dressed as nobles. The next day, the King was recognized and arrested at Varennes. He and his family were paraded back to Paris under guard. The Assembly provisionally suspended the King. He and the Queen remained held under guard. In addition, the King's younger brother, Charles-Philippe, who had already left France, conspired abroad with other monarchs, demanding the king's total liberty and dissolution of the Assembly, or face invasion from abroad. The more the *émigrés* agitated abroad, the more dangerous the royal family's position became.

The National Assembly finally promulgated a constitution and required the King to pledge to defend it, which he did. This Constitution, however, was not a success. While the old regime was deposed, the government that replaced it was not the shared vision of a people united. The Legislative Assembly of the new Constitution first met on October 1, 1791, and degenerated into chaos less than a year later. It consisted of about 165 constitutional monarchists on the right, about 330 who favored a republic on the left, including slightly more moderate Girondists and a more radical small group of Jacobins that came to be known as the Montagnards, or the Mountain, and about 250 deputies unaffiliated with either faction.

In Paris itself, things became even more radical, as the working class called the *sans-culottes*, without the britches (that the upper classes wore), working with some of the more radical members of the Assembly, began to take over the city government of Paris through the Paris Commune. In this increasingly radical climate, Louis XVI again made mistakes in dealing with the radicals. He tried to use his weak veto power over new legislation that would punish émigrés and take away some of the privileges of the clergy. The Legislative Assembly and the Paris Commune were furious. On the night of August 10, 1792, insurgents, supported by the Commune, assailed the Palace of the Tuileries. The King and Queen were taken prisoners. A rump session of the Legislative Assembly made up almost exclusively of the radical left, suspended the monarchy.

Reign of Terror, 1793-1794

Now the Girondists and Montagnards were in charge of the reformed government and declared yet another legislative body — the National Convention. But of course, there was too much factionalism to form an effective government; there was too much fear of the hostile monarchies that surrounded France who were inflamed by the arrest of the French royal family; and there was too much suspicion and intrigue in all political circles. The new Jacobin-dominated government saw royalist conspiracies everywhere and, on January 17, 1793, condemned King Louis XVI to death for "conspiracy against the public liberty and the general safety." He was executed, beheaded by guillotine, on January 21, 1793. On October 16 of the same year, Louis's Austrian-born queen, Marie Antoinette, followed him to the guillotine.

The radicals began to turn on each other. The most radical of the Jacobins, the Montagnards, mobilized the mob power of the *sans-culottes* and began to purge the government of the more moderate Girondists. Their mechanism for terror was a small group called the Committee of Public Safety, which had been created by the Convention; it was a "revolutionary dictatorship." Prominent Montagnard members of the Committee included the radical Jacobins Georges Danton and Maximilien Robespierre. For two years the committee unleashed what is called the Reign of Terror. At least 18,000 people met their deaths under the guillotine or otherwise, after accusations of counter-revolutionary activities. The slightest hint of counter-revolutionary thoughts or activities could place one under suspicion. The trials that followed were little more than show trials with no legal scruples being followed. Members of the Paris Commune treated the parading of the convicted and their executions as a public fair.

But the Girondist opponents of the Montagnards resisted through violence of their own. On July 13, 1793, the assassination of Jean-Paul Marat — a Montagnard leader and journalist known for his bloodthirsty rhetoric — by Charlotte Corday, a Girondin, resulted in a further spiral of political violence, with deputies accusing each other and condemning their fellows to the guillotine. A prominent radical, Georges Danton, himself came under suspicion for corruption and was removed from the Committee, later guillotined in the spring of 1794. On July 27, 1793, Robespierre, who styled himself "the Incorruptible," headed the Committee and became the face of the Revolution.

On June 24, the National Convention adopted the first republican constitution of France, variously referred to as the French Constitution of 1793 or "Constitution of the Year I." But it was readily ignored, as the dictatorial Committee of Public Safety coped with the most urgent business at hand — civil and foreign war. This meant building armies and feeding the country. On August 17, the Convention voted for general conscription, which mobilized all citizens to serve as soldiers or suppliers in the war effort. On September 9, it established *sans-culottes* paramilitary forces, the revolutionary armies, to force farmers to surrender grain demanded by the government. On September 17, the *Law of Suspects* was passed, which authorized the charging of counter-revolutionaries with vaguely defined "crimes against liberty." On September 29, the Convention extended price-fixing from grain and bread to other essential goods, and also fixed wages. The *Ventôse Decrees* of 1794 proposed the confiscation of the goods of exiles and opponents of the Revolution and their redistribution to the needy.

These dictatorial measures helped to mobilize the country for war and avoid immediate military defeat against the Austrians, Prussians, British and Spanish, who were arrayed against them. The radical government moved quickly to expand the size of the army and replace many aristocratic officers with younger soldiers who had demonstrated their ability and patriotism in the field, a very popular move. The rapidly reforming army managed by 1794 to put down revolts that were cropping up in the countryside. However, despite success on the military side and these numerous efforts to appease the populist forces abounding in Paris and the countryside, in 1794, the public began to turn against the Jacobins. Robespierre saw his own popular support erode dramatically by the summer of that year.

On July 27, 1794, some of the Girondists who survived the Terror managed to organize a coup — the Thermidorian Reaction — which led to the arrest and execution of Robespierre. They staged their own purge, banning the Jacobin Club, and executing many of its former members in what was known as the White Terror. And they had the Convention approve yet another Constitution, on August 17, 1795; a plebiscite ratified it in September, and it took effect on September 26, 1795.

The Directory, 1795–1799

The Constitution of 1795 created the Directory, as well as the first bicameral legislature in French history. The parliament consisted of a Council of 500 representatives and 250 senators, or the Council of Elders. Executive power went to five "directors," named annually by the Council of Elders from a list submitted by the Council of 500. With the establishment of the Directory, the Revolution might seem closed. After six difficult years, the nation desired rest and the healing of its many wounds. Those who wished to restore the monarchy and those who would have renewed the Reign of Terror were insignificant in number. The possibility of foreign interference had vanished.

Nevertheless, the four years of the Directory were not a period of stability. The atrocities of the recent past had made confidence or goodwill between parties impossible. Self-preservation and intrigue continued to dominate everything political. The directors frequently ignored the Constitution of 1795, and when elections went against them, they appealed to the sword. The directors themselves were notoriously corrupt and the general maladministration of the Directory heightened their unpopularity.

What they did do rather well was to throw in their lot with military leaders and a provocative foreign policy to retain their power. State finances were so ruined, they could only meet their expenses with the plunder and tribute of foreign countries the French army could attack and intimidate. This encouraged more belligerent foreign policy. After all, If peace were made, the armies would return home and the directors would have to face the exasperation of the rank-and-file who had lost their livelihood, as well as the ambition of generals who could, in a moment, brush the directors aside.

It was only a matter of time that a young general and fortunate soldier named Napoleon Bonaparte would, in fact, do just that — brush them aside. On November 9, 1799, in conspiracy with a few directors, foremost among them the corrupt Paul Barras, Bonaparte staged a coup that installed the Consulate (1799-1804). The Consulate was in fact a joint dictatorship, which very quickly devolved into a dictatorship of one man — Napoleon Bonaparte — who eventually declared himself emperor in 1804.

Reading: Napoleon Bonaparte, 1769-1821
Causes of the Revolution

Napoleon Bonaparte was perhaps the most important figure in Europe at the beginning of the 19th century. He influenced not only the politics of his time, but also the military, the arts, culture, law, diplomacy, and technology. Though he was a leader of France, he actually was born on August 15, 1769, on the island of Corsica in the middle of the Mediterranean, which was under French sovereignty. At a very young age, Napoleon climbed the ranks of political power during the French Revolution via the route of the French army, becoming first consul, or de facto dictator, of France in 1799–1804 and ultimately emperor in 1804–1814.

The Jacobin Years, 1788-1791

Napoleon completed his training at military academy in 1788, shortly before the outbreak of the French Revolution. While Napoleon seemed to believe that political change was necessary, as a military officer, there was little evidence that he engaged in any activities that forwarded the causes of the Revolution in its first two years. But in April 1791, while a lieutenant garrisoned at Valence, he joined the local Jacobin Club, a group that initially favored constitutional monarchy, and soon became its president, making speeches against nobles, monks, and bishops.

By June of 1793, Napoleon seems to have completed his transformation to a full Jacobin. In his work *Le Souper de Beaucaire* (Supper at Beaucaire), he argued that all who favored a republic should rally round the Jacobins and abolish the monarchy. The army by this time was split between republican and royalist officers, and a civil war raged across France. In August republican troops were temporarily held at bay by a combination of royalist and British forces at Toulon, when the commander of the republican artillery was wounded. Napoleon took command and drove the British forces out, to much acclaim. On December 22, 1793, he was promoted to brigadier general at age 24.

In the next two years, 1794-95, Napoleon's fortunes were erratic. He had hitched his star to Maximilien Robespierre, who was executed along with many of the more radical republicans. But he captured a ray of good fortune in October 1795. As the conservatives rose to take control of the French Revolution, Paul Barras, who had been entrusted with dictatorial powers by the National Convention, was looking for a commander of the troops of the interior. He turned to Napoleon, who proved his loyalty to Barras by vigorously shooting down the columns of radicals who marched against the National Convention. He was soon hailed as the savior of the National Convention and the republic.

The Directory, 1795-1799

Barras and the new conservative government, called the Directory, relied on Napoleon for his military prowess. Napoleon augmented his new power by marrying one of the more politically influential women of the French salon, Josephine Tascher de La Pagerie, who kept him well-informed of politics in Paris. The Directory soon gave him control of the Grand Army, and he whipped the ill-equipped, ill-fed men into shape for a campaign in Italy. Early on Napoleon showed a genius for military logistics, giving as much attention to supply lines as he did the frontline battles. Taking this army into Italy, he showed another genius — the ability to win just enough battles to intimidate his opponent and negotiate very advantageous armistices and treaties. Finally, along the way, he converted many of the monarchies in to constitutional republics, which gave him and his armies the reputation of liberators and disseminators of the high goals of the Enlightenment and the French Revolution.

Battle of the Nile

While their brilliant general had been quite successful on land, the Directory was concerned about the British navy's control of the sea around Europe. The directors wanted an invasion of the British Isles, but in February 1798, Napoleon convinced them that France should strike at the sources of Great Britain's wealth by occupying Egypt and threatening the route to India. The expedition had some early successes, especially at Alexandria, but the British under Admiral Horatio Nelson destroyed Napoleon's fleet, leaving him stranded on land he had conquered. In early 1799, Napoleon tried to break out of this box but was unsuccessful. Heartened by his defeats at the Nile, the British, Austrians, Russians, and Turks formed an alliance against France.

In the meantime, the Directory in Paris was showing signs of unraveling. One of the directors, Emmanuel Sieyés, asked Napoleon to return to France and restore order. "I am looking for a sabre," he said. Napoleon left his army in Egypt on August 22, 1799, arriving in Paris on October 14. Things had quieted down by the time Napoleon arrived, but Sieyés and Napoleon still conspired to stage a coup on November 9–10, 1799. The other directors were forced to resign, the members of the legislative councils were dispersed and a new government, the Consulate, was set up. The three consuls were Napoleon, Sieyès, and Pierre-Roger Ducos. But it was Napoleon who was henceforth the master of France.

The Consulate, 1799-1804

Though he had been in the limelight of French politics for a while, Napoleon, now 30 years old, was something of an unknown quantity. Three things were clear, he was a good commander, a better diplomatic negotiator, and above all an insatiably ambitious man. A lot was expected of him — bring back peace, end disorder, and consolidate the political and social "conquests" of the Revolution. But Napoleon was less a man of the Revolution than he was of the Enlightenment and a believer in men of talent, such as himself. He was a ready-made "enlightened despot."

The Consulate was a dictatorship. Sieyès composed a constitution to give it a gilded surface, but it gave immense powers to First Consul Napoleon Bonaparte, leaving only a nominal role to his two colleagues. The first consul appointed ministers, generals, civil servants, magistrates, and the members of the Council of State and even was to have an overwhelming influence in the choice of members for the three legislative assemblies, though their members were theoretically to be chosen by universal suffrage. When submitted to a vote of the people in February 1800, the constitution won by an overwhelming majority.

Yet, the Consulate's governmental reforms, undertaken at Napoleon's instigation, was to have a enduring effect on France. Napoleon established a clear hierarchical administration from the Council of State, through the prefects of the *départements*, or districts, and the judges of the judicial system. The police organization was greatly strengthened. The financial administration was considerably improved: instead of the municipalities, special officials were entrusted with the collecting of direct taxes. The franc, the French currency, was stabilized; and the Banque de France, owned partly by shareholders and partly by the state, was created. Education was transformed into a major public service.

In addition, Napoleon negotiated a Concordat of 1801 with Pope Pius VII and ended the opposition of the Catholic Church to the developments in France. The Concordat established the lay affinity of the French government for the first time. One of Napoleon's most significant accomplishments was called the Napoleonic Code, or the codification of the civil law. Completed in 1804, it gave permanent form to the great gains of the Revolution: individual liberty, freedom of work, freedom of conscience, and the lay character of the state, and equality before the law. It allowed divorce but granted only limited legal rights to women.

The army received the most careful attention. The first consul continued practices established in the Revolution: recruitment by forced conscription, the mixing of the conscripts with old soldiers, and the eligibility of all for promotion to the highest ranks. The creation of the Academy of Saint-Cyr to produce infantry officers made it easier for the sons of bourgeois families to pursue a military career. Moreover, the École Polytechnique, founded by the National Convention, trained artillery officers and engineers. Meanwhile, Napoleon continued to organize the army and in the summer of 1800 scored several triumphs in Austria. Feeling themselves bereft of allies, the British signed the Peace of Amiens on March 27, 1802.

At the height of his power, Napoleon put forward a referendum: "Shall Napoleon Bonaparte be consul for life?" In August an overwhelming vote granted him the prolongation of his consulate as well as the right to designate his successor. The French Revolution was for all intents and purposes over, but the rise of a militarized France would continue. Napoleon used Amiens as a cover for continued provocative actions and acquisitions of territory on the European mainland; there was little the British seemed to be able to do. It came down to the tiny island of Malta in the

Mediterranean Sea. According to the Peace, the British were to return Malta to France. Citing Napoleon's provocations in violation of the treaty, they refused to leave the island. Franco-British relations became strained, and in May 1803, the British declared war.

The Empire, 1804-1814

Napoleon was successful in obtaining the life consulate because of his ability to negotiate the Peace of Amiens. Now, the breakdown of this peace and the prospect of war would lead to the formation of a French empire and himself as emperor. Interestingly, it was the British who may have accelerated Napoleon's grab for more power by financing a plot to assassinate him. It was unsuccessful. But Napoleon's advocates argued that he should convert the life consulate into a hereditary empire, because an heir would remove all hope of changing the regime by assassination. He readily accepted the suggestion, and on May 28, 1804, the empire was proclaimed.

Napoleon changed very little of the Consulate's work on government organization, but as emperor he did revive some of the institutions of the French monarchy. For one, he insisted on being consecrated by the Pope himself. But when the Pope attempted to put the crown on his head, the audacious Napoleon took the crown and placed it on his own head. Princely titles were brought back for the members of Napoleon's family in 1804, and an imperial nobility was created in 1808. To suppress the opposition, Napoleon instituted strict censorship on the press. Because of the censorship, Napoleon did not have as good a handle on French opinion, as he drew France into a series of military struggles against his main enemy, the British, and most particularly the powerful British navy.

Battles Against the Coalition, 1803-05

Still far inferior to the British navy, the French fleet needed the help of their ally, the Spanish. A Franco-Spanish fleet under Admiral Pierre de Villeneuve found itself blockaded by the British navy in the port of Cádiz in the south of Spain in July 1805. Villeneuve tried to run the blockade, but on October 21, 1805, he was attacked by Nelson off Cape Trafalgar. Though Nelson was killed in the battle, the Franco-Spanish fleet was totally destroyed. The British had won a decisive victory, which gave them almost total control of the sea from that point forward.

But the French army also had its own victories. Napoleon ordered it to attack Austria. He won at the Battle of Ulm and entered Vienna on November 13, 1805. On December 2, in perhaps his greatest victory, he defeated the combined Austrian and Russian armies in the Battle of Austerlitz. The Prussians lost to Napoleon at Jena and Auerstedt in October 1806. The Russians were routed at Friedland in June 1807. The Russian emperor Alexander I, sued for peace, creating a vague alliance with Napoleon.

The Peninsular Campaign, 1808-1812

Napoleon tried a new tactic of stifling the British economy, establishing a "continental system" that forbade all trade from the European continent with the British Isles. He ordered the confiscation of all goods coming from English factories or from the British colonies and condemned as fair prize not only every British ship but also every ship that had touched the coasts of England or its colonies. The one country that refused to comply was Britain's old ally, Portugal. Napoleon decided to attack the Portuguese by land and actually took over the government of his weak ally, Spain, on the way to Portugal in 1807, naming his brother Joseph king of Spain.

However, the Portuguese and Spanish resisted. The British navy took the Portuguese royal family to its American colony of Brazil, and the Portuguese navy and army came under the leadership of the British. The Spanish populace began a spontaneous insurrection in response to the presence of French troops. The insurrection spread and Spanish republicans formed an alternative government in Cádiz. In 1809, the British general, the Duke of Wellington, led his own and Portuguese forces and coordinated with Spanish guerilla fighters in both regular army battles and insurrection campaigns that ultimately wore down the French. By 1812, the French army found itself retreating from the Iberian Peninsula.

Russian Disaster, 1812-13

To consolidate his claim to empire and his relations with Austria, he repudiated his wife Josephine, who had not provided him with a child, and married an Austrian princess who gave him a son and heir. But in 1812, his former ally, the Russian Emperor Alexander I, began to turn on him. Napoleon responded by massing his forces in Poland to intimidate Alexander. After some last attempts at agreement, in late June his Grand Army — about 600,000 men, including contingents extorted from Prussia and from Austria — began to cross into Russia. The Russians retreated, adopting a scorched-earth policy. Napoleon's army did not reach the approaches to Moscow until the beginning of September. The Russian commander, Mikhail Kutuzov, struck back at Borodino on September 7. The fight was savage, bloody and indecisive. A week later Napoleon entered Moscow, but found the Russians had abandoned it. On that same day, a huge fire broke out, destroying the greater part of the town. Moreover, throughout the winter, Alexander unexpectedly refused to treat with Napoleon, even though Napoleon held his Russian capital. Without provisions to sustain his army, Napoleon was forced to withdraw through a brutal Russian winter. By the time the French army retreated back across the Russian border, it consisted of 10,000 men.

In Germany the news of Russian disaster unleashed an outbreak of anti-French demonstrations. The Prussian contingents deserted the Grand Army in December and turned against the French. The Austrians also withdrew their troops and adopted an increasingly hostile attitude. And in Italy the people began to turn their backs on Napoleon. Even in France, signs of discontent with the regime were becoming more frequent. Arriving in Paris on December 18, 1812, Napoleon proceeded to stiffen the empire, raising money and levying new troops.

But the French were losing their enthusiasm for empire. In the next two years, Napoleon tried to negotiate his way out of difficulties, but the Spanish and Russian conflicts had depleted his forces of men and he could no longer command the upper hand as he had in the past. All of Europe was now arrayed against Napoleon. At the Battle of Leipzig, also called the Battle of the Nations, in October 1813, Austrian, Prussian. Russian, and Swedish forces met Napoleon and tore apart his Grand Army. At the same time the British were attacking his homeland defenses on the French side of the Pyrenees.

The Abdication and Downfall, 1814-1815

In January 1814 France was being attacked on all its frontiers. By the Treaty of Chaumont of March 1814, the allies — Austria, Russia, Prussia, and Great Britain — took the unusual step of binding themselves together for 20 years, pledging not to negotiate separately and promising to continue the struggle until Napoleon was overthrown. When the allied armies arrived before Paris on March 30, the foreign minister and former Napoleon ally, Charles-Marie de Talleyrand, lost no time in treating with the allies. Persuaded that further resistance was useless, Napoleon finally abdicated on April 6, 1814. According to the terms of his abdication, Napoleon received the Mediterranean island of Elba as his own sovereign principality, an annual income of two million francs to be provided by France, and a guard of 400 volunteers. After a hazardous journey, during which he narrowly escaped assassination, Napoleon arrived at Elba on May 4, 1814. He was age 45 years old.

In France, Talleyrand and other leaders were trying to restore the junior members of the French royal family but were running into resistance. Though in 1814 the majority of the French people were tired of Emperor Napoleon, they had no wish for the return of the Bourbons. They remained strongly attached to the essential achievements of the Revolution. Old hatreds were revived, resistance organized and conspiracies formed. While the allies paid little attention to the troubles in France, Napoleon was following the politics closely.

Decisive as ever, Napoleon dramatically returned to France on March 1, 1815. As he crossed the Alps, republican peasants rallied round him, and near Grenoble he won over the soldiers dispatched to arrest him. On March 20 he was in Paris. If Napoleon had allied himself with the anti-monarchy Jacobins, as he had done 25 years before, he might have rallied the people. But he did not, possibly because of his own conservative background, possibly because of his experience as emperor. Enthusiasm ebbed fast. Nevertheless, Napoleon mustered an army that marched into Belgium and defeated a Prussian army at Ligny on June 16, 1815. However, two days later he and his army faced Wellington and his hardened British troops at the Battle of Waterloo. A Prussian army arrived to reinforce the British, and Napoleon went to defeat.

What to do with Napoleon a second time? The allies were agreed on one point: Napoleon was not to go back to Elba. A British ship took him to a remote island in the southern Atlantic Ocean called St. Helena. Though the climate and his accommodations at St. Helena were quite good, an energetic man like Napoleon soon found the reclusive life of an exile unbearable. Napoleon showed the first signs of illness at the end of 1817; he seems to have had an ulcer or a cancer of the stomach. There has been continuing controversy about the cause of his death, but the evidence used by some to support the theory that Napoleon was poisoned is not considered conclusive by many scholars. By April 1821, Napoleon was dictating his will. On May 5, 1821 he died.

The Legacy

As soon as the emperor was dead, his legend grew rapidly. Memoirs, notes, and narratives by detractors and advocates followed and seemed to run with the tides of the time. During the revival of the monarchy under Charles X in 1815-30, criticism of Napoleon was predominant. When the second or July Monarchy of 1830 was established, the son of the new king Louis-Philippe was sent to St. Helena to bring back Napoleon's remains, and he was entombed in Paris. Finally, the advocates of the republic triumphed in 1848, and Napoleon's own nephew, Louis-Napoleon, won election to the presidency of the Second Republic with an overwhelming majority. In 1851 he carried out a coup of the republic and established himself emperor in the Second Empire.

Napoleon was an unusual, benevolent dictator, different than the many who followed him to power in Europe and the Americas. He built up the institutions of French government and laid the foundation for a modern republic. However, also laid at his feet is the human toll paid for his ambition. The Napoleonic Wars of 1800–15 cost France alone about 500,000 casualties, or 1/60th of the population, and another 500,000 imprisoned or missing. There is no telling the total non-French losses where his armies roamed, across the rest of Europe as well as the Americas and the Middle East.

Reading: Industrialization and the Social Question

In comparison to the shocking events of France in 1789, the industrial "revolution" is a somewhat misleading term. Industrialization in Europe was a relatively slow and uneven process, starting in Great Britain and a few pockets of northern Europe in the late 18th century, and spreading to the east and south of the continent. It might seem more appropriate to call it the industrial *evolution* more than revolution. But just as the Enlightenment led to the production of new ideas and sensibilities that would influence societies and politics around the world, industrialization fundamentally changed the way many people lived. In his 1844 book *The Condition of the Working Class in England*, Friedrich Engels (1820-95) called industrialization a "revolution" for it had promised to transform "the whole of civil society."

Industrialization would come to determine the conditions under which most Europeans lived and worked, the goods they bought, the food they ate, even the norms of daily interaction, and the "classes" they associated with. Industrialization also redefined human beings' relationship with nature, changed global conceptions of time, and eventually even reordered space. And, as industrialization in Europe required resources from and trade with distant economies, it also changed the way Europeans engaged with the world. The legacy of the Industrial Revolution is clear today: from the buildings we live in to our use of transportation, from our obsession with technology to the clocks on the wall, much of 21st century daily life would be unthinkable without this process.

British Industrialization

There is much disagreement about why exactly industrialization took off in Britain in the late 18th century. But some factors certainly made for prime conditions for economic growth. Europe underwent a demographic transformation that saw the population as a whole nearly double between 1700 and 1850. The highest regions of growth were in Western Europe. Population in Britain, for example, nearly tripled in this period. Epidemic diseases like smallpox and plague became far less common. The consumption of tea and coffee, both requiring boiled water, made water-borne maladies like cholera less common. Birth rates also rose, in part due to the fact that 18th-century Europeans started marrying earlier in life, meaning that couples had more years to reproduce. Improved agricultural practices made famines unlikely and eased chronic malnutrition.

Improvements in agricultural practices, especially in Western Europe, also eventually led to a surplus of labor in the countryside. Thanks to Enlightenment-era innovations in the science and technology of farming, engineers drained swamps to render more land arable; chemists developed better fertilizers. Communities increasingly found it more efficient to combine small plots of land into larger "enclosures" that enabled more diversified crops and better control of production. In some regions, efficiency lowered food prices, leaving families with money for discretionary spending. It also left agricultural workers with more time on their hands to work in occupations unrelated to farming.

While transformations in agriculture were a key precondition to industrialization, a change of mentality about the economy was a necessary intellectual transformation. In early modern times, most people did not produce much more than they could themselves consume. Mercantilism, the dominant economic theory of the day, regulated and restricted trade by controlling guilds, setting tariffs, and creating monopolies that stifled competition. In 1776, Adam Smith, a Scottish philosophe, wrote *The Wealth of Nations*, which challenged the mercantilist system on moral and intellectual grounds. He argued that men naturally wanted to "truck, barter and exchange one thing for another." Self-interest, long considered morally questionable, could in fact cause social good, wealth as opposed to poverty. Economic freedom, Smith argued, would make societies wealthier, stronger, and more virtuous. This formed the basis of classical economic liberalism, what Smith called "laissez-faire" economics. It hinged on the idea that states had no place in the regulation of economies.

Many would-be entrepreneurs embraced Smith's ideas, especially in Great Britain. The country was well suited to industrialization. It was politically stable, possessed excellent means of transport along waterways, rivers, and the sea, and was rich in natural resources, including coal. The wealth of slave economies, especially in the production of sugar, tobacco, and cotton, also meant that industrialists in Britain had cash to invest in new ventures. Britain also had new markets and sources for raw materials in India, where it had traded for over a century. Industry began with textile production in "cottage industries" – literally small production set up in the homes of people who had extra time to work. Technological developments in spinning and weaving, as well as in water and steam power, led to the building of larger factories. These new factories expanded exponentially the amount of material that could be produced. As one measure of growth, Britain's appetite for raw cotton from American expanded from five million pounds in 1750 to nearly 600 million pounds a century later.

Expansion in textiles fed further innovation and industrialization. The spirit of the Enlightenment inspired inventors to create more efficient ways to clean (cotton gin, 1793) and spin (spinning jenny, 1764) cotton. New machinery demanded more robust sources of power, first water mills and then steam. The use of steam engines required coal mining. Coal was difficult to transport, necessitating the building of railroads, which required iron. Railroads were complex and expensive, requiring further technological advances and more sophisticated financing, leading to investment firms and banks.

Over the course of the century, economies were transformed, first in Great Britain, then in the mid-19th century across the continent, in France, the Netherlands, and the German states, with industry arriving in Russia on the eve of the First World War. Industrialization changed many aspects of life. Railroads literally shrunk the distance between regions making it possible for people to travel more and even become tourists. Transport also made consumer goods, even from very distant parts of the world, more readily accessible to Europeans. But certainly, industrialization brought far less appealing changes, as well. New industries required hundreds of thousand of new workers, many of whom came from the countryside where jobs were scarcer. The division of labor associated with industry meant that families that had, in rural areas, often worked together were now separated and stripped of any control over their schedules. Working hours were long (up to 12 hours a day), with women and children placed in difficult and often dangerous jobs. Urban areas built up around industrial centers, where laborers often lived in squalid conditions.

Overseas Markets

Industrialization had significant impacts on how Europeans defined themselves at home and engaged with the world around them. Abroad, the new economic system required Europeans to rely on overseas markets and people in increasingly invasive ways. The need for resources, including metals, cotton, silk, and even foodstuffs, led European merchants to increase trade, especially in Asia over the course of the century. In turn, the same merchants delivered goods to new foreign markets hungry for finished goods made in the factories of Europe. This interaction deeply impacted local economies outside of Europe, driving communities to change their modes of living and production to respond to western economic interests. Where this process happened without European intervention, regions sometimes remained autonomous. Places where local elites challenged European intervention often faced the likelihood of being colonized.

Non-Europeans were also forced to respond to Europe's new labor needs. When the British abolished the international slave trade in 1807 and emancipated slaves in 1838, they needed a new source of labor to work overseas plantations. In the 1840s, the British created an Asian contract labor system – also known as indentured servitude – that moved over a million primarily Indian workers to plantations in the Caribbean, Mauritius, South Africa, and elsewhere. Other imperial powers, including the French, followed suit, recruiting indentured laborers from China, Indochina, and elsewhere to work in a variety of overseas possessions. Ostensibly "free" labor, indentured servants were nonetheless often exposed to the harsh treatment given to slaves, sometimes being kidnapped, transported across the seas in the holds of ships, and forced to work in inhumane conditions.

Population growth in Europe, combined with periodic swings in the economy, also left many Europeans unemployed and desperate during the course of the century. Millions responded to the challenges brought by industrialization by seeking new lives abroad. Fewer than two million people emigrated from Europe in the three centuries before 1800. By contrast, the 19th century saw more than 50 million Europeans move to the United States, Canada, Australia, Argentina, Brazil, Cuba, and South Africa. This diaspora occurred in waves, with the early emigration of nearly 10 million people from Ireland, especially during the deadly years of the Potato Famine in the 1840s, the German states, and Scandinavia. Economic downturn later in the century witnessed many millions leaving Italy, Spain, and Eastern Europe. This extraordinary movement of people fundamentally shaped the cultural, religious, and political perspectives of destination countries in North and South America, South Africa, and the antipodes.

The Social Question

For those who stayed at home, industrialization gave rise to a radically new way of defining identity in European society: class. In the years of the French Revolution, the political dissatisfaction of the sans-culottes was shaped by their experience as urban workers. But they lacked a coherent sense of class-consciousness. Industrialization, with its homogenization of workers' experiences, its disparity of incomes, and the rise of new political leaders committed to workers' needs, expedited the development of working class identity. The "social question" – that is, the question of how to improve the plight of the working classes – was closely tied to the formation of a new ideology of socialism.

Socialism, as an ideology, did not come entirely – or even largely – from workers themselves, but often from one-time entrepreneurs who had grown disenchanted with the world made by industrialization. Much early socialist thought challenged liberal economic theories, including Adam Smith, in one important way: socialists rejected the idea that human nature was driven by self-interest. Instead, man's natural state was communal. Many early socialists, often called "Utopian" or "Romantic" socialists, set out to produce a fairer, more equal society for workers and factory owners, often through the creation of small communities. Their efforts responded to the social dislocation caused by industrialization. Christian ideals, such as helping the poorest members of society, met with the technical knowledge and secular values of the Enlightenment ideals of secular humanism. Early socialists were reform minded, rather than radical. They did not seek to turn back the Industrial Revolution, but to make it a more equitable and humane process. In fact, many utopian socialists believed in the promises of science and industry to improve people's lives.

An important shift in socialist thinking came in the mid-1800s with the dissemination of the ideas of Karl Marx (1818-83). Marx rejected many early versions of socialism as weak and unscientific. Instead, he insisted that socialism had to be understood in terms of history. Relying on Enlightenment precepts, he argued that history is a rational, linear process that moved forward through class struggle toward a determined end. The most recent moment was defined by capitalism – the economic system of Industrial Europe – that pitted the bourgeoisie, the owners of the means of production, against the proletariat, the workers whom he imagined to be a single, unified class. Unlike other socialists who tried to reform industrialization, Marx predicted a coming revolution, which would be led by the proletariat. When the workers gained class-consciousness through their dispossession, they would emerge as the "grave diggers" of the bourgeoisie. The new world order would put an end to private property and individual interests and usher in real equality and pure communism. While Marx's prediction of a proletarian revolution did not come to pass in the 19th century, his writings inspired political parties and labor movements to challenge the forces of liberalism across the continent and, indeed, world.

Reading: Global Migration 1500-1900

Humans have been on the move since they left Africa 40,000 years ago. But human migration in the world before 1800 generally has been gradual and the movements mostly to adjacent regions. The advent of international migration, from continent to continent, has happened in the last two and one-half centuries. There had been a few exceptions before, particularly the forced migration of African slaves to other parts of the world. But the 19th century saw the first large-scale, voluntary human movements from homelands to far away places. And the 20th century after WWII saw migrations larger than the world has ever known. Immigration is a major feature of world history, and it is useful to understand how and why people began to migrate.

Localized Migrations, 1500-1800

Most movement of humans prior to 1800 were motivated by push factors. Often people were trying to get away from war or famine. But the factor that seems to have caused mass movement was more often state-sponsored, often forced, migration. Monarchs and emperors encouraged laboring people to move and settle into regions that were relatively sparse within their kingdoms. Sometimes, the reason was economic, to relieve population pressure in one part of the kingdom and improve development in another; and sometimes it was for defensive reasons, to improve the security of a frontier.

Western Eurasia

Internal European migrations in the 16th and 17th centuries of this kind have been estimated at about four million. The bulk of these migrations seem to have been Russian peasants, following Russian expansion in the direction of the Caucasus, when tzars added the central black-earth and steppe regions near the Lower Volga and Don rivers to the Russian empire; later Germans were encouraged to locate to the steppes. Around 50,000 migrants from the Asiatic part of the Ottoman Empire colonized the Balkans at the beginning of the 16th century, mostly nomadic Turkish tribes but also Tatars, who settled in Bulgaria. In the early 17th century, some 270,000 Kalmyks moved from western Mongolia to the borders of the Caspian Sea in European Russia.

People also simply migrated on their own to get away from real or imagined religious persecution, often with the blessing of monarchs. Notable examples of this phenomenon were the mass migrations of Protestants from the Spanish Netherlands to the Dutch Republic after the 1580s. When Spain expelled the Jews from the Iberian Peninsula, many settled in northern Europe and eventually England, while others established large communities in the Levant, the eastern Mediterranean. The French crown expelled the Huguenots from France in the 1580s, and many resettled in Switzerland. Since the 14th century, the Serbs started leaving the areas of their medieval kingdom as it was overrun by the Ottoman Turks and migrated to the north, to the lands of today's Vojvodina (northern Serbia), which was ruled by the kingdom of Hungary at the time. The Habsburg monarchs of Austria encouraged them to settle on their frontier with the Turks and provide military service by granting them free land and religious toleration. Some 250,000 English and Scotch Protestant colonists in the period 1560-1690, also moved to predominantly Catholic, northern Ireland, not to move away from persecution but to keep Ireland more firmly in English hands.

Eastern Eurasia

Asian migrations particularly in China were even more often state-sponsored and localized. It had long been the practice of Chinese emperors to require the migration of people from the highly populated southeast of China into less populated areas of the western and northern frontiers, often to create defenses against the perennial problem of marauding tribes. The Han emperors (206 BCE-220 CE) moved about a million people this way, or more than three percent of the entire population. In a 50-year period from 1370 to 1417, the Ming-founding Emperor Hongwu ordered 11 million people (16 percent of his population) to move from the Shanxi plateau and the Yangtze River Delta to the more barren inner lands of the west and northwest. Ming emperors created colonies of soldiers and their families, called *wei* or *suo*, along the remote stations of the Great Wall.

In the interregnum of violence and dislocation between the Ming and the Qing Dynasties in the mid 1600s, peasants began to move south and away from the northern Manchu armies of the Qing. Once established, the Qing Dynasty (1644-1911) Emperors Kangxi, Yongzheng, and Qianlong used preferential policies of free land and relief from taxes, rather than force, to encourage Chinese settlement into more remote regions of the large empire. By 1776, immigrants to Sichuan Province and their descendants reached six million, accounting for more than 60 percent of the province's population.

But there was also a steady, voluntary Chinese diaspora to Southeast Asia that began in the Ming and increased in the Qing period. They were mostly Chinese traders and merchants, taking advantage of the Indian Ocean trade, and they took second wives in the ports of Champa (northern Vietnam), Cambodia, Borneo, Java, and Sumatra. The descendants of these second families, with constant influxes of more Chinese immigrants, formed a significant Chinese community abroad. The communities maintained their distinct Chinese culture. When early Portuguese, Dutch. and English traders entered the Indian Ocean ports, they often found well-established Chinese guilds and a *kapitan china*, or leader of the Chinese merchant community, who represented its interests to local and colonial authorities.

International Migration, 1500-1800

While merchants, traders, and soldiers were always the vanguard of international migration, they mostly formed a trickle. The development of the Silk Road by land and sea across Central Asia in the Medieval period provided an opportunity for Europeans, like Marco Polo, to go to Asia. The profits of the Silk Road also encouraged European crusaders of the 11th through 14th century to settle in several islands of the western Mediterranean and create small trading empires. The real international travelers of this time, however, were the Arabs, the backbone of trade across North Africa and the Indian Ocean supported by their coreligionists in communities from Morocco to Indonesia. But for all western Eurasians, including Arabs, the journey to the East was long, difficult, and filled with all kinds of opportunities to die. Therefore, it is not entirely surprising that large-scale migration was possible only when long-distance travel by sea was developed. The Portuguese opened up this particular chapter in human history. In the 1400s, a state-sponsored program of sea exploration began with Prince Henry, a younger son of the Portuguese royal house. Portuguese sailors and commanders hired by the prince developed the small but effective ship called the caravel. It combined square and lateen sail rigging in such a way that it could navigate the open oceans for long distances.

The African Slave Trade

By the mid 15th century, the Portuguese had learned to sail the eastern Atlantic well enough to discover and settle several island chains — the Azores, the Madeiras, and the Cape Verdes Islands — and were determined to sail down the coast of Africa. Initially, their goals for Africa were two, and neither included slavery. First, they wanted to round the continent of Africa to reach the Spice Island trade of the Indian Ocean, thus breaking the trade monopoly of the Turks and Venetians. Second, they wanted to break the hold of Arab Saharan traders over West African gold.

Having accomplished both by 1500, they soon learned that it would be relatively easy to also cut out the Saharan Arab traders on another commodity and create a new market network — supplying African slaves to Europe. The Portuguese brought hundreds of thousands of West African slaves to Iberia and Italy between the 1440s and the 1640s. In some cities, they made a significant demographic impact: for example, in Lisbon in 1550, 10,000 people (some ten percent of the population) were black slaves. Most of these were domestic slaves, but the Portuguese also took over as the suppliers of thousands of African galley slaves to Mediterranean shippers. We have no exact records, but the Portuguese may have brought as many as 300,000 slaves into Europe by the 1550s. It was a trifle, however, compared to the next phase of slave exploitation.

The Portuguese, aided by Genoese merchants, soon learned that the soil and climate of their recent conquest, the Madeira Islands, was perfect for a product that was in great demand in Europe — sugar from sugarcane. But the intense and dangerous labor of sugar production was too much for the small European settlement population of Madeira, and the Portuguese began to bring in slaves to do the heavy labor. In the process the Portuguese developed what we call plantation slavery — large tracts of land wholly devoted to the production of one global commodity and the labor provided almost entirely by slaves. Sugar was so profitable that care of the slaves and slave families, as one would do for domestic slaves, was not essential. All that was needed was a constant supply of mostly male slaves who led short and brutal lives growing and processing the sugar cane. The Portuguese soon began a sugar industry in northeast Brazil and aided the Spanish as they began the production of sugar on the islands of the Caribbean, another suitable climate for sugarcane. Soon the British and French captured Caribbean islands of their own and began truly large-scale sugar factories on Barbados, Jamaica, Martinique, and other islands.

Slavery was essential to the new migration in the Americas for two major reasons. As soon as Europeans came, they spread diseases among the indigenous Americas, resulting in a demographic collapse of the population. Second, European monarchs in the 16th and 17th centuries did not want massive emigration of their citizens to the Americas and tightly controlled it. The citizens themselves were also well aware of the dangers of living in the Americas, from indigenous attacks to tropical diseases to the overall primitive conditions. Moreover, the new lands were not readily domesticated with small farming; the climate and soil was too different from Europe. So, the policy of European settlement soon became extraction of resources needed in Europe, such as sugar and silver, fueled with slave labor and managed by small bands of traders, planters, and low-level administrators, many of whom formed families with the indigenous and black populations. The one exception was religious refugees, like the Puritan communities of New England, and later convicts sent to Australia, where the crowns of Europe saw some benefit to getting rid of such people.

European Emigration to the New World

From 1570 to 1700, there were 1.5 Africans arriving in the Americas to each European. European emigration was extremely slow to get started. From 1492 to 1650, only 500,000 Spanish immigrated to Spanish America. By 1700, one would have found only 70,000 Portuguese settlers in Brazil. Though the British had founded colonies in North America and the Caribbean in the early 17th century, only 257,000 British actually left home to become a part of British America. But it was not just the crown discouraging emigration. One of the main problems for poorer Europeans was the price of the ticket on sailing ships. Therefore, many white laborers had to immigrate as indentured servants; ship owners paid the passage and then sold the servants to American planters who demanded bonded work for as many as seven years. Though there were women indentured servants, by far most of the servants were men.

But the re-populating of the Americans with Africans and Europeans began to pick up steam in the 18th century because of three factors. First, the population of Europe in the 18th century increased significantly, particularly as a result of the cultivation of new food crops brought from the New World in what is known as the Columbian Exchange. European crowns began to lift restrictions on emigration to the colonies to get rid of the excess population. Second, and perhaps most importantly, the price of transportation across the Atlantic steadily declined, allowing more and more working class people and families to avoid indentured servitude while still migrating. In the Americas, extraction industries in fishing, lumbering, agriculture, and mining were much more developed as was commerce in the large towns and cities like New York. They competed for European labor, paying much better wages than could be had in Europe. And cheap frontier land was readily available to the young and adventurous.

Third, the plantation economy was growing and expanding into new American crops besides sugar, such as tobacco, indigo, rice, and cotton, demanding more and more African slave labor. The forced importation of African slaves reached its height in the last decades of the 18th century. As a result of these new influxes, American population grew exponentially. The population of the British American colonies reached 1.2 million in 1750 and doubled by 1770. In Brazil in 1818, the total population was 3.5 million, of which a little over one million were white and 2.5 million were Africans and African descendents.

Migration in the Nineteenth-Century

Obviously, steamship companies had four to ten times more supply of passenger space to move people by the late 19th century, and the price of the passenger ticket plummeted. But even with low prices, the companies had empty spaces. They hired recruiters and brokers to go into the interior of countries where the companies were doing business and attract passengers with promises of work, wealth, and opportunity in another part of the world. These brokers could be found in many ports in Asia, Africa, India, and Europe. Because of recruiters, to this day the Chinese refer to California, an important destination for Chinese immigrants, as "gold mountain."

A second crucial factor was the end of the slave trade. Both the United States and Great Britain had abolished the trade by 1807. The British further abolished slavery in the empire in 1833. The British navy regularly trolled the Atlantic to board slave ships of other countries and returned Africans to Africa, severely hampering the trade in the Atlantic. But British plantations and factories around the world still needed labor, so the government encouraged brokers to entice poor laborers in one part of the empire to work in British plantations, mines, and factories in other parts, sometimes using indentured servitude. It began with Indians from Bengal to sugar plantations in the island of Mauritius in the Indian Ocean in the 1830s and 40s. Later, Indians, often called "coolies," were sent to British Guiana to replace manumitted slaves. Between 1837 and 1917, 1.5 million Indian indentured workers migrated within the British empire to Kenya, South Africa,

Uganda, and Trinidad and Tobago to work on plantations. It is estimated that as many as two-thirds stayed in their new lands.

Europeans on the Move in the 19ᵗʰ Century

From 1815 to 1932, 60 million people left Europe to go to other parts of the world. Some returned but most stayed and settled in their new homes, primarily in "areas of European settlement," such as the US, Canada, Brazil, Argentina, Australia, and Siberia. Records indicate that over 65 percent went to the United States. Over half of the emigration before the 1870s was from the British Isles, with much of the remainder from northwestern Europe. As migration increased along with new transportation technologies in the 1880s, regions of intensive emigration spread to South and East Europe. Large numbers of Italian, Poles, and Jews entered the US in its high point of immigration in 1880-1910. These European populations multiplied rapidly in their new habitats; much more so than the populations of Africa and Asia. As a result, on the eve of WWI, 38 percent of the world's total population was of European ancestry.

The impact of immigration was greatest in the far north and south of the Americas, where the indigenous American populations were more sparse. In 1910, foreigners in the US were 14.7 percent of the country's population or 13.5 million. By 1881, 14 percent of Canada's population was foreign-born, and the proportion increased to 22 percent in 1921. Argentina had a much smaller population, but the foreign-born had a huge impact, making up 30 percent of the population by 1914, fully a third were from Italy. In Brazil the proportion of European immigrants in the national population was much smaller, peaking in 1920 with just 7 percent, mostly Italians, Portuguese, and Spaniards at two million foreign-born. Though in the US today, many believe the percentage of foreign-born are quite high, it is actually about 13 percent, close to historic highs for the US but not greater than the early 20ᵗʰ century.

Asian Emigration in the 19ᵗʰ Century

In the 1840s, the Qing emperors tried mightily to stop European companies from enticing Chinese citizens into indentured servitude and migration. But China had two major problems. First, there had been very rapid and dramatic increases in the Chinese population in the first two centuries of the Qing Dynasty, especially between 1749 and 1811 when the population doubled from 177,495,000 to 358,610,000. By 1851, the population had reached about 431,896,000, and the state was having difficulty feeding all of its citizens. Second, the Qing Dynasty was rapidly slipping into decline in mid century, suffering from European encroachments on its sovereignty, the disastrous Taiping Rebellion, and debilitating famines. Naturally, many Chinese wanted to move away from the great troubles.

Though the government tried to punish them, local Chinese smugglers, called "crimpers," worked with European brokers in westernized ports such as Macao and Hong Kong, smuggling hundreds of thousands of Chinese to the Americas in European and American vessels. Between 1847 and 1874, 250,000 Chinese were brought to South America to work in the guano and sugar fields. Another 550,000 went to California, British Columbia, and Australia primarily to build railroads. Chinese "coolies" also migrated to Singapore, at the instigation of the many Chinese traders who were well established in those communities. Laborers were particularly attracted to the prospect of work in the tin mines and rubber plantations of the Malay Peninsula. They stayed, remained loyal to China, and were referred to as "Straits Chinese," after the Malay Straits.

At the end of the 19ᵗʰ century, the Chinese government realized that overseas Chinese could be an asset, a source of foreign investment, and a bridge to overseas knowledge. They relented on their previously restrictive emigration policies, which was already undermined by decades of smuggling. But now emigration could flow readily. Among the provinces, Guangdong had historically supplied the largest number of emigrants, estimated at 8.2 million in 1957, about 68 percent of the total overseas Chinese population by then. Within Guangdong, the main immigrant communities were clustered in seven districts in the Pearl River Delta: four districts known as Sze Yup and three known as Sam Yup. Because of its limited arable lands, with much of its terrain either rocky or swampy, Sze Yup was the "pre-eminent sending area" of emigrants during this period. Most of the emigrants from Sze Yup went to North America, making their Chinese dialect Taishanese, the main language spoken in Chinatowns in Canada and the US.

Though the Chinese were the largest immigrant community in the 19th century, Japan, a country not well-known for emigration, increased its immigrant profile in the 19th and early 20th centuries. Today, there are about 2.5 million Japanese emigrants and people of Japanese descent living in countries around the world. The modern waves of Japanese emigration began in 1868 when 153 Japanese journeyed to Hawaii to work on sugar plantations. But the Meiji government prohibited such emigration because these first Japanese were treated like slaves. A new treaty with Hawaii in 1885 provided for better work conditions and three-year contracts. Over the next nine years, about 29,000 Japanese went to Hawaii to work on sugar plantations. In 1899, 790 people left for contract work in Peru, starting a wave of Japanese Immigration in Latin America, particularly to Brazil. There are now roughly 1.5 million Latin Americans of Japanese ancestry, at least half of whom trace their ancestral origins to the island of Okinawa. Brazil has the most: 1.3 million. Peru has about 100,000. Argentina has about 50,000. Mexico is estimated to have 30,000. Late 19th- and early 20th-century Japanese migration, resulted in nearly one million Japanese immigrants and people of Japanese descent.

Reading: Europe, 1815-48
Metternich and the Post-Napoleonic Congresses

The years from 1815 to 1848 provided a much-needed respite from the endless wars of the Napoleonic Era. When a coalition of European powers finally managed to defeat Napoleon for the last time, all the rulers wanted to do was return Europe to "normal" — no war, no equality of the classes and no revolutions or even great change. In short, they wanted stability, and the monarchs and major diplomats of Europe began with a reorganization of Europe undertaken at a series of meetings, the most important of which was the Congress of Vienna. The leader of this restoration of "normal" was Prince Klemens von Metternich, a high-ranking diplomat in service to the Austrian emperor. Metternich's highest goal was to establish a century of "peace, stability, and security" in Europe and was certain that only autocratic monarchs in firm control of their countries could accomplish this.

Modern historians have credited him with establishing what he called a "congress system" and we today would call a peace conference. Powerful nations would work out their differences in a series of meetings followed by multi-party agreements. Metternich also seemed to understand that the peace of Europe, with so many powerful nations in a single continent, needed a set of rules acknowledging a "balance of power" — less powerful nations deferring to the great powers, the great powers acting in responsible ways and all parties actively attempting to avoid war. This was an improvement on the 18th century practices of great nations going to war to demonstrate their superiority and making two-party agreements, often in secret, that sowed discord. However, historians also acknowledge that Metternich's and his fellow diplomats' firm and active opposition to the new 19th-century ideas of liberalism, republicanism and socialism also probably made the monarchies brittle and unable to withstand revolutionary pressures that exploded later in mid century.

Nevertheless, the Congress of Vienna established a practice of the great powers meeting when tensions in Europe began to crop up and, in so doing, the period 1815-1848 was a age without much war. In 1818, the Congress of Aix-la-Chapelle decided that the great powers could withdraw their military forces that had been occupying France since Napoleon's defeat. In 1820, as a reaction to the evident collapse of the government of Naples, Metternich called another meeting, the Congress of Troppau. Metternich wanted to stop the revolution in Naples from spreading. At Troppau, Austria, Prussia and Russia allied to restore the King of Naples. Britain, though anti-revolutionary, was less inclined to be bound by continental commitments. Thus, they stayed out of intervention in Naples, as did France. In the early 1820s the Bourbon government of Spain seemed especially fragile in the face of revolutionary actions. At the same time, Greek nationalists sought more actively to establish a Greek nation in Turkey. To deal with these troublesome developments,

Metternich called the Congress of Verona in 1822. The congress also allowed France to send an army into Spain to end the revolt and stabilize the Bourbon king. The revolution in Spain was quickly smashed. Then they easily put down the Greek revolutionaries, who really did not have the military power to take over Turkey at this time anyway.

Conservative Years, 1815-1830

In France, the newly established King Louis XVIII, whose brother Louis XVI had been executed during the French Revolution, certainly didn't want another revolution in France. He did his best to balance the tense situation following Napoleon's defeat. On both sides, Louis granted amnesties, hoping to "start over" in France. The wealthy, however, remembering the Revolution, became passionately anti-revolutionary, even reactionary. The reactionary element only increased after the King's nephew, the Duke of Berry, was assassinated in 1820. In 1824, Louis XVIII died, and was replaced by the assassinated Duke's father, Charles X. Unlike the moderate Louis, Charles was a hard-core reactionary, and hated all the changes taking place in France, even the ones Louis had initiated. Charles believed himself to be a monarch appointed by God, and he started trampling on basic elements of liberalism like the French constitution.

Poland was a state recreated by the Congress of Vienna and ruled by the Russian Czar Alexander I. Initially, its government was quite liberal. Though ruled by Alexander, Poland had a constitution. Alexander considered himself an "enlightened despot" and spoke often of granting freedom to the people, but he soon found that when he did give the people some self-government, they didn't always agree with what he wanted them to do. Liking liberal reforms in theory more than practice, Alexander increasingly curtailed Poland's right of self-government. Frustrated in its desire for self-rule, Polish nationalism began to rise. Secret societies developed, and a university movement got underway. Alexander's secret police suppressed all such groundswells of revolution.

In Germany, nationalists motivated by Romantic ideas, such as the belief in a special German Volksgeist, hated the results of the Congress of Vienna, which was satisfied to leave Germany fragmented. Dissatisfaction centered among students and intellectuals, who began to form highly nationalist clubs called Burschenschaft. In 1817, the Burschenschaft held a national meeting at Wartburg, finally convincing Metternich that German nationalism was a force to be reckoned with. When the German nationalists began assassinating reactionary leaders, however, Metternich intervened by pushing the Carlsbad Decrees through the German congress, the Bund, in 1819. The decrees outlawed the Burschenschaft and pushed them underground. Secondarily, the decrees increased government regulation of the universities, limiting what was taught, and made way for government censorship of German newspapers. The Carlsbad Decrees quieted the German nationalist movement for about a decade.

In Great Britain, in 1815, the aristocrat-dominated Parliament passed the Corn Law, which raised tariffs on grain to make imports impossible and enrich large landowners. The high tariffs also raised prices beyond the reach of the working class. In December 1816, starving workers rioted in London. Meanwhile, in Manchester, the ascendant industrialists who dominated the city had been hoping to get Parliamentary representation for some time. Realizing how discontented the workers were, the industrialists helped organize 80,000 workers to demonstrate at St. Peters Field against the Corn Law and for universal male suffrage. The protest was peaceful, but British soldiers nonetheless fired into the crowd, killing several. The event became a national scandal, called the Peterloo Massacre. The Tory Parliament, frightened of the potential for worker revolts, passed acts in 1819 aimed at stopping mass political organization. Not appeased, a group of workers decided to try and assassinate the Tory cabinet. This group, known as the Cato Street Conspiracy, was discovered in 1820. Several members were executed.

Intellectual Ferment and the Beginnings of Revolution

Militarily and politically, the congresses established a veneer of stability, but underneath there was a torrent of new intellectual ideas about government and the sharing of power. Though not plagued by rampant wars, the years 1815-1848 can be seen as a more subtle battle between conflicting worldviews. On one side were the powerful and entrenched members of the Old Regime, who opposed change of any kind. On the other side were the forces of change: the middle class created by the dynamics of the Industrial Revolution, liberals, socialists, republicans, radicals, romantics, and nationalists. The struggle of ideas erupted in the form of various small-scale revolutions, first in 1830 and then on a more widespread scale in 1848 — the year of revolutions.

The Industrial Revolution and Liberalism. Economically, the Industrial Revolution was beginning to create a new class of entrepreneurs and middle-class businessmen who were not content to let aristocrats rule for them. Moreover, their need for labor led to large movements of men and women who had farmed the countryside and now came into the cities seeking work in the manufacture of textiles and iron. Great Britain, especially the North where the Industrial Revolution began, led the way. While the conservative Tory Party ruled, the British parliament proved to be more resilient than its continental partners in absorbing the lower classes into the existing political structure. While the years 1815 to 1848 marked a period of particular industrial acceleration for Great Britain, Germany, France and the Netherlands also began to establish an industrial sector. Burgeoning middle and laboring classes began to champion a range of political ideologies, but generally they were in favor of a liberal philosophy of self-government that would take the place of the arbitrary rules of monarch and aristocracy.

Beginning in Spain and France during the 1820s, liberalism soon spread to England. Its advocates were businessmen and professionals who wanted modern, efficient self-government, although they were not always for universal male suffrage. They wanted freedom of the press and freedom of assembly. They wanted constitutions and "laissez faire" economic policies, such as free trade and low tariffs. And they were generally against unions.

Socialism. The counter to liberalism was socialism, which sought economic equality for all, and was very much against the free market ideals of liberalism. Socialism looked at the free-market economies of western Europe in the midst of the Industrial Revolution and saw exploited workers leading miserable lives while manufacturers profited enormously. Socialists felt that with the rich profiting so much, the poor should get some of the benefits, since worker's labor supported the entire system. Therefore, they wanted to nationalize parts of the economy, such as industrial and financial sectors, giving these areas of the economy over to government control. Thus, the benefits could be distributed more equally to the various members of society. For example, Robert Owen, a manufacturer in Manchester, grew upset at his workers' living conditions and began paying higher wages than other manufacturers did, and he treated his workers well. In 1825, he founded New Harmony, Indiana, an experimental socialist community in the United States. Such socialist entrepreneurs were often called Utopian socialists in their desire to create ideal societies within a capitalist system.

Radicalism and Republicanism. Radicalism appeared in the 1820s in England as the "Philosophical Radicals." This principled and unconventional group, consisting partially of workers and partially of industrialists, had its greatest leader in the colorful Jeremy Bentham. The Radicals were anti-church and anti-monarchy and favored more political equality. They were a force unto themselves until 1832, after which they merged with the British liberals. The European counterpart to Radicalism was usually referred to as Republicanism, which grew out of the French Revolutionary tradition. Republicanism sought complete political equality in the form of universal suffrage and they also opposed monarchy and the Catholic Church.

Romanticism and Nationalism. A young intellectual movement called Romanticism, rose up in reaction to the intense rationalism of the 18th-century Enlightenment. Romanticism challenged the ideal of universal standards for all mankind, and led to the glorification of the unique "national genius" of each ethnic and linguistic group. Thus, it was also during 1815 to 1848 that the modern phenomenon of nationalism was explicitly formulated. Tired of existing as a loose federation, many people in the fragmented German states hoped for German unification. The various Italian states sought Italian unification. Numerous groups within the ethnically diverse Austrian Empire dreamed of forming their own nation. The possibility of nationalists achieving their goals greatly frightened the reactionary rulers of Europe, who knew how destabilizing these changes might be.

Nationalism was the most powerful of all the "isms" in this period. France and Great Britain's strong nation-states had inspired jealousy throughout the rest of Europe; other nations, disorganized as they were, wanted to unify. German intellectuals living in (and hating) the loosely organized Bund provided much of the vocabulary for nationalism, stating that each nation had a particular "Volksgeist," or national spirit. Soon, just about every European language group wanted to have their own nation. Quickly outlawed by reactionary forces, nationalist groups formed secret societies such as the Italian Carbonari and German Burschenschaft. In Eastern Europe, the Poles wanted their own state, and in Austria, the Magyars wanted their own kingdom of Hungary. Throughout the Austrian Empire, the various language groups revived the study of their languages and hoped to carve their own nations out of the empire. A particularly potent nationalist force known as Pan-Slavism began to circulate among various Slavs in Russia, Poland, and Austria. All of these Eastern European groups began a renewed interest in their own cultures. European nationalist groups distributed propaganda leaflets and plotted rebellions. Often, nationalism combined with other ideologies, from liberalism to socialism.

Conservatism. Not all ideologies advocated change. The final important "ism" of the period was conservatism, which was championed by the British parliamentarian Edmund Burke. While Burke did not favor monarchs and did favor a strong parliamentary government, he was extremely suspicious of democracy, believing that the lower classes lacked the judgment essential to self-government. He was appalled at the violence and chaos of the French Revolution and the principles of liberty and equality that led, in his opinion, to that bad outcome. Burke is regarded as the father of modern conservatism, which today represents democracy with all the attendant civil rights, specific institutional controls on the majority that prevents wild shifts in government policy and also slow, slow change guided by traditions.

The Road to Revolution
Metternich's "congress system" began to fail in the late 1820s and the early 1830s. Interestingly, it was on the periphery of Europe that one could see the first evidence of great powers exercising independence. In Greece, nationalists again pushed for independence from Turkey. But this time Great Britain and France, hoping to stop Russian expansion in the Balkans, decided to join in, against Metternich's wishes. By 1829, an independent Greece was internationally recognized. In addition to the Greeks, several Balkan states gained independence and Egypt broke out of Ottoman rule. Meanwhile, in Europe, conservatives began to feel the challenge of lower classes.

In France, the reactionary Charles X had reigned since assuming the throne in 1824. Charles X's reactionary policies antagonized much of the French population, who were used to liberal and republican reforms. Charles thought of himself as divinely appointed to restore the "old ways," and he accordingly gave more power to the aristocrats and Catholic clergy. When the French Chamber of Deputies moved against these changes, Charles dissolved them, passing the four "July Ordinances" in 1830 that disenfranchised the middle class, dissolved their Chamber of Deputies and censored the press. The middle class and radical republicans from the working classes quickly took to the streets of Paris in the July Revolution, rioting and setting up barricades. Charles X quickly abdicated, and the rebellion's leaders moved quickly to install a constitutional monarchy bringing in the more pliant Duke of Orleans, Louis Philippe, who accepted constitutional monarchy.

In France, socialism was spreading rapidly, and the working public became more and more interested in the memory of highly radical leaders like Robespierre. Writers like Louis Blanc began to glorify the act of Revolution. The July Revolution rippled through Europe, starting revolutions in Belgium and Poland. Belgium's revolution was essentially successful. The country ended up with self-government as long as it remained a neutral state, and the other powers agreed not to invade it. Polish nationalists, looking to the successful revolutions in Belgium and France, also decided to revolt in 1830, but Czar Nicholas quickly crushed the rebellion.

In Great Britain, rising tensions were retarded somewhat by the fact that the British had long had a constitutional monarchy and a parliament that had proved periodically to be responsive to the demands of the people. In fact, the dominant conservative Tory Party had its share of "liberal" Tory leaders, such as Robert Peel. Liberal leaders targeted the infamous corn laws of the wealthy landowners and the "rotten boroughs" of southern England that gave it far more political representation than it deserved compared to manufacturing cities like Manchester. In the 1830s, a reform bill came up which would remedy these problems, but it was quashed by Prime Minister Wellington. Wellington's action led to rioting. Parliament realized it had to pass the bill, which it reluctantly did in 1832. The redistribution of British political power with the Reform Bill of 1832 brought a flood of other reform laws that served the middle and working class. In 1833, the Factory Act limited use of child labor; the Poor Law in 1834, established poor houses for unemployed workers — the beginnings of a welfare society, In 1847, a Ten Hours Act passed into law, limiting the number of hours women and children could work per day.

Nevertheless, British workers were only somewhat placated and advocated for more. Though illegal, workers formed labor unions to negotiate for better wages and conditions. Some started to advocate seriously for the overthrow of the wage-labor system, in order to replace it with socialism. A reform bill was drafted in 1838, called the Charter. Its advocates, the Chartists, demanded six reforms: annual elections to the House of Commons; universal male suffrage, secret ballots, equal representation in boroughs, worker representation in Commons and salaries for representatives in the commons, so workers could afford to be a member. The bill did not pass, but the Chartists continued for another decade to collect signatures from the public. Although unsuccessful in this respect, the Chartist Movement helped to build the British labor movement. Instead of taking to the streets in revolt, British workers had learned to organize and press for reform within the political system. This was not the case on the continent and all came to a head in the year 1848.

The 1848 Revolution
Paris. In France, Louis Philippe's government had allied with the middle class, a disappointment to the workers who had manned the barricades in 1830. Only one in 30 adult males could vote, and Louis Philippe staunchly opposed enlarging the voting base. Popular discontent finally resulted in the February Revolution of 1848. The working classes again put barricades up in the streets, and an unruly Paris mob frightened Louis Philippe into abdicating. The Radical Republicans then managed to get the provisional government to pass socialist programs. In May, the military turned against lower class agitators. In late June, three days of especially violent class warfare broke out in Paris with the army finally restoring order.

In late 1848, the French began to draw up a new constitution. The constitution included provisions for a strong president, who would be elected via universal male suffrage (all adult males would vote). Among the candidates was Louis Napoleon Bonaparte, Napoleon Bonaparte's nephew. He had no real platform; he merely said that his uncle, Napoleon had been liberal and that he would be liberal. Since the name Bonaparte still resonated so strongly among the general population of France, Louis Napoleon won. Though claiming to be liberal, the newly elected president was mostly interested in re-establishing order. After gaining support by promising universal male suffrage, he promptly got rid of socialists in the government. He encouraged religious influence in school teaching, and then, after becoming confident of his support base, he declared himself Emperor Napoleon III. The revolution in France ended with a new government, but once again a new dictator.

The Austrian Empire. Like the July Revolution of 1830, the February Revolution of 1848 reverberated throughout Europe, resulting in a series of revolutions, most powerfully in Germany and Austria. Vienna, the capital of the ethnically diverse Austrian Empire, was a leading cultural center in Europe. Full of artists, composers, writers, and intellectuals, Vienna was truly the jewel of the Austrian Empire. Yet the various ethnic groups in Austria, including Hungarians, Serbs, Czechs, Slavs and Italians, had become increasingly nationalist over the preceding decades, and by now they all yearned to express their individual volksgeist and gain independence from Austria. Prince Metternich was still chancellor in 1848, working hard for decades to keep the Austrian Empire together. But the diverse ethnic groups were beyond considering themselves as Austrian nationals.

In March 1848, a radical Hungarian Magyar group led by Louis Kossuth began a vocal independence movement. Kossuth's fiery speeches were soon printed in Vienna, where they were a sensation and soon became an uprising. Metternich, monitoring the revolutions throughout Europe, had become fearful and decided to flee Vienna. The situation probably wasn't as bad as he thought, but once news got out that Metternich had left, the Austrian revolutionaries got truly excited. Austrian Czechs and numerous Austrian-controlled Italian states followed the Magyars' lead. Some of the revolutionary excitement also spilled into Prussia, where, to ease the pressure, the Prussian King Frederick William IV promised a constitution. On March 15, Kossuth's Hungary was granted independence under Habsburg rule. The Czech movement in Bohemia soon received the same status, and Italian states like Milan soon overthrew Austrian occupation.

In the latter half of 1848, however, the revolutionary forces began to lose ground. In Prague, a conference of Slavic nationalists grew violent and Emperor Ferdinand of Austria brought his army to smash it. He followed by sending the army to retake the rebellious Italian states of Lombardy and Milan. Serbo-Croatians in independent Hungary soon rebelled against Kossuth and asked the Hapsburgs for help. While another rebellion in Vienna in December led to Emperor Ferdinand's abdication, his even more autocratic son Franz Joseph quickly appealed to the Russians to march into Hungary and crush Kossuth and the Hungarians. The 1848 revolutions in Austria came to an end, restoring order in the Austrian Empire and leaving it a bastion of very conservative monarchist rule under Franz Joseph.

Germany and Prussia. In Prussia, the old king, Frederick William III, had always been opposed to giving the Prussian people a constitution and his son. Frederick William IV, followed his suit. However, the success of Prussia in the last few decades had been almost entirely due to the skilled group of bureaucrats and administrators serving the government, and all of these administrators were pushing hard for a constitutional monarchy.

In March 1848, rioting began in Berlin, as the 1848 revolution fever crossed from Austria into Prussia. Frederick William IV quickly mobilized the disciplined Prussian army to suppress the revolution. However, he was persuaded to take a somewhat more liberal stance and allow the election of a Prussian assembly. The new more radical assembly wanted to unite Prussia with all of Germany and to grant the Polish minorities living in eastern Prussia a right of self-government. But Frederick William IV decided that the experiment in democratic government had gone too far and dissolved the Prussian Assembly, summarily ending the Prussian revolution.

The 1848 revolutions, however, inspired a parallel nationalist movement in Germany. In May 1848, a group of German nationalists met at the Frankfurt Assembly. The goals of the assembly included creating a unified Germany that was liberal and constitutionally governed. The Frankfurt Assembly issued the Declaration of the Rights of the German People, based on the Declarations of the Rights of Man in France and the Declaration of Independence in the United States. Following the nationalist rather than the Enlightenment ideal, this declaration ignored the universal rights of all mankind and simply proclaimed the rights of Germans. In 1849, they then offered Germany to the Prussian King Frederick William IV. Though Frederick wanted the territory, he knew that his acceptance would lead to war with Austria and make him into a constitutional monarch, neither of which he desired. He turned the offer down. Germany remained fragmented after 1848, and the rulers of the various small German states came back to power.

Reading: The Rise of Nations

This struggle – between the forces of liberal capitalism and the working classes – would profoundly influence the political landscape for decades to come. The point of conflict was the nation. The Enlightenment and French Revolution helped define the idea of a nation. In its struggles over the obligations of citizens, the symbols of the Revolution, and even political participation, the revolution gave meaning to what is often called an "imagined community" – that is, an imagined bond that unites those who are members of the nation and excludes from the community those who are not. More than simply a group of people living under a common state, nations possessed a sense of shared comradeship, often defined by a sense of community, citizenship, shared history, or even a biological belief in shared blood.

Liberalism and the Nation-State

In the 19th century, nations in Europe did not simply come into being; they were made. In some countries, like Britain or France, there was a longstanding state with a fairly fixed geography where nations would take shape. But elsewhere – in central and southern Europe – it was more complicated. Italy and Germany, for example, were nothing more than collections of small states that first had to be unified. And their paths to unification were remarkably different. It took years of political negotiations and even civil wars to finally unify these states into single nations. In most European countries, nation-building was closely tied to political power and the continued aspirations of liberal elites – largely urban and educated. But as in the French Revolution, who would enjoy full citizenship was often a point of conflict.

Despite the efforts of conservative monarchies to restore the Old Regime, the liberal genie had been let out of the bottle after the French Revolution. Middle-class businessmen and professionals still wanted greater influence on the political process, and organized societies and parties across Europe, especially in Britain, France, Italy, the German states, and in pockets across the Austrian Empire. They were inspired by the Enlightenment ideals of rationalism and progress and were eager to end state regulation that they believed interfered with industrial economies. In the early 19th century, however, many liberals were more cautious of revolutionary activity. They looked warily back to the Terror, believing it to have been caused by workers' demand for a role in politics. With Europe's working classes expanding to meet industrialization's labor needs, the fear of a popular revolution was even more potentially threatening.

The year 1848 witnessed revolutions of varying sizes and outcomes in France, Italy, the German states, Austria, Hungary, Denmark, Romania, and elsewhere. The catalyst for this revolutionary moment was France, where liberals demanding suffrage staged demonstrations for three days in February. King Louis-Philippe (1773-1850) sent in his soldiers, but many officers were sympathetic to the demands of the revolutionaries. The king fled and a provisional government was established. Workers, many of whom were jobless, immediately demanded a stake in the new government, taking to the streets to demand it. The young government was unable to meet their demands and during a few, bloody "June Days," the liberal government turned on the workers, killing thousands in the streets of Paris. In a bizarre replaying of the first French Revolution, Louis Napoleon, the nephew of Bonaparte, entered politics and soon won the backing of many in France who feared socialism and instability. In 1851, he dissolved the National Assembly, staged a coup, and declared himself Napoleon III, Emperor of France.

Elsewhere in Europe, revolutions were perhaps less dramatic, but they represented important efforts for groups of liberals to experiment in political action. As in France, most of the revolutions failed in part because liberals and conservatives feared inclusion of the "masses" who threatened to undermine economic and political order. In the wake of 1848, many liberals, and even socialists, across the continent adopted a different strategy to gain power. Rather than revolution, they looked to win power more gradually, through reform of the established form of government. Even in France, many liberals increasingly entered into service of state bureaucracies and honed their legislative skills in liberal institutions like bar associations, Masonic lodges, and charitable organizations. Rather than remaking their nations through radical means, they chose to redefine the nation in a way that furthered their ideals and interests without risking violence. They chose to rebuild their nations in their own image and to rewrite national myths to reflect their values.

Across Europe – whether in Britain and France or in newly unified Italy and Germany – people still had to be convinced to feel part of the nation. Language was the first hurdle. When Italy was unified in 1861 only two percent of Italians spoke standard Italian. That same year, about a quarter of Frenchmen spoke no French; most spoke regional dialects. Into the late 19th century, there were efforts to improve and standardize education – making it free and compulsory. Textbooks were written to teach national history, folklore, and myths. Universal military conscription helped men feel like members of the nation as well; the army brought together men from disparate regions, forced them to speak a common language, and moved troops around the nation – allowing them to see the country that united them. At the same time, flags, national holidays, national monuments, and statues of national heroes all aimed to provide citizens with shared symbols. Imperial conquests abroad showed the power and superiority of national communities.

In saying that national identities had to be made, we should not underestimate their potency. Decades of indoctrination into the nation would make for European populations willing to fight and die for their imagined communities. In important ways, the nationalism of the 19th century made the carnage of the 20th century possible. When European countries went to war in 1914, hundreds of thousands of men, cutting across class, ethnic, and religious differences, volunteered to fight. Liberal and socialist, secular and religious, urban and rural – all fought side by side in the trenches of the First World War. In many ways, the promises and aspirations of the Enlightenment remained unattainable as the 19th century came to a close. Across Europe, liberty remained elusive for women, colonized subjects, ethnic and minorities, and the poor. Equality in rights and wealth became an increasingly utopian dream. But the nation made fraternity, at least temporarily in the face of war, an ideal that many found worthy of dying for.

Reading: The British in India

On November 1, 1858, Queen Victoria (1819-1901) issued a proclamation declaring that the British Crown would, from that date on, take charge of the lands of India formerly controlled by the East India Company. This ushered in the era of the British Raj (1858-1947). Regarding the future of India as envisioned by the Crown, the proclamation states the following:

"We desire no extension of Our present territorial Possessions; and while We permit no aggression upon Our Dominions or Our Rights, to be attempted with impunity, We shall sanction no encroachment on those of others. We shall respect the Rights, Dignity, and Honour of Native Princes as Our own; and We desire that they, as well as Our own Subjects, should enjoy that Prosperity and that social Advancement which can only be secured by internal Peace and good government. We hold ourselves bound to the Natives of Our Indian Territories by the same obligations of Duty which bind Us to all Our other Subjects; and those Obligations, by the Blessing of Almighty God, We shall faithfully and conscientiously fulfill."

The proclamation was an attempt to calm Indians fearful of what might be in store for them in the wake of the Sepoy Mutiny: a large and bloody rebellion against the British presence in India that began a year earlier. The statement also heralded a profound shift in the nature of British-Indian relations, as the Queen's government would now take full and direct control from the defunct leadership of the East India Company. The sentiments expressed by Queen Victoria are rich in 19th-century Victorian views about British power and the ability to export the more "advanced" aspects of British civilization. Though perhaps sincere at the time, it is clear that those without prior experience or interest had little idea of the realities of the manner in which the East India Company had functioned, or what it would mean to exercise such power thousands of miles away, with a small number of men, over a civilization of complex political, religious, and social structures. Despite these challenges, India would become the "Jewel in the Crown," of an empire upon which the sun never set.

The British East India Company

By the time the British Government took direct control, India had been visited and partially colonized by the British for over two hundred years. The East India Company initially received a charter in 1600 from Elizabeth I (1533-1603), who was in the final years of a long and transformative reign. By this time, the English had far more experience at sea, had successfully fought off a Spanish invasion in 1588, and were eager to break into trade with Asia -- a trade heretofore monopolized by the Spanish and the Portuguese. It also suited Elizabeth that an entity other than the Crown would take on the cost and risk of such a venture.

The Charter created the *Governor and Company of Merchants of London, Trading into the East Indies*. The name would change in 1709 to the *United Company of Merchants Trading to the East Indies*. The company was given a monopoly on trade with the "East" (at the time a rather vague geographical notion). The company would be run by a governor, who would be aided by a deputy and a committee chosen by an assembly of stockholders. The first ships set sail and, by 1615, English ships were consistently in minor conflicts with the Portuguese.

Power Transitions En Route to British Control

The traditional interpretation of British success in India is that a technologically superior power, Britain, invaded a "backward" power whose leadership was in decline. This view has its origin in the late 19th-century Western ideologies of empire. At worst, it belies the subcontinent's history. At best, it is a poor reflection of a much more complex story.

Seventeenth-century India was ruled by the Mughal Empire, founded in 1526 by Babur (1483-1530). Mughal leaders were focused on continued conquest as a means to solidify their power and to provide constant new wealth to sustain their armies and infrastructure. Because of this, they did not often try to change the civilizations they encountered, but rather sought loyalty, men for their armies, and the peaceful payment of taxes.

Islam expanded under the Mughals, proving as popular in India as it had in other regions made subject to Muslim rulers. Though Buddhism had largely fallen out of favor by this time, Hinduism continued to flourish alongside Islam as the major religions of India. Often the largest impact on conquered peoples was in the field of architecture, the prominent example being the Taj Mahal, a tomb for the most beloved wife of Mughal Emperor Shah Jahan (1592-1666).

The Mughal emperors never enjoyed the kind of dictatorial power, often referred to as "Asian despotism," that outsiders ascribed to them. Once they reached beyond Northern India, where their influence was strongest, into the Deccan and further south, they encountered mostly poor, rural territory. Because of the lack of resources and the sheer size of the sub-continent, they relied on local leaders to sustain their authority and, like many empires built on constant expansion, eventually became overstretched. When the British began to press for further engagement, the

Mughals were used to a European presence. They were used to delegating authority, and eager for opportunities to gain more wealth.

The Beginning of the East India Company

The history of the East India Company bears a direct relationship to how British rule developed India. The most current interpretation of this history is that, while neither the company nor its men engaged thoughtfully in empire building, in seizing every opportunity to expand British power and to protect the company's financial interests, empire building is exactly what they did. In 1615, the English received permission to open a company "factory" (essentially a business complex) in Surat. In 1617, the Mughal Emperor Jahangir (1569-1627) received a resident British ambassador. Among the more popular trade items were pepper, indigo, spices, and textiles. Eventually, tea would overtake the market. Because the English did not produce anything Asia wanted to buy, they received an exemption to trade gold and silver.

The English presence solidified when Charles II (1630-85) received Bombay as part of his new wife's dowry and leased it to the East India Company in 1669. The English also had "presidencies" at Madras and Calcutta, opening Indian Ocean trade with China and the Spice Islands. To maintain control, the company also created an army made up mostly by *sepoys* — indigenous soldiers commanded by British officers. Company men were willing to take risks to enhance both the company's wealth and their own private fortunes. They often forayed into new territory, making side deals and negotiating with local princes, establishing common practices that would translate into indirect rule.

A key change occurred when, in 1715, Mughal Emperor Farrukhsiyar (1683-1719) granted a *Firman* to the East India Company, allowing the company to trade without paying duties (up to a designated sum), and use their own currency. By then, the company had both a civilian and military wing, which became essential as the British fought the French in a series of 18th-century wars that spilled over into India. India became fraught with conflict and instability. As the wealth produced by the company was integral to government finances, the British government became more intrusive in company affairs, and the company essentially became an arm of the state. As men like Robert Clive (1725-74), who began on the civilian side of the company but switched to the military wing as fighting broke out with the French, conquered more territory in India, the company created relationships with local Indian leaders. These leaders often sided with the English against the French and vice versa for their own aggrandizement, again formalizing relationships that would lay the foundations for the British Raj.

In London, long-term worries about monopolies, combined with fears of the company extending its mandate, led to a series of legislative attempts to bring the company under more direct supervision. This trend continued into the next century, ultimately leading to Queen Victoria's proclamation in 1858. The company was susceptible to such interference, as the cost of its conflicts outweighed its revenue capacity. The company was close to bankruptcy after the Seven Years' War (1754-63). To combat potential monopolies, the Regulating Act of 1773 appointed a governor-general to be assisted by a council made up of men not associated with the company. It also created new courts to administer law and oversee disputes. In 1784, Parliament passed the East India Act, which gave the British government more control over political dimensions of the company's activities in India.

In the first half of the 19th century, new land acquisitions continued and the British government was even more involved in the workings of the company. The 1820s and 1830s in Britain saw the emergence of a powerful evangelical movement. Men like William Wilberforce became involved in reform movements to abolish the slave trade, reform prisons, and end the gin addiction common among the poor. Simultaneously, the British spoke of bringing Western advancements to India, which would lead to prosperity for everyone. This was the new ideology of the empire, a "civilizing mission" that would reach full force later in the century.

British Reforms

Reformers influenced British policy in India with their emphasis on the use of English, Western education, and the spread of evangelical Christianity. In 1835, Thomas Macaulay, Member of Parliament and author, penned his "Minute on Indian Education," which argued for the use of English in educating Indians. He went so far as to say that he had never met an Eastern scholar who would "deny that a single shelf of a good European library was worth the whole native literature of India …." European-style schools were opened in the major cities and many young Indian men were sent to Europe for an education. Evangelicals worked to spread Christianity, and pressed for permission to send missionaries to India. The first Christian missionaries were allowed in India under the new Charter of 1813, and though they did not gain converts quickly or in large numbers, their presence did raise concerns among Muslim, Hindu, and Buddhist religious leaders. These fears seemed justified as the British mounted a campaign against cultural practices like *sati*, a Hindu custom where a widow would throw herself on the funeral pyre of her dead husband. *Sati* was ultimately banned in India, though modern scholars debate whether the issue existed mostly in the English imagination; it was not a common practice.

The reformist sentiments of the 1820s and 1830s added a new and destabilizing dimension to the British presence in India. The East India Company had been more interested in profits and stability, and generally accepted and used local customs to their own benefit. Combined with the increasing rate of modernization, tensions in India were on the rise. In 1857, Northern India erupted in violent rebellion against the British. This came to be known as the Sepoy Mutiny, the Great Rebellion, and, by some Indians, as the First War of Independence. The outbreak of violence was sparked when Sepoys heard rumors that their new ammunition cartridges were greased with pig and cow fat. Because soldiers would have to bite the ends of cartridges before they could be loaded, this was an affront to both Muslims and Hindus serving in the British forces. Though the cartridges were quickly changed, rumors continued to spread. Once unleashed, the rebellion mushroomed into a manifestation of deep resentment to British rule in India.

By 1857, the British presence in India was stronger, more official, and less tolerant of indigenous practices. Western technology began to change the nature of British rule as steamships and railroads, (and later the telegraph) bound India closer together and sped up the rate of communication. By 1848, most of the strongest powers in India had been made subject to the British through outright annexation or through policies such as the "Doctrine of Lapse," which was used to take territory after the death of the local prince. The regions that retained a local leader followed the policies set forth by their British advisers. The presence of Christian missionaries and attacks on local customs, like *sati*, gave the impression that traditional religious practices were under attack. Meanwhile, British moves to "modernize" and "westernize" India disrupted traditional social, economic, and political structures. These forces came together and found expression in the Sepoy Mutiny.

The British Empire in India

Ultimately, the Sepoy Mutiny convinced the British that they must create a more formal empire in India. The rebellion remained localized in Northern India and initially had much success. Meerut and Delhi were quickly taken, and the 82-year-old Mughal Emperor, Bahadur Shah II (1775-1862) gave the rebellion his blessing, despite having no material support to offer the mutineers. The fighting was extremely violent and atrocities were committed by both sides. When it was over, Bahadur was exiled.

The British eventually brought enough force to bear to end the rebellion and take back opposition strongholds. In August 1858, Parliament passed the Act for the Better Government of India which transferred power from the East India Company to the British Crown. India would now be governed by a secretary of state for India aided by a cabinet of 15 and represented in India by a viceroy.

In November 1858 came Victoria's proclamation. In addition to promising to allow local princes to maintain their territories, the proclamation also offered a general amnesty. It ended with the following words:

"When, by the Blessing of Providence, internal Tranquility shall be restored, it is Our earnest Desire to stimulate the peaceful Industry of India, to promote Works of Public Utility and Improvement, and to administer its Government for the benefit of all Our Subjects resident therein. In their Prosperity will be our Strength; in their Contentment Our Security; and in their Gratitude Our best Reward. And may the God of all Power grant to Us, and to those in authority under Us, Strength to carry out these Our Wishes for the good of Our People."

By mid-century, Britain took on all of the attributes associated with the Victorian Era. Brazenly confident in its superiority, enormously wealthy due to industrialization, and the most powerful nation in the world thanks to the Royal Navy, Britain judged other civilizations through its own lens. This is not to say that Britain was without its issues. Labor disputes became more common throughout the century, England's relationship with Ireland remained tense, and there was consistent worry about Britain's subversive and criminal classes. Britain also faced increasing competition from other European powers who sought to grow their empires.

The British Raj

The era of the British Raj saw a small number of British civil servants, between 900 and 1500, control a huge landmass and large population of subjugated peoples. This was made possible by indirect rule, which used local princes to carry out British policy in return for position and wealth. It was supported by a large military presence, still made up mostly of Indians, and bolstered by the presence of the British navy. The navy was made more effective with the opening of the Suez Canal in 1869. Indian rajas and maharajas (king and great king respectively), worked with the British to maintain the imperial economy.

This system was unique and in many ways was connected to the history of the East India Company and to the subcontinent's history, which had fascinated the English since the early days of contact. An interest in India's languages, religions, and customs waxed and waned, but a connected Aryan past suggested to British theorists that the peoples of India should be treated differently than the conquered peoples of other regions -- particularly Africa, which saw more settler colonies. Rooted in now debunked racial "sciences" of the 19th century, these ideas initially promoted education as means of advancement and many elite Indian families sent their sons to England for an education. Racial ideology of the time, however, meant that Indians could not be equal to Britons, as the original Aryans had intermingled with indigenous populations. Thomas Metcalf argues in *Ideologies of the Raj* that "as the effects of racial degeneration could never be eradicated, India's peoples, even though Aryan in origin, had now to remain forever distinct, different, and inevitably inferior." This idea seems to have encouraged a return to the policy of accepting and using indigenous systems, rather than imposing purely British models. Elite Indian men were given official titles and even knighthoods, which symbolically linked them to England's history but real power remained with English diplomats and civil servants.

British policy became increasingly heavy-handed after 1870 for several reasons. First, the racist theories of the 19th century were now an accepted way of classifying people. Second, the goals and personalities of several Indian viceroys tended toward centralizing power and rooting out discontent. Third, there was increasing competition for empire as Europe's "scramble" for new territory hit a fevered pitch. The white and nonwhite populations of India were incredibly segregated. The British secluded themselves in white enclaves where, outside of interactions with servants, they lived much as they had at home, except for the oppressive summer heat. When the heat came, the British moved the seat of the government to the mountains because of the cooler climate. This separation helped maintain distance between the white rulers and the indigenous subjects. Some British legislation was even more deeply embedded with obvious racial ideologies of the day.

The particular interests of the individual viceroys could also produce periods of harsh rule. Viceroy Robert Bulwer-Lytton (1831-91), for example, issued the Vernacular Press Act, which allowed the government to shut down newspapers that spoke out against British rule. Some viceroys were more liberal in their approach and sometimes Indian policy swayed back and forth with the British elections of the age. Perhaps the greatest change in British rule after 1870 was the changing nature of European empires. Competition for power ran rampant in the late 19th century. Bolstered by nationalist ideology and jingoism, holding an empire meant having power, and everyone wanted to take part. The Scramble for Africa is the best example, but in India, it had to be the Royal Titles Act of 1876 which proclaimed Victoria the Empress of India.

Lord Curzon and the Height of British India

The final decades of the 19th century brought both a high point of imperialist ideology under Viceroy George Nathaniel Curzon (1859-1925) and the birth of modern Indian nationalism. Lord Curzon was the embodiment of 19th-century British imperialism. He had no doubts about the superiority of British civilization and had seemingly been training for the job in India all his life. He had often spoken of India as the fulcrum of British power and had spent years studying the region in preparation for service there.

As viceroy, he continued to build up India's infrastructure, building railroads and canals. He tried to secure the British position in Afghanistan and Tibet, with mixed results. The British had tried on previous occasions to secure Afghanistan and keep the Russians, who also had expansionist desires, at bay. They never had much success.

Curzon also worked to bring order and efficiency to British administration. This brought him to Bengal. Bengal was a large, historically important, and wealthy region. Population growth, however, had made it unwieldy and, in Curzon's mind, in need of more attention. He decided to partition Bengal into two territories, roughly along religious lines between Muslims and Hindus. The Indian response was profound and well-articulated by the English-educated elites of the region. Protests erupted throughout India in opposition to the partition. Protestors participated in marches, organized boycotts of British goods, and engaged in more violent attacks on British officials. The movement became known by the word, *swadeshi*, meaning produced at home. The successor of Lord Curzon, Gilbert Elliot-Murray-Kynynmound, Earl of Minto, took over as tensions peaked over the partition. As a reformer, and part of a Liberal administration, his appointment ushered in an era of increased participation of Indians in the administration. Indians could now be elected to some provincial legislatures and to more official positions. The partition of Bengal was brought to an end in 1911.

Indian Nationalism

The Indian nationalism at the heart of the protests was rooted in an appreciation for India's rich history, a shared experience of British colonialism, and exposure to Western education. Religious leaders were at the heart of nationalist movements, focusing attention on India's past leaders, organizing festivals rooted in Hindu and Muslim tradition, and offering a narrative of a glorious civilization interrupted by the European encroachment. Anti-colonialism also brought nationalists together in opposition to the high imperialism of the late 19th century. Dadabhai Naoroji (1825-1917), an Indian intellectual, highlighted the "drain" of wealth from India to Britain throughout the colonial period. This "drain theory" blamed the British for poverty in India. Though in modern texts its facts are challenged by some historians, the theory fit within the nationalist, anti-colonialist message of the time. Western education also proved vital for the rise of nationalism in India. When elite Indian men traveled to England for education, they became aware of Enlightenment thinkers, revolutionary ideas from Europe's past, and 19th-century European nationalism.

The Indian Nationals Congress, founded in 1885, would become the main home of early Indian nationalists. In its early years, the Congress tended to be moderate in its approach, favoring liberal reforms like a free press and the right of association. Its leaders argued for a gradual approach that worked with colonial authorities in hopes of eventually achieving self-rule. One of its main goals was more access to higher positions in the civil service. These moderates promoted the use of written letters of protest and petitions. For some, this was not enough. Nationalists like Bal Gangadhar Tilak (1856-1920) rejected the moderate view that there were positive aspects of British colonialism. He advocated a focus on India's past and believed in taking stronger action against British power, particularly the use of the boycott. In the end, extremists were more susceptible to running afoul of the British government -- moderates continued to dominate the movement.

To nationalists like Tilak, the promises of Victoria's proclamation must have been seen as unfulfilled. Though the British could reconcile blatant imperialistic goals and paternalism, by the end of the 19th century, much of the Indian population viewed such ideas with disdain. As the 20th century dawned, nationalism was ripe in India just as England headed into the cataclysm of World War I and, in 1915, as Mohandas Gandhi returned home.

Reading: The Age of Imperialism, 1850 -1914 (Topical Essay)

James P. Daughton is an award-winning historian of European imperialism. His research on the role of the complicated relationship among missionaries, liberal republicans, and governments in European empires in the late 19th century has broken new ground. The aiding European colonialism has broken new ground on the subject. Daughton is interesting in a variety of topics on European intellectual history, including imperialism, capitalism, humanitarianism, and the role of the city in the emergence of ideas in the modern world.

This essay explains the intellectual origins of European imperialism and the way that it played out on several continents, especially the Scramble for Africa, the name historians give to the rapid domination of European imperialists in Africa. Among the major imperialists in the late 19th century was Cecil Rhodes. His outright advocacy of British colonialism in southern Africa is depicted in a Punch cartoon, showing him bestriding Africa. The cartoon alludes to the famous colossus statue that supposedly stood over the harbor of the eastern Mediterranean island of ancient Rhodes.

European influence over the globe expanded more rapidly in the 19th century than in any other period of history. In a remarkably short span of time, between 1850 and 1914, Europe emerged as the dominant power in the world. A look at the map makes clear the rapidity of the process. In 1800, Europe possessed its "old colonies" established in the 16th and 17th centuries in North and South America. British influence in India was far from complete. And a number of ports scattered around South and Southeast Asia and Africa were under the control of the British, French, German, Dutch, Spanish, and Portuguese. A century later, by contrast, European empires had staked claims to the entire continent of Africa, save for Liberia and the Kingdom of Ethiopia. The British and French either possessed or strongly influenced Indochina, Malaya, Thailand, and Burma. Australia, New Zealand, and many archipelagos across the Pacific were claimed by European powers. And Europeans had leased ports in China, increased influence in the Ottoman Empire, and solidified rule across South Asia. In all, European empires acquired over 10 million square miles of territory – a space far larger than Europe itself.

The extraordinary speed with which Europe's empires grew was not lost on contemporaries; it led to the coining of a new term in the 1880s – "imperialism" – that captured the sense of an unrelenting, ideological process. What motivated this huge acquisition of land? The origins of and reasons for European global expansion were complex. Some individuals who were marginalized from European societies by the processes of modernization, like religious missionaries, played key roles in motivating overseas expansion. But in important ways, European imperial power mirrored the extraordinary changes that had been taking place in Europe since the late 18th century. Enlightenment thought, industrialization, and the rise of nationalism were all key components of the age of imperialism. Each shaped how Europeans understood, managed, and celebrated their interaction with peoples and powers around the world. And, just as the 19th century left unanswered many questions about who would be included and excluded from participation in the nation, imperialism presented new paradoxes by bringing tens of millions of non-European "subjects" into states ostensibly founded on liberal values.

An important set of preconditions of imperialism can be traced back to the Enlightenment. The curiosity about understanding nature and society, as well as recording knowledge from geographically and temporally distant cultures, brought Europeans into contact with many parts of the world. Settlement in the Americas and exploration in the Pacific brought new knowledge of distant societies. The Enlightenment practice of setting up institutions of learning led to a great interest in the language, art, religion, and histories of what was called "the Orient," a geographically large and culturally diverse region that stretched from North Africa to the Asian subcontinent. Greater knowledge inspired fascination and even fantasies about "the East" and "Oriental" societies that Europeans imagined to be brutal, erotic, and backwards in comparison to their own. The growth of Orientalism coincided with and even facilitated greater European interaction, first via trade and travel, and later through more direct imperial engagement. This region was perhaps an early example of how Europeans identified knowledge with political power, but it was certainly not the last. Later in the 19th century, the colonization of Africa would include geographers, linguists, and ethnographers whose studies would inform colonial policies.

If knowledge of distant societies was an effective strategy for imperialists, Enlightenment philosophies were far less useful to would-be colonizers later in the 19th century. Many classical liberal thinkers of the 18th century were deeply critical of empire building. Adam Smith, the great economist, was doubtful of pejorative arguments that Europeans were superior to the rest of the world. Rather, he argued that societies are, first and foremost, rational responses to material circumstances and that they developed through stages. Non-European societies were not backwards or inherently inferior, but simply at an earlier stage of development. More importantly, Smith argued in *The Wealth of Nations* that colonialism was detrimental to everyone involved: it was expensive, required military force, and rested on prejudices. It also promoted unnatural economic practices as empires were too often built on protectionism, monopoly, and state intervention. Finally, Smith questioned whether empires would treat non-Europeans with justice and humanity. This was a concern shared by a number of other 18th-century commentators who suggested that national reputations would be mired by the great distance of colonies: when men are far from home, it was believed, they are more prone to behave in violent, immoral, and unfair ways.

For the inheritors of the liberal economic tradition, imperialism in the late 19th century had to be reimagined. The Industrial Revolution had made economic expansion into foreign markets both easier and more pressing. Technological advances in shipbuilding and weaponry marked a clear advantage for European merchants and militaries. As industrialized European nations produced larger quantities of finished goods, like textiles, machinery, arms, and chemical products, they increasingly looked abroad for cheap raw materials to buy and for new markets in which to sell these products. Also, booming industrial economies produced excess capital that could not be entirely reinvested in European ventures. Many believed that colonies were the answer: they could absorb excess capital, expand markets, and promote prosperity. But many colonial supporters remained all too aware of the classical critiques offered by Adam Smith and others.

One way that liberals justified imperialism was to claim it would increase happiness. John Stuart Mill (1806-73), a leading philosopher and proponent of utilitarianism, argued that colonialism was defensible because it would increase the wealth and prestige of Britain, while improving the lot of non-Europeans, as well. Mill and his father both had business interests in India. His views reflected a new chauvinism in the mid-19th century that saw a much starker dichotomy between civilized and savage societies than Adam Smith would have allowed. Dividing societies between "progressive" and "stationary," Mill stopped short of claiming that inferior societies were beyond help. Rather, he argued that European humanity could improve them. Colonialism, then, was not only justified, but in fact presented a moral obligation that required more civilized nations to improve the lives of indigenous populations.

Liberal justifications for imperialism like Mill's, then, became enmeshed in new definitions of the nation. If a nation were great – that is, economically, politically, and morally superior to other peoples of the Earth – then it needed a robust colonial empire. In the wake of the abolition of the slave trade, and just as their economies started to turn away from goods produced on plantations, Britain and France turned their attention to new regions abroad. The British East India Company, with increasing support from the crown, intensified trade with India. As the century progressed, the presence of British officials in India started to change relations with local people.

The British asserted their superiority in a number of ways. They introduced laws prohibiting a number of Indian practices, including *sati* or widow burning. The British developed a civil service, but promotion up the hierarchy was racially determined, insuring only white men held positions of power. They developed the country economically through building infrastructure and schools to educate future bureaucrats. But many of these programs solidified further British profits and power more than they helped Indians. In 1857, amid growing tensions and resentment of British power, Hindu soldiers mutinied against their white officers. After initial successes, the Sepoy Rebellion, named for the soldiers involved, was savagely put down by British reinforcements. The uprising nonetheless led to the establishment of the British Raj, or rule. The British state officially took control from the East India Company and made India a full-fledged colony. Queen Victoria would later be named Empress of India.

India, the "jewel in the crown" of the British Empire, inspired other European powers to acquire overseas possessions as well. In 1830, in an attempt to prove the vitality of the Restoration monarchy, the French invaded Algeria, but it took two decades of bloodshed for them to establish a stable presence there. With the British in India, the French looked to increase their influence over Indochina as a means of eventually doing business in China. And throughout the second half of the century, the British and French jockeyed for influence over islands in the Pacific. By the 1880s, a kind of "great game" had begun whereby European countries competed to counter one another's new claims.

At the same time, a new taste for exploration and improved prophylactic medicines to combat tropical diseases allowed for the so-called "Scramble for Africa." European states backed adventurers and rogues who claimed sovereignty of territory on behalf of different nations. Claims to territory in parts of Africa started to come so quickly and by such disparate means that the great powers of Europe finally met in 1884-85 to discuss how best to proceed. The Berlin Congo Conference mapped out spheres of influence and established rules as to what counted as legitimate territorial claims, including requirements to develop local economies and "civilize" new colonial subjects. It is often imagined that Europeans sat down at a map and divvied up Africa among themselves. In fact, colonization was more complex, requiring both the presence of European explorers on the ground and interested politicians at home. But the Berlin conference did help shape the map: it legitimized French claims to West and North Africa, British presence in East and South Africa, Belgian King Leopold II's claim to the Congo, and German possession of smaller territories across the continent.

A byproduct of both Enlightenment values and nationalist aspirations, the desire to "civilize" became central to the ideology of European imperialism by the end of the century. The British pursued what Rudyard Kipling coined in his 1899 poem "The White Man's Burden," a supposedly selfless – and even painful – commitment to educate, cure, and develop their subject populations. For the French, the "civilizing mission" was a national "duty," as the pro-colonial politician Jules Ferry (1832-93) put it, to spread to the empire the values of the French Revolution, as well as the scientific and cultural genius of France. The Germans, Portuguese, and even the Belgians under the notoriously callous Leopold II all had their own rhetoric to prove the humanity of colonialism.

In some instances, Europeans were earnest in their desires to help colonial subjects. Colonial states outlawed slavery and intervened in ethnic and political rivalries. Missionaries, doctors, and civil servants set up hospitals, orphanages, and schools. But colonial rule also caused social dislocation of its own: indigenous cultural, political, and linguistic traditions were undermined or outlawed; taxes forced men and women to abandon their ways of life to earn money from colonial employers; government projects often forced colonial subjects to work in miserable and dangerous conditions; and the reconfiguring of local economies to feed European trade disrupted local markets, increasing poverty, and occasionally even causing famine.

Ironically, the language of "civilizing" colonial people also acted to justify their continued oppression. Europe's assumed position of bestowing the trappings of civilization on lesser peoples acted to solidify perceived racial differences rather to help moderate them. Men and women in need of European guidance were men and women unprepared to be citizens. And in fact very few colonial subjects ever had the hope of becoming citizens of their metropolitan governments, even after serving in colonial armies or completing advanced education. On the whole, colonial subjects could not vote. They had no direct input on colonial policies. Many of them, particularly in Africa, were not even guaranteed protection before the law. Throughout the 19th century, people living under European colonial rule faced the possibility of administrative harassment, imprisonment without cause, and even torture. The rewards of liberty and justice, so championed in Europe, were all too infrequently found in the empire.

The realities of colonial rule, however, remained obscured to most Europeans. For people in the cities and countryside of Europe, the empire was a place of mystery, intrigue, and adventure. It gave rise to stories of exploration and conquest, to medical breakthroughs, to heroes of the nation. Accomplishments in the empire – such as efforts to find the source of the Nile or to cross the Sahara – became the subjects of newspaper articles, speeches, and books that not only championed individual achievement, but also reflected well on the nation as a whole. The construction of great railroads, opera houses, and government buildings in places as diverse as Brazzaville, Hanoi, and New Delhi proved that European technology, industry, and culture knew no boundaries. The final decades of the 19th century witnessed both the ascension of European global power in political, economic, and military terms, as well as Europeans growing faith in their own civilization. If the dangers of such hubris were not evident in their conquest for global power, they would become so soon enough, closer to home, in the trenches of the First World War.

Reading: The Atlantic Revolutions and Independence
Scholars have debated what the term "revolution" means for a couple of hundred years, particularly with regard to political events. The word comes from *revolutio*, which in Latin means "a turn around." But some turnarounds are greater than others. A great revolution, such as the French and Haitian Revolutions, completely undoes the prior political power of the society and replaces it with people, usually from the lower ranks of society, who have not held power before. On the other hand, the American Revolution and the Wars of Independence in Latin America were *coups d'etat*, overthrows of the leadership of a country or in this case colony. Some members of the colonial elites who were of European background and born in the Americas, called Creoles, rebelled and battled the mother country for control and leadership of the colonies. In all cases in the Americas, the rebel Creole elites won. The fifty years from 1770 to 1824 were a period of more than a dozen of these two types of revolutionary struggles on both sides of the Atlantic, which is why this is called the Age of Revolution. There were a few themes that the Atlantic Revolutions share.

International Context
First, the revolts on each side of the Atlantic were definitely connected to one another. It has often been remarked that the European intellectual movement called the Enlightenment, which championed human and political rights, inspired rebel leaders across the Atlantic. But even more important for colonial rebels were the opportunities to break away from Europe that were made possible because of the titanic 18th-century struggle between Great Britain and France for mastery of Europe, first in the Seven Years' War (1756-63) and then in the Napoleonic Wars (1803-16).

Civil War

Second, all the revolts were civil wars, pitting one faction against another. In France, it was a class struggle between the lower and upper classes. In Haiti, slaves revolted against their masters. In the cases of the Wars of Independence, the rebel Creoles had to battle their colonial compatriots who were loyal to the mother country as well as the European armies. Civil war was most pronounced in the American Revolution and the Wars of Independence in Mexico and Peru, where there were significant numbers of officials from the mother country.

The Leadership of the Creole Elite

Finally, the rebellions were not only opportunistic, none of the leaders had a plan for what would come next or what kind of society they wanted. Many of the declarations and manifestos of independence or human rights came months and years after the rebellions began. The documents were often cries for more justice and equity but not plans for a new way of governing. Rebel leaders often disagreed as to the type of government. Lofty ideas of liberty contested with parochial local interests that involved slavery, land, territorial claims, labor systems, and individuals' rights to participate in governance. In the end, while there was much rhetoric about liberty and equality, none of the Atlantic Revolutions resulted in an actual democracy. It would take decades before the liberated societies evolved into something like democratic republics for all of the people living in them.

The American Revolution

Up to the mid 18th century, Great Britain hardly attended to its British North American colonies. If anything, the crown's interests were more focused on its increasingly valuable island colonies in the Caribbean. But in the Seven Years' War (1756-63), the British waged war with France around the world in the Philippines, India, the Caribbean, and Canada, with the western frontier of the thirteen British American colonies being a major theater of war. The British won victory after victory around the world in these contests including acquiring much of the French colonial lands east of the Mississippi River. They had invested the modern equivalent of millions of pounds in securing that frontier. After more than a century of neglect, British officials and officers returned to Great Britain impressed with the economic potential of the colonies. The British believed it was time for British Americans to become better integrated into the British economy and geopolitical interests of the empire.

The international Context. While British Americans were quite proud of the empire's victories in the war, they were less convinced that they had a role to play in securing those victories. But British leaders did not think it was fair that the colonies paid only one shilling of tax per capita to the empire, while British citizens paid 26 shillings per capita. Moreover, the imperial government needed more revenue to finance the national debt, which had soared from 73 million pounds before the war to 137 million pounds after the war. And more debt was mounting as the British had to station 10,000 troops to garrison the territories they had conquered from the French in North America. A particularly vexing issue was the disposition of those conquered lands. Land-hungry colonists wanted to head out west to survey, sell, and buy the land. Each encroachment into the new territories set off an Indian war that the British army had to quell with more and more soldiers. The crown established a Royal Proclamation of 1763, a treaty with the Native American groups that colonials would not cross the line to settle the new territories. The colonists naturally violated the treaty at every turn, creating tensions not only with the Native Americans but also British colonial officials and Parliament.

The Leadership of the Creole Elite. Victory in the Seven Years' War had turned out to be a double-edged sword. On the other side, the British had grown too confidant of the power of their army and navy and could hardly imagine a rebel threat from the colonists. The removal of the French from North America had taken away the common enemy of the British officials and the colonists. They soon began to bicker with one another, particularly over a series of fees or indirect taxes that the British tried to impose after 1770. One must also remember that the years of neglect had allowed the colonists to begin to develop their own local governments, schools, churches, and other institutions. In the Americas, the Creole elite of the British colonies was probably the most effective home-grown leadership. One could even argue that American colonists participated more in self-government than those in the British Isles. A man had to have land to vote in elections at the time. Only one in four men in Britain had the vote, but at least half to two-thirds of British Americans had the franchise. Moreover, the colonies had no natural aristocracy. The elite was simply the wealthier and better educated among the colonists. Therefore, the colonies had as a matter of habit and course, a more democratic style to their political environment.

Civil War. But the elite was not united in support of independence. The rebels called themselves the Patriots and were about 40 percent of the population, while the Loyalists who wanted to stay in the empire represented about 25-30 percent of the colonial population. The battle between these two groups was brutal, particularly along the western frontier and particularly when it involved Native American allies. After the revolution, the Loyalists in many cases were forced to emigrate to Canada and the Caribbean. The war finally ended when the British public fatigued of the high cost of blood and treasure. But international circumstances again played a decisive role — the French navy came up from the Caribbean in support of General George Washington's land troops, delivering a fatal blow to the British at Yorktown, forcing the British to sue for peace.

The French Revolution(1789-1799)
Here again, events across the Atlantic helped set the stage for the French Revolution. The success of American revolutionary political ideas inspired the educated lower classes in France to throw off the yoke of feudal government of the French monarchy and aristocracy, often called the the *ancien régime*. But even more important, as with Great Britain, the military cost of helping the Americans in 1783 and the lingering debt of the Seven Years' War forced the French crown to raise regressive taxes on its citizens, the poorer paying a higher rate than the wealthy and more privileged. Aggravating the situation was the fact that France suffered several years of drought in the 1780s and there was famine in the countryside, causing food shortages in the cities.

Problematic Leadership. But most historians of the French revolution recognize that the rhetoric of liberty and equality swept up the people and provided them with governing aspirations for which they had no practical experience. The French government was a feudal system of monarchy, aristocracy, and clergy; the crown had long ago dismissed the old institution of the people, the French equivalent of Parliament called the Estates General. In the first phase of the revolution (1789), the crown was forced to reconvene the Estates General, which was dominated by representatives from the educated middle class — teachers, lawyers, shopkeepers, and low-ranking military officers — who were inspired by the Enlightenment ideas of liberty and equality but knew little of how to compromise their politics and organize a government. The result was a second phase (1790-94) called the Reign of Terror, in which political factions — from conservative to radical — began to execute political opponents; at least 15,000 and perhaps as many as 40,000 died. The factions were particularly radicalized by reports that conservatives and aristocrats abroad were encouraging the other crowns of Europe to attack France and restore the monarchy. This threat finally led to the imprisonment and execution of King Louis XVI and Queen Marie Antoinette.

Civil War Averted and Replaced with New Imperialism. In the third phase, or the Thermidorian Reaction (1795-99), a moderately conservative executive council called the Directory took over the reigns of the state to restore order. But the committee was rife with corruption and autocratic figures. By 1799, one member of the committee, General Napoleon Bonaparte, organized a coup d'etat, and thus the fourth phase of the revolution, the Consulate, began leading to the dictatorship of Napoleon, and then Napoleon crowning himself as emperor in 1803. Of course, after a decade of failed civilian government, the people threw their support behind the institution and the man who delivered them their greatest success — the army. And the French armies were brilliant. They marched across Europe and into the countries of the Mediterranean destroying monarchies and spreading the ideas of the French revolution. But Napoleon and the French had simply replaced an oppressive monarchy with a dictatorship. The French Revolution's greatest success was that it ended the credibility and stability of the European ancien regime; it did not establish the Enlightenment ideal of a democratic republic. Led by Great Britain, a coalition of crowns across Europe defeated Napoleon at the Battle of Waterloo, and France suffered through another 50 years of intermittent despotic monarchies and failed republics.

The Haitian Revolution

The Haitian Revolution is difficult to imagine without the French Revolution. Haiti is the western half of the island of Hispaniola in the Caribbean. The Spanish conceded this territory to the French in 1697, who called it Saint-Dominique. The French colonized it with slaves and sugar plantations that had a reputation for being some of the most brutal in the New World; fully a third of imported slaves died within a few years. While 32,000 whites, or *blancs*, lived in Saint-Dominique, they were vastly outnumbered by the more than 500,000 slaves, most of whom were born in Africa and retained their African culture. There was also a small but important population of 25,000 free blacks and mulattos, or *gens de coleur*, many of whom owned slaves. Inspired by the revolutionary events in France in 1789, the *gens de coleur* began to agitate for more rights. For the next two years the French National Assembly debated both the rights of free blacks and mulattos and the issue of manumission of the slaves. In May 1791, they gave rights to the former but not manumission to the latter.

By August 1791, thousands of frustrated slaves rose in rebellion. Within weeks, the number of slaves who joined the revolt reached some 100,000. In the next two months, as the violence escalated, the slaves killed 4,000 whites and burned or destroyed 180 sugar plantations and coffee and indigo plantations. In September 1791, the surviving whites organized themselves and struck back, killing about 15,000 blacks in an orgy of revenge. Though demanding freedom from slavery, the rebels did not demand independence from France at this point, rightly calculating that the French government would grant them freedom in order to quell the black rebellion in 1794.

Leadership in the Creole Elite. Since 1789, numerous mulatto and black leaders led factions of the revolt, fighting each other as much as the French. The most successful was Toussaint Louverture, a former slave, slaveholder, and a military leader. In the 1790s, he gradually gained control of the whole island from his various rivals and gave nominal allegiance to France while pursuing his own political and military designs. In May 1801 he named himself "governor-general for life." This would prove to be the pattern with the new Haitian leaders. A military leader would consolidate power through conquest, become the dictator, and eventually become emperor, a plan Louverture had before he died. The homegrown leaders of Saint-Dominique and their formerly-slave citizens felt more acutely the aspirations of liberty and freedom than they understood the making and maintaining of a government of all the people.

When Napoleon Bonaparte consolidated his power in 1801, he attempted to restore the old regime, slavery, and European rule by sending an army to Saint-Domingue that included his own brother-in-law. Toussaint tried to arrange an armistice in May 1802 but ended up in a French prison, dying in April 1803. In his absence, his lieutenants, Jean-Jacques Dessalines and Henry Christophe led a black army against the French in 1802. They defeated the French commander and a large part of his army. Debilitated by yellow fever and malaria, the French withdrew from Saint-Dominique but maintained a small presence in the eastern part of the island until 1809.

Civil War. On January 1, 1804, the entire island was declared independent. Dessalines renamed the country Haiti from an older indigenous name. It was the first nation of former slaves in world history and the second independent republic in the Americas. Many European powers and their Caribbean surrogates ostracized Haiti, fearing the spread of slave revolts. More important, nearly the entire population was utterly destitute—a legacy of slavery that has continued to have a profound impact on Haitian history. Moreover, Haiti was plagued by factionalism. Regions of the island often would continue to break out in open revolt. The "gens d' coleur" refused to submit to the rule of former slaves-become-dictators (and emperors).

In October 1804 Dessalines assumed the title of Emperor Jacques I, but in October 1806 he was killed while trying to suppress a mulatto revolt, and Henry Christophe took control of the kingdom. Civil war then broke out between Christophe and Alexandre Sabès Pétion, who was based at Port-au-Prince in the south. Christophe, who declared himself King Henry I in 1811, managed to improve the country's economy but at the cost of forcing former slaves to return to work on the plantations. In 1820 his soldiers mutinied, and he committed suicide. It was not until 1825 that

France recognized Haiti's independence, and then only in exchange for a large indemnity of 100 million francs.

The Wars of Independence in Latin America (1807-1824)

After three centuries of colonial rule, independence came rather suddenly to most of Spanish and Portuguese America. Between 1808 and 1826 all of Latin America except the Spanish colonies of Cuba and Puerto Rico slipped out of the hands of the Iberian powers who had ruled the region since the conquest. The rapidity and timing of that dramatic change were the result of a combination of long-building tensions in colonial rule and a series of external events.

The international Context. Even before the British in the 1770s began to integrate the thirteen colonies into the larger empire, the Spanish government instituted reforms in the 1740s.

Many Creoles felt Bourbon crown policy to be an unfair attack on their wealth, political power, and social status. Creoles reacted angrily against the crown's preference for Spanish-born officials, peninsulars, in administrative positions. After hundreds of years of proven service to Spain, the Creole elites felt that the Bourbons were now treating them like a recently conquered nation. In cities throughout the region, Creole frustrations increasingly found expression in ideas derived from the Enlightenment. Still, these ideas were not, strictly speaking, causes of independence. Rather, European diplomatic and military events provided the final catalyst that turned Creole discontent into full-fledged movements for Latin American independence.

When the Spanish crown entered into an alliance with France in 1795, it pitted itself against England, the dominant sea power of the period, which used its naval forces to reduce and eventually cut communications between Spain and the Americas. In 1808 Napoleon turned on his Spanish allies and imprisoned both King Charles IV and his son Ferdinand. The Spanish political tradition centered on the figure of the monarch, yet, with Charles and Ferdinand removed from the scene, the hub of all political authority was missing. The Spanish in Spain tried to set up a government more or less in exile in southern Spain beyond the reach of the French army. While some Creole leaders came to Spain to join in the Cortes, or new Spanish government, they found that the peninsular Spaniards were not willing to given them the autonomy they wanted.

Interestingly, Spanish troubles had already led to Brazilian independence. In 1807 the Spanish king had granted passage through Spanish territory to Napoleon's forces on their way to invade Portugal. The immediate effect of that concession was to send the Portuguese ruler, Prince Regent John, fleeing in British ships to Brazil. Arriving in Rio de Janeiro with some 15,000 officials, nobles, and other members of his court, John transformed the Brazilian colony into the administrative center of his empire.

Leadership in the Creole Elite. During 1808–10, *juntas*, committees of temporary governance, emerged all across the Spanish colonies to rule in the name of the king. But the aspiring leaders were either groups of peninsulares or combinations of peninsulars and Creoles who did not always trust each other. In Mexico and Uruguay caretaker governments were the work of loyal peninsular Spaniards eager to head off Creole threats. In Chile, Venezuela, Columbia, and other colonies, by contrast, it was Creoles who controlled the provisional juntas. By 1810, however, the trend was clear. Without denouncing Ferdinand, Creoles throughout most of the region were moving toward the establishment of their own autonomous governments. By 1812 a British-Spanish insurrection and military expedition dislodged Napoleon from Spain. Ferdinand VII came back to power and sent Spanish troops to take back control of the colonies. Over the next decade and a half, Spanish Americans had to defend with arms their own movement toward independence.

Perhaps the most famous of these Creole military and independence leaders and heroes was Simon Bolivar of Venezuela, also called the Liberator. From Argentina proceeded another powerful force, this one directed by José de San Martín. After difficult conquests of their home regions, the two movements spread the cause of independence through other territories, finally meeting on the central Pacific coast. From there, troops under northern generals finally stamped out the last vestiges of loyalist resistance in Peru and Bolivia by 1826.

The independence of Mexico, like that of Peru, the other major central area of Spain's American empire, came late. As was the case in Lima, Mexican cities had a powerful segment of Creoles and peninsular Spaniards whom the old imperial system had served well. Between 1808 and 1810, peninsulars had acted aggressively to preserve Spain's power in the region by taking over the government. Nevertheless, homegrown independence movements emerged under two radical priests, the Creole Miguel Hidalgo y Costilla and the mestizo José María Morelos y Pavón. Each appealed directly to the indigenous and mestizo populace, which sufficiently frightened the Creoles in Mexico City into joining peninsulars to suppress the revolts.

Final independence, in fact, was not the result of the efforts of Hidalgo, Morelos, or the forces that had made up their independence drive. It came instead as a conservative initiative led by military officers, merchants, and the Roman Catholic Church. Confident in their ability to keep popular forces in check, Creoles finally turned against Spanish rule in 1820–21. Two figures from the early rebellion played central roles in liberating Mexico. One, Vicente Guerrero, had been an insurgent chief; the other, Agustín de Iturbide, had been an officer in the campaign against the popular independence movement. The two came together behind an agreement known as the Iguala Plan. Centered on provisions of independence, respect for the church, and equality between Mexicans and peninsulars, the plan gained the support of many Creoles, Spaniards, and former rebels. Unfortunately, Iturbide tried to install himself as Agustín I, Emperor of Mexico. Guerreron joined another former insurgent Guadalupe Victoria and overthrew Iturbide, establishing a republic in 1824.

Civil Wars. In all of the wars of independence there was a struggle between the peninsulars, the Creoles, and the popular masses, including indigenous people, slaves and free blacks. Civil war generally raged when two of the three banned together to fight the third. In Mexico it was the temporary alliance of Creoles and peninsulars against the indigenous, blacks, and poor whites. In Venezuela, Bolivar's armies were led by both Creoles and some mulatto leaders. The troops included Creoles, free blacks, and some former slaves and indigenous people. They fought Spanish troops and loyalists. Creole elites generally emerged as the leaders of post colonial societies but even then most liberal leaders like Bolivar,expressed strong doubts about the capacity of his fellow Latin Americans for self-government. "Do not adopt the best system of government," he wrote, "but the one most likely to succeed." Thus, the type of republic that he eventually espoused was very much an oligarchic one, with socioeconomic and literacy qualifications for suffrage and with power centered in the hands of a strong executive. Across Latin America, independent republics formed that were consistent with colonial administrative centers and districts. Local Creoles in the major cities dominated and government was oligarchic in nature, not particularly enlightened and not democratic.

Reading: African Scramble, 1881-1914
New imperialism

New imperialism is a term that has been used by historians to describe the form of dominance of European countries when they captured and consolidated their power over parts of Africa and Asia in the 19th century. New imperialism had some features that were similar to traditional colonialism in the 18th century and before but also some new characteristics that reflected modern economic and political realities. In this reading, the effects of new imperialism were most evident in Africa. In the mid 19th century, Europeans controlled mostly trading posts along the African coast but little else. By 1870, European nations had taken over about 10 percent of the continent, mostly Portugal in Angola and Mozambique, Great Britain in the Cape Colony (now South Africa) and France in Algeria. By 1914, however, the entire continent was in European hands; only the African nations of Ethiopia and Liberia maintained their independence. This rapid imperialization of Africa in 1881-1914, a little over three decades is called the "African Scramble."

Technical and Economic Reasons

First, technological advances were very important in making possible the physical expansion into remote areas of Africa. Europeans brought their steamships, railroads and telegraphs, so that they could travel up rivers in the interior areas with armies and settlers. Medical advances also played an important role, especially medicines for tropical diseases. The development of quinine, an effective treatment for the dreaded disease of malaria, made vast expanses of the tropics more accessible for Europeans. This was quite different than previous and traditional colonialism in Latin America and Asia, since the tropical zone was not as extensive in those areas. Nevertheless, the Europeans needed communication and transportation systems into the Congo and other interior areas to harvest and bring out the tropical products that were important to the Industrial Revolution and global markets — rubber, gold, diamonds, cotton, copper, palm oil, cocoa and tin.

What is less understood was a popular argument at the time that Africa was a pending market for European finished goods. By the 1870s, European merchants and manufacturers were beginning to create oversupply of manufactured products and did not have sufficient markets to sell what they produced. In addition, in 1873-96, European markets were hit with a series of recessions that is often referred to as the Long Depression. The reaction of European and American governments was to become more protectionist and limit trade, which only exasperated the problem. Great Britain as the lead manufacturing country was hurt the most and was, thus, more conscious of a need to open global markets beyond Europe.

Some diplomats and financiers reasoned that Africa offered Britain, as well as Germany, France, and other countries, a potential open market that might solve this problem. Moreover, many investors argued that capital invested in emerging markets like Africa often supplied a much better return on the investment because of cheap materials, limited competition, and abundant raw materials. Many historians, however, have argued that private investment, other than Cecil Rhodes's famed De Beers Mining Company in South Africa, was not actually that great in Africa even in the height of the African Scramble. The new imperialism was most advocated by governments, pursuing state-led development, rather than private, "corporate" investors. These state-led developments reflected the larger geo-political ends of the great powers.

Geopolitical Rivalry

To the great powers, especially Great Britain, the eastern half of Africa between Egypt and gold and diamond-rich South Africa seemed to have great geopolitical value, particularly in securing the flow of overseas trade. Britain was under political pressure to secure lucrative markets against encroaching rivals in China and its eastern colonies, most notably India, Malaya, Australia and New Zealand. Thus, it was crucial to secure the key waterway between East and West — the Suez Canal. But it was also important to acquire naval and military bases across the Indian Ocean region. The growing navies, and new ships driven by steam power, required coaling stations and ports for maintenance. Defense bases were also needed for the protection of sea routes and communication lines, particularly of expensive and vital international waterways such as the Suez Canal. The new colonies were seen as assets in this contest of the "balance of power" in the world, as well as useful as negotiable chips when international bargaining was required. Colonies with large native populations were also a source of military power; Britain and France used large numbers of British Indian and North African soldiers, respectively, in many of their colonial wars and would do so again in the coming world wars.

National Prestige

In the age of nationalism, there was also pressure for a nation to acquire an empire as a status symbol; the idea of "greatness" became linked with the sense of duty underlying many nations' strategies. Controlling land became a goal in and of itself. By the end of the 19th century, Europe added almost 9,000,000 square miles – one-fifth of the land area of the globe – to its overseas colonial possessions. Between 1885 and 1914, Britain took nearly 30 percent of Africa's population under its control; 15 percent for France, 11 percent for Portugal, nine percent for Germany, seven percent for Belgium and one percent for Italy. Nigeria alone contributed 15 million subjects to Great Britain, more than in the whole of French West Africa or the entire German colonial empire. There was more than a fair share of envy about British colonial successes.

European Conquest

Germany. Germany was a latecomer to African colonization. As Germany was not united until 1871, it could not act in as concerted a way as Great Britain and France. However, after 1880, it managed to maneuver its way into parts of Africa not yet touched by the others. The powerful German Premier Otto von Bismarck had little use for colonies before 1884, regarding them as a waste of effort. But he was gradually prevailed upon to acquire Cameroon and Togoland, German Southwest Africa and German East Africa or Tanganyika, though not with much enthusiasm. However, the grandson of the German king, Kaiser Wilhelm II, was a thoroughgoing imperialist. He came to power in 1888, soon pushing aside Bismarck and his more conservative policies. Wilhelm had a taste for what German colonial advocates called weltpolitik (world policy), the aim of transforming Germany into a global power through aggressive diplomacy, the acquisition of overseas colonies and the development of a large navy. Germany became the third largest colonial power in Africa by 1914, but the empire was short-lived. After WWI, they lost the whole of their overseas territories to WWI victors, mostly Great Britain and France.

Italy. Italy's first colonial interests were primarily in the horn of Africa. It took possession of parts of Eritrea in 1870 and 1882. Unlike the other European powers, Italian armies had more difficulty conquering African territories, suffering a defeat in the First Italo–Ethiopian War (1895–1896). But it did acquire Italian Somaliland in 1889–90 and the whole of Eritrea by 1899. In 1911 Italy shifted its attention to North Africa and engaged in a war with the Ottoman Empire, in which it acquired Tripolitania and Cyrenaica (modern Libya). The Italian leader and early supporter of fascism, Enrico Corradini, justified these conquests as an expression of the rise of the middle class and nationalism in Italian politics. Later in 1935-36, the Fascist Benito Mussolini waged the last colonial war, the Second Italo-Abyssinian War, finally occupying its nemesis Ethiopia, the last African territory besides Liberia that had successfully resisted European rule.

Belgium, Early explorations of the interior of Africa were generally individual efforts. In the case of the famous David Livingstone, it was missionary work as well as exploration. In the case of the second most important explorer of the period, Henry Morton Stanley, it was newspapers and colonial societies who paid for his expedition to locate Livingstone in the early 1870s and explore the upper reaches of the Nile River. Though Stanley's accounts of his travels and advocacy for African colonization sold newspapers, no European government had much interest in these early schemes, except Léopold II of the small country of Belgium. From 1869 to 1874, Leopold secretly sent Stanley to the Congo region, where he made treaties with several African chiefs along the Congo River. Encouraged by Stanley's efforts, in 1876, Leopold organised the International African Association (the Congo Society). By 1882 Stanley had enough territory under treaties to form the basis of the Congo Free State. Léopold II personally administered the Congo Free State, not Belgium. Through merchants and adventurers he contracted, he extracted enough ivory and rubber to fund his political ambitions in Europe.

Though the French, the Portuguese and the British also sent expeditions into the Congo, trying to capture colonies and monopolize the trade in tropical products, none were able to dislodge Leopold's and Stanley's early efforts. Leopold acquired 890,000 square miles of the Congo and allowed his colonial concessionaires to run an economic terror regime in the Congo Free State, including mass killings and forced labour. Finally, the scandal was too much, and Belgium, under pressure from the Congo Reform Association, ended Leopold II's rule and annexed it in 1908 as the Belgian Congo. The Leopold period in the history of the Congo is perhaps the most notorious example of colonial brutality in Africa. Up to eight million of the estimated 16 million native inhabitants died between 1885 and 1908. The brutal methods of the concessionaires, along with the introduction of disease, resulted in the loss of up to 50 percent of the indigenous population.

France. The French thrust into the African interior was mainly from the coasts of West Africa (modern day Senegal) eastward, through the Sahel along the southern border of the Sahara, a huge desert covering most of present-day Senegal, Mali, Niger, and Chad. Their ultimate aim was to have an uninterrupted colonial empire from the Niger River to the Nile, thus controlling all trade to and from the Sahel region, by virtue of their existing control over the caravan routes through the Sahara.

The French and the British were also vitally interested in building the Suez Canal to link the Mediterranean Sea to the Red Sea and out into the Indian Ocean. Its virtues were evident, as it would allow the easy shipment of goods back and forth from the Far East to Europe without having to take the long voyage around Africa. The French diplomat, Ferdinand de Lesseps, negotiated the concessions from Isma'il Pasha, the Khedive of Egypt and Sudan, in 1854–56. Later, in 1869, when the canal was finished, the Khedive borrowed enormous sums from British and French bankers at high rates of interest. In 1875, he was forced to sell his block of shares in the Suez Canal and the British snapped them up. When Isma'il repudiated Egypt's foreign debt in 1879, Britain and France seized joint financial control over the country, forcing the Egyptian ruler to abdicate, and installing his eldest son, Tewfik Pasha, in his place. But Tewfik soon faced opposition from his own people for allowing himself to become the puppet of foreign interests. To the south, in the Sudan, a charismatic leader, Muhammad Ahmad, led the Mahdist Revolt, severing Sudan from Egypt in 1881. That same year, the Egyptian army revolted against Tewfik in the Urabi Revolt. Tewfik appealed for British military aid, which put down both revolts by 1898. But the price the Egyptian elite paid was that the British would administrate Egyptian governmental affairs for years to come and colonize the Sudan.

Great Britain. In the 1890s, Great Britain also added to its colonial possessions in Africa — Nigeria in the western part of Africa and Kenya and Uganda in the eastern part. The British Cape Colony (South Africa), which they first acquired in 1795, provided a base for the subjugation of neighboring African states and the Dutch colonial settlers who had been there since the 17th century. At the time, they were called boers, the Dutch word for farmers, and later Afrikaners. The Afrikaners migrated north into the interior to avoid the British and found their own republic. The British tried to encircle the Afrikaners by annexing an interior province, the Transvaal, in 1877, and then defeating the African native Zulu tribes in 1879 and annexing their territories. Finally, the British and the Afrikaners went to war, the First Boer War, in 1880-81. The Afrikaners proved themselves quite effective in guerilla fighting and caught the British off guard. The subdued British government negotiated a peace that gave the Afrikaners self-government in the Transvaal though tensions continued. A Second Boer War was fought between 1899 and 1902, about control of recently discovered gold and diamond fields in the Transvaal. This time the Afrikaners lost and were absorbed into the British Empire. But by 1910, the British parliament decided to recognize the independence of what came to be known as the Union of South Africa. Ultimately, the Afrikaner community became very influential and even dominant in the politics of the new nation.
The goal of the British in the late 19th century had been to link their possessions in South Africa with various African territories along the eastern half of Africa — Botswana, Zimbabwe, Lesotho, Swaziland, and Zambia — finally with Kenya, through the Nile Basin up to Sudan and Egypt. This direct "red line" from Egypt to South Africa was made most famous by Cecil Rhodes. Along with Lord Milner, the British colonial minister in South Africa, Rhodes advocated such a "Cape to Cairo" empire, linking the Suez Canal to the mineral-rich southern part of the continent by rail. Though hampered by German occupation of Tanganyika until the end of World War I, Rhodes successfully lobbied on behalf of such a sprawling African empire and captured the imagination of British politicians for a couple of generations.

The Berlin Conference (1884–85)

The acquisition of the Congo in the late 1870s and the occupation of Egypt in 1879 are now considered the first major moves in what came to be the precipitous scramble for African territory. The subsequent schemes and plots of governments and individuals to build empires in Africa always endangered the peace of Europe. Thus, in 1884, Bismarck convened the Berlin Conference to discuss the African problem — how each country would acquire African territory without getting in each other's way. The conference diplomats put on a humanitarian façade by condemning the slave trade, prohibiting the sale of alcoholic beverages and firearms in certain regions, and expressing support for missionary activities. But mostly, their aim was to lay down a set of rules of competition for African territory. They agreed to Leopold's demand that the Congo was to become the Congo Free State, a neutral area where trade and navigation would be free but administered by him as a private individual. No nation was to stake claims in Africa without notifying other powers of its intentions. And no territory could be formally claimed prior to being effectively occupied. Though the Berlin Conference tried to manage the competition among the great powers, they actually ignored the Berlin rules when convenient and on several occasions war was only narrowly avoided by hasty subsequent conferences.

Native Revolts

Nativist revolts also troubled European sovereignty in Africa. Following the Berlin Conference, the British, Italians, and Ethiopians sought to claim lands owned by the Somalis in the Horn of Africa, a particularly important geo-strategic area on the Indian Ocean. They met the resistance of Mohammed Abdullah Hassan, a Somali religious leader who gathered Muslim soldiers from across the Horn and united them into a loyal army known as the Dervishes. This Dervish army enabled Hassan to carve out a powerful state that repulsed the British Empire four times and forced it to retreat to the coastal region. Finally, the British defeated the Dervishes in 1920, but only as a result of effective use of air warfare that the British had learned in WWI. Germany also found itself fighting a guerilla-style war with Herero and Namaqua native peoples in German Southwest Africa. The result was a genocide of horrific proportions. In total, as many as 65,000 Herero, or 80 percent of the population, and 10,000 Namaqua, or 50 percent, starved, died of thirst, or were worked to death in camps between 1904 and 1908.

The Colonial Lobby and Racial Jingoism

It took a couple of decades for the enthusiasts of colonial empire to capture the imagination of Europe. Like Bismarck, various important political leaders, such as William Gladstone, actually opposed colonisation as a distraction from more important national projects. Other politicians opposed the new imperialism because the expansion of national sovereignty on overseas territories contradicted the unity of the nation-state which promised the privileges of citizenship to its population. Thus, a tension began to surface between, on the one hand, the universalist will to respect human rights of the colonised people, as they may be considered as "citizens" of the nation-state, and, on the other, the imperialist drive to cynically exploit populations deemed inferior. Colonial lobbies emerged to legitimise the Scramble for Africa and other expensive overseas adventures and were quite successful. By the end of World War I, the colonial empires had become very popular almost everywhere in Europe: public opinion had been convinced of the needs of a colonial empire, although most of the Europeans would never see a piece of it. Popular exhibitions, starting with the famed Great Exhibition in London in 1850 to the world fairs in several capitals near the end of the century, can be seen as arms of colonial propaganda and were instrumental in bringing forward these popular sentiments predisposed to the new colonialism as a modern development.

Some of these exhibitions of the "modern" world would be abhorrent today. Indigenous people from Africa were brought to Europe and put on display for scientific and leisure purposes. Karl Hagenbeck, a German merchant in wild animals and a future entrepreneur of most Europeans zoos, in 1876, sent one of his collaborators to the newly conquered Egyptian Sudan to bring back some wild beasts and Nubian villagers for display in successful exhibits in Paris, London and Berlin. Such "human zoos" could be found in Hamburg, Antwerp, Barcelona, London, Milan, New York City, Paris, etc., with 200,000 to 300,000 visitors attending each exhibition. "Negro villages" would be presented in the Paris' 1878 and 1879 World's Fair. The 1900 World's Fair presented the famous "living" diorama of Madagascar, while the Colonial Exhibitions in Marseilles (1906 and 1922) and in Paris (1907 and 1931) would also display human beings in cages, often nude. A good example of the scientific racism and racist jingoism of the time involved Madison Grant, head of the New York Zoological Society. In 1906, he created an exhibit at the Bronx Zoo that exposed a Mibuti man, the pygmy Ota Benga, alongside the apes. Another exhibit placed Ota Benga in a cage with an orangutan and labeled him "The Missing Link" in an attempt to illustrate the popular theories of Social Darwinism, that Africans like Ota Benga are closer to apes than were Europeans.

Reading: Imperial Russia and the Making of a Nation (Topical Essay)

Tsar Peter the Great, ruler of Russia from 1682 to 1725, inherited a country suspicious of Western European ways. When he returned from a tour of Europe in 1698, the intimidating, 6′ 7″, monarch cut off the beards of the noblemen who greeted him. He then decreed that all townspeople wear "Western dress," even specifying petticoats for the women and German shoes for the men. He decided that Russians beginning in 1700 would mark time with a Western-style calendar. And as of 1721, he would be called "emperor." Peter unequivocally proclaimed that Russia — geographically spanning Europe and Asia — would turn its gaze Westward and remake itself as a European empire.

Throughout the 18th century, this strategy of intensive borrowing from the West worked: as a European empire, Russia could win wars and utilize the resources of its Russian and non-Russian populations. But in the 19th century, Western Europe developed a new political model, the nation, which had the power to sow both prosperity and social chaos. Russia tried to reinvent itself once again, generating major reforms, rich explorations of national identity, and fantastic novels. However, looking Westward also complicated Russia's efforts to become a nation — economically, politically and culturally. For Russia, knowing what lay on the path ahead brought burdens as well as benefits.

Europeanization under Peter I and Catherine II

Although Peter the Great is often remembered for his flamboyance, his policies generally led toward a pragmatic goal: winning wars. In an earlier era, Russia might have looked toward the rich civilizations to its south and east, but the rising powers of Peter's day lay to Russia's west, in Europe. So Peter sent the sons of the nobility to Europe to learn "how to navigate a vessel in battle," and enticed European military experts to settle in his new capital city, St. Petersburg, with its Dutch canals and baroque architecture. He looked to Sweden, Denmark and Prussia when restructuring the government into nine departments in 1717 and creating the Table of Ranks in 1722, a system that forced even the nobility to serve the state to earn their ranks. He reorganized Russia to create a regular navy, a standing army, and a permanent bureaucracy to run the country while he was busy fighting.

But what good were new Western buildings if you put the same old people in them? Although not totally isolated, the Christian Eastern Orthodox Russians were as wary of the "Lutherans" (Protestants) and the "Latins" (Catholics) as they were of Muslims. In a population of about 10 million, around 90 percent were either serfs, tied to noble lands, or state peasants tied to state lands. Both serfs and masters believed that Russia's greatest strength was its piety. They honored the God who had created them in His image, down to their unshaven chins. But if Russia was to compete with the West, Peter needed a compliant nobility, skilled in Western technology but also dazzling at a Parisian ball. So the noblewomen had to put on ballgowns and the noblemen had to shave. The peasants could pay a small tax and keep their beards.

And to compete with the West, Russia needed an "empire." All great European powers were building empires in distant lands. In terms of size and diversity, Russia met traditional definitions of an empire. By the end of Peter's reign, Russia's territory reached from Lutheran Germans near the Baltic Sea, to Muslim Tatars on the Volga River, to Shamanistic Chukchi in far eastern Siberia. Like most multi-ethnic empires of the time, Russia relied on indirect rule: encourage the local elite to integrate into the Russian nobility, but mostly allow regions to keep their leaders, language, and religion — as long as they remained quiet and productive.

Russia lacked an overseas empire, but that problem was solved through creative labeling. Why are Europe and Asia two continents? What began as ignorance by the Ancient Greeks, who assumed a great body of water lay north of the Black Sea, was perpetuated by the arrogance of medieval Europeans who liked the idea of a geographically distinct European Christendom. Before Peter, Russians didn't care about Europe or maps. But geographer Vasilii Tatishchev, tasked by Peter to describe the empire, wanted a clear division between Europe and Asia. So he found one: the Urals, a relatively low mountain range. West of the Urals would be Europe and east of the Urals would be Asia. Thus, Russia was firmly situated in Europe, with an empire over in another continent, Asia.

Some historians argue that in other ways Russia's transformation into a European country was more flash than substance. Russia was enormous and under-governed. Decrees were ignored when possible and then abandoned after Peter's death, especially out in the countryside. Peter's response to a shortage of funds and manpower was often coercion. St. Petersburg, the symbol of Russia's new Western orientation, was built with slave labor. In other ways, Peter strengthened Russia's autocracy, a form of government in which the ruler's word is law. With a decree of 1722, the tsar could even choose his successor. New propaganda portrayed the tsar not just as God's emissary, but as an "earthly god." And peasants got little besides a poll tax levied on every male. Clearly, Peter was uninterested in parliaments and constitutions.

However, by 18th century standards, Russia measured up as a European empire. Europe was still mostly ruled by monarchs with no desire for an empowered citizenry in search of common national goals. They wanted obedient subjects whose bodies and possessions could be harnessed, often to fight and fund wars.

Perhaps Peter's most fitting successor was Catherine the Great (r.1762-96), despite being a German-born princess who gained the Russian throne by deposing her husband, Peter the Great's grandson. While lacking Peter's capriciousness, she, too, combined vision with action. Married at 15 to a strange boy (she claimed he enjoyed court-martialing rats) who was hostile to Russian sensibilities, Catherine studied Russia's language and politics, and then supported the coup that made her empress. Though some insist that once again Westernization was a veneer masking Russian autocracy, Catherine fit the mold of an 18th-century enlightened European empress.

In the spirit of the Enlightenment sweeping Europe, she corresponded with leading French philosophe Voltaire; in 1767 convened a Legislative Commission, with elected representatives from the nobles, merchants, non-Russian minorities, and even state peasants to advise her on rationalizing Russia's law code (an effort abandoned after 18 months); in 1785 provided charters to clarify the rights and duties of townspeople and nobility; and in 1786 instituted a national co-ed public school system (albeit with a shortage of teachers and funds).

However, for Catherine, as for Voltaire, enlightenment did not mean democracy. She opened her Instructions to the Legislative Commission with two fundamental principles: "Russia is a European State" and in Russia, "The Sovereign is Absolute." She dealt with a peasant uprising (1773-75) led by a Cossack posing as her dead husband, by publicly decapitating, drawing and quartering the leader, and then giving local lords freer rein to control the countryside. In 1772, she joined enlightened European rulers in Austria and Prussia in taking pieces of Poland. In 1783, she annexed Crimea, assured by her close advisor that all European powers were "carving up Asia, Africa and America." And in keeping with the Enlightenment passion for uniformity, Catherine took steps toward homogenizing the empire, extending Russian statutes into Ukraine and the Baltics, which for the local peasants mostly meant new taxes and more serfdom.

Although the autocrat's powers in vast Russia remained limited, Catherine furthered Peter's project of developing a well run and expanding European empire, in which the elite held its own in European ballrooms and embassies, the military was respected, and the provinces were orderly and prosperous. Getting everyone on the same page, from bearded peasants to French-speaking Russian nobility, from Poles to Bashkirs to Jews, was at most a distant goal.

Nationalism and the Nation-State in the 19th Century

Then Europe changed. France's political revolution in 1789 and England's industrial revolution in the early 1800s promoted new means of harnessing resources: subjects were replaced with citizens, and peasants with factory workers. The French Revolution's "Declaration of the Rights of Man" proclaimed: "sovereignty resides essentially in the nation," not in a king or queen. This new conception of nation fundamentally contradicted the old principle of empire. Nations comprised not lords and servants, not a conglomeration of peoples, but brothers and sisters with a common identity and equal rights.

Impassioned citizens and booming factories promised prosperity and global domination, but also misery and upheaval. By the 1860s, European countries were taming their political and economic revolutions by remaking themselves as nation-states. A nation-state was present in people's daily lives from the policemen on their street to the pension that staved off starvation in old age.

Nation-states also actively promoted state-friendly nationalism. When you read in the newspaper about your country's latest imperial conquest or the victory of your team in burgeoning national sports, you were proud to be British. Or French. Or German. Perhaps you forgot about the factory owner or landlord, a fellow countryman, who threatened to fire or evict you. In a nation, all were on the same page — or at least, often believed they were.

These nation-states only partially reformed their empires to match. Although Europeans portrayed themselves as bearers of "civilization," those living in European colonies largely remained subjects, not citizens, expected to provide the rubber, palm oil, or cotton that fed the Industrial Revolution.

Russians devoted much energy in the 19th-century to becoming a nation. Russia's most innovative, though ultimately unsuccessful, attempts to reinvent itself as a nation occurred in the cultural sphere. In 1819, shortly after Russians ejected Napoleon from Moscow and helped liberate Europe, the poet Petr Viazemskii coined the term *narodnost* (from the term *narod*, meaning "the people") to name the unique character he was certain his people possessed. But what was this narodnost, this national character?

Nicholas I (r.1825-1855) knew from experience that musings on such topics could turn seditious. The day after he became Emperor of Russia, a small group of officers staged the country's first revolution, proclaiming the Russian people's natural right to liberty. Nicholas hanged five Decembrists (named for the month of their revolt), exiled others to Siberia, and then secretly formed committees to investigate Russia's current conditions and plan for reforms, including the eventual freeing of the serfs.

In public, Nicholas tried to put an end to debate on Russia's national character with an official slogan crafted in 1832: the Russian people had faith in "Orthodoxy, Autocracy, Narodnost.'" By nature, Russians love God and the tsar. This formulation settled little, claiming as it did that narodnost was defined by faith in narodnost. To give content to the elusive concept, the state poured funds into the study of Russian history and literature. But every study added fuel to the disagreements about Russia's past and future.

In the 1840s, young men, most of them privileged, argued the matter in Moscow's elite homes. They dubbed each other Slavophiles and Westernizers. The Slavophiles, some proudly sporting peasant-style beards, insisted that Russia should nurture its unique spirit, trampled on by Peter's Westernizing ways. The Westernizers countered that Russia could only progress as a European nation.

In the following decades, as Russians explored their national identity, they raised fundamental questions about the West's so-called progress. Does progress necessitate the reign of science and materialism? If so, are all of our actions reduced to scientific cause and effect? As Fyodor Dostoevsky's mad narrator put it in *Notes from the Underground* in 1864, are we merely piano keys, tuned to play a particular note? Is there no room for spontaneity or faith? And as Anton Chekhov asked in *The Cherry Orchard* (1903), must our heroes be those who chop down orchards to build and sell vacation homes? Could Russia's national identity, its purpose, lie in revealing a better path, one that incorporated the West's achievements yet salvaged the precious from the past? Could modernity have a soul? These concerns were only fully appreciated after two world wars dampened Western enthusiasm for unbridled progress.

The state, meanwhile, finally moved from slogans and secret reform projects to action after humiliating defeat in the Crimean War (1853-56). Like the United States, in the 1860s Russia launched a massive effort to forge a single nation from disparate parts. The era of The Great Reforms began with a stunning act of reform from above: in 1861, two years before Abraham Lincoln's *Emancipation Proclamation* in the midst of civil war, Alexander II (r.1855-81) emancipated the serfs. In theory now all Russians would navigate a single free-market economy. As of 1864, Russians elected representatives to town councils to build schools, hospitals, and roads; and all except the peasants (considered unready to abandon customary law) met in the same law courts, with a jury of their peers. With universal conscription (1874), all men served six years in the army. Though the autocracy remained untouched, Russia was starting to become one nation, with an economy, legal system, military, and even a small measure of political participation, shared by all.

Sort of. What was to be done about the non-Russians in the expanding empire? By 1897, the year of Russia's first census, the empire's population was about 128 million, including around 11.5 million Catholics, 5.2 million Jews, 13.9 million Muslims, and over 68 million people — from Poles in the far west to Tajiks in Central Asia — whose native language was not Russian. Increasingly the state's response was that everyone was going to need to become more Russian.

Russification wasn't so easily accomplished. Many Poles or Baltic Germans considered themselves more European and more civilized than their Russian rulers. Russians worried they were right. Relations with Finland, part of the empire since 1809, turned from amicable to hostile when the state rewrote the Finnish constitution in 1899 to deprive the territory of its traditional autonomy. Plus, the "state" consisted of people with conflicting views of Russianness. In some state-supported schools in Kazan, Muslim children worked on mastering the Russian language, while their teachers avoided any attempt to convert them from Islam; in others, non-Muslim children learned the lessons Russian Orthodox Christianity, taught in their native dialects. Did Russification entail a change of language or religion? Of course, every European imperial nation-state bred contradictions, but they were more easily glossed over when they occurred across a sea.

The other group that proved difficult to incorporate into a Russian nation? The most Russian of the Russians, the millions of peasants still in their felt boots and long beards, largely untouched by Peter the Great's cultural revolution. Russian elites went in search of narodnost, and found it enchained on their own country estates. That couldn't be a good thing. But elites worried what a nation of Russian peasants would bring. If peasants gained a voice, would they prop up the tsarist regime, as some hoped and others feared? If the peasants left the villages to become factory workers, would Russia gain a modern economy but lose its national soul? Every dispute about the fate of the Russian peasantry was an argument about the future of the Russian nation.

Late 19th-Century Modernization Dilemmas
Ironically, having a roadmap to progress provided by Western Europe only complicated matters. Many Russians believed they had only to look to the West to see where each step would lead. If the peasants represented Russia's past, Western Europe represented Russia's potential future. And what did that future hold? Capitalism and constitutions; smoke stacks and military success; exploitation, alienation and revolution. While Russians disagreed about the various items on the list (for example, the tsars and revolutionaries didn't see eye-to-eye on the desirability of toppling kings), they faced the same dilemma: could Russia get the good without the bad?

With their eyes focused on what they believed to be their possible future, Russians at times made decisions that conflicted with their own goals and created the strangest of bedfellows. Most Russian Marxists, enemies of capitalism, insisted that Russia must become capitalist like the West. After all, Marx insisted that only the factories of advanced capitalism would produce the workers to create a revolution and the technological advancement to guarantee prosperity that would ultimately provide for "each according to his needs." Even after a revolution brought down the tsars in 1917, most Marxists stuck to this script: capitalism must come before socialism.

Perhaps even more surprising were the two groups that found common cause in impeding Russia's transition to capitalism: the tsars and the populist revolutionaries who killed a tsar, Alexander II in 1881. Like the Marxists, the populists wanted socialism, but they saw no reason to drag Russia through the miseries of capitalism to get there. Echoing Slavophilism, they insisted Russia could chart a unique path using a Russian institution, the peasant commune — village assemblies through which peasants dispensed justice.

Since the 1840s, Russians in search of narodnost had idealized one feature of the commune. If the commune noticed, for example, that Ivan had a small family but much land, and Fyodor had a big family but little land, it might give part of Ivan's land to Fyodor. Historians are still investigating how often or peacefully this occurred, and whether the goal was to guarantee none would starve or to ensure all paid their share of the obligations to state and master. But the populists looked at this land redistribution and decided, if that isn't "to each according to his needs," what is? If only the repressive state were removed, Russian peasant socialism could be unleashed. The icing on the cake would be showing Western Europe that the Russian nation's destiny was to lead, not follow.

The tsars also placed their wager on the commune, though for different reasons. When Alexander II freed the serfs in 1861, land was given to the commune, not the individual peasant. What began as a temporary measure to protect the peasants during the transition to private ownership and a market economy in a later era became permanent. With their eyes on the revolutions and labor movements to the West, Alexander III (r.1881-94) and some in his government worried that Marx was right: the factories of capitalism created a socialist proletariat. The solution? Keep the peasants out of the factories and in their communes. After all, they were certain the peasants were by nature not socialists, but monarchists.

The state tightened the grip of the commune, even as it promoted grand projects to modernize the country. In 1893, just two years after beginning construction of the Trans-Siberian Railway to connect Russia from west to far east, Alexander III approved a law forbidding peasants from selling their land without permission from two-thirds of the commune. Many in the government argued against such measures, insisting that the commune, far from protecting peasants, kept them impoverished, and undermined a key goal of emancipation — ending peasant isolation and creating a unified nation. Some even worried that the populists were right and the commune was a hotbed of primitive socialism.

After a revolution in 1905 forced the last tsar, Nicholas II (r.1894-1917), to accept Russia's first albeit limited parliament, one mystery was finally solved. The peasants, when allowed to vote, didn't love their tsar all that much. They mostly voted for the anti-monarchist parties that promised to give them more land. Nicholas took the lessons of revolution and elections to heart, changing the electoral law to give the peasants fewer votes, and, at long last, agreeing to break up the communes.

Was Russia by this point doomed to violent revolution? Debate continues. Recent research suggests that the peasants, especially after 1861, were neither as isolated nor as economically stagnant as once portrayed. And almost 50 years after the Great Reforms, peasants and their former masters at last had begun to live in one economic system. Though Nicholas II kept the title "autocrat" and representation was definitely not equal, men from across the empire could attempt to reconcile their conflicting visions of Russia's destiny on the floor of the parliament. Perhaps with enough time, Russia could have found a way to be a nation of many.

Instead, partly due to the delaying tactics of the previous century, Russia had less than a decade left. Then came World War I. This was more than a nascent nation could withstand. In February

1917, in the midst of war, the Russian monarchy collapsed. In October 1917, the Bolsheviks, a group of radical Marxists led by Vladimir Lenin, seized power with a formula to outwest the West, getting all of the good and none of the bad — and no waiting for the right time. They promised that this time, Western workers would follow Russia's lead, igniting a world-wide socialist revolution. Both empires and nations would vanish as workers of the world willingly joined together in an egalitarian future. As it turned out, these dreams were illusory.

Reading: Latin America, 1500-1900

Latin America is, by definition, the parts of the Western Hemisphere that were colonized primarily by the Spanish and Portuguese crowns in the 16th and early 17th centuries and additionally in the late 17th and 18th centuries by the French, British and Dutch. Phases of Latin American history describe the disruption and demise of the many indigenous groups that lived on these continents in 1492, the year Columbus landed in the West Indies, the efforts of the Europeans to exploit the peoples and natural resources, and the final 19th century phase when the descendents of European settlers, called Creoles, declared and enforced their independence from Europe.

Settlement and Governing of the Colonies

The slow subjugation of North, Central and South America to European nation-states commenced in 1492 and lasted well into the 18th century with the most remote and western parts of the continents colonized very late. But the major areas of Native population in Mexico, in the Andes, in the Caribbean and in northern South America were essentially settled and under the control of Europeans by the second half of the 16th century. The less populated and rural regions of North America, Brazil, Argentina and Chile were part of the second phase of steady European conquest in the late 16th and throughout the 17th centuries.

Viceroyalties and Shareholding Companies

The governments that the Spanish and Portuguese established were designed to create as much wealth as possible from the resources of the New World for their respective crowns. Spain was the wealthier power and had more experience governing peoples beyond the Iberian Peninsula, in Italy and the Low Countries, using a system of *audiencias*, or courts and legislative bodies at the local level, and viceroys, at the broader regional level. For his viceroy, the king appointed a nobleman that he believed he could trust, acting as an "alter ego," knowing what the far away king would want and do in any specific situations. This gave the viceroy considerable power, though the crown conducted audits of his behavior and management at the end of each viceregal term. Initially, there were two viceroyalties -- New Spain (Mexico) in 1521and Peru (in the Andes) in 1542 -- which were the most populous and wealthy areas of indigenous habitation in the Americas at the time of the conquest. Later as the Spanish extended their conquests and their governmental reach, two more viceroyalties were established -- New Granada (modern-day Columbia and Venezuela) in 1739 and La Plata (modern-day Argentina, Uruguay and Paraguay) in 1776.

The viceroy had a governing council to assist him. But as the empire became more complex and populated, the viceroys increasingly had to depend on the several audiencias in each of the viceroyalties, stationed in important secondary cities of the viceroyalties. The audiencias became controlled by Creoles, or Spaniards born in the New World, unlike the viceroy, who was almost always born in Spain. Despite the growing independence of the Creole elites in their audiencias, both the viceroy and the Creole ministers believed it was in their best interests to remain loyal to the crown, and the crown and their viceroys were clever enough to deal out many privileges and benefits to their powerful Creole subjects to ensure that loyalty.

The Portuguese crown was not wealthy and thought of their colonies in the Americas as commercial adventures that had to be managed by commercial men and shareholding companies who were exclusively contracted to the crown to exploit the colony and provide a regular payment to the crown. As such Brazil, the major Portuguese colony in South America, was somewhat haphazardly run and it was not until the 1570s that the Portuguese finally discovered the way to make Brazil a worthwhile project. In the northern part of the colony called Recife, near the mouth of the Amazon, sugar could be grown. However, indigenous labor had not proved effective; rather African slaves had to be brought from the Portuguese colonies in West Africa. The crown was then able to capitalize financially on both sugar and human slavery. Only later in the 18th century when gold was discovered near the city of São Paulo did the south of Brazil become populated with settlers.

Indigenous Demographic Collapse

In the early period of conquest, especially in Mexico and the Andes, the Spanish were aided by the demographic collapse of indigenous populations from exposure to deadly European diseases. Indigenous leaders, especially in the most populated areas, were unable to resist Spanish aggression when as many as 50 to 90 percent of their people died from the small pox, measles, and other epidemics in 1520, 1548, 1576-1579, and 1595-96.

In his famed treatise of World HIstory, *Guns, Germs and Steel*, Jared Diamond explains the significant geographic advantage Europeans had over the pre-Columbian American peoples in the conquest. One can see the geographic advantage by looking at a world map. Note that the landmass of Afroeurasia, the Old World, is continuous and laid out west to east. It is easy for culture, technology, and agricultural developments to travel with people and be shared across a west/east axis. Moreover, more agricultural crops thrive in the moderate climate of the temperate zones than they do anywhere else. In the New World, there is not a continuous landmass across the temperate zones and not much sharing between the two major civilizations -- Mexico and the Andes -- one in the northern and one in the southern hemisphere.

Why is this geographic fact important to Diamond? The stable agricultural centers of the Old World gave humans long exposure to diseases endemic in agricultural animals -- pox and flu particularly -- so that populations all across Afroeurasia built up antibodies and immunity. New World people became sitting ducks for the vast waves of diseases that the Europeans brought with them. Plus the Old World was populated twice as long as the New World -- 40,000 years compared to 20,000 years -- and for this longer period of time Europeans were able to share and gain technologies and cultural developments that traveled easily from east to west and back. Note that it was less easy for people in the New World to transfer their culture and technology across climate zones from North to South, and thus the two relatively independent civilizations. Among technology that was shared widely in Afroeurasia was iron and steel and then armaments. Thus, guns, germs and steel overwhelmed the indigenous people who came in contact with Europeans, especially in the 16th century.

Presidio and Mission

Once the Spanish moved into an area and subjugated a population of Natives, they implemented what was called the *presidio* and mission system. The presidio was the Spanish fortification or military base where military officers and soldiers were kept in barracks. The mission was usually in the same place behind the same walls. The various brotherhoods of the Catholic church -- Franciscans and Dominicans, later Hieronymites and Jesuits -- built a church, a school for Native children, dormitories for domiciled Natives, especially women, and various commercial operations to support the church -- candle making, leather goods, cloth spinning and weaving, food making, etc. To support the care and feeding of Spanish personnel, outside the presidio-mission was a rancho del rey, or king's ranch, a tract of land used to pasture horses and other beasts of burden, as well as raise cattle to supply meat for the European diet (which the Natives did not share) and crops such as wheat and cotton.

The Spanish presidio-mission method, which the Portuguese shared to a certain extent, used both overwhelming technical power and soft conversion to bring the Natives to heel and keep them in a dependent position. With their conversion efforts, the Spanish soon brought the children of the former Native leadership into their orbit, creating a community of go-betweens and a culture of dependency that solidified their control. Though the Spanish could control effectively a region of large numbers of Natives with this system, which required a few dozen Spaniards, as always the problem was that there were not enough Spaniards in the Americas to establish more of these outposts, so the conquest by presidio-mission slowly took three centuries. One of the last projects of conquest was the mission complexes of California in the 1760-1820 period.

African Slavery

Human labor to exploit the natural resources and treasures of the New World was a major preoccupation of Europeans. They first tried with Native labor. The Spanish implemented the encomienda system, where the crown granted lands and the Natives that lived on those lands to conquerors for their exploitation. While the Spanish crown did not consider the Natives slaves legally (they were conquered people rather than chattel), only a small percentage were wage laborers. This reversed by the beginning of the 17th century, when dwindling numbers made their labor more scarce and valuable. In commodities that the Natives were familiar with such as the mining of silver in the Andes, they provided most if not all of the labor that the Spanish needed.

However, their declining numbers and unfamiliarity with some forms of labor and European products meant that Natives could or would not supply all the Europeans' needs. Thus, the Spanish began to import African slaves as early as 1501 in their first colony of Hispaniola, an island in the Caribbean. There, they were employed in the mining of gold but later in other colonies were used to harvest products -- cattle, cotton, coffee, gems and pearls, indigo, sugar, etc. The Spanish observed the treaty boundary between themselves and the Portuguese -- the Treaty of Tordesillas -- which reserved the African slave trade to the Portuguese but most of the land in the New World (except Brazil) to the Spanish. Thus, the Portuguese and later the English did most of the enslaving in Africa and transporting across the Atlantic to form the international slave trade. While the Spanish did not import slaves, they had a brisk internal slave trade that moved slaves all about their territories.

Slave Economies

During the nearly four centuries in which slavery existed in the Americas, Brazil was responsible for importing 35 percent of the slaves from Africa (4 million) while Spanish America imported about 20 percent (2.5 million). These numbers are significantly higher than the imported slaves to the United States. In the US, we have one of the few phenomenon where slavery grew beyond the importation rates and this is due to slave breeding. In Brazil and the Caribbean, slave owners did not see an economic incentive to breed slaves and so they allowed slaves to die at a higher rate, especially in the areas where sugar was raised. At the same time, there seemed to be an enormous number of runaway slaves due to a lack of governmental response, and greater levels of manumission (granting a slave freedom). While the Latin America and Caribbean societies had fewer slaves than the United States at any given time, Latin American slaves made up a higher percentage of the overall population. The sparse white upper class of Latin American societies constantly feared for uprising among not only slaves but Indians and the poor of all racial ethnic groups.

Over 70 percent of slaves in Latin American worked on sugar cane plantations but also worked in the production of tobacco, rice, cotton, fruit, corn and other commodities. Thus, the majority of slaves brought to the Americas from Africa were men who could handle the brutal work of sugar cultivation and production. Black slave populations were extremely low in Cuba and Puerto Rico until the British took Havana, Cuba, in 1762. After that, the British imported more than 10,000 African slaves to Havana, using it as a base to supply the Caribbean sugar market and its 13 North American colonies. A weakened Spain was forced to open its slave trade to the powerful English, who began to dominate the Caribbean economies in the late 18th century.

Slave Revolts

Latin America experienced many more slave revolts than in the thirteen colonies of the future United States. The first open black rebellion occurred in plantations in 1521 on the island of Hispaniola, which was quickly put down. It was followed by a major slave rebellion on the island of Puerto Rico in 1527, as dozens of slaves fought against the colonists in a brief revolt. The few slaves who escaped retreated to the mountains and secluded with some surviving Taino Natives in a renegade community, which the Spanish called a *maroon*. In the islands and later in the hinterlands of Venezuela, Columbia and Brazil, escaped slaves were able to survive and even do quite well in maroons (the Portuguese equivalent were called *quilombos*), creating governments, militias and even small industries beyond the grasp of the colonial governments.

One important reason for more slave revolts in Latin America was the relatively larger number of recently imported African slaves. Upon arrival in Brazil the various "tribal" groups were not separated like they were in the North American colonies. Recently sold Latin American slaves were more likely to recreate much of their own African culture in a new land. Since most of the slaves in Brazil were African-born and from the same "tribal" (ethnic) group, escaped slaves were able to organize into large paramilitary units and more effectively defend themselves in quilombos in the Brazilian rainforests Because they shared the same ethnic background, they were able to communicate and discuss plans for affirmative action against the slave regime in Brazil.

The most important of these African tribal communities was the Yoruba, which had its own large cultural and imperial domain in Southwest Nigeria. The Yorubas comprised about 40 percent of all Africans arriving in the New World. The Yoruba left the largest African religious system that survives in the New World today in Brazil, Cuba, Haiti and New Orleans. One of the major reasons you had more of a tradition of slave resistance in those countries was because of the role of African religion as a unifying force for enslaved Africans.

Castas and Miscegenation

With the increased dependency on enslaved Africans and with the Spanish crown opposed to enslavement of Natives (except in the case of rebellion), slavery became associated with race and racial hierarchies, with Europeans hardening their concepts of racial ideologies. *Casta* was an Iberian word that meant "lineage" or "breed." From the Middle Ages, lineage was often associated with purity of blood, meaning a person free of Jewish heritage. In the New World, it would come to mean a person free of African ancestry. For the Spanish, they distinguished between themselves as *gente de razón*, or people with reason, and the Native, *gente sin razón*, or people without reason. Therefore, while Natives were not logical people to the Spanish, they were not so low socially as Africans.

The Spanish developed a complex hierarchy of four major categories and described miscegenous blendings of people derived from those four categories: *peninsular*, a Spaniard born in Spain; Creole, a person of Spanish descent born in the New World; *indio*, a person who is descendent of the original inhabitants of the Americas; and the lowest category, Negro, or a person of black African descent, whether enslaved or free. There were dozens of terms that reflected mixtures of these categories, such as *mulatto*, a mix of Spanish and African, mestizo, a mix of Spanish and Indian and then even more blended categories, such as *morisco*, a mix of a Spaniard with a mulatto, or three-quarters Spanish, or an *albino*, a mix of Spaniard with a morisco, or seven-eighths Spanish, as well as many mixtures of Indians with blacks.

In the 18th century, a genre of castas paintings emerged, depicting the various categories of racial mixing in the Americas; most of these paintings were from Mexico. The two consistent themes in the depiction of couples and children in these paintings was, first, it was possible for Native children to become white or Spanish by mixing over several generations with Spanish, and, second, that the child with some Negro blood could rise, though not as high as the person with indigenous ancestry. The latter is an important distinction because in Latin America, the castas system allowed the person to increase social standing with the right kind of racial mixing, whereas in North America, even the slightest amount of Negro blood would condemn the person to the lower ranks of society.

Independence

The colonization of the Americas was not the result of the kind of dense government we would know today, where a central government can directly and deeply affect the local society in terms of taxes, finances, regulations and laws. Neither the Spanish nor the Portuguese crowns could administer lands thousands of miles from their capitals in that way. Instead, they relied on a system of viceroys and audiencias, forming reliable and stable collaborations and partnerships with Creole elites, which often required compromise and tolerance on the part of the crown and allowed the Creoles considerable independence, if they remained loyal to king and country. And historians today speculate that this fine equilibrium of mutual interests between the colonies and their mother countries would have been stable enough to make colonization last for several more decades, if it were not for the upheaval of Europe in the Napoleonic Wars in 1799-1815. Napoleon overran the Iberian Peninsula, arresting Spain's king and crown prince, the future Ferdinand VII, and driving the Portuguese king and crown prince to Brazil. Independence, therefore, was pressed on the Latin Americans because of a sudden and complete absence of government from the mother countries.

Structural Independence of the Colonies

But we should not assume that independence was inspired by Enlightenment ideas about liberty and equality as possibly inspired the American Revolution. Except for a few cases, such as the revolutionary leader Simón de Bolívar, independence leaders were more shaped by a desire to maintain and protect the independence and power in finance, communication, military leadership, laws, etc. that they had been experiencing in the later colonial period. There was a struggle between elites, especially in the capitals who had exceptionally good relations with the viceregal government, and those in the secondary cities and rural areas where the Creole elites were well established in patterns of control.

European Revolution and Colonial Independence

The Napoleonic Wars were a series of wars fought between France (led by Napoleon Bonaparte) and alliances involving Great Britain, Prussia, Spain, Portugal, Russia and Austria at different times, from 1799 to 1815. These wars were devastating to the Iberian powers. In May 1808, Napoleon captured King Carlos IV and his son, King Fernando VII, and installed his own brother, Joseph Bonaparte, on the Spanish throne. This event disrupted the political stability of Spain and broke the link with some of the colonies which were loyal to the Bourbon Dynasty. In the colonies, the local Creole elites took matters into their own hands organizing themselves into juntas, or government committees, claiming "in absence of the king, Fernando VII, [that] their sovereignty devolved temporarily back to the community."

At first, the juntas swore loyalty to the captive Fernando VII and each ruled different and diverse parts of the colony. Most of Fernando's subjects were loyal to him in 1808, but after he was restored to the Spanish crown in 1814, his policy of restoring absolute power alienated both the juntas and his subjects, especially when he sent armies from Spain to the colonies to retake power. In Argentina, the local governments managed to throw off the Spanish yoke early and march across the Andes to free Chile and then march from the South toward Peru, the old stronghold of Spanish power in South America. Simon Bolivar led an army of Creole, mestizo, and Afro-metizo troops to free Venezuela, Columbia, Ecuador and finally march from the north to south to capture Peru in 1824. In Mexico, a horrific bloody battle commenced between Creoles and peninsulares, with the Creoles fighting for a constitutional government finally getting the upper hand also in 1824.

Imagining Republics

How do people of diverse backgrounds imagine themselves no longer a colony but now a republic? In the United States, the 13 colonies had difficulty thinking of themselves as a single republic and not as separate colonies. The compromises in the American Constitution that gave substantial power and representation to states, which were former colonies, demonstrate that they do not imagine anew, they simply try to adapt the familiar concepts of power and law to the new concept of a single entity with additional powers, that is the federal government. It was the same for the Latin Americans. When the rebellions were finally over, the Creole elites declared new republics out of what had been divisions of the old viceroyalties into the smaller audiencias, the strongholds of the Creole elites.

Today's map of the countries of South and Central America demonstrates this mirror of audiencia power. The viceroyalty of La Plata did not become the new republic of La Plata; it broke into smaller republics of Argentina, Uruguay and Paraguay, which had been audiencias. The viceroyalty of Peru became Peru, Bolivia, Chile and Ecuador, all former audiencias. New Granada became Columbia and Venezuela. New Spain broke into the major republic of Mexico and eventually smaller countries in Central America. The various Spanish islands of the Caribbean all became separate nations except the slave colonies of Cuba and Puerto Rico, which remained colonies of Spain. In 1822, Brazil broke from Portugal but became a kingdom in its own right under the son of the

Portuguese king, which kept the large colony intact. In 1889, Creole elites deposed the king and declared Brazil a republic.

Ultimately, it was the Creole elites who emphasized the local nature of governance who triumphed in the age of independence. They gave themselves power, but instead of democracy and equality they mostly devolved into dictatorships under a series of strongmen who presented only the veneer of a republic. The dictatorial pattern would remain well into the 20th century, in fact, into the 1970s and 80s, when middle class and working class coalitions tried to and continue to try to bring the promise of the republic to Latin American countries.

Unit 13: East Asia, 1700-1919

Hugh Shapiro, University of Nevada, Reno

Reading: The Early Qing Empire, 1644-1796

Learning How to Rule

This logistical conundrum of ruling China that faced the victorious Manchus was in fact a perennial problem. China's first unification, circa 200 BCE, was in one sense precocious, having unified a subcontinent well before the technical means to rule such a large area existed. From late antiquity, one strategy for maintaining political control was the control of the intangible, of symbols, and symbolic control became woven into the very DNA of China's political culture. Sumptuary laws, an enduring practice, strictly regulated who could display what types of icons or wear which clothes or erect specific architectural features on the home. Even certain words were reserved for the political elite; their careless use signaled/implied sedition. The Manchus were mindful of these types of puzzles, and strategized to overcome them. The very word "Manchu," to wit, was fiction, an ethnic-political label invented by the Jurchen leaders as a way to lend cohesion to the disparate tribes and nations that were joining their cause of the "Great Enterprise," of conquering China, south of the Great Wall.

And the newly invented Manchus would not be the first unprecedentedly powerful army to conquer China and then fail, seeing it all slip away. The Mongols, for all their stunning military prowess, lasted only 89 years in China as the Yuan Dynasty (1279-1368). Yet the Manchus were serious students of history, and they were determined to avoid what might become a short-lived pillage of China, only then to be hounded back to the steppe. To this end, one generation before their conquest of China and the establishment of the 267 year-long Qing Dynasty north of the Great Wall, the Manchus created a shadow government explicitly mimicking the Confucian administration of the Ming state.

The Manchus aimed to educate themselves on how the Chinese state functioned. By understanding the levers of power that made China's empire governable, and discovering where these levers were, the conquerors hoped to hit the ground running in their bid to govern the empire in a lasting fashion. In laying the groundwork for long-term success in China, the Manchus made one more shrewd decision. On the cusp of the invasion, they enjoyed a decisive military advantage. Even so, they waited for an historically auspicious moment to attack.

The propitious moment materialized during a massive internal rebellion against the Ming state, specifically when Chinese rebel Li Zicheng attacked the capital with his enormous ragtag army, causing the last Ming emperor to commit suicide. The Manchus now possessed their righteous cause. They swept into China avenging this heinous crime — the violent death of an emperor. By defeating the rebels, punishing their regicide, and reestablishing order, the Manchus likened themselves to the virtuous Han forces that had crushed the illegitimate, cruel Qin Dynasty in 207 BCE. Punishing rebel iniquity and saving the people: they performed this careful choreography not solely for contemporary opinion. Equally, they acted out the revenge drama for future historical memory.

In doing so, the astute Manchu invaders deftly inserted themselves into the grand epic that was China's dynamic imperial history. History in China was a tangible force/presence that acted on people, influencing life and death choices. After all, it was the specter of condemnation by disapproving historians of the future that pushed the last Ming emperor to kill his daughters and hang himself from a tree. By authoring a plausible narrative to justify their invasion, the Manchus insinuated themselves into China's historical imagination. They cast themselves as forces of virtue as their forces stormed into China and set about destroying the Ming armies, massacring civilians and murdering any remaining Ming royalty they captured.

Innovative Qing Rulers

While the new Qing state did go on to follow the proven pathways of Confucian administration for which it had assiduously prepared, it did not simply adhere to Ming custom. To the contrary, it departed from tradition and employed innovation in important ways. In social life, for example, Manchu women did not bind their feet, as was widely practiced among China's elite. Yet Manchu women, too, wished to be beautiful, because the bound foot was perceived as the quintessence of feminine allure. As a solution, Manchu women invented a platform shoe that mimicked the bound foot, the horse-hoof (*mati*) shoe. Imagine the long-term health benefits for Manchu women in not binding their feet, and the implications for the agency of women. The Manchus also made other pragmatic adjustments in political life.

At the very core of the Confucian patriarchy was political succession, witnessed in the sacerdotal transfer of power from father to son, from emperor to prince. However, primogeniture contained an innate flaw: the heir apparent, the first-born son, might be unfit to rule. In China's high antiquity, leaders understood the perils of transferring power solely along the paternal bloodline. Instead, the culture heroes and the founders of China's earliest historical dynasties passed power not to their children, but rather to the meritorious.

Departure from this practice in the 3rd millennium BCE with the turn towards the transfer of power to the eldest son, is considered, within China's political culture, the equivalent of eating the forbidden fruit and expulsion from paradise. Implicit in this critique is that all subsequent governments contained a fundamental defect, a nepotistic kernel of moral corruption. The Manchus abandoned this practice, and rightly so. Take one son of the Yongzheng Emperor (r. 1723-35), in line for succession. He enjoyed lying in a coffin feigning death, as his friends caroused. In this case the fourth son, Aisin Gioro Hongli, went on to take the throne, becoming one of China's most celebrated emperors, Qianlong (r. 1735-96).

The ingenuity of this small adjustment in how emperors were enthroned lay in its valuation of merit over hierarchy and tradition. Even though the "great man" view of history can sometimes be overstated, the "three emperors" of the Qing state merit special mention. Kangxi, Yongzheng, Qianlong: father, son, grandson. This formidable triumvirate lent meaningful stability to the Qing imperium for nearly 140 years (r. 1661-1796). The curiosity of these energetic leaders and their openness to foreign ideas is hinted at by their intimate relationships with European Jesuits who enjoyed access to the highest levels of Qing society. Many served as doctors, or as astronomers, or in the case of Italian Jesuit Giuseppe Castiglione (Chinese name, Lang Shining), as a court painter who melded European sensibilities with the aesthetics that he encountered in China. Yet the high Qing emperors remained attentive to indigenous practice in China, to wit, Confucianism, as an idea of governance.

Committed practitioners of Confucian statecraft, Kangxi, Yongzheng, and Qianlong, took seriously the idea that benevolent government should rest lightly on the people. In 1712, the Kangxi emperor froze the rate of land tax extracted from the countryside to prevent future government from becoming a burden on the people. It was one-half century into Kangxi's rule, and the recovery from the destruction of the Ming collapse and the Manchu invasion was well underway. In time, the number of officials assigned to run the empire would also be frozen, for the same reason — preempting fiscal burdens on the population.

Clearly, the high Qing emperors pursued the paternalistic ideal of the enlightened sage rulers, showing magnanimity, self-mastery, wisdom, and moderation. Kangxi's grandson, for example, the Qianlong emperor, a Confucian monarch and devout Buddhist, wished to discuss ideas with the Dalai Lama, the spiritual leader of Tibetan Buddhism. Qianlong prepared thoughtfully for this meeting. First, he studied the Tibetan language for 15 years; he wished to speak directly with the Dalai Lama. Then, when the Tibetan religious leader visited Beijing, Qianlong aimed to make him comfortable, offering him a complex of temples a few hours north of Beijing. They were modeled precisely on the Potala Palace in Lhasa in Tibet and built to one-third scale of the original structure. Qianlong hoped that the Dalai Lama would decide to stay, shifting his official residence from the

Tibetan plateau to north China, within easy distance of the capital. The Dalai Lama met with Qianlong, accepted the hospitality at the "little Potala Palace" (Putuo Zongcheng Temple), but after a month or so, the Dalai Lama expressed his desire to return to Tibet. Qianlong allowed him to go.

The Legacy of Qing Territorial Expansion

Yet the high Qing emperors did not always display such restraint. Take the ongoing troubles on China's other western frontier, far north of Tibet, in Dzungaria, in what is today northern Xinjiang, the Uyghur Muslim northwest. Qing armies perennially clashed with the Dzungar Khanate, last among the steppe empires of Central Asia. Over the three generations of the Kangxi, Yongzheng, and Qianlong reigns, the campaigns were waged by father, son, and grandson. It was under Qianlong, in the mid-1750s, that Qing armies finally annihilated the Dzungar nation. Dzungaria essentially ceased to exist, both as a political entity and as a lived culture. Often described as a genocide, this final solution marked the permanent integration of what became known as Xinjiang, the Uyghur homeland, into the Qing imperium. And territorial expansion is perhaps the Qing's most lasting contribution to the China that we see today.

The Qing gave China its modern territorial shape. Qing expansion of China's territory was dramatic, more than doubling the size of the Ming. Most conspicuously, Qing armies and diplomats brought Tibet, Xinjiang, and Taiwan into the Qing imperium. In fact, Qing territory was significantly larger than China's today, for it also controlled Mongolia, the second largest landlocked country in the world after Kazakhstan. The Qing movement into the "frontiers," such as Taiwan, was much like the American expansion into the West or Russian expansion into Central Asia and Siberia. Taiwan, the island off the Chinese coast, however, was elevated to the status of a Chinese province only in 1887, after Japan and France showed geopolitical interest in the area. This territorial expansion in part accounts for why China's borders touch more countries than any other state in the world and the concomitant complexity of its geopolitical challenges.

Population, Technology, Economy

Population is another index of Chinese society's prosperity/flourishing under the Qing. Witness the tripling of China's population from the late Ming — one hundred million — to late Qing — three hundred million. This spike in population is the result of a multiplicity of factors, most pointing to a society experiencing overall social health. At the base must be China's highly efficient system of farming, driven by the quintessential family farm. Their use of irrigation, fertilizer, and legumes such as soybeans, used to re-fix nitrogen in heavily worked soil, was enhanced by the introduction of New World crops such as corn and the potato. Their farming skills plus new crops enabled the opening up of new land on previously unused hillsides. State policies encouraged farmers to develop farm land on the frontier. They also promoted the development of an "internal" frontier, the land in core areas that had been passed over.

The Qing state invested heavily in hydroworks, such as along the mighty Yellow River, attempting to contain and harness that massive waterway that unpredictably careened and whiplashed across the north China plain. At the micro level, small groups developed waterworks seen in local dikes and also the remarkable reclamation of land in silt-rich estuaries, such as the fertile Pearl River Delta near Hong Kong. Here farmers ingeniously harnessed the flow of river sediment, enabling the formation of rich farmland out of shallow bays and coastal waters. Agricultural experts visiting from the United States in the early 20th century were so impressed by China's efficient use of land and the skilled processing of grain by local farmers that American expert F.H. King in the 1930s recommended to the Roosevelt administration to adopt some of China's approach to grain production and distribution. But efficient farming was only one, albeit critical, factor.

China also boasted efficacious medical knowledge and pharmacology. Public health was further boosted by a philosophy of moderation in daily regimen, seen in exercise and diet. The social practice of boiling water for tea also played an important role in general well-being. Laborers from China working on the American railroads in the 19th century survived in much higher rates than laborers from Europe, who did not habitually boil drinking water. (Instead Europeans and early Americans relied on distilled and fermented liquors, which were safer than unboiled water.) The absence of domestic strife and war in core areas of China in the 18th century was also a great boon to the Qing Dynasty.

The enduring legacy of the Qing's population growth is incalculable. It was on this enormous early modern base that China grew to 450 million, circa 1950, and then tripled under the People's Republic of China to reach today's gargantuan 1.4 billion. In other words, the pro-natalist policies of radical Maoism from the 1950s to the 1970s indeed produced China's 20th-century population explosion. Yet, without the earlier Qing-era demographic momentum, China today could not have born this population burden. China's enormous environmental, economic, and increasingly political footprint is the direct result of its population, and is changing the future of the world. This might be China's most tenacious legacy.

Qing China also constituted a large share of the economic gross world product (GWP), growing from China's enormous domestic economy and extensive international trade. The Qing presence in the global imagination was legendary. We can read Voltaire's deep admiration for Confucian ethics and techniques of government and observe the broad-based chinoiserie, or European imitations of Chinese motifs, an aesthetic phenomenon that reverberates to this very day.

Europeans hungered for products from China, as they had for centuries. Recall that the very word for porcelain in Europe is "China," just as the word for China in Greco-Roman antiquity was seres, or silk. In a very tangible way, European desire for Asian goods structured modern global history, motivating Columbus's voyage and many other types of paradigm-shifting undertakings, such as the European rounding of Africa and entering the Indian Ocean. Yet Europe of the late 18th century was much more confident, worldly, and aggressive than Europe of the late 15th century. It is not entirely surprising, then, in 1795, that England, an emerging global power, sent an emissary seeking an audience with the great Qianlong emperor.

Representing King George III, the very king who lost the American colonies, Lord George Macartney was charged with transforming, or normalizing, England's relationship with China. King George III demanded two things. First, that England and China interact as equals, dispensing with the antique ritual structure of the "tribute system" by which lesser countries sought munificent, magnanimous favor of China, the greater country. Second, that the old "cohong" system run out of Guangzhou (Canton) be abandoned. The cohong system strictly regulated European trade: merchants were denied direct access to China's market, and instead had to go through middlemen, which was costly and restrictive. From England's point of view, their demands were rational and fair. How did the Qianlong Emperor respond?

Reading: The Meaning of the Bound Feet of Chinese Women (Topical Essay)
The History of Women in China
Precisely when the practice of foot binding began in China we do not know. But it does appear to have started taking root during the fabulously wealthy yet geopolitically retiring Song Dynasty (960-1279). The Song was the dynasty that invented gunpowder, dazzled Marco Polo, and then fell in the Mongol invasions.

Before foot binding, women in China did whatever men did. They led armies, participated in war, rode horses, played polo, danced the Sogdian swirl, shot the bow and arrow, participated in official state functions, organized ribald drinking parties, openly patronized brothels, and displayed themselves proudly in public. Consider these pre-foot binding luminaries. Princess Pingyang led 70,000 warriors in 617 CE, playing a critical role in overthrowing the Sui Dynasty and founding the great Tang. China's most celebrated *femme fatale*, Yang Guifei (d. 756), is immortalized by her poetic genius, Bai Juyi (d. 846) wrote the *Song of Everlasting Sorrow (Chang Hen Ge)*. The poem describes her subtle beauty; yet Yang Guifei was not delicate, her activity was not stymied. Painter Qian Xuan (d. 1305) immortalizes her as a woman who would readily climb on a horse for a long ride, *Yang Guifei Mounting a Horse*. These are things subsequent Chinese "beauties" would not do. China's only female emperor, Wu Zetian (d. 705 CE), was pre-foot binding; she even founded her own dynasty, the Zhou (690-705)! Centuries later, in the post-foot binding era, even the singularly powerful Dowager Empress Ci Xi (d. 1908), who dominated politics in Qing China for decades, could not become emperor. Confucian scholars who ran the empire had become too suspicious of women. They would not countenance women holding power openly.

The First Six Hypotheses

There are many explanations for foot binding. Here are 13 hypotheses on its origins.

First, there is the idea of fashion disseminating from the elite down into the mainstream. In this particular telling, foot binding originated in the Five Dynasties and Ten Kingdoms period (900s CE), between the great Tang and Song Dynasties. The story is told that a certain emperor especially loved one particular dancing girl, who had tiny feet. Witnessing the favor that the emperor showered on this dancer, the other courtesans sought to emulate her small feet so as to win the favor of the emperor. They began binding their feet up. As elsewhere, the fashion proclivities of the elite are said to have trickled down to the rest of society. However, no evidence exists to prove that this story is true.

Second, some historians believe that there was a correlation between the rise of foot binding and economic growth. The Song Dynasty (960-1279) witnessed an economic revolution that gave rise to an unprecedented concentration of wealth and capital. The Song economy constituted a significant part of total global economic output. With this economic explosion, Song society witnessed the rise of outrageous conspicuous consumption. New concentrations of wealth enabled rich merchants to amass huge fortunes. However, possessing a mansion filled with beautiful objects was not enough. Some scholars hypothesize that this new wealth led to the commodification of women. In this scenario, the wealthy could afford to take a person who was generally required to have some practical function, and turn this person into an object. With bound feet, a woman could not work. Binding the feet thus turned that person into an object of beauty, without practical value, but having artistic and prestige value to the man.

Third, consider the relationship of Confucian morality to foot binding. In a nutshell, having bound feet was a way for a woman to prove her own virtue and chastity. In this scenario, with bound feet, it is difficult to go outside and get into trouble. With bound feet, women tended to stay indoors more, and when they ventured out, it was usually not by themselves, as they needed attendants to help them walk.

Fourth, Confucian morality also manifested anxiety regarding women's sexuality. Her confinement to the home meant that she would not be seen by other men outside the home and family.

Fifth, there is also a fetish argument. With all bodily obsessions, as with taste, and cultural behavior in general, there is a strong element of randomness. In different eras, society is attuned to different parts of the body. The adoration of one era will perplex another. During the late colonial American era, for example, men paraded their masculinity by displaying proudly their calf muscles. (Incidentally, today in Bhutan, the size of a man's calf is sometimes used to ascertain his health.) Without question, the problem of foot binding in China can hardly be separated from the idea of a foot fetish. Indeed, copious love poems address in graphic detail the spellbinding, erotic virtues of the foot, and that its constituent parts contain all the essential parts of the human body.

Erotic painting of the late imperial era also expressed this idea, that the foot was perceived as the most erotic part of the woman's body. In one painting, a man sits serenely on a rock in a garden, leaning against a tree, his pants down around his ankles. His penis is erect. This detail is front and center of the painting. Standing next to him is a woman, her clothing is loose and suggestive. We can see her vagina, but it's a minor detail of the painting, easily missed. The real action is this: her bound foot, still wrapped in formal garments, is planted on the man's thigh, just next to his erectness. This dominates the erotic painting. Her foot next to the man's erect body. It is clear that these are the erogenous zones of the human body that mattered. And for woman, that most sexualized part is the foot.

The beauty argument is the sixth hypothesis. In this scenario, the foot is not only erotic, it is aesthetically the most beautiful part of the body. Indeed, elderly women in China are on record as stating that they wanted their feet bound because, "we wanted to be beautiful." This sentiment was echoed by the women of the Manchu nation, which conquered the Ming (1388-1644) and established the Qing Dynasty (1644-1911). Once in China, Manchu women were forbidden from binding their feet because of the debilitating mutilation, another example of Manchu sensible pragmatism. However, Manchu women still wished to be beautiful. Instead of binding their feet they invented a shoe that mimicked the shape of the bound foot, the "horse-hoof" (*mati*) shoe.

The Seventh Through Thirteenth Hypotheses

Seventh, the natalist argument must be considered. According to the natalist hypothesis, the woman's body must perform one singularly important function: the reproduction of a male heir. All other concerns regarding the woman's body are secondary. Bear in mind that a woman's position in her husband's household was not secure until she gave birth to a son who survived. Failure to produce a son would become legal basis for a husband to divorce the wife. Even in the absence of divorce, a position of a childless wife in the family was badly compromised. Recall, too, that it was in the Song Dynasty that witnessed the rise of the OB/GYN specialty in China's medicine. We see intense social, and medical, attention focused on reproduction of a male heir. Thus, in this analysis, a woman's body, and its attendant reproductive capacity, is simply too important to be left for mere pleasure. Therefore, the site of erotic pleasure migrates to a different part of the body, in this case the foot.

Eight, there exists the anatomical or sexual pleasure argument. In this hypothesis, the bound foot forced a change in the way that women walked. The bound foot forced a woman to walk on her heels. In this analysis, the forced change in locomotion changed the muscular structure of the pelvis and inner thighs. This muscular transformation is said also to somehow transform the structure of the reproductive organs in a way that made sex more pleasurable for men.

The hypergamy argument offers a ninth explanation. In this hypothesis, mothers bound their daughter's feet as an act of love, to help them advance in the world. Hypergamy means "marrying up," and there is little disagreement that with the profound social valuation of small feet, a girl's chances for a "good marriage" could pivot on the size of her feet. The monumental Ming Dynasty novel, *Jin Ping Mei, The Plum in the Golden Vase* (1617), contains an explicit episode of this dynamic. A *Marriage Proposal*, takes place in the inner courtyard of an affluent gentleman's home. The spacious courtyard is well-appointed, showing all the signifying accoutrements of the man's elite station, his leisure, his refinement. Over an altar is a painting of the Goddess of Mercy, Guan Yin Bodhisattva. We see tasteful objects of art, a slice of a rare stone mounted on antique wood, elegant furniture, the large "strange stones" (*qishi*), rocks excavated from rivers or lakes, a Bonsai tree, and a maid attending to the guests with refreshments. At center stage is a granny (*laopo*), a well-connected busybody, resourceful, cynical, unscrupulous, and not to be trifled with. This granny is proffering a "bride," a young woman whose main allure the granny brazenly displays. Lifting up the woman's skirt, the granny reveals her small feet. The man can hardly conceal his lascivious glee at the prospect of a bride with small feet.

Tenth, there is the home-yarn-spinning-and-cloth-weaving-cottage-industry argument. In this hypothesis, foot binding was not about sex, concepts of marriage, beauty, nor Confucian oppression of women. Instead, it was about the labor requirements of the home spinning and weaving cottage industry. The rough contour of this argument is this: by crippling her daughter, a rural mother prevented the girl from running around outside. Thus, she could wring a bit more work out of her daughter, doing "hand work" at home such as spinning cotton, before the daughter married away, where she would continue this type of work. Support for this argument suggests that foot binding faded away at the precise time when mechanized spinning machines arrived in China, thus eliminating the need for home spinning labor. This argument is extremely depressing, nihilist even, yet might be bolstered by the harsh statement in some Chinese literature that daughters are a net loss because they will marry out and into someone else's family. Thus, the grim saying that one is raising "other people's daughters." Add to this poverty and life near the edge of destitution, which sometimes makes people take desperate measures. Bride burning in India, for example, the practice of murdering brides who fail to bring an adequate dowry to the marriage, is not widely practiced across society. The practice is focused in the social group that exists just above destitution, the lowest rung of the lower middle class. This low social group lives in constant fear of slipping into complete poverty, perhaps to the dissolution of the family. In the context of grinding poverty, the mutilation of a child's feet might appear as a practical tactic for the survival of the family.

Eleventh, we have the empowerment argument. In this scenario, foot binding constituted a realm controlled by women. Men were excluded from this space and women managed all aspects of the experience.

Twelfth, there exists the preparation for the difficult life of a woman argument. Life as a laboring daughter-in-law and then a toiling mother promised to be arduous. In one analysis, the terrible pain of foot binding prepared girls for the harsh life of womanhood. In this scenario, surviving the torture of the bound foot showed toughness, in the same way that smallpox scars from surviving the disease showed a robust constitution and likelihood of enduring the hardships of adulthood.

Thirteenth, let us examine the hypocrisy argument; Confucian hypocrisy, that is. As a philosophy, as guiding principles for living, Confucianism demanded a rigorous, hard-to-uphold moral code. In this scenario, the aspiring Confucian gentleman, unable to adhere consistently to benevolence and virtue, forced women to adhere to ever stricter moral and ethical standards, thus fulfilling his duty as a proper gentleman, allowing himself to be free to pursue what he desired. An added contradiction, or perhaps hypocrisy, is the Confucian tenant against body mutilation. An age-old idea, coming down from the late classical age, was that the body was a gift from one's parents, and should not be casually damaged. The Buddhist practice of shaving the head is a violation of this idea and thus lent some resistance to men becoming monks. This value remains potent today, seen in social resistance to blood and organ donation and the disapproval of tattoos and related body art.

When the Qing Dynasty collapsed in 1911, it brought down with it practices and attitudes holding on from the past. The imperial exam ceased to exist, men stopped shaving the front on their heads and growing a queue down the back. To their credit, the early Qing rulers had attempted to outlaw foot binding in the 17th century, but had failed. The deep-rooted practice was finally outlawed in the first year of the ill-fated Republic, in 1912. Women in cities stopped binding their feet. The countryside was another matter. The centuries-old practice continued in some regions, down to the late 1940s, and in some places, even later. Thus, even today, one can occasionally encounter elderly women with bound feet, though this is becoming rare. The updated legal code of 1935, *The Criminal Code of the Republic of China*, contained indirectly worded prohibitions against foot binding.

After 1949, women were fully enfranchised in the new constitution of the Communist People's Republic of China, with important rights such as being able to choose a marriage partner. The slogan, "Women hold up half the sky," popularized the official position that women could no longer be excluded from the mainstream, that one half of the population must no longer be crippled.

Reading: The Long 19th Century in China, 1793-1919

Britain's problem in its relations with China was centuries-old, and other merchant states shared its grievances. Even during the Ming Dynasty, hundreds of years in the past, European traders sourly nicknamed China the "silver coffin." It was where money flowed to, and it stayed there, falling out of circulation. A stunning one-half of the all the silver mined in the Americas ended up in China's coffers. In the European system, ideal trade involved barter, the exchange of objects, such as Great Britain's wool for China's silk, and not a unilateral flow of money. The problem was people in China preferred wearing silk to wool. Britain was, therefore, forced to pay cash for silk. Qianlong's negative response to British requests, therefore, did not entirely surprise Lord Macartney. The emperor denied British ideas of trade graciously: he sent food from his table and bestowed parting gifts upon the embassy. Yet Qianlong's famous reply, translated and carried across the globe, rang haughty to George III's ears: what Britain seeks is "a useless undertaking; we have everything we need." Whether Qing China possessed everything it needed is a moot point. What it did indisputably possess was what Britain and other nations sought. And that was tea.

Opium for Tea

Tea was the culprit. British consumers loved it too much. Consider this: the typical British household spent five to ten percent of its annual budget on tea. This level of expenditure is akin to what contemporary Americans spend on health care or food or transportation. British society was so addicted to the hot beverage that the British parliament passed a law compelling the British East India Company to store in its warehouses one year's supply of tea in order to meet national demand in the event of a disruption of the supply from Asia. This reveals the same logic behind the Strategic Petroleum Reserve in the United States or the Strategic Pork Reserve in China: tea was essential to the normal functioning of British society.

Tea from China was legendary, and the British spun tall tales about all aspects of its procurement. In one fantasy, resourceful villagers in China trained monkeys to pick tea leaves. Less humorous to the British was the resulting trade imbalance. Merchants were desperate for a product that would sell in China so that they could stop spending so much silver for tea. The solution: opium.

Opium, however, does not grow in Great Britain, the climate is not right. But it does grow in India, then a British colony. The opium solution, then, would not only wreak havoc in China, it also laid waste to large portions of Indian agriculture which were turned over to opium production, a cash crop for export. This immiserated and starved large numbers of Indian farmers, a factor in what one scholar terms, "Victorian holocausts."

The opium scheme proceeded in the following fashion. First, the British East India Company (BEIC) established a monopoly over opium production, largely in Bengal. Then, it exported the product on ships to the very southern reaches of the Qing empire, deep in the south near Guangzhou, and later Hong Kong, far from the political center in the north. An illegal item, the BEIC off-loaded the opium onto smaller vessels, either traffickers from China's underworld, or other foreign agency houses, such as the company Matheson Jardine, the largest importer of opium into China, which then smuggled the drug into China via the myriad small waterways that laced this part of the country and were difficult to police.

By 1800, on average, two million pounds of opium entered China each year. American firms in China such as Russell & Co. also sold opium on a massive scale. But American merchants enjoyed a slight advantage, for they enjoyed access to three items that the beau-monde, or elite, in Qing China desired: Spanish bullion, ginseng (from the Appalachian Mountains), and furs, especially sea otter pelts, from the American northwest. However, with its new product, the British did not require plants or pelts. By the 1820s, the illegal opium trade was paying for all the tea purchased from China bound for Great Britain.

The Qing state viewed opium as a grave problem. Outlawing the drug had failed, as did trade retaliation, such as in 1821, when tea exports were suspended. None of it stemmed the opium tide, which was harming Qing society in diverse ways. Fiscally, the unprecedented flow of silver out of the country emptied coffers, triggering a destabilizing inflation. Addiction to the drug-plagued transport workers, police, soldiers, city dwellers, and officials. Bureaucratic corruption followed opium profits. Public service posters militated against the drug, admonishing communities with dramatic illustrations.

A painting of the time, *Decline of an Opium Smoker*, for example, narrated the heart-rending injury that opium addiction provoked. In this painting, a dignified grandmother beats her wastrel son with a cane while the agitated grandfather looks on. The addict's virtuous wife destroys his opium pipe with a kitchen cleaver. A traumatized child weeps as the family falls apart. Broken items lay on the ground. Opium shatters a family, just as it promises to destroy the nation.

In Great Britain, the opium trade was not occurring in a moral vacuum, it had divided public opinion. Large numbers of Britons perceived the opium business as pure wickedness. A debate raged in both the House of Commons, and it finally came to a vote: Should the opium trade be banned? It was a close ballot. By a single vote, parliament voted to allow the trade to continue.

In 1837, opium smuggled into China reached three million pounds. The Qing court of the Daoguang Emperor (1782-1850) had decided to take a new type of action.

The First Opium War (1839-42)

Commissioner Lin Zexu was both erudite and morally upright, an impeccable choice to carry out the Daoguang Emperor's vision of ending the opium blight once and for all. Sent from Beijing, the formidable and respected official arrived at faraway Guangzhou (Canton) in 1839. Imperially commissioned, he set about arresting over one thousand Chinese drug dealers and destroyed thousands of opium pipes. But Commissioner Lin's attempts to negotiate with the foreign merchants came to naught, even after offering to exchange their opium for tea. So, he forced them to surrender their warehouses of opium. The agent of the throne then destroyed it in a highly public manner. His small army of workers adulterated the two million pounds of confiscated opium with lime and washed it out to sea, apologizing to the ocean deities for polluting their dominion.

Commissioner Lin also wrote an open letter to Queen Victoria, wondering rhetorically if it was not hypocritical for a principled monarch as herself to allow her subjects to poison another nation for filthy lucre. Even if the commissioner's letter had reached the Queen, it is unlikely to have quelled the frenzied rage of the foreign merchants whose treasured opium had been so horrifically desecrated and flushed away. Keep in mind that a man could be hung for simple theft in Victorian England. The stealing that Commissioner Lin was accused of was an act of war.

And war he got, though this clearly was neither his intention nor the Qing court's. A state-of-the-art British ironclad warship, the *Nemesis*, attacked Qing war junks. Importantly, this very war vessel that helped decimate the Qing fleet was not of Great Britain's Royal Navy; it was part of an enormous private army controlled by the BEIC. (Imagine if American companies who did international trade such as Halliburton, Exxon, or Verizon maintained their own private armies.) The *Nemesis* had been constructed in secret and kept off the BEIC's list of ships, evidently commissioned for the purpose of smuggling opium into China.

The ship's shallow draught enabled it to travel up small Chinese rivers. In war, the ship's design proved useful at pursuing smaller vessels into shallow waters, as did its deadly armament. Eventually, the British state joined in the fray in earnest and China and Britain bloodied each other over the course of several years. In the end, however, Britain's victory was categorical. China's defeat in 1842 marked a profound, tectonic shift in China's modern history. China's loss of the Opium War brought on a geopolitical dark age.

The Advantages of the European Nation-States

The defeat brought about much soul-searching in China. A much smaller nation that had deployed its forces halfway around the world laid bare deep structural problems within the Qing imperium. At the very least, European military technology had long surpassed China's. True, China boasted key military innovations of global significance. It had invented gunpowder, the first iron-barreled gunpowder weapon, multi-stage rocketry, land and water mines, the first semi-automatic weapon (a crossbow), the flamethrower (powered by the double action piston bellows), as well as an array of technically advanced defensive weapons, such as the geophone that detected the acoustic footprint of enemy tunneling, and delivery systems to send poison gas into those tunnels, to name only the most conspicuous inventions. There was even evidence that the British ship design that had defeated China had borrowed from Chinese technology.

However, for the previous centuries, endemic warfare in Europe had produced paradigm shifting military advances, on land and sea. The rise of Napoleon and the wars against his grand army accelerated this phenomenon. By comparison, the once unstoppable early Qing military had stagnated; it was antiquated, outgunned, and outmaneuvered. However serious was this military weakness, the Qing suffered an even more problematic disadvantage vis-à-vis the newly powerful European nations. Deep structural problems in the Qing state dated to its origin in the mid-17th century.

Two global crises had rocked much of the mid-17th-century world: a worldwide cooling, a "mini- ice age," and a global monetary crisis. Both had shaken societies from Ming China to Cromwellian England. The chaos and upheaval forced traditional European dominions, the ancient régime, to restructure, and they emerged as much more efficient nation-states, able to mobilize resources on an unprecedented scale. This was seen in the state's new ability to tax the populace, to conscript troops, and to exploit natural resources, such as coal. The western nation-states' restructuring enabled them to harness the more limited resources of their smaller countries much more efficiently, to punch above their weight, seen for example, in the fielding of national armies, funded by streamlined taxation, supported by newly exploited resources.

China's passage through the turbulent 17th century yielded a very different type of solution. In a nutshell, when the Ming Dynasty collapsed, the Manchus did exactly the opposite of their European counterparts. They fixed the system (that broke elsewhere). The Manchus rescued the old Confucian monarchy, resuscitated it, making it run even better. However, and this is key, the Manchus intentionally avoided the type of centralizing institutions that would enable, for instance, the fielding of a national army. The Manchus viewed such a capacity as dangerous: given their minority-as-rulers position, it might be turned against them. (Interestingly, a later Chinese leader, Chiang Kai-shek, the leader of the Nationalists who lost to the Communists in the 1940s, grappled with an analogous dilemma.)

Thus, after the reestablishment of social order by the end of the 1600s, the Manchus spread their military power thin, allowing large forces to be amassed only when required by specific emergencies. After a crisis passed, the forces were dispersed back to separate localities. Not constructing a national army (that they feared would turn against them), backfired when the Qing were faced with powerful European armies and navies.

Qing ability to mobilize nationally was further thwarted by its limited tax infrastructure. The freezing of taxes in 1712, at the time a humanitarian act, severely hampered Qing efforts to concentrate resources in times of crisis. Corruption plagued bureaucratic China, too, for a related reason. The high Qing emperors had also frozen the number of officials who could serve. Thus, an "unofficial" bureaucracy emerged; it was tolerated by officialdom because it undertook much of the day-to-day work of the empire. These myriad jobs did not officially exist and thus were unsalaried. The men carrying out the work, then, found their own means of support through bribes, gifts, skimming, and a slew of other well-established practices. It was corruption, yet to function, the system required it.

Mid 19th-Century Disasters

Other early Qing successes also morphed into ecological disasters. Opening up marginal land, on hillsides, for example, initially increased the amount of food being produced. After several generations, though, the terraced hillsides began to erode. In north China, eroded soil flowed down the denuded hillsides into streams that fed the mighty Yellow River. The amount of particulate-dissolved soil in the river at times reached 50 percent of total volume. The river smashed through dikes and whipsawed across the North China Plain. Catastrophic flooding inundated so much arable land that many farmers simply abandoned agriculture and took up fishing. Others took up banditry.

The 19th century also witnessed exceptionally damaging weather, specifically the El Niño Southern Oscillation (ENSO), which parched the earth and caused drought-induced famines. Areas not stricken by famine still coped with extreme weather, combined with overuse of the land. Visitors to rural areas in the north reported seeing farmers sweep dust off the streets and place it back on the fields. Heavy use was exhausting the land's fertility; it also stressed social relations. Many places witnessed three levels of ownership of a single tract of land. The deep soil belonged to an absentee landlord; the subsoil belonged to local landowner; and the surface, was the responsibility of a tenant farmer.

Population growth, resulting from successes of the 18th century, put additional strain on existing arable land. A long-term demographic phenomenon ensued, sometimes expressed as the High Level Equilibrium Trap. The trap expresses the process by which a highly efficient system of farming collapsed under the demographic strain of the 19th and early 20th centuries. In essence, rice agriculture in China benefited from intensive labor. Thus, as China's population went from 100 million to 300 million, the land absorbed labor efficiently and generated an agricultural surplus that supported the burgeoning population. The larger population, in turn, turned its labor to the land. However, at a certain point, no matter how much labor was invested in farming, the land reached a point of diminishing returns.

Tragically, China's demographic momentum pushed the population up to 400 million by the mid-19th century. The resource base was simply unable to support the population. People ended up working for less than subsistence wages. This situation provoked despair, starvation, famine, outbursts of social violence, and civil war. Such was the stressed economic, social, and environmental situation when the bellicose and powerful new enemy, the British, crushed the Qing military.

The Beginnings of British New Colonialism
The British had shrewdly sailed their warships up the coast, bombarding vulnerable fortresses. Their close proximity to the Beijing imperial court caused panic, and the Qing finally sued for peace — anything to get the invaders to return to the malarial south where they belonged, far from the capital. The subsequent Treaty of Nanjing (1842) reads like an obituary for Qing sovereignty. It was the first of many succeeding "unequal treaties" to be imposed on China by violence. It established the original architecture of foreign interference with and penetration into China. Consider its major points.

To uphold the new treaty system, Great Britain, and then other countries that joined in, deployed brutal gunboat diplomacy. Because the Yangzi River was large enough to accommodate ocean-going vessels, large warships could pull alongside major cities that resisted British colonialism, such as Nanjing, and blast away at civilians, sometimes massacring thousands, until the offending official or state agency backed down. Dissatisfied with trade and access, a Second Opium War was waged from 1856 to 1860. This time the British allied with the French. The grim legacy of the Opium Wars continues to haunt the Chinese public and state imagination to this very day.

The many capitulations to the British and other powers was a source of great resentment among the common people of China. British imperial policy, the weakness of the Qing emperors, and the many famines and ecological disasters partly inspired a massive rebellion and civil war in China between the Qing state and rebels called Taipings, who wanted a social and moral invigoration of

Chinese society along Christian principles, along with the overthrow of the Qing Dynasty. The Taiping Rebellion lasted 15 years, from 1850 through 1864.

Qing Attempts at "Self-Strengthening"

The dynasty survived the Taiping Rebellion; however, the 15-year conflict killed upwards of 30 million people and devastated the economy. Entire areas of the country were laid to waste, devoid of people. The mid-century disasters broke the imperial back of the Qing dynasty. Yet from the 1860s to the 1890s, it optimistically pursued a policy of "self-strengthening," with the aim of catching up to the wildly powerful nations of the West. Much of the vision and heavy lifting was carried out by ambitious, capable provincial officials given a new type of autonomy from the throne. Chinese officials such as Li Hongzhang loyally served the Qing imperium as he built arsenals and shipyards, often employing foreign expertise and deploying foreign weapons systems. The first Sino-Japanese War of 1894-5 put the new tools of "self-strengthening" to the test.

The entire world had been following the events leading up to the hostilities between China and Japan. Both countries had acquired state-of-the-art weapons and ships from Germany, France, and Great Britain. The European powers watched to see how the weapons systems performed in battle. (A similar phenomenon happened in the Cold War a century later, when the US and USSR watched conflicts among allied states; for example in the Middle East, when Israel used American weapons against the USSR-backed Syrians.) Meiji Japan's decisive victory over Qing China in 1895 dealt an incalculable blow, both politically and psychologically. Not only had decades of self-strengthening failed, it had been by the hand of Japan, which China perceived as a much junior partner in East Asia.

Self-strengthening had been hobbled by a conceptual burden, summarized as "Chinese essence, Western tools." The main idea was to borrow the useful technology from Western civilization while maintaining the core Confucian essence of Chinese society. Yet to genuinely "modernize," to catch up, China's reforms would require a much more totalistic approach. Meiji Japan, in its own modernization program, had not made this mistake. And acting as the Europeans had, Japan wrested commercial advantages from China and exacted an immense war indemnity — 8,000 tons of silver (five billion USD today). This disbursement ended China's military modernization efforts, while it funded Japan's efforts to push ahead. Japan also annexed Taiwan, and other Chinese territories, which it colonized until 1945.

Turn-of-the-Century Turmoil

In 1895, the Qing began sending Chinese students to Japan, for intensive study, aiming to learn what Japan had clearly learned: foreign technical and organizational know-how. The Qing, however, continued to misread geopolitics. At the turn of the century, the Boxer Rebellion (1899-1901) erupted. An organization called the Society of the Righteous and Harmonious Fists, rebelled against the foreigners, killing missionaries and their converts in the countryside, and then foreigners everywhere. The Qing state initially opposed the boxers but then took their side, in a misguided hope of riding the anarchic millenarian violence to victory over the foreign powers. All it did was aggravate foreign aggression in China. In 1900, the combined foreign powers marched into Beijing, eight nations in all. At that point they could have easily toppled the Qing Dynasty; yet they did not. It was better for business to keep a weakened Qing on the throne, preserving the status quo of a China that could not defend itself against foreign demands and aggression.

After the utter catastrophe of the Boxer Rebellion, a chastened Qing attempted to reform itself more systemically, in the first decade of the 20th century. They did enjoy some wins, such as controlling a devastating epidemic of plague in the far northwest, under the brilliant direction of Malaysian-born, Dr. Wu Liande. But this was followed by humiliation, as Imperial Russia and Imperial Japan fought the Russo-Japanese War of 1904-5 on Chinese territory, as if China's government already did not exist. The Qing could do nothing about it.

The Early Chinese Republic

In the final analysis, the reforms were too little, too late and all the new policies did was to elevate expectations the enervated state could not meet. Private societies, many with Western-educated leaders, such as Dr. Sun Yat-sen, agitated for regime change. In 1911, the "Xinhai" Revolution basically ended the Qing Dynasty. Sun Yat-sen was elected "provisional president" of the new Chinese Republic but in 1912 was forced to abdicate to Yuan Shikai, who controlled the largest army in the country. Militarist Yuan Shikai had served the Qing too long to be fully invested in electoral politics, and in 1915 he attempted to install himself as emperor, even riding to the Temple of Heaven for his investiture in an armored car. Upon his death in 1916, there was no other strong man who could hold things together and the fledgling republic broke into regional satrapies run by military magnates, and then into full-blown warlords.

In World War I (1914-8), China sided with the Allies, sending 140,000 carefully selected men to work as stretcher bearers, trench diggers, transporters of munitions on the European battlefields. When the war ended, at the Versailles Peace Conference, China sat with the victors. In 1919, China reasonably expected that the German-occupied territories in China, in and around Qingdao, would be returned to its control. After all, Germany had lost the war and was losing all of its colonies. Instead, in what was an intensely hurtful and disappointing backroom betrayal, Japan was awarded Germany's former territories in China.

The decision at Versailles had global consequences. First, outrage in China reached a fever pitch. For the first time, mainstream people who generally stayed out of politics took to the streets in what became a massive, nation-wide protest, igniting what is loosely known as the May Fourth Movement. This was the birth of mass nationalism in China. Second, the irresponsible behavior of the victorious nations at Versailles left many students, intellectuals, leaders, and political figures in China disillusioned with the western democracies. It was a significant factor that nudged China towards Communism, with implications for China's future that were profound.

Reading: The Meiji Restoration
The Challenge to the Japanese
Japan observed the disturbing events on Asia's mainland with trepidation. Starting in 1839, invading foreigners had shattered the Qing military and forcibly rewritten the law of China's Qing Dynasty. If these upstart, dangerous foreigners, the British, so handily defeated the mighty Qing state, imposing an alien and humiliating treaty structure on China, what would befall Japan, a much smaller country? In terms of territory, the Qing Empire was larger than the United States is today with a population of 300 million. Japan was smaller than the state of California with a population of 30 million. There was little question that "the British were coming;" it was only a matter of when, and how many other nations would pile on pressure, just as they would be piling it on in China. Recall that by 1900, the armies of eight nations marched on and then occupied the Qing capital of Beijing, causing the imperial court ignominiously to flee the city. How could the Tokugawa government avoid such a disaster?

Tokugawa Japan was thus geopolitically insulated as the British ripped apart the Qing order a mere five hundred miles away, the distance from San Francisco to San Diego. As China had done, but for different reasons, Japan had not kept up militarily, and would be outgunned if they engaged in any conflict with the new European powers. Precisely the opposite to Europe's endemic warfare, which had driven its rapid technical and military progress, Tokugawa's prolonged peace, the very absence of war, engendered a bloodless new martial art. This was the practice of Kendo, the martial art of bamboo sword fighting, as a way to maintain fighting skills in the absence of actual conflict. In addition, in other areas, the long Tokugawa prosperity witnessed important social advances.

For starters, Tokugawa society enjoyed exceptionally high levels of literacy, which nurtured a well-developed culture of reading. High literacy would prove key to Japan's rapid modernization. The economy, moreover, was regionally integrated and cities such as Edo (Tokyo) and Kyoto hosted sophisticated urban cultures, with widespread curiosity about foreign science and technology. Add to this, despite its official disengagement from the outside world, the Tokugawa leadership maintained excellent intelligence on nearby events in China. Even Japan's written language was designed to accommodate the absorption of new and foreign ideas as neologisms, or new words One of its three writing systems, Japan's phonetic alphabet *katakana*, was designated solely for the translation of foreign ideas. These and other factors would contribute profoundly to the speed and success of Japan's headlong bid for modernization when Japan turned to that purpose. A forceful push came in 1853, with the uninvited and unwelcome arrival of the American naval commander, Matthew Perry.

The Reformers and Their Plan

The reformers who incited war were upstarts in the exact meaning of the word. They hailed from provincial domains remote from central power, Satsuma and Chōshū, territories located in the far southwest of the country, closer to Korea than to Kyoto. Alienated from the power structure, these determined men, largely in their 20s, used their modern, foreign weapons to defeat a punitive expedition sent by the Tokugawa Shogunate in 1866. They had acquired this firepower with funds from clandestine trade with the Ryukyu island kingdom, to Japan's south, which China claimed as a tributary state. The final battle of the Boshin War of 1867-68 took place off the shores of Hokkaido, the northernmost island, near a French design-inspired star fortress originally built to counter Russian expansion. The imported weapons used by the new Meiji army proved decisive in their defeat of the Tokugawa loyalists, including a Gatling gun and an ironclad ram warship, built surreptitiously in the shipyards of Napoleon III, originally bound for the Confederate side of the US Civil War. As far as civil conflicts go, the Boshin War was relatively short with several thousand casualties. At the time, observers expressed relief, it could have been much worse.

The men of Satsuma and Chōshū, such as Itō Hirobumi, justified their campaign under the rubric of centralizing power in the imperial institution, in the person of the emperor. Indeed, the centralization of power had been a key aspect of European modernization. But the ambitions of what became known as the "Meiji Restoration" (from 1868) were much more far-reaching. Their goal: quickly open up and modernize Japan so that it could survive in the brave new world of aggressive, violent, well-organized nation-states coming out of Europe and North America. It involved a totalistic reformulation of Japan's economy, social structure, military, education system, culture, body politic, and even identity, how to dress, behave, speak.

With great intensity, the new Meiji (1868-1912) leadership set about radically remaking Japanese society. The samurai, a millennium-old group integral to the existing order, were stripped of their special legal status of carrying weapons in public. More critically, the samurai were divested of their prerogative to enforce the law when they perceived it being broken. Inherited attitudes, though, did not necessary metamorphose as nimbly as official policy, and the Meiji authorities militated against lingering respect for the disenfranchised warriors.

To this end, in 1875 the state published a public service message aiming to guide people towards modernity, advising how to be, how to fashion identity. In the publicly posted image, three figures stand side by side. The first figure is a samurai, wearing a sword, traditional garb, and straw sandals. The caption over his head reads: "unenlightened." The second man is "half enlightened." He wears a mass-produced cap, totes a Western-style umbrella, and in one hand holds a pocket watch. The watch is an important detail: it bespeaks "internalized" time, as opposed to externally experienced time, such as responding to a town bell or a clock tower. Internalized time was vital to modern industrial life. External time meant rising with the sun and working according to the seasons, an agricultural mode of existence. Internalized time, on the other hand, carrying time and experiencing it individually until it merged with one's consciousness, was essential to industrialization and capitalism, which required efficiency, productivity, and precision. To achieve these ambitious goals, for Japan to survive, the new Meiji citizen must internalize time. The third man is "enlightened." He sports a top hat, Western clothes, a walking stick, leather shoes, and a moustache. He even walks a dog, which itself is walking upright. The message: be dignified and modern, not backwards and uncivilized, as the old samurai.

The Meiji leadership deployed fact-finding missions to Europe, such as the Iwakura Embassy, which from 1871 to 1873 traveled through European capitals, studying how society, government, and education was organized in those impressive powerful countries. The Embassy returned to Japan with ideas, impressions, proposals, conceptual blueprints. Meiji promulgated a new constitution and legal system, constructed on European models (deciding that the American one was too democratic). European governments took note of Japan's conscious emulation of its institutions, and they liked it. Although racism ran deep and remained an impediment to normal relations, there was something of a "you're one of us now" attitude in European capitals. Add to this: Europeans were not interested in Japan as an object of plunder. In the 19th century, power was measured in territory. The big prizes were the Ottoman Empire, India, Africa, and China. Japan was territorially small and possessed no discernable resources of interest. Plus, unlike China, rivers in Japan were shallow and thus not navigable by large vessels. This rendered any penetration of the country more difficult. The result of all of this is that Japan suffered little of the aggression and violence that Europeans visited on places such as China and India. Indeed, Meiji's problems would come from within.

Loosening class restrictions, and the attendant end of the samurai class, was designed to liberate Japan's citizens into modernity, to free up potential for development and discovery. For some samurai, though, the losses proved too much to bear, including the once energetic leaders of Meiji, such as the formidable Saigō Takamori. The "last samurai" rebelled against the Meiji state and his onetime comrades in arms, in the Saigō Rebellion of 1877. However, the proud warriors were brutally defeated by the new national army's conscript troops, the "dirt farmers" whom the warriors looked down upon. Efficiently transported to the battlefield in large numbers by the new railways, the conscripts and their officers brought to bear the killing machines of modern warfare: artillery with exploding shells and accurate rifles. And common conscripts were now better educated.

Education became compulsory, and by 1900 the country had achieved nearly 100 percent in basic literacy. Foreign advisors were retained to develop industry, banks, infrastructure, universities, factories, shipyards, and arsenals. With rapid industrialization, Japan began mass producing silk, becoming a competitor with China. The sewing machine emerged as a powerful symbol of transformation of daily life. By late Meiji, circa early 1900s, women spoke on telephones and rode bicycles in the countryside. As in Europe and elsewhere, the bicycle lent considerable freedom from parents and neighbors, and became tied to the idea of sexual freedom. Dirigibles could be seen flying over hectic marketplaces, messages were cabled via telegraph, people studied foreign languages, wrote with fountain pens, read bound books, and dressed in mass-produced textiles. The pace and texture of life was "modern."

Japan's Meiji modernization project also contained a robust weapons program. A mass-produced woodblock print from 1889 portrays urban citizens strolling leisurely on a Sunday afternoon, watching the demonstration of a water mine explode in the water nearby. This print exemplifies that the issue of national security, building up military and the science of war, became a mainstream issue, popularly recognized in Meiji society. Indeed, compulsory military service for men was broadly accepted. And Japan's military achievement was impressive. A pioneer in ship-based aviation, by the 1930s Japan boasted the best carrier pilots in the world. Japan was not simply emulating the dominant nations of the age; in key areas, Japan was leading. (In science, too, Japan began to innovate; the jet stream, for example, was discovered by Wasaburo Oishi).

Perhaps the best way to grasp the enormity of the Meiji Restoration is this: it's still being scrutinized today as an efficient model of development for emerging countries. And the sweeping transformation not only remade Japanese society, it also rocked the geopolitical order. Consider that in 1853 Commodore Perry refused to bow an inch from the waist. Yet, half a century later in 1906, the grandson of Queen Victoria herself, Prince Arthur, kneeled at the feet of the Meiji Emperor, solemnly presenting him with a jealously guarded royal honor, the Order of the Garter.

Not since the age of Chinggis Khan had people west of the Urals performed such humility in the presence of an Asian monarch, when Russian aristocrats kissed the spurs of Mongol overlords or when Marco Polo (in his telling) prostrated before Kublai Khan. What inspired the mighty British Empire to bestow upon the Meiji Emperor an honor that to this day no person in North America has ever received? Succinctly: Japan's defeat of Russia in 1905.

The Emergence of Reformed Japan

The Russo-Japanese War of 1904-05 was an astonishing exclamation that Japan had, in fact, achieved "modernization." Ten years prior, Japan had crashed the East Asia political order by defeating the great Qing Empire on land and at sea in the First Sino-Japanese War of 1894-95. Few observers predicted that outcome, least of all China, which itself was coming off 30 years of self-strengthening, which alas, proved a failure. Japan's defeat of Russia in 1905 was even more astounding to the audience of international powers. The war was hard fought and horrifically costly in men and money, to both sides. Tsarist Russia sent men along the freshly laid Trans-Siberian railway into what became described in St. Petersburg as the "meat grinder" of northeast Asian battlefields. The fighting on land was brutal, such as the nightmarish Battle of Mukden (Shenyang), which saw 600,000 soldiers clash, the largest land battle fought before World War I. The sea battle, on the other hand, started and ended in one day.

Russia's ill-fated Baltic Fleet had spent six disaster-laden months sailing around the globe, to reach the war. Early in the journey, in the North Sea, the jumpy fleet had attacked a group of fishing trawlers, mistaking them for Japanese torpedo boats. England used this mishap to deny use of the Suez Canal, forcing the Russian fleet to circumnavigate Africa, adding thousands of miles to the voyage. England also shared military intelligence with Japan. When the Russian fleet finally reached the Straits of Tsushima between Japan and Korea, Admiral Tōgō Heihachirō sprang a devastating ambush, annihilating the Baltic Fleet and destroying any hope Russia harbored of winning the war. Of Russia's 36 warships in the battle, only three escaped. At the time, this was the largest pre-Dreadnought naval battle in history. And the international community capitalized on the opportunity to dissect the relative merits of competing weapons systems in the conflict.

The fighting, however, was also destabilizing to the global order, and collective relief at its conclusion was expressed by awarding Theodore Roosevelt the Nobel Peace Prize for presiding over the Treaty of Portsmouth that ended the conflict. Indeed, the Russo-Japanese War was so bitter, costly, and disruptive that it played a role in precipitating the Russian revolution of 1905. Japan, on the other hand, experienced an incalculable boost in the international community.

Japan's victory over Tsarist Russia also transformed the Meiji state's image of itself, in ways that played out with global significance over the next half century. For decades leading up to the turn of the 20th century, an idea in philosophical circles had been circulating in Japan, summed up as *datsu-a ron*, meaning, "throwing off Asia," or "leaving Asia." The idea was that in light of the radical changes wrought by the Meiji Restoration, Japan was no longer part of Asia. Rather, it was closer to Europe, still something distinct, not European, but unquestionably not "Asian." During the 1895 and 1905 wars, first with China and then with Russia, dynamic, color images widely circulated in the print media showing variations on this theme.

In battle, Japan's troops showed moral superiority, to wit, the Japanese officer who saved a Chinese child as he battled Chinese troops. ("Even in heat of battle we show humanitarian love"). (Though it is not entirely clear how carrying the baby into battle actually is a rescue). We witness Japan's troops physically overpower Russian troops in hand-to-hand combat. In sea battles, Japan's warships destroyed a hapless enemy ("Sending Russian ships to the bottom of the sea"). Moreover, in these images the facial features, body habitus, and overall appearance of Japan's officers and diplomats become indistinguishable from their European and Russian counterparts. Chinese officials, conversely, are portrayed as obsequious, bent, fawning, old-world, humiliated, not merely trounced militarily but morally crushed. After the victory over Russia in 1905, the idea of *datsu-a ron*, of throwing off Asia, pushed into the mainstream, to the level of state policy.

A state-sponsored idea of Japan's moral and physical superiority continued to grow in political and military-industrial circles. By the 1930s, it morphed into something powerful, and dangerous, the Great East Asia Co-prosperity Sphere. In this formulation, Japan was the only (righteous) force capable of liberating Asia from European and American imperialism. Once Asia was liberated from colonial occupation, it would thrive collectively under Japan's aegis. Japan's subsequent invasion of China and Southeast Asia and the attack on the United States in 1941 ended in horrific catastrophe, for virtually all sides. However, and this fact is obscured by the violence and suffering of the war, Japan did achieve the dismantling of European colonial holdings in the Pacific and Southeast Asia.

From this perspective -- Japan prying colonies away from the imperialists and then colonizing the areas themselves -- we can see that the Meiji Restoration set Japan on a path of not only emulating European institutions governing society, education, the economy, and the military. It also began a trend of emulating the distinct paradigm of European colonial imperialism which had done much to structure the modern world. And Japan's decolonization and then recolonization of Asian territories began well before the world war of the late 1930s and 1940s, before the idea of the Great East Asia Co-prosperity Sphere.

In 1895, under the Treaty of Shimonoseki, Meiji Japan hewed Taiwan from Qing China, which itself had only colonized the island in the 17th and 18th centuries, following attempts by Holland and Spain. In 1910, Japan annexed Korea, having earlier cleaved it from China's sphere of influence. Then, in 1914 at the outbreak of the First World War, Japan seized Germany's colonial possessions in China at Qingdao. The control of these possessions were then formalized by the Treaty of Versailles in 1919, which inflamed public opinion in China. In 1914, Japan also captured Germany's island possessions in the South Pacific. Germany had come late to the colonial game, and it had purchased the Pacific islands from the Spanish Empire, as it collapsed under American onslaught. These marginally significant islands, including Saipan and the Marianas, brought Japan deep into the Pacific; they became major battlegrounds between Japan and the US.

In 1931, Japan invaded and then colonized China's Manchuria, an immense, strategic, and resource-rich territory. This paradigm of development was invented in Lisbon and Amsterdam and then expanded by London, Paris, Moscow, and Washington. It was the murderous conflagration that became the Pacific War (1937-45), as World War II is known in Japan, and witnessed the global working out of this path of development that for Japan had begun with the Meiji Restoration.

Overview of Era 8: Order and Disorder, 1900-present

Joshua Weiner, American River College

At the outset of the 20th century, humanity's mastery over the Earth was greater than ever. Science was increasingly cracking the mysteries of nature, technology was growing by leaps and bounds, and seas, mountains, jungles, and deserts were less and less significant as real barriers to human communication and interaction. Indeed, much good would come through this emergent mastery, but even as there were some positive developments, the legacies of history can never be truly escaped. The modern world was, after all, constructed on a shaky 19th-century foundation of unprecedented imperialism, increased nationalistic fervor, deep-seated racial ideas, and a hyper-competitive system of industrial capitalism. Add to this were ideological struggles among conservatives who sought to preserve an old (mostly imagined) order, liberals who thought that progress could best be achieved through incremental political change, and radicals who believed that real social progress could only come through revolution. Thus, even as incredible technical and scientific feats would mark the century, such feats were not necessarily accompanied by the growth of wisdom. This point was eloquently made by the great Indonesian nationalist Sukarno in his address to the 1955 Bandung Conference, when he asked about the progress achieved in the first half of the 20th century:

"[H]as man's political skill marched hand-in-hand with his technical and scientific skill? ...The answer is No! The political skill of man has been far outstripped by technical skill, and what he has made he cannot be sure of controlling."

For all our achievements, therefore, humans proved incapable of constructing a stable world order within an increasingly globalized world. Ironically, many of the most concerted attempts to establish order helped create conditions that contributed to disorder. European alliances meant to maintain borders and protect national interests ended up helping to precipitate World War I. Imperial policies intended to construct order in colonies instead exacerbated tensions among colonized people and led in to civil war and even genocide in some post-colonial nations. A global economic order based on free trade had increased the power of multinational corporations and enriched the few at the expense of the many. We will explore this tension between order and disorder by focusing on the Age of Crisis that covered much of the first half of the 20th century, the post-World War II dissolution of colonial empires and the emergence of new nations that occurred within the context of the Cold War, and the dizzying pace of globalization that has created a degree of interconnectedness that would have seemed impossible even 50 years ago.

The Age of Crisis (Anxiety)

In 1922, just four years after the end of World War I, the French poet and philosopher Paul Valéry wrote of a crisis that had outlived the fighting. He noted that, "something deeper has been worn away than the renewable parts of a machine." It was a crisis of the Mind:

[Parchment]
"The storm has died away, and still we are restless, uneasy, as if the storm were about to break. Almost all the affairs of men remain in a terrible uncertainty. We think of what has disappeared, we are almost destroyed by what has been destroyed; we do not know what will be born, and we fear the future, not without reason. We hope vaguely, we dread precisely; our fears are infinitely more precise than our hopes; we confess that the charm of life is behind us, abundance is behind us, but doubt and disorder are in us and with us."

Valéry's fears of a storm "about to break," would prove prescient. The post-war settlements that were supposed to settle the issues that led to WWI instead tended to exacerbate old tensions while creating new ones. Any lingering hopes for the establishment of a new global order were definitively crushed by the coming of the Great Depression in 1929. By the mid-1930's, political radicalism, military expansion by Japan and Italy, the remilitarization of Germany under Adolf

Hitler and the Nazi Party, and civil wars in China and Spain all contributed to a sense of global disorder and impending crisis.

When World War II did erupt in 1939, even the most pessimistic observer could not have predicted the horrors it would unleash. The actions of Nazi Germany, in particular, were so extreme in their violence and dehumanization of entire populations as to necessitate a new word. In 1944 the word "genocide" was invented by the Polish-Jewish lawyer Raphael Lemkin to describe Nazi attempts to exterminate entire groups of people and most especially the Jews. While not as systematic as the Nazis, the armies of Imperial Japan perpetrated massacres of civilian populations, used humans as guinea pigs in scientific experiments, and forced hundreds of thousands of mostly Korean and Chinese women to serve Japanese forces as sex slaves. Even the nations that stood up to Japan and Germany committed their own moral transgressions. The Soviet Union committed thousands of murders and rapes on civilian populations as they forced the Germans to retreat in 1944-45. The British led massive bombing raids on civilian populations even in strategically insignificant German cities, like Dresden. The US forced 120,000 American citizens of Japanese descent into concentration camps during the war with military cause, and then killed 130,000 Japanese citizens by dropping two atomic bombs on Hiroshima and Nagasaki. The point is not to draw a moral equivalence but to point out that WWII was brutal everywhere, killing 50-80 million and leaving the monumental task of creating stability out of the ashes.

The Cold War and the New Nationalism

When Valéry spoke of the "doubt and disorder within us" at the end of WWI, he was thinking of the European mind not the minds of the majority of humanity in Africa and Asia. Their minds were also unsettled, however, and many had come to question the merits of western civilization. Europeans like Valéry who had been so assured of European progress in the pre-war years may have been shocked by the brutality and inhumanity they witnessed during the world wars, but what seems shocking to insiders can often seem obvious to outsiders. As early as 1909, for instance, the Indian leader Mohandas Gandhi wrote of British rule that, "unless its whole machinery is thrown overboard, people will destroy themselves like so many moths." Reflecting back on the war years, Aimé Cesaire, who grew up in the French colony of Martinique, remarked that what truly shocked Europeans about Hitler was not that he committed war crimes, but that his crimes were

"against the white man, the humiliation of the white man, and the fact that he applied to Europe colonialist procedures which until then had been reserved exclusively for the Arabs of Algeria, the coolies of India, and the blacks of Africa."

This is all to say that by the end of World War II, fewer people were left who were willing to make a positive case for the continuation of the old imperial system. The result was that in the decades that followed the war, the world went through a long process of what is called *decolonization*, within which former colonies achieved independence from imperial rule. To get a sense of the scope of this process, when the United Nations formed in 1945, there were only 51 member nations, while today there are 193. Although many of these nations came into being amid difficult circumstances, in nearly every one, those who experienced the day of liberation did so with a sense of optimism, passion and revolutionary fervor.

Jawaharlal Nehru, India's first prime minister, was well aware of the challenges and opportunities that came with freedom. When his country achieved independence on August 14, 1947, he stood before the country's new constituent assembly and gave one of the century's greatest political speeches. Known as "The Tryst with Destiny," the speech managed to be hopeful without shying away from the difficult realities before the Indian people:

"We rejoice in that freedom, even though clouds surround us, and many of our people are sorrow stricken and difficult problems encompass us. But freedom brings responsibilities and burdens and we have to face them in the spirit of a free and disciplined people... . The future beckons to us. Whither do we go and what shall be our endeavour? To bring freedom and opportunity to the common man, to the peasants and workers of India; to fight and end poverty and ignorance and disease; to build up a prosperous, democratic and progressive nation, and to create social, economic and political institutions which will ensure justice and fullness of life to every man and woman."

The hope, optimism, and idealism that helped turn colonies into nations would rarely be enough to overcome the massive challenges that these new nations would face. The old imperial system, marked as it was by political exploitation and limited educational and economic opportunities had done little to prepare colonies to emerge as modern nations. So, while decolonization brought political independence to former colonies, it was much more difficult to escape from the threads of European and American cultural and especially economic influences that still entangled them.

One of the best ways to understand the gap between the hope and promise of decolonization versus the reality is through the term "Third World." Coined in the early 1950's, the term was intended to describe countries that were aligned neither with the United States nor its allies (the "First World") or the Soviet Union and theirs (the "Second World"). At the time, leaders from these non-aligned countries often embraced the term and even wore it as a badge of pride. At the aforementioned Bandung Conference of 1955, in the same speech quoted above, Sukarno called upon the independent nations of Africa and Asia to set a new course for the world free from the Cold War politics of their era:

"What can we do? We can do much! We can inject the voice of reason into world affairs. We can mobilise all the spiritual, all the moral, all the political strength of Asia and Africa on the side of peace. Yes, we! We, the peoples of Asia and Africa, 1,400,000,000 strong, far more than half the human population of the world, we can mobilise what I have called the Moral Violence of Nations in favour of peace."

Over time the term itself lost its original connotation and came to be more frequently associated with poverty, corruption, political instability, and economic weakness. As much as the new nations of the post-war era hoped to be able to rid themselves of the old legacies of imperialism and remake the world in a new image and based around a new order, as Nehru noted of his own country in his Independence Day address, "The past clings to us still."

Globalization

When we first discussed globalization, we saw a world that was becoming more connected even as the pull of global forces was still relatively weak and many societies continued to exist outside those forces entirely. As the centuries progressed, globalization's influence would only grow. Over the course of the 20th century the last remaining isolated societies were dragged into a web whose strands allowed interaction and influence to spread at an unstoppable pace.

As always, technological innovation has been the great driver of globalization in the last century. In particular, the immense improvement of communication and transportation networks have completely revolutionized the ability of humans to interact and spread information across distance. Today there are nearly a billion cars on the roads worldwide, roughly four billion airline passengers, another four billion internet users among whom three billion are active users of social media, and perhaps six billion people who have access to mobile phones. All of this means that humanity is experiencing a degree of connectivity that is both unprecedented and shows no sign of slowing down.

The ability to move rapidly, communicate instantly, and share constantly has created a strange kind of world. On the one hand, boundaries both natural (forests, mountains, bodies of water, deserts, etc.) and human-constructed (national boundaries) are less significant than ever before. On the other, that very breakdown of boundaries has caused many to react through a kind of retrenchment: hardline nationalism, religious fundamentalism, and the building of walls both literal and metaphorical.

For others, it is not the idea of increasing connectivity and interaction that worries them, but the means and manner in which it occurs. So much of the process, after all, is driven by multinational corporations (MNCs) whose concerns are mainly things like profits, stock prices, and market share. To the MNCs local cuisines, art forms, manners of dress, languages, and forms of entertainment simply represent competition. When the goal is to sell the most products to the most people, local tastes, traditions, and even languages can act as a hindrance to that goal.

As globalization continues to progress, the great question still to be answered is -- to what end is it taking us? Is it possible to have a globalized world in which we recognize each other's shared humanity while respecting and preserving those elements that make a community unique? Will it instead result in a bland homogeneity? Or, most disastrously, will the fear of the changes wrought by globalization further encourage a retreat into fundamentalism, nationalism, and violence to protect a world that never was or is already lost? The story of globalization is far from complete.

The 20th century was a time of tremendous and unprecedented change. It was an era in which humanity faced some of its greatest crises while also accomplishing some of its greatest triumphs. We now live in a world in which we know more about ourselves, our world, our history, our universe than ever before. The great hope for us as a species is that all of this knowledge will help us develop solutions to some of the most vexing problems of human existence, that it will help us finally definitively turn the tide against the forces of disorder. As we face new crises and opportunities in the 21st century, it is vital that we understand our past if we wish to construct a better future.

Unit 14: World Wars and Decolonizations , 1900 – 1945

Pamela Radcliff, University of California, San Diego

Reading: Wars, Mass Violence, and Genocide

One of the major trends of the first half of the 20th century was a dramatic increase in mass violence, both on the battlefield and against civilian populations. This trend can in part be blamed on military technology. There were new inventions, from the machine gun to the atom bomb to the gas chamber. This trend, however, was also rooted in ideological systems that placed a lesser value on certain human lives and the parallel expansion of nationalism and state power.

Concepts like "total war," the "civilianization of warfare," "genocide," "totalitarianism," and "brutalization" have been coined to frame some of these trends. Yet scholars disagree about the definitions and the precise turning points. Many view World War I as the key turning point in the escalation of mass violence, both as the first "total war" and as a point of departure for a culture of "brutalization" that smoothed the path to WWII. Others argue that "total war" began with Napoleon. Still others assert that "brutalization" began in the colonial "dirty wars" at the turn of the 20th century. These blurred the distinction between combatant and civilian.

World War II has often been seen as the key turning point in the "civilianization of warfare," but mass civilian killings were present earlier. They were seen in the colonial wars, WWI, the Spanish Civil War, and in the Stalinist regime in the 1930s. The upshot is less a linear story of gradual and inevitable escalation to a "war without limits" than a multiple narrative of points of origin that culminated, both statistically and in geographical scope, during and after WWII.

Colonial Wars

There is a good case to be made that colonial campaigns at the turn of the 20th century mark important turning points in mass violence against civilians. Key examples can be found in German Southwest Africa, Spanish Cuba, and British South Africa. In German Southwest Africa, the suppression of a revolt by Herero tribespeople between 1904 and 1907 resulted in the death of between 75 to 80 percent of the population. Some died in battle. Some died of thirst in the desert while fleeing from the army. Others died in internment camps where death rates were 45 percent. In Spanish-controlled Cuba, the independence movement (1895-8) was suppressed with a brutal pacification campaign that included "reconcentration," or the massive forced relocation of half a million people. They were put into what were sometimes called concentration camps, which resulted in the deaths of up to 170,000 civilians, or 10 percent of the population. Reconcentration emptied the countryside and forced the poor rural population into cities where the priority was surveillance, saving money, and troops, not the welfare of the people.

During the Second Boer War (1899-1902), British armies employed a "scorched earth" policy to eradicate the human and material support infrastructure for the enemy's guerrilla war. To this end, the British burned crops, destroyed homes, and interned more than 100,000 Boer women and children and another 100,000 black Africans in concentration camps. Entire regions were depopulated, leading to more than 27,000 Boer deaths (most of them children) and at least 14,000 black African deaths. These deaths were all due to inadequate food rations, exposure, and disease.

As important as the bare statistics is the question of how to define or label these mass deaths. They occurred in a wartime context but transgressed the conventional boundaries of military casualties. The available terminology runs from massacres and atrocities to final solutions, which include deportation and genocide. While massacres and atrocities are single events, perhaps arising out of a specific context and moment, final solutions and genocide point to overarching plans. The intent is the dehumanization of the enemy population and the pursuit of their total domination or annihilation. Each case of colonial war has to be evaluated on its own terms, but some scholars have argued that at least a few cases rise to the level of final solutions.

What explains this ratcheting up of violence against civilians? For the Herero case, one historian has emphasized the impact of transferring Germany's military culture of total annihilation of the enemy to the colonial context. In the colonies, the lack of civilian controls and an unconventional enemy created a dynamic of escalating violence. More generally, other scholars have pointed to the rising influence of a biological racism that undercut the colonizers' claims to "civilize" their colonial subjects, or to the expansionist dynamic of imperialism itself. Challenging the Enlightenment assertion of a common human capacity, the late 19th century view of distinct races (and genders) constituted a "crisis of universalism" that also implied a lesser value for some human lives. While it is important not to establish facile automatic links from the Herero to the Holocaust, it can be argued that these "dirty wars" set precedents that eased the path for future escalation.

World War I

The First World War (1914-8) was a major turning point in the lethal nature of warfare itself, with more battlefield deaths than in all the major wars between 1790 and 1914. About 10-11 million soldiers were killed or died from their wounds, compared to 500,000 in the US Civil War or 400,000 in the Napoleonic campaign in Russia. There were several reasons for the high death rate. They lay in the combination of new weapons, particularly the machine gun, the military strategy that grew out of the new form of trench warfare, and the sheer length of the conflict. The machine gun, first used in colonial wars by the British, could shoot up to 500 rounds a minute compared to the 10 rounds of a bolt action rifle. Another new weapon was poison gas, whose horrors were immortalized in Wilfred Owen's poem, "Dulce et Decorum est." Later came tanks and airplanes. The technological transformation of warfare led some to talk of a new dynamic of mass industrialized killing. At the same time, neither side pursued total annihilation of the enemy, and most POWs survived the war.

The war began in August 1914 as a classic "war of movement" led by cavalry forces. By November, however, the French victory at the Battle of the Marne on the western front had stopped the German advance and stalemate set in. The two armies dug in along a 475-mile trench line, which remained essentially static for the next four years. Soldiers wrote about the "troglodyte" world of trench warfare. These men lived below ground in damp, rat-infested tunnels, often knee-deep in water that smelled of the rotting flesh of soldiers and animals never buried.

During battles, the soldiers faced the terror of climbing "over the top," passing through the barbed wire, and across no man's land, where they were exposed to machine gun fire from the opposing trench. In the Battle of the Somme (mid-1916), 60,000 British troops died in one day. The Eastern Front never bogged down into trench warfare, but the new weapons made sure the battles were equally costly. Thus, in the German offensive against Russia at the end of 1915, half a million Russian soldiers died. In addition to the high casualty rate, the war in the East was equally indecisive, with neither side able to "break through" with decisive victories until the entry of the US and the exit of the Russians. Thus, the US entered the war in the West (April 1917), sending two million troops. The Russian Bolsheviks signed a separate peace in the East (March 1918). The war finally ended when the armistice was signed on November 11, 1918.

Without challenging World War I's special role in the escalation of battlefield violence, recent studies have highlighted the harsh treatment of civilian populations. It at least foreshadowed the trend in WWII, although to a much lesser degree. German, Turkish, Russian, and Italian armies committed various atrocities against civilian populations, including the willful destruction of cultural monuments, massive deportations, a network of internment camps, and, of course, the beginning of what most scholars call the Armenian genocide (1915-23).

The Ottoman, and then Turkish, government embarked on a purposeful if somewhat haphazard effort to eliminate its Armenian population. Some were massacred and others died in forced marches. There was an estimated total of one to one-and-a-half million mortal victims. Hundreds of thousands of Greek residents of Anatolia were also forced to flee in the same "Turkification" campaign, leading to tens of thousands more deaths. More broadly, occupation policies, especially by German armies in the East, have been called "proto-colonial." Proto-colonial means that occupation tended towards the systematic exploitation of civilian populations that were increasingly viewed as expendable.

This focus on violence against civilians in WWI has opened a debate about how innovative WWII really was in the "civilianization of war." The now classic "brutalization thesis" argues that WWI inaugurated a new era of ruthless and extreme politics in which the wartime language of annihilation was transferred to political enemies, creating a mentality that led directly to WWII and the Holocaust. Hitler and Mussolini themselves exemplify this profile on an individual level, both embittered and radicalized by their wartime experience. But others point to the significant discontinuities between the wars, especially in terms of the qualitative and quantitative leap in violence against civilians, which constituted one-sixth of the deaths in WWI and two-thirds in WWII. Thus, practices that appeared haphazardly and unevenly in WWI mushroomed into systematic, deliberate, and widespread mass killings and brutal exploitation of civilians, especially, but not only, by the fascist powers.

World War II

It is thus the global escalation of civilian violence rather than the introduction of new practices that mark World War II as a turning point. This is so even though the widespread mass murder of civilians was already present in individual countries, in the Spanish Civil War, and in Stalin's "liquidation of the kulaks," or independent farmers. The escalation was partly a result of another generation of military technology and strategy, including widespread use of tanks, strategic aerial bombardment of non-military targets, nuclear weapons, and gas chambers. They also stemmed, however, from racist, collectivist, and ultra-nationalist ideological systems that classified entire groups of people as either expendable or active threats.

Democratic, communist, and fascist regimes all practiced mass killing of civilians through the employment of strategic bombing, culminating in the two atomic bombs dropped on Hiroshima and Nagasaki. Estimates of deaths include 400,000-600,000 Germans killed by Allied bombs, 60,000 British killed by German bombs, and 500,000 Japanese killed by US fire bombs. As a direct result of the atom bombs, another 90,000-150,000 were killed in Hiroshima and 40,000-80,000 in Nagasaki. Some have argued that the US's willingness to use atomic weapons on Japan was facilitated by a racist framework that also justified the wholesale internment of 110,000-120,000 Japanese and Japanese Americans (60 percent) in the US.

What distinguished the mass killings of the Axis powers of Germany, Italy, and Japan were deliberate policies to exploit civilians to the death or to eliminate them. Japanese occupation forces conscripted millions of other Asian peoples and POWs into forced labor, including up to 200,000 so-called "comfort women," who were subjected to forced prostitution or rape. Civilian massacres were also routine, most famously the so-called "Rape of Nanking," in which up to 300,000 Chinese were murdered in the initial stages of Japan's China campaign. The Japanese armies also practiced human experimentation, testing biological weapons on prisoners, as with the infamous Unit 731, which caused up to 3,000 deaths. Estimates of total civilian deaths caused by the Japanese army range from three to ten million. Even without a concerted plan to eliminate entire peoples, a racist disregard for the human value of those considered to be inferior had devastating consequences for civilian mortality rates.

In Europe, the rapid Nazi military victories of 1939-41 set the stage for an occupation policy explicitly based on a new racial world order. The concept of racial hierarchy had long been central to European culture, but it had been mostly applied to colonial peoples. The Nazis were the first to systematically establish a racial hierarchy within Europe and to explicitly argue that lower races existed only to serve the higher "Aryan" race. Especially in the East, the Nazis treated the Slavic populations as expendable, useful only as slave labor. Some 10-12 million people, two-thirds of them from the East, were conscripted into forced labor, many of whom did not survive the war. It was on the Eastern Front as well that German armies fully participated in systematic massacres of civilians, both Slavs and Jews. Older claims that most killings were carried out by special "fanatical" units have been thoroughly debunked, with plentiful evidence that regular army units not only did much of the civilian killing but were also much more likely to express racist or dehumanizing perspectives about the enemy than soldiers in WWI.

Reading: The Spanish Republic and the Civil War

Pamela Radcliff is professor of history at the University of California, San Diego. She has spent much of her career studying the Spanish Civil War. The civil war was a forerunner to World War II, with Russia on the side of the Loyalists, along with idealistic Americans in the Abraham Lincoln Brigade, and Nazi Germany on the side of the Spanish fascists. Radcliff has not confined her studies to politics; she has also explored the art of Spain during the civil war. Recently, Radcliff has applied her decades of expertise in Spanish in publishing a book on modern Spain.

The image is of surviving members of the famous Veterans of the Abraham Lincoln Brigade holding their banner. In January 1937, the brigade numbering over 2,500 Americans, went to Spain to defend its fledgling democratic republic against a Fascist coup led by Francisco Franco.

Exemplifying the major themes of the "crisis of meaning" and war and mass violence, Spain serves as an excellent if lesser known national case study of the broader trends of the era. Even though Spain did not participate in either of the two World Wars, and had lost the vast majority of its colonial empire before 1900, it ended up consumed by the ideological struggles and mass violence that defined the period.

The Spanish Republic

Within global and European history, Spain had moved from the center to the margins over the course of the 17th through the 19th centuries, as the once dominant global empire receded from the world stage. Culminating in the humiliating loss of its last overseas colonies in the Antilles to the US in 1898, the imperial eclipse was accompanied by a pessimistic discourse of national failure that dominated Spanish history for most of the 20th century.

The most hopeful moment of optimism in the first half of the century was the declaration of the Second Republic in April 1931, one of the most ambitious of the new democratic experiments that emerged after WWI. Within five short years, however, the Republic was engulfed in a brutal Civil War, with democrats and left-wing revolutionaries on one side and fascists, Catholics, and conservative nationalists on the other.

The war ended on April 1, 1939, with the victory of the Nationalists, under the leadership of Francisco Franco, whose dictatorship lasted for almost 40 years. With no effort to integrate the losing side, the conflicts that could not be resolved through democratic means during the Republic were forcibly excised from the political realm. As elsewhere, the ideological crisis of meaning was resolved through war and mass violence, but in contrast to the other fascist powers, all the violence was turned inwards against the Spanish people.

In April of 1931 when the Republic was proclaimed, many Spaniards felt optimistic about the prospects of democracy. The major challenge, as in many other parliamentary democracies of the era, was to construct a majority coalition among a range of disparate political groups with different views and expectations of "democracy." The Republic experimented with two different majority coalitions, in the First Biennium (April 1931-Nov 1933), the Second Biennium (Nov 1933 to Feb 1936) and the Popular Front (February to July 1936), which marked a return to the first coalition.

During the "First Biennium," the Republic was led by a left-leaning coalition government with a social democratic platform that aimed to integrate the secular urban middle classes, the urban working classes and the rural poor, especially in the south. At the beginning, this coalition was both broad and heterogeneous, reaching from the Socialist party to Liberal democrats. While this governing coalition did not consolidate, the first biennium constituted a coherent legislative period, with an ambitious reform agenda anchored by secularization, social welfare, and regional autonomy initiatives.

The "Second Biennium" took shape in reaction and response to the politics of the first phase, experimenting with a different majority coalition that leaned to the right, appealing to Catholics, businessmen, landlords, and the rural peasant communities of the northern part of the peninsula. In the November 1933 elections, conservative sectors of the population had a new option, the CEDA, which ran a campaign in defense of religion, social order, and private property. The CEDA's official position towards the Republic was "accidentalist," meaning conditional support as long as their interests could be defended through parliamentary channels. The new government was led by a liberal democratic party, which formed a minority government supported by an informal alliance with the CEDA. The new government claimed to offer a "Republic for all Spaniards," in contrast to the social and secularist version that had alienated many Catholics and frightened the propertied classes.

The third brief phase of the peacetime Republic was the Popular Front, which reunited the democratic and socialist alliance of the First Biennium (with the addition of the Communist party (PCE)), but in the more charged context of growing polarization, workers' impatience at the slowness of reforms, the Nazi takeover in Germany, and the rise of fascist and authoritarian movements everywhere. Campaigning on catastrophic threats of fascist or communist revolution, the two major "left" and "right" coalitions each received almost the same number of votes. Belying the "fascist" vs. "communist" rhetoric of the electoral propaganda, the support for the parties bearing these names remained insignificant.

In any case, the victorious left-leaning coalition was no more successful in stabilizing the Republic than in 1931. The refusal of the Socialists to join a coalition government (in contrast to 1931), and of the "right" parties to accept electoral defeat, and, most definitively, a military conspiracy, brought an end to this last phase of the peacetime Republic.

The question of why neither of the majority coalitions could stabilize the democratic Republic is hotly contested, with debates about which period and which political actors deserve most blame for undermining the democracy. From the left perspective, the first biennium agenda constituted the only viable and authentic democratic project of the Republic. All on the left also blame right wing resistance to a "social" democracy that threatened elite privileges. They would also agree that what they call the second "black" biennium had no democratic project, and that the CEDA was at best conditionally democratic and at worst authoritarian or even tending towards fascism.

In contrast, from the conservative perspective, it was the first biennium coalition that was non-democratic, with an "exclusionary" Constitution that alienated the Catholic half the population with its anti-clerical principles and an at best "conditionally" democratic Socialist party. This narrative argues that the Second Biennium did represent an alternate "liberal" democratic project, although there is debate as to whether the CEDA could have consolidated as a Christian democratic party. Equally contested is the Popular Front era, viewed as either the last chance to rescue democracy from a descent into fascism or as an uncontrolled spiral into disorder, social revolution, and violence.

Whether the Republic could have consolidated if certain individual and collective actors had behaved differently will continue to generate heated speculation. Without trying to resolve the debates over responsibility, it is easy to see how the ideological struggles of the period took shape in ways that undermined the ability of the democratic system to consolidate: from competing visions of social vs. liberal democracy, to the "conditional" democratic support of left and right wing parties, to the difficulty of finding a majority coalition in a population deeply divided by class, religion, and rural/urban mentalities.

Whether it was inevitable or the result of bad political decisions, these competing goals could not successfully be contained within a democratic framework. Either way, the Republic was a messy and contradictory democratic experiment that contained elements that were both promising and challenging for any version of democratic consolidation.

Military Rebellion
The most crucial decision in undermining the fragile democracy was the military rebellion launched on July 17, 1936. Planned as a surgical coup against the Republican government, it instead devolved into a brutal civil war. Everyone would agree that the Civil War was a tragic and momentous turning point in Spain's history. On the most basic level, it was a demographic catastrophe that cost half a million lives in battlefield deaths, repression and disease, and another 200,000 to exile.

In political terms, it ended Spain's democratic experiment and inaugurated a forty-year repressive right wing regime that broke with the trajectory of post-WWII western democratic Europe and joined Portugal in a Southern European zone of dictatorship. And, of course, it left the legacy of a fratricidal conflict that continues to shape current politics and society. Not surprisingly, explaining the significance and outcome of such a tragedy continues to generate enormous scholarly as well as popular interest. In the competing moral narratives about Spain's 20th century history, conservatives argue that the Nationalists saved Christian civilization from communist takeover, while for the left the war sealed the victory of fascism over democracy.

Why the Outcome of the Conflict
Beyond this meta-debate about the significance of the Republic's defeat, historians have focused most of their energies on explaining the outcome. There is general agreement that some combination of unfavorable external and domestic factors put the Republicans at a significant disadvantage and ultimately led to their defeat. In terms of external factors, the foreign aid and military support provided by the fascist regimes for the Nationalists was countered by a policy of non-intervention on the part of the western democratic powers of Britain, France, and the US, a deficit only partly filled by inferior Soviet aid.

In terms of domestic factors, the Nationalists were more successful in pursuing a unified, efficient, and effective war effort, while Republican divisions about both goals and methods, especially between democrats and left wing revolutionaries, undermined efficiency and effectiveness. Not surprisingly, conservatives tend to accentuate the importance of domestic factors, especially Republican "disorder," while the left emphasizes the debilitating impact of non-intervention on Republican survival.

So how do we evaluate the "meaning" of this bloody conflict? It seems clear that the answer lies somewhere between the competing moral narratives of "fascism vs. democracy" or "Christian civilization vs. communism," but it is difficult to pinpoint the exact balance of forces and it is no surprise that Spaniards remain deeply divided. Did Spain lose the opportunity to consolidate a democratic regime that would have joined post-war Western Europe? To imagine this outcome would have required not only functional pluralism among the fractured Republican groups but letting go of the exclusivist rhetoric that permeated their language. Moreover, a Republican victory in 1939 would have left them bereft of international support, unless they held on as an anti-fascist democracy until 1945, when Spain may have been able to benefit from the Marshall Plan.

As tentative as this alternative imagined path is, it seems to offer more possibilities for a better outcome than the Francoist victory, although those who are convinced that a victory of the Republic would have led to a Soviet satellite regime would disagree. It is, however, difficult to view the unforgiving and extremely repressive Nationalist victory as the best option available to Spain in the 1930s. This conclusion would suggest that Spaniards were simply incapable of attaining the minimal degree of consensus necessary for a functioning democratic state, but one could point to the counter examples of countries like Italy and Germany, whose political systems were transformed in the more favorable context of a post-allied victory.

The precise circumstances under which the Republic could have won the war are also difficult to define, although everyone would agree that a combination of mutually reinforcing unfavorable factors led to its defeat. It seems hard to sustain the conviction that everything would have been fine if only the democracies had decided to support the Republic, given the level of internal challenges, from political fragmentation to military ineptitude and logistical inexperience, not to mention the alienation of practicing Catholics. But there is no question that non-intervention exacerbated all of these problems, in addition to increasing the Republic's dependence on the USSR and thus the power of the controversial Communist party.

For the Nationalists, it seems equally hard to sustain the position that their victory depended solely on the foreign aid from fascist powers. Equipped with about the same amount of resources as the Republican side, the centralized and efficient Nationalist organization was able to channel these into a coordinated military and logistical strategy that gained at least passive acceptance by many non-Republicans and bested the Republican armies on the battlefield. At the same time, it is impossible to imagine the Nationalist victory without this foreign aid, since a rebellion against an elected democratic government would have had no international standing among non-fascist powers.

However one ranks the importance of the various domestic and international factors, none of them worked in the Republic's favor, not even its status as the democratically elected government. What is also clear is that the outcome marked a huge fork in the road in Spanish history, whose consequences are still being played out today.

Reading: World War i: A Military History

The battles of World War I were quite different than the strategies and tactics of the battles of the 19th century in Europe. Most of the previous wars featured battles that looked similar to the kind that Napoleon Bonaparte fought at the beginning of the 19th century — speedy battlefield movement, combined arms assaults between infantry, cavalry, and artillery, relatively small numbers of cannon, short-range musket fire and bayonet charges. The saying that "generals always fight the last war" may not be true today, but certainly seemed the case in the 19th century. Napoleonic tactics continued to be used well after they had become technologically impractical. The mismatch between new devastating armaments and the old-school military tactics led to large-scale slaughters during many struggles, including the American Civil War (1861-65), the Austro-Prussian War (1866) and the Franco-Prussian War (1870).

In contrast, WWI was a highly defensive war, which emphasized the protection of troops in massive trench systems on the Western Front between France and Germany. There were foreshadowings of the kind of tactical trench warfare of WWI in some trench battles in the Crimean War in southern Russia in the 1850s, the trenchworks around Richmond, Virginia, late in the American Civil War and in the Russo-Japanese War in Manchuria and Korea in 1904-05. But WWI represented a much more extensive use of trench warfare than ever had been seen before. The military strategies and tactics of WWI seemed to have three periods. The first phase was the initial strategy of mobility and rapidly advancing armies, similar to 19th-century battles, from the beginning of the war in August 1914 to the rapid retreat to trenches by the end of that year. The second phase was much longer and seemingly quite static for three years, from early in 1915 to the end of 1917. Finally, the third phase saw the return to more mobile and fluid warfare throughout 1918 until the end of the war in November of that year.

First Phase: Initial Mobilization (1914)

Records demonstrate that many military commanders on both sides envisaged a conflict that would last about 18 months, which would have been about on par with most conflicts in the previous century. The campaigns that they designed demonstrated rapid, coordinated movement of forces across large amounts of territory between Germany, France and Belgium. But in the summer and fall of 1914, these campaigns uniformly failed.

The German plan (best referred to as the Schlieffen-Moltke Plan after the military chiefs who designed it) entailed moving the bulk of the German field army westwards to defeat France quickly by wheeling through Belgium and outflanking the modern fortresses the French had built along the Franco-German border to the south. The less modern Belgian fortresses around Liège and Namur were overcome quickly by German mobile heavy artillery, and the French had left their northern frontier behind the Belgians largely unfortified.

In that same month of August while the Germans attacked, the French army with the British Expeditionary Force (BEF) advanced into Alsace, Lorraine and the Ardennes, territories along the French and German boundary a little to the south of the German attack. But they were driven back with enormous losses. The French commander, Joseph Joffre, however, transferred forces from his east flank to the center of his line, and in September counter-attacked at the First Battle of the Marne. By the end of 1914, the Western Front, the line between the two armies, now began to take the shape that it would generally hold for three years. The Germans were in control of Belgium and parts of northern France, but the French and British held the boundary line between France and Germany to the south. Paris, the clear object of the German advance, remained firmly in Allied hands, though it had experienced a close call in August 1914 and was close enough to the Front to be in a constant state of anxiety.

Why had the two sides failed to make the highly mobile advance that each so clearly strategized. From the beginning of the war, the Germans had to contend with its Russia problem. Even though the Russian army was no match for any of the western powers, it was an ally of the French and British. Germany had to worry about possible coordination between the allied enemy on both its eastern and western borders. This was enough to create caution in German military chiefs. During the First Battle of the Marne, the German commander, Helmuth von Moltke the Younger, unnecessarily diverted two corps from his right flank in the west to fight against the Russians in the east. He delegated the decision to retreat from the Marne to a staff officer, Colonel Richard Hentsch, who authorized it prematurely. But even these mistakes probably do not answer fully the question: What stalled the German advance?

For one, the French seemed to have learned a lesson from their loss to Germany in the Franco-Prussian War in 1870. They mobilized their army quickly bringing forces that were almost as large as Germany's. France also had invested heavily in their railways, allowing the French commander Joffre to move his troops laterally and swiftly to points where they were needed. On the other hand, the German army was often a hundred miles in advance of its railheads, depending on only 4,000 large freight trucks to transport troops along the line, most of which were broken down. The Germans also had difficulty bringing up basic supplies to the front, for example, to feed the troops and horses. The French also had a better telegraph network, while the Germans not only could not communicate as well, their wireless messages were often intercepted. When Joffre found his troops bogged down, unlike Moltke, he kept his nerve and successfully implemented a fall-back plan, using his resource advantages effectively.

Nevertheless, the French also could not make effective advances. Both sides found themselves better at defending than advancing, and it was 19th-century technological improvement in armaments that was the fundamental reason. Rapid-firing rifles with smokeless magazines could fire 15 times a minute from up to half a mile away, giving concealed infantry great advantages. Machine guns could fire across a field 2,500 yards long and 500 wide, mowing down anything or anyone in the radius. Quick-firing field artillery guns had improved greatly. The French 75mm field gun could deliver, with a trained crew, up to 20 rounds a minute. German light field howitzers in the Battle of Ardennes showed what terrible damage could be done to advancing troops on foot.

While the Germans found themselves against a strong defensible Franco-British wall in the west, against Russia, they were able to use their technical knowhow and their superior military tactics to better advantage. Initially, the Russians had a little success because they faced an Austro-Hungarian force (part of the Central Powers) that was much smaller than their own and only about one tenth the size of the German field army. They defeated an Austrian incursion into Russian territory but also overran many of the eastern provinces of Austria, partly because the Austrians divided their efforts between fighting on the Russian front and quelling their internal problems in Serbia. But Russia had poor military leadership; their decision to expand their attack to include the Germans diluted their numerical advantage. The German VIII Army defeated the Russians at the Battles of Tannenberg and the Masurian Lakes. In these battles, it was the Germans who had superior interior rail links and intact telegraph networks, whereas the invading Russians blundered forward along forest tracks and broadcast unencrypted radio messages. Once the Germans came to Austria-Hungary's aid, the Russian advance was halted and Russia went on the defensive, scorching the earth behind them to deprive Germany of needed resources in the field.

When the fighting fronts stabilized in winter 1915, the Germans held most of Belgium and 4.5 percent of France, including key industrial areas in Lorraine and French Flanders. On the eastern front, the Russians were driven out of Poland and their previously conquered territories in Austria, losing hundreds of miles of Russian territory, but still holding the line against further German advances. To end the war on favourable terms the French and British allies understood that they had to expel the Germans from the western territories and hope that Russia could hold the line. They also realized from the first few months experience of war that this task would be extremely difficult. The Allies, however, had some strategically important military accomplishments beyond the stalemate on European land. By the beginning of 1915, they had destroyed most of the German warships operating outside the North Sea. They had also severed Germany's and Austria's overseas trade links. And thanks to the British and French colonies, the Allies could bring in reserves from all over the globe. Troops from India held one third of the British Western Front sector in the winter of 1914-15. If the Allies could mobilize their resources, they held a longer-term advantage; but whether this would suffice against the Germans' stronger territorial position and greater operational effectiveness remained unclear in January 1915.

Phase 2: Stalemate (1915-17)

What is not particularly well known is that both sides had already suffered hundreds of thousands of casualties in those few months at the end of 1914. In fact, the initial phase of relatively mobile warfare saw the greatest daily losses of the war. The French suffered 27,000 soldier deaths on one day alone — August 23, 1914. It was no wonder that soldiers seeing the thousands mowed down with deadly shrapnel bursts spontaneously began to dig trenches. By the end of 1915, 475 miles of opposing trench systems had been dug, extending from the North Sea to Switzerland.

The Germans were determined to hang onto the gains they had made in their initial phase but stalled drive into France in 1914, so they were the first to use systematic trench-building. The

German high staff also considered it an efficient way to hold the western front so that they could re-deploy troops, when needed, to the eastern front in Russia. For their first trenches, German engineers chose ridges, so their soldiers could observe enemy artillery positions and force their enemy to attack uphill. Trench lines also began and ended near railheads and along the coasts so that soldiers could be transported directly into the trenches and be easily extracted and re-deployed to danger points where the enemy might be penetrating the line. By 1916, these defense systems became so elaborate that there were usually three lines — a forward, a main, and a support trench, with interconnecting communication trenches between them. There were field gun batteries in the rear as well as machine guns and barbed wire further forward. In drier parts of the front, the defenders built trenches as much as 30 feet deep; in areas with high water tables, such as Flanders, they built concrete pillboxes, that is a raised small hut hardened with concrete to protect against small-arms fire and grenades. Attackers found over and over again that these defensive structures were simply too strong to overcome.

Trench warfare would not have worked without the important difference between WWI and earlier 19th-century wars — much larger numbers of soldiers and men in the field. In WWI, it was not unusual for there to be 5,000 combatants per mile of front. Moreover, advances in medicine meant wounded soldiers were more likely to return to the field. Also, the French and British were able to bring in laborers from their colonies around the world to dig trenches and pillboxes, build railways, supply munitions and feed soldiers, freeing up those soldiers to fight. Early on both sides had periodic shortages of munitions, but the demands of war prioritized the design and building of better production and manufacturing facilities behind the lines and at the homefront. And the soldiers and laborers stayed in the field year round rather than withdrawing to winter barracks and quarters.

Trenches were characteristic not just of France and Flanders but also of almost every other campaign theater. They formed in the Gallipoli peninsula, where after Turkey entered the war on the side of the Central Powers, Allied forces tried unavailingly during 1915 to break through to Constantinople. In the Trentino and on the Isonzo, trenches developed after Italian forces, on the side of the Allies, made some advances against Austria-Hungary in May 1915. In Macedonia in the Greek peninsula, after Allied forces advanced inland from Salonika in the autumn, soldiers hunkered down in trenches. In Poland, military chiefs on both sides of the Eastern Front ordered the digging of trenches, although the Eastern Front had half the density of manpower and was less rigid than its western counterpart. In the Eastern Front, force-to-space ratios and quantities of heavy weaponry were generally lower than in the west, but here too the firepower revolution gave the defender the tactical edge.

In 1915-16, both the Allies and the Central Powers vigorously pursued technology breakthroughs that would end the impasse. The Germans introduced poison gas in April 1915, and the British at the Battle of Loos in September 1915. But the canisters were thrown only when a favorable wind presented, a highly dangerous proposition to soldiers releasing the canisters. By 1916, however, chlorine gas was being launched with artillery shells so that they would explode further away from friendly forces. But already effective gas masks were being developed. Gas warfare was terrible but provided no outstanding advantage to its practitioners.

Tanks, which would be such an important technology in WWII, were a very new technology in WWI. They had been designed to help the advancing infantry to break down trench barriers. But the early models moved barely faster than walking pace and were subject to breakdown. Much more effective were advances in the production of heavy artillery, especially six-inch calibre shells, which could send bursts over longer distances and were often guided by aerial reconnaissance and photography. It took over two years, but by 1917 the French, Germans and British all possessed many more guns and were far more proficient at using them. Armies also learned how to lay down a "creeping barrage," that is a curtain of field-gun and machine-gun fire just ahead of the advancing infantry until the soldiers could storm their target.

These technologies and new tactics were developing throughout the three-year middle period of stalemate. An equilibrium still held and the lines hardly moved, but it was not a period of endless and mindless repetition of the same tactics, as it is often portrayed. Under the surface there was a lot of learning going on and the cumulation of new tactics, technologies and armament production would eventually break the equilibrium. It was an equilibrium that was fundamentally due to the Germans having a third of their men pinned down in the Eastern Front, and the French and British with too few to take advantage and liberate their territories conquered in 1914.

On the seas, from spring 1915 the Allies imposed a blockade on the Central Powers but it was not complete; Germany continued importing food and supplies from its neutral neighbours. The German High Seas Fleet avoided an engagement with the larger British navy because they were hoping to preserve it to pressure the British in possible peace negotiations. The Germans seemed to have an inferiority complex concerning the British navy. In May 1916 the sea battle at Jutland in Denmark could actually have been considered a German win, but the German high command interpreted it as a narrow escape and they were loath to risk their ships again. German u-boats were too few to inflict serious losses on Allied shipping until 1916, and they were hobbled for two years, fearing that American objections to "unrestricted" submarine warfare, that is, torpedoing anything afloat and without warning, might bring the Americans to the Allied side. But in February 1917, the Germans became pessimistic about the land war in Europe and began to defy the Americans on the high seas. They launched a no-holds-barred campaign, intercepting and attacking all shipping around Great Britain. Ultimately, this turned American opinion against neutrality and allowed President Wilson to declare war in April 1917.

Phase III: Return to Movement (1918)

To understand the breaking of the 1915-17 pattern of stalemate fighting, however, it is necessary to look away from tactics toward strategy, most importantly, command strategy that used much of what had been learned in the previous three years. In early 1918 suddenly armies went on the move again. First, between March and July the Germans launched five great offensives, also known as the Ludendorff offensives, after the legendary German commander. They advanced almost 50 miles, threatening the key British railway junctions at Amiens and Hazebrouck before advancing almost halfway to Paris.

The Ludendorff Offensives were surely responding to a strategic advantage the Germans had gained in the fall of 1917. Throughout 1917, Russia was in turmoil, food riots and rebellions raging on the homefront and troops mutinying on the Eastern Front. Tzar Nicholas II abdicated in March 1917. The Germans hoping to knock out Russia from the war, allowed the Communist Revolutionary leader Vladimir Lenin to return home to Russia in a train traversing Germany, ending his exile in Switzerland. By October, Lenin and other leaders staged the Russian October Revolution and took over the government. They negotiated a ceasefire with Germany in December 1917. Germany moved a half a million men from east to west. This gave them the coveted numerical majority on the Western Front and they had good reason to use in their offensives of the late spring 1918, before American troops could arrive in strength to give the Allies the numerical advantage.

Effective use of artillery was a critical factor in the temporary success of the Ludendorff Offensives. Through painstaking trials with each gun, the Germans had learned to dispense with ranging shots, preliminary shots that allowed soldiers to adjust the guns to hit the target. and could deliver without warning an intense and accurate bombardment, lasting hours rather than days. These bombardments were designed not to destroy their enemies' positions but to silence their batteries (drenching them with poison gas shells), paralyse their command centers, and suppress front-line resistance. The accompanying "Stormtroop" infantry tactics were assaults by specialist squads equipped with portable machine guns, grenades, and flamethrowers, which would bypass the opposing strong points and drive on as far and fast as possible. Aircraft would direct the artillery and carry out ground strafing. But the German army had difficulty sustaining these advances. They had few tanks and trucks and suffered from gas and rubber shortages. Supply shortages and broken supply lines repeatedly halted their columns.

The Ludendorff Offensives cost the German field army more than a million casualties, and it dwindled from 5.1 million to 4.2 million men. Though the French and British armies, now on the defensive, also suffered hundreds of thousands of losses, the Americans brought in troops to fill the gap, as the Germans feared. During the summer over 250,000 American personnel reached France each month, and by November they would number nearly two million. In July 1918, the Allies again outnumbered their German enemy, and they used similar artillery tactics to the Germans, with the addition that they had many more heavy guns and could now launch major attacks in rapid succession or even simultaneously. The Allies also had more and better tanks, which they could now deploy in the hundreds rather than dozens. Tanks proved themselves able to save lives and make it easier to attain surprise.

Under General-in-Chief Ferdinand Foch in late September, the Allies unleashed four major attacks from Flanders to the Argonne along the major German railway lines. In the face of this multiple onslaught, the Germans could not transport their reserves quickly enough, and on September 28, 1918, the German co-commander Erich Ludendorff suffered a nervous breakdown. Ludendorff also suffered from the news from the Balkans, where the Allies attacked in mid-September and forced Bulgaria to sue for a ceasefire. Now the Central Powers were nearly split — Germany and Austria-Hungary in the northwest and the Ottoman Empire in the southeast with its precious supply of oil. In late September 1918, British forces destroyed the Turkish armies in Northern Palestine and drove north into Syria, as well as advancing on Mosul. Finally, the Italians, who with British and French assistance had repelled a final Austro-Hungarian offensive in the June 1918 Battle of the Piave, went on to the attack in October at the Battle of Vittorio Veneto, in the midst of which Austria-Hungary disintegrated as a political entity and hundreds of thousands of its troops surrendered. The German high command, which was mostly Ludendorff and Paul von Hindenburg, agreed that they must seek an immediate ceasefire.

The Allied victories depended on adequate manpower and troop morale. They also required abundant weapons and munitions, manufactured primarily in Britain and France, although American war loans and raw materials (particularly oil and steel) were indispensable to the production effort. A further precondition was command of the seas, the u-boat menace being at its deadliest in April 1917 but thereafter subsiding. The convoy system, where ships crossed the Atlantic for mutual defense introduced in the summer 1917, was the most important single factor in defeating the submarines. In many ways the Allied victory was also a triumph of political leadership particularly in 1918 with American President Woodrow Wilson, British Prime Minister David Lloyd George, French President Georges Clemenceau, and Italian Prime Minister Vittorio Orlando.

By 1918 the character of warfare had been transformed in Europe. The all-arms aspect of Allied operations that combined armour, artillery, airpower and infantry would be familiar to a soldier today in a way that the war in 1914 would not. By the fall of 1918 the Allies and Americans were well aware that the struggle was less a triumph than a close-fought thing that at that moment was greatly in their favor. They had no desire to extend the fighting into Germany and prolong the war, so they signed an armistice on November 11, 1918.

Reading: The History of World War II in Its Great Battles
The Two Theaters of World War

What is the difference between a world war and other wars? World wars affect directly or indirectly the other parts of the world beyond the warring nations. While the theater of belligerence might be confined to one geographic area, it is drawing in the areas where there is no violence but there are changes or disruptions due to the war — diplomatic and political intrigue, alliance troops being called up to support the actual warring nations, danger on the high seas, immigration of refugee populations and economic recession or rapid growth because they are is supplying oil, food or munitions to the warring parties.

Comparing WWI and WWII, one can argue that the European-based conflicts of WWI did draw in other parts of the world, such as the British colony of India, Middle Eastern countries that supplied oil to the conflict, and the United States which finally came in on the Allied side. But Latin America, Africa and most of Asia were not drawn in very much to the four-and-one-half year conflict. Not so, the six years of WWII. There were two major theaters of war — Europe and the Pacific — and more than half of the countries of the world were involved directly while most of the rest were indirectly affected. The warring countries went severely into debt during the conflict, buying enormous amounts of goods and services from around the world. In the last 36 months of WWII, a million people a month were dying around the world directly due to the war.

Militarily, WWI presented strategic and tactical problems in overcoming stalemate and trench warfare on land. WWII presented much more diverse geographic fields of battle around the world, more innovative military strategies and the technical capability to wage more war at sea, in the air and on the land. It is difficult to summarize the range of military operations of WWII, but it is possible to create a descriptive narrative of the ten major and most consequential battles of WWII. The battles recommend themselves not only because of their military tactical and strategic importance in determining victory during the war but also their political consequences after the war.

France, May 1940

The war in Europe began on September 1, 1939 when the armies of the Nazi German government invaded Poland. Poland's ally, Great Britain responded with an ultimatum to Germany to cease military operations in Poland by September 3rd or it would declare war on Germany. The Germans ignored the ultimatum and the British declared war, followed within a week by France and several members of the British Commonwealth — Australia, New Zealand, South Africa and Canada. To keep himself out of a two-front war, Adolf Hitler cleverly had negotiated a pact with Josef Stalin, premier of the Soviet Union, to remain neutral and, in exchange be allowed to conquer parts of Poland and Eastern Europe for himself. Hitler then demanded that the French and British sue for peace or he would attack France in the spring. When the Allies could not conclude a satisfactory peace deal with him, Hitler made plans for an invasion of France.

In April 1940, Germany invaded Denmark and Norway to protect its supply lines in the Baltic Sea in preparation for the French invasion. Disappointed by this development, the British government appointed for prime minister the most hawkish and anti-Hitler of its ministers, Winston Churchill. In May 1940, the German army used a tactic — blitzkrieg or lightning war — a version of which it had tried unsuccessfully in WWI. It invaded France with a large army through the narrow corridor of the Low Countries of Belgium, the Netherlands and Luxembourg. But this time they executed the strategy perfectly and invaded the north of France in less than four weeks. Paris was in Nazi hands by the middle of June. Meanwhile Hitler's ally, Fascist Italy invaded the southeast of France, and French Fascist sympathizers in the southwest and center of France formed the independent Vichy government, for all intents and purposes a puppet of Germany.

Tactically, the Germans' blitzkrieg through France had shown that they were the best in the world at mobilized warfare. But strategically the invasion of France was incomplete. In the winter of 1940, the British had moved their British Expeditionary Force (BEF), the bulk of their army, into France in an all-out effort to defend their ally. The BEF was overwhelmed along with the French army in the blitzkrieg that followed, with the result that the two armies were stranded on the beaches of Dunkirk in northern France. The Germans delayed moving in for the kill, and Churchill managed to muster a huge armada of civilian and naval seacraft to evacuate the armies back to Great Britain. By not finishing off the Allied army at Dunkirk, Hitler had only knocked off one of his two foes and the failure weakened Stalin's confidence in the Germans. It can be argued that the May 1940 offensive was strategically the most important battle of WWII: from that point forward, the end goal of the war would be the liberation of France.

Battle of Britain, August-September 1940

Geographically, Germany had a much more difficult problem in Great Britain than in France because the English Channel protected against invasion and the British navy was strong enough to throw such an invasion back. Therefore, Hitler's strategy for an invasion of Great Britain was to weaken Great Britain first. He sent the Luftwaffe, or German air force, over southern England in daily bombing raids of harbors, airfields, and manufacturing centers, while German u-boats prowled the English Channel, the North Sea and the North Atlantic to search out and destroy British commercial and navy ships

The goal of this strategy was to soften up the British enough to force them to peace negotiation or lay the groundwork for an invasion in September 1940. But the British Royal Air Force (RAF) managed to fight the Luftwaffe to a standstill in what would be called the Battle of Britain. In a few months, the RAF shot down 1,733 German plains compared to only 915 British planes. Ultimately, the RAF in a short time put together their advantages to create a seamless air defense system over southern England that established the goal of all air warfare — air superiority. The British had over 50 radar stations and numerous blimps that gave them excellent air intelligence. British pilots were fighting over familiar territory closer to home: if they survived shooting down over England or the Channel, they were rescued and returned to the fight, whereas German pilots became prisoners. Being closer to home allowed the British pilots to fly more sorties and become more experienced. British fighter planes, especially the Spitfires, proved to be more maneuverable than German aircraft. In September, the exasperated Germans tried night-bombing of civilian populations, a terror tactic they called the blitz, but it was unsuccessful in breaking British resolve. Hitler called off the invasion of Great Britain that same month; British air superiority had forced his hand. With an implacable enemy in the west, Hitler turned his attention to the potentially treacherous Russians to the east. Hitler decided over the winter to attack the Soviet Union as his next strategic move in the spring, hoping to knock Russia out quickly and protect his rear.

Operation Barbarossa, June–July 1941

By the end of September 1940, the Germans had negotiated a Tripartite Pact with Fascist Italy and Imperial Japan, later known as the Axis. A few efforts were made to include Russia in the Axis, but mutual suspicion between the autocratic capitalists of the Axis and Communist Russia hindered the talks. Unknown to Stalin, Hitler and the German high command in December decided to invade the Soviet Union in the spring of 1941 in a campaign known as Operation Barbarossa. The Germans amassed forces on the Soviet border and crossed over on June 22, 1941. The very short summer of Russia and need for drier land to accommodate German tank warfare was the reason for what seems like a late start. But to be successful, Operation Barbarossa had to accomplish its goals within a few months. Thus, the Germans sent their armies in three directions -— to the Baltic Sea and Leningrad (formerly St. Petersburg), to Moscow (the capital of the Soviet Union) and to the Ukraine and Stalingrad (formerly Volgograd). The Germans and their Eastern European allies of Hungary and Romania, along with Italy, brought a massive army and took a massive risk.

Barbarossa was essentially blitzkrieg but on a much larger territorial and human scale — the largest military offensive in human history. It was successful in the first phase — the occupation of all of western Russia, including the city of Kiev. Resource-wise, this was the most valuable part of the country, the real object of Hitler who wanted to re-populate it with Germans. But Germany could not hold western Russia without defeating the three major Russian cities further to the east and north — Leningrad, Moscow and Stalingrad — and in the process break the back of the Red Army of the Soviet Union. The failure to do either by August-September 1941 was the undoing of Barbarossa. Instead of rushing forward to attack the far more powerful and numerous Axis army, Russian commanders defeated the three-pronged blitzkrieg by staging a fighting retreat for 400 miles into Russia, but holding the line in front of and in the major cities. The costly fighting retreat greatly delayed the Axis troops in their objectives, ensuring that the German army would be caught in the Russia winter of 1941-42, the worst winter in the 20th century.

Battle of Moscow, December 1941

In October 1941-January 1942, Marshall Zhukov, the Red Army commander, stopped his fighting retreat and set up defensive lines around Moscow. His army was greatly helped both by the onset of winter and the army's ability to replenish its ranks with new troops from the east, gaining a slight numerical advantage on their foes. Once he halted the German advance, he began to mount a counteroffensive against the German front lines, known as the Battle of Moscow. Zhukov pushed the German army back and forced them into winter encampments in western Russia. The Battle for Moscow represented probably the second most important battle of WWII, because it established a stalemate on the Eastern Front of the European theater of WWII. The Soviets were not able to completely throw the Germans out of the western part of their country until 1944, but they had successfully turned the tables on the German blitzkrieg and forced them into a bloody and costly war of attrition. Though the Allies ultimately defeated the Axis powers everywhere, most historians regard the German losses on the Eastern Front at the hands of the Red Army as the factor that truly took down the Third Reich. Moreover, the Soviets joined the Allies in June 1941, followed by the United States in December 1941. From May 1940 to May 1941, Great Britain had been fighting Germany nearly alone, but just six months later, they had a formidable alliance with two of the most powerful armies in human history — the Red Army and the United States army, navy and airforce.

Pearl Harbor, December 7, 1941

While Barbarossa brought the Soviets into the Allied camp, it was the Japanese attack on Pearl Harbor, December 7, 1941, that turned a reluctant American public into enthusiastic allies and created the Pacific theater of WWII. For two years, Imperial Japan had pressured China and Southeast Asia with invasions and harsh occupation measures. The US did not send troops, since the public preferred neutrality in 1939-41. But Roosevelt was able to retaliate against the Japanese with trade embargoes on iron ore, steel, oil, rubber, etc., and gave financial aid to the Chinese Nationalists (just as he had been giving financial and munitions aid to the British for nearly two years). The Japanese hostility toward the US grew with the bite of the embargoes.

Finally, the Japanese high command made the strategic mistake of trying to knock out the American Pacific fleet. Tactically, it was a brilliant, if highly risky plan by Admiral Isoroku Yamamoto. Though most people regard Pearl Harbor as a single battle, it was actually part of a simultaneous attack on the American-held Philippines, Guam and Wake Island and British-held Malaysia, Singapore and Hong Kong on December 7-8, 1941. Yamamoto's aim was to destroy the American and British fleets in these locations to give Japan time and opportunity to take over much of Southeast Asia and consolidate its hold on China. At Pearl Harbor, Yamamoto sent his six top-of-the-line aircraft carriers with 400 planes shrouded by cloud cover across the northern Pacific to an area northwest of Hawaii. In seven hours on that Sunday of December 7, his fleet completed four aerial strikes at the American naval base at Pearl Harbor and several related airfields; the first two destroyed most of the best battleships of the American Pacific fleet.

The great advantage to Japan was that the US had made the mistake of congregating its fleet in Pearl Harbor, easy to attack by aerial bombing runs. The disadvantage was that the three major American aircraft carriers — Enterprise, Lexington and Saratoga — were absent from Pearl Harbor. Yamamoto believed that by destroying the majority of the American battleships at Pearl Harbor, he would deliver a devastating blow. Instead, much of the rest of the Pacific War would be fought between aircraft carrier groups — the aircraft carrier, surrounded by battleships and their powerful artillery, and loaded with hundreds of aircraft that could send devastating aerial strikes miles from its homebase at sea. Perhaps no technology advanced more in the years since WWI than the sophisticated sea-going weapon of the aircraft carrier.

Midway, June 1942

In the months after Pearl Harbor, the Japanese had the run of the southeastern Pacific, capturing European territories and island nations. The American army in the Philippines was defeated at the Battle of Bataan in April 1942, large numbers of soldiers surrendering. With such success, the Japanese decided to send their fleet of six aircraft carriers again to strike directly at the American navy in the hopes yet again of destroying the aircraft carriers. This time they wanted to attack Midway, an isolated northern Pacific island that contained an important American airbase, draw in the American aircraft carriers to attempt Midway's rescue and then ambush them. This was one of the first all air-sea battles where the aircraft carriers were miles apart and never saw each other. The Japanese ambush, however, did not work. Instead, it was the American carriers who hid themselves more successfully. They sent aerial, squadrons that located the Japanese carriers at a key moment when they lacked aircover. A few squadrons of American torpedo bombers dropped dozens of bombs, point-blank, on the wood decks of the Japanese carriers and destroyed four of the six. While American carriers also took hits and one was abandoned, the blow to the Japanese fleet was insurmountable and hobbled them for the rest of the war.

But the American Pacific navy could not take advantage of Japan's weakness right after Midway. The worst problem for the Americans was that they were fighting also in Europe. The American high command and President Roosevelt, along with their British allies, judged that defeating the more powerful German army was the higher priority. Forces and allocated funds demonstrated this priority. In the course of the war, the US spent 75 percent of its war funding and its troops in Europe and only 25 percent in the Pacific. Thus, the American navy took another year and half before it began to really bring the full brunt of the fight to the Japanese. They put together a plan for the defeat of Japan that featured the aircraft carriers and an "island hopping" or capturing strategy, taking back slowly each of the small island territories and nations that the Japanese had seized in 1941-42. But one can argue that the victory over the Japanese fleet at Midway gave the American navy the time it needed to employ this systematic and efficient plan of attack against Imperial Japan.

Operation Torch, November 1942

Given the German "priority," the Americans at first favored a straightforward, large-scale attack on Germany through France. The Soviets were also demanding a second front. The British, on the other hand, argued that military operations should target peripheral areas to wear out German strength. They advocated bringing a heavy bombing campaign against German cities, spending armament instead of soldiers. Besides, the Allies needed more time to marshall their forces and build ships for what would clearly be a difficult crossing of the English Channel. Thus, the Americans agreed to begin by driving Axis forces out of North Africa and then move north to attack the weaker Axis ally, Italy, or what Churchill called the "soft underbelly" of the Axis.

Back in 1940, Fascist Italy had taken control of some areas of North Africa, but the British defeated the Italian army decisively. Italian defeats prompted Germany to send armies under the command of Erwin Rommel into North Africa. This began one of the great tank wars of WWII. The tank that was so cumbersome in WWI was now an effective weapon of troop support. The desert climate proved to be a perfect geography for rapid advances and maneuverings of troop and tank squadrons. Rommel's Afrika Korps, with their superior Panzer (tanks), soon drove the British back to western Egypt. But in August 1942, the British succeeded in repelling a series of attacks on their stronghold at El Alamein and, a few months later, commenced an attack of their own, dislodging the Axis forces from Egypt and driving across Libya.

The Americans joined this battle (their first battle in Europe) with their landings in North Africa — Operation Torch. American and British forces drove the retreating German and Italian armies into the Tunisian peninsula and then conquered the remnants in May 1943. This opened the way for the Allies to attack Sicily and eventually the Italian peninsula. Again, German armies had to be sent to Italy to stave off the Allied advance into the underbelly of Europe. Operation Torch was important not only because it gave American tank armies and commanders the opportunity to practice the tactics associated with mobilized tank warfare, but also because it introduced the US into Middle Eastern affairs, which became essential during and after the war.

Stalingrad, November 1942 to January 1943

Despite the fact that the Russian counter-offensive in the Battle of Moscow effectively stopped the German advance, a large German army remained in western Russia, particularly in the southwestern Ukraine region of the Soviet Union. The Germans regrouped and tried to push into the oil fields in the Caucasus, driving toward Stalingrad on the Volga River and nearly taking the city by mid November 1942. The Soviets decided to make their stand there. Again, they used the winter for their offensive and planned an encirclement of the German Sixth Army at Stalingrad. By early February 1943, the German Army had taken tremendous losses, their front line pushed back outside Stalingrad. German troops were caught in a pocket and the Sixth Army was forced to surrender. All of Europe understood the significance of Stalingrad. From that point, the German army was on the defensive in lands it had conquered and would stay on the defensive in Europe for the rest of the war — Stalingrad was the turning point. The Russians followed with victories in the summer 1943 in the city of Kharkov, which demonstrated that the Red Army was perfecting offensive strategies that coordinated the use of men and munitions over large terrains in a way that was not evident before the battles of Moscow and Stalingrad.

Normandy and Operation Bagration, June–July 1944

Finally, the Americans, the British, the Free French and the nations of the British Commonwealth marshalled their forces in Great Britain during the spring of 1944 for a summer assault on the northern French coast of Normandy. In a war of firsts, this was the largest amphibious assault to take a beachhead in history. The assault took place on June 6, 1944, but the night before, the Allies parachuted 24,000 airborne troops into France behind enemy lines. The next day, over 120,000 troops with tanks and heavy armor landed on five beaches along the Normandy coast. The assault did not accomplish its goal of taking several inland towns on the first day. In fact it took weeks in some cases. But the Allies had established a redoubt on French soil, never giving it up. Nearly a million Allied forces poured through the beachhead in France by the end of June, which later led to a relatively rapid liberation of Paris. The assault on German territory began in the winter of 1944-45, with the Germany army suing for peace by May 1945.

But western Allied forces were not the whole story of the final capitulation of the Third Reich. Three weeks after D-Day, the Russians attacked Germany through Belorussia in a campaign called Operation Bagration. Bagration involved even more soldiers than D-Day, and no doubt the nearly simultaneous attacks on Germany from east and west were of mutual help to each other in splitting German manpower and attention. Where earlier in the war, the Red Army depended on fighting retreats and a strategy of attrition, in Operation Bagration, they began to use effective operational tactics called "deep battle." Deep battle was offensive but not the same as blitzkrieg, which pushed all of the army through a narrow line of territory into the heart of the enemy. Deep battle was carried across a very wide front line with a series of smaller but sharp frontal attacks on the enemy in unsuspecting places along the battle line, reserve forces pouring through the gap to hold the territory. It was designed to confuse the enemy and force it to re-deploy defensively to a large number of areas. The Red Army had used deep battle to a lesser extent in the battles of Moscow and Stalingrad. But in Bagration, they took it to a much wider front line and effectively used it for the rest of the war, relentlessly pushing the German army back across the wide expanses of western Russia, Eastern Europe and Germany, until it liberated the German capital of Berlin in late April 1945.

Hiroshima and Nagasaki, August 6 and 9, 1945

The last battle of WWII was not actually a battle at all but a vitally important technical development that would have the widest and most important consequences after the war — the nuclear bombing of the Japanese cities of Hiroshima and Nagasaki on August 6 and 9 in 1945. The United States had developed a nuclear bomb by the end of WWII, because certain refugee physicists who had fled Nazi Europe understood that the Germans might have the ability to build a nuclear weapon. With the help of Albert Einstein, they communicated this possibility to President Roosevelt in August 1939. After joining the Allies, the American government decided to attempt to build a nuclear bomb and in early 1942 organized a military-research team, the Manhattan Project, to bring this about. The Project brought together over a thousand scientists, military personnel and technologist who for over three years had the goal of building the "bomb" before Germany could. After Germany surrendered in May 1945, it became clear that it had no similar nuclear project. However, WWII continued on against Imperial Japan, which had decided not to surrender with its Axis allies in the spring.

During the late spring and summer of 1945, the American army knew that its island-hopping campaign would eventually be successful and Japan was doomed. But they also noticed something rather terrifying — the closer they got to Japan, the more bloody and difficult it was to capture islands, particularly those with Japanese civilians. The desperate Japanese were sending suicide missions against American soldiers not only on land but also in the air with kamikaze pilots, whose sole purpose was to fly themselves and their planes into American ships. Two battles on islands close to mainland Japan — Iwo Jima and Okinawa — were some of the worst of the war. American command estimated that the battle to occupy Japan could take the lives of millions of Japanese and Allied soldiers. Vice President Harry Truman had become president upon the death of President Roosevelt in April 1945. It would become his decision to use the atomic bombs on smaller cities in Japan to force them to surrender or to follow the conventional strategy of a military assault on Japan. He chose the former. On August 6, 1945, a single plane, the Enola Gay, left Okinawa. carried one of two bombs the Manhattan scientists had developed and dropped it on the city of Hiroshima, killing instantly about 50,000 people. The military government of Japan refused to surrender. On August 9, a second bomb was dropped on Nagasaki, killing more than 35,000 instantly. Emperor Hirohito forced the Japanese government to surrender to spare more Japanese lives and the war ended.

In the aftermath of Hiroshima-Nagasaki, the major powers of the world understood that they had to develop nuclear weapons of their own to remain major powers. The Soviet Union, Great Britain, France, and eventually China developed nuclear weapons in the next two decades. Strangely, the development of nuclear arsenals around the world seems to have helped to prevent massive conventional world wars in the last 70 years. The reason is mutual assured destruction, or MAD. Each major power knows that if it drops a nuclear weapon on a foe, killing hundreds of thousands instantly and perhaps millions with radiation sickness over time, the foe will do the same. Since the major powers have hundreds of such bombs, they could theoretically kill all human life on earth. Thus, nuclear diplomacy has kept a tenuous peace among the major powers, having built itself on the terrible assumptions of the MAD doctrine.

Reading: The Crisis of Meaning: Artistic, Philosophical, and Political
Artistic and Philosophical Crisis

Another major theme of the first half of the 20th century is a "crisis of meaning" that was experienced both within the dominant western civilization and in the subordinated colonial world. The crisis of meaning was linked to the escalation of mass violence and the apparent contradiction between the "Enlightenment project," with its comfortable assurance of rational human nature, progress, and universal values, and the reality of senseless brutality on the ground, from trench warfare to the gas chambers. Within the "west," WWI marked the crucial turning point. It was a war of annihilation between the supposedly most advanced peoples and nations. As such, it defied rational explanation.

Some people were simply shocked by the devastation of the war. Psychologist and philosopher Sigmund Freud, however, viewed it as proof of his new theory that human beings were not essentially rational creatures. Instead, humans were internally divided between the rational and the irrational, with a powerful "unconscious" nurturing our darkest instincts for death and destruction. Indeed, the war convinced many others of Freud's more pessimistic view of human nature. Freud had been read only in medical circles before the war. In contrast, his major philosophical work, *Civilization and its Discontents* (1930), became one of the most important books of the era.

Freud argued that the progress of civilization had involved a trade-off. On the one hand, people's deepest instincts for the "rule of force" had been repressed. In return, they enjoyed the security of living under the "rule of law." Instead of the optimistic Enlightenment vision that the "rule of law" could triumph over the "rule of force," Freud insisted that the destructive urges remain, in society as in the individual. The result was a constant struggle for the survival of civilization itself, in which the outcome was anything but certain. Still, Freud argued that civilization had to keep up the struggle to repress the irrational and destructive impulses as necessary to any peaceful co-existence. Indeed, he was a big supporter of the League of Nations as a global "rule of law" to prevent another war.

In contrast, many other artists and intellectuals of the early 20th century embraced the crisis of meaning more fully, arguing that the entire Enlightenment project and its world view was dead. With no objective universal set of rules for society and no rational order, the only truth we could know was subjective, that is, reflecting a particular point of view. By implication, the dominant political system of liberalism was also doomed. It relied on rational human individuals and universal truth (as in the U.S. Declaration of Independence: "We hold these truths to be self-evident..."). Not surprisingly then, many of the artists and intellectuals of this generation became political as well as cultural rebels, abandoning liberalism and embracing one of the anti-liberal political movements of the era, particularly fascism or communism.

Three major artistic movements of the period that exemplify these trends are Futurism, Dadaism, and Surrealism. Futurism was launched as both an artistic and philosophical movement in the *1909 Manifesto*, with an explicit embrace of speed and its destabilizing qualities. One of their favorite metaphors was the automobile, not as a product of rational technological invention but as a symbol of brute force and exhilaration. Instead of fearing the potential chaos, Futurists cheerfully abandoned the certainties of the past. In relation to these themes, Futurist paintings tried to capture the dynamism of objects in motion, expressing change, mutability, and the refusal to acknowledge a stable, fixed material reality that could serve as an anchor for truth and reason. In Boccioni's *Riot in the Galeria* (1911), for example, the seething crowd is blended together in a psychic display of energy that is clearly more important than the (unknown) reason for the riot. Indeed, "riot" is in itself a word that exemplifies irrational anger.

Dadaism contained a similar embrace of uncertainty and irrationality, with a desire to shock and break through the limited confines of rational thought. Dada was a nonsense word, chosen at random to express the nonsensical nature of the world. Artists were encouraged to penetrate the rational surface using spontaneous methods like collage and stream of consciousness to draw out the disorder of our emotional depths. Similarly, Surrealism tried to plumb the murky recesses of the unconscious. A prime example is Salvador Dali's grotesque painting, *The Spectre of Sex Appeal* (1929), in which a monster-like figure moves across a desert landscape like the powerful sexual desires that dominate the brain. In sum, these movements do not offer a coherent alternative world view. Instead, they are a chaotic and multi-pronged attack on the certainty of an Enlightenment project that had claimed to be leading human society towards a more rational world order.

Political Crisis: Communism

It is within this larger context of a philosophical crisis of meaning that the alternative political movements of communism and fascism make sense as a collective response, despite their important differences. Beginning with communism, the best way to understand its anti-rational spirit is to contrast it with its 19th-century Marxist roots. Lenin shared Marx's basic goals of a working-class revolution leading to an egalitarian future, but he shifted the emphasis on how to get there.

For Marx, history moved according to rational laws of nature, with powerful structural forces pushing human society towards a more evolved future. The unjust capitalist economic system, he argued, was creating the very class (i.e., the proletariat, or working class who filled the factories of the new industrial economy) that would overthrow it. Thus, the growing contradictions of an economic system that produced its own enemy would inevitably destroy it. Once capitalist industrial society and the proletariat had fully developed, a political revolution was bound to unfold naturally. To express his certainty, Marx called his theory "scientific socialism."

By 1914, however, Marxism had reached an impasse, with large socialist parties that seemed no closer to the revolution than they had been 60 years earlier. It was Lenin that helped break this impasse by shifting the emphasis in Marx's theory from scientific inevitability to the force of action. Lenin's concept of "insurrection as an art" nicely exemplifies this shift with its implication that revolution was a creative act, not the working out of the laws of history. This seemingly simple shift opened up a whole new set of possibilities within Marxist theory.

Thus, for example, according to Marx's timetable Russia was not ready for a socialist revolution. It had a tiny proletariat and an incipient industrial economy. Nevertheless, Lenin argued that Russia was ready, judged by what he calls the "revolutionary spirit of the people." Turning Marx's theory on its head, the political seizure of power would precede the economic transition from feudalism to an industrial capitalist economy. While for Marx the power of socialism was its scientific inevitability, for Lenin power was about the excitement of heroic action. This excitement in and of itself was one reason why communism attracted many people in an era that glorified spontaneous action over staid reason. However, although communism mobilized millions across Europe, before WWII there was only one successful communist revolution.

Fascism

In a general way, fascism spoke the same language of action and will. It promised to integrate the masses into a heroic community, even though its goals were very different. Fascism was unlike communism, which was a makeover of an existing movement. Fascism was the major political innovation of the first half of the 20th century. It was arguably the biggest threat to the liberal democratic West. The fascist revolution in Italy (1922-5) began to challenge the model that liberal democracy was gradually spreading through Europe and later would spread through the world as the epitome of rational political organization. By the 1930s, liberal democracy was on the defensive, and most of the newer and even some older democracies had been replaced by authoritarian regimes, including fascist versions in Germany (1933) and Spain (1939). Nazi Germany's expansionist aims, which many argue follow directly from fascist ideology, spread fascism across the continent before it was defeated in 1945.

At the heart of fascism was an aggressive ultra-nationalism that sought to channel all individual energies into the aggrandizement of the nation. Beyond mere patriotism, ultra-nationalism implied a Darwinian struggle of the fittest. Instead of Marx's theory of "class struggle," fascists believed in the struggle among nations for domination. It follows from this nationalist framework that fascists were both anti-liberal and anti-communist. Instead of the liberal "pursuit of happiness" for each individual, fascism insisted on service to the nation, while communists were despised for dividing the nation into warring social classes.

Determining who belonged to the nation was not always obvious, however. The German Nazis distinguished between "us" and "them" using racial categories. Jews were specifically targeted as an inferior race that was defiling the "purity" of the German race by intermixing. The Italian Fascists began with a more cultural understanding of national identity, although Italy did adopt anti-Semitic policies in the 1930s-40s as it increasingly came under Nazi influence. Scholars still debate over whether the differences between Nazism and Italian fascism justify viewing them as distinct genres or as subsets of a common fascist typology.

Common to both Italy and Germany was the innovative combination of mass political mobilization and authoritarian charismatic leadership. Thus, the movement actively sought to win followers and impose absolute obedience at the same time. The leader principle signified that the leader was endowed with almost mystical authority. There was a terroristic side to both the seizure of power and to fascist rule, with political police, the disarticulation of opposition movements, and the arrest of their leaders. But on the other hand, by seeking mass consent, the fascist movements sought willing and active adherence. To this end, fascist movements mounted impressive propaganda campaigns. In fact, fascists were among the first to effectively utilize the techniques of modern propaganda and spectacle, from banners and uniforms to parades, posters, and mass rallies. Scholars still debate the balance between terror and consent in fascist rule, but both Hitler and Mussolini took seriously the challenge of winning hearts and minds.

In the first half of the 20th century, many people were attracted by the heroic spectacle of either fascism or communism, but by the end of WWII, the picture had changed significantly. In the western half of Europe, interest in democracy was revived. Meanwhile, the dangers of extreme anti-liberalism and its indifference to individual life became brutally clear, a tendency that some post-war scholars labeled "totalitarianism." On one extreme, "totalitarianism" extinguished all individual autonomy, while on the other, pure individualism left individuals without any protections. Political systems in the second half of the century continued to struggle with finding an acceptable balance between the community and the individual.

Reading: National Liberation/Decolonization

An important theme for the many peoples living under colonial rule at the beginning of the 20th century was the transition from colony to independent nation. While most of the process of decolonization occurred later in the 20th century, there are several important vanguard cases whose paths towards independence would serve as models going forward.

The first was the Mexican Revolution (1910-7), almost a century after the country achieved formal independence from Spain. Despite formal independence, Mexico was still struggling to create a coherent nation state that could protect itself against neocolonial intervention. Thus the Revolution fits under the rubric of independence struggles. The other two important cases were the Chinese Revolution (1911-49) and the Indian independence movement (1919-47), both of which culminated in the late 1940s. Each of these foundational movements charted a different path of anti-imperialist nationalism, which set the parameters for the later tidal wave of decolonization from the 1960s. By that point, anti-imperialist national liberation had become the primary political force in the non-western world.

China

The Chinese revolution that erupted in 1911 overthrew a centuries-old imperial order that had lost most of its power and prestige against encroaching economic imperialist power. While China was never formally incorporated as a colony, it had been divided up into "economic spheres of influence." In these spheres, foreign powers controlled access to markets and raw materials, set tariffs, and had rights to establish military bases and foreign laws in their territories. Even though this economic imperialism left China politically independent, it had so undermined the legitimacy of the old order that the empire quickly collapsed. Between 1911 and 1949, competing movements sought to define the parameters of a Chinese nationalism that could both unite the country and establish its independence. As the victorious Mao Tse Tung proclaimed at the establishment of the People's Republic in 1949, "ours will not any longer be a nation subject to insult and humiliation. We have stood up."

The victory of Mao and the Communist Party against the Guomindang (Chinese Nationalist Party) came after a long civil war. It can be explained as an outcome of a variety of factors, including the social and economic appeal of the CCCP and the invasion of the Japanese army in the 1930s. Both of these movements originated in western ideologies. However, the question is to what degree China's path to national liberation remained within these contours. While there is certainly evidence for western imitation, the victorious CCCP also put its own stamp on the communist model, adapting it to local circumstances.

Mao started his political education with western ideas, beginning with vaguely democratic and liberal beliefs, but he became disillusioned after the Paris Peace Conference, which did not return China's foreign-controlled territory. He helped found the CCCP in 1921 after reading Marx and Lenin. Over the next few years, Mao and his comrades followed the Russian model of organizing workers and students in China's coastal urban centers under the banner of both anti-capitalism and anti-imperialism. However, when that movement was crushed in 1927 by the GMD, the CCCP under Mao's leadership adopted a new strategy of mobilizing peasants. For Marx, peasants were irrelevant to the revolution; for Lenin, peasants supported the workers. In China, a country with even fewer industrial workers than Russia, the poor peasants became — by necessity — the main revolutionary class.

At the same time, the anti-imperialist side of the communist movement was further strengthened with the Japanese invasion, when the CCCP waged a guerrilla war against the imperial power. By the time Mao bragged about China standing up, he was acknowledging that nationalism was as important as anti-capitalism for a communist movement that had, in the European context, always been internationalist in its aims. The result was a powerful model of communist nationalism which was taken up by a variety of poor agrarian countries like Cuba, Angola, and Vietnam. As with China, their situations were far removed even from Lenin's adaptation of Marx.

The question is whether Maoism, over the course of its evolutionary adaptation in surviving the Civil War, created an indigenous revolutionary ideology. Or does it simply fall along a spectrum of communist movements? How one answers this question goes back to the issue of whether political initiative had shifted to the non-western world, or whether the "West" was still providing the framework within which 20th-century global politics could be imagined.

India

In contrast to China's communist nationalism, India epitomized the liberal democratic nationalist path to independence. In its 1948 Constitution, the new Indian nation state embodied the basic elements of representative government, pluralism, civil rights, and the rule of law. At the same time, the Indian path was not simply a carbon copy of the western original. Just as communism had been adapted to the Chinese context, so liberal democracy was mixed with elements from indigenous culture and tradition. From the founding of the Indian National Congress in 1885, which met to propose reforms to British rule, to the shift towards independence in the years after WWI, there was an ongoing tension between a dependence on western tools and models provided by the British and creative adaptation.

The dependence on western tools and models was evident in the very structure of the first INC meeting. The British-educated elites who attended the conference spoke in their common language of English and accused the British imperial government of not upholding its own principles of self-government and freedom. Later, there were several turning points that pushed the INC from its initial reformist stance to an independence movement, but all evolved from the idea that the British were unwilling to relinquish their double standard.

The most important turning point, however, was WWI. The British appealed to Indians to fight for the Empire, and over one million volunteered. But as the war dragged on and anti-war sentiment grew, the British took the fatal step of promising "the progressive realization of responsible government in India." However, after the war, not only was there no progress towards "home rule," the British seemed determined to violently repress any political discussion in India. A dramatic illustration of this refusal was the so-called Amritsar massacre in April 1919, when British troops fired on an unarmed protest against arbitrary rule, killing 400-500 civilians. In the tradition of imposing the rule of force instead of the rule of law in the colonies, the massacre brutally exposed the double standard for all to see.

The INC turned towards independence in the wake of British hypocrisy in implementing its own principles. Meanwhile, the emerging leader, Mohandas Gandhi, also insisted that resistance was required for religious reasons. Thus, when he raised the call to rise against the British rulers, he argued that Hindus who failed to resist would jeopardize their souls. At the same time, Gandhi was a British-educated lawyer who was fully conversant in liberal democratic principles.

Returning to India from South Africa in 1915, Gandhi quickly rose to prominence in the nationalist movement. This role was a result of his ability to bridge the gap between a minority British-educated elite and the vast largely illiterate (88 percent) majority who could understand his religious vocabulary and the spiritual nationalism he created. Although India was a religious quilt of Muslims, Sikhs, Jains, Buddhists, and Hindus, Hinduism was enough of a majority religion to provide an at least partially unifying form of popular national identity.

In Gandhi's spiritual nationalism, political independence had to begin with the spiritual transformation of the people. Specifically, he argued that until the Indian people had learned their own self-respect, they couldn't demand it from the British. Thus, the freedom movement began with what he called the "preparation of the people," putting them in a state of spiritual readiness to demand freedom. In contrast, Marx had argued that people could not be spiritually free until political and economic oppression had been abolished. The technique of preparation was called "satyagraha," or the search for truth. It purified the heart of the searcher and was meant to change the heart of the enemy as well.

One of the central tenets of spiritual readiness was the willingness to suffer for one's beliefs, which put non-violence at the center of his philosophy of resistance. Over the course of the following years, Gandhi pursued this preparation with collective satyagraha campaigns that involved hundreds of thousands of people. They boycotted British goods and the making of Indian cloth. They would not pay taxes, quit government jobs, and so on. The point was to convince the British it was not worthwhile to maintain their evil rule and teach Indians to rely on themselves and come together as a nation.

While Gandhi's spiritual nationalism put an indigenous stamp on India's democratic model, it also helped create the potential for serious divisions along religious lines. Even though Gandhi himself preached religious tolerance, the mobilization of Hindu identity in the service of Indian nationalism created suspicion on the part of religious minorities that they would not be treated equally. The immediate result was the so-called partition of the empire into a Hindu state (India) and a Muslim state (Pakistan), but religious conflict continued to plague Indian democracy. Hardly unique to India, most democracies maintain an unstable tension between the individualist and universalist goals of diversity and the specific markers of collective identity that draw communities together.

Mexico

The third vanguard case of anti-imperialist nationalism took shape in the Mexican revolution that broke out in 1910. Even though Mexico had been formally independent since 1824, the revolution had a strong anti-imperialist agenda. In schematic terms, early 20th-century Mexico suffered from the impact of a dual imperialist legacy. The first phase of Spanish imperialism had left behind a vastly unequal two-tier social structure in which one percent of the population owned 85 percent of the land. Creole elites were at the top of the hierarchy and the indigenous population at the bottom, as famously represented by Diego Rivera in his public murals.

The second phase, later coined by Ghanaian President Kwame Nkrumah in his 1965 book as "neocolonialism," consisted of relations of economic and political domination and subordination that arose after independence. Since the Latin American countries participated in one of the earliest phases of decolonization, they were also among the first to experience the impact of "neocolonialism," a problem generally associated with the post-WWII era decolonization.

In the mid-19th century, it was British financial interests that played a major role, imposing a free trade system that flooded the markets with British industrial products while extracting raw materials in return. By the end of the 19th century, US financial interests came to the fore. Thus, in Mexico, by 1910, 20 percent of national territory was owned by foreigners in addition to 94 percent of all mines, railroads, ports, and banks. Two-thirds of all economic investment came from foreign sources. The Mexican Revolution was the first serious attempt to address the dual imperialist legacy. It was later followed by the Cuban revolution in 1959 and the Sandinista revolution in Nicaragua in 1979, each of which looked back in some way to the Mexican case.

Like the other nationalist movements, the Mexican Revolution drew on western political ideas, but as in the other cases, the protagonists adapted them to fit better local conditions. Similar to the Chinese case, there were competing groups who rallied around liberal constitutionalism on the one hand and egalitarian redistribution on the other. The so-called Constitutionalists represented elite economic interests who were mainly interested in wresting control away from foreign powers. The Zapatistas represented poor indigenous peasants who wanted to redress the other imperial legacy of social inequality.

The upshot was a compromise that produced a hybrid model, neither liberal, nor democratic, nor communist. On the one hand, the Constitution recognized pluralism, representation, and individual civil rights, while on the other hand, it sought to acknowledge and redress the marginalization of specific groups. In particular, workers and peasants were explicitly identified as disadvantaged populations deserving of special government intervention, such as land redistribution.

Implemented by subsequent administrations, especially that of Lazaro Cardenas (1934-40), special collective representation was instituted. This arrangement meant reserving a number of legislative seats for worker and peasant candidates. The hybrid model also applied to the stance towards neocolonialism, in which the Constitution tried to achieve a balance between Mexico's integration into the global economy and its pursuit of economic independence, with measures to limit foreign investment and intervention. The first test case of this compromise came in 1938, when Cardenas decided to expropriate the US oil companies for refusing to abide by Mexican labor laws while promising not to pursue a general policy of expropriation.

In addition to the innovation of the hybrid model itself, the agenda of the Zapatista camp, as expressed in the Plan de Ayala and the agrarian program, was rooted in the specific structure of

Mexican society. Thus, in some ways, the Zapatistas were similar to the communists in China. They demanded major redistribution of wealth from rich to poor. At the same time, their peasant leader, Emiliano Zapata, framed this project as a recovery of indigenous rights and traditions, not as a Marxist class struggle. Thus, expropriation of haciendas would lead to the re-creation of the ejido system of communal farming. This language of recovery and restitution was very different from the Marxist narrative of moving forward towards the next higher social order. As a result, it reflected the distinct constellation of Mexican society in contrast to China. Just as the Chinese CCCP under Mao put its own stamp on the Marxist tradition, so did the Zapatistas create their own version of a social revolution legitimated by the past rather than the future.

What conclusions can we draw about global history during this era from this brief examination of mass violence, the crisis of meaning, and national liberation movements? While these trends undoubtedly made it impossible to return to any simplistic notions of human progress, they also produced creative responses that demonstrate resilience and adaptation. Thus, out of the devastation of fascism, genocide, and total war, the post-war order tried to construct international institutions like the United Nations and laws like the Genocide Convention that they hoped would prevent such future catastrophes. It would take another few decades for the communist bloc of Eastern European countries to collapse in 1989, leaving democracy as the aspirational global political system at the end of the 20th century. And while decolonization/national liberation did not lead to the full empowerment of "third world" peoples, it definitively ended the era of formal empires and enshrined the principle of a world of sovereign nation states. Like all historical eras, it was defined by contradictory impulses and consequences that defy any simple "lessons" to carry forward into the future, even as it left its powerful imprint on the rest of the century.

Unit 15: The Bipolar World and its Demise
Katherine A. S. Sibley, St. Joseph's University

Reading: The Making of the Post-War World Order, 1945-63
World War II Legacy
In 1945, a new world began, drawing on the vision laid out in the war with the Atlantic Charter (1941), Declaration of the United Nations (1942), the security and economic agreements of Dumbarton Oaks and Bretton Woods (1944), as well as the UN Charter of 1945. All of these initiatives were created or dominated by the leading allied powers of World War II, including the United States, the Soviet Union, Britain, France, and China. Yet these new agreements and institutions, with their emphasis on social security, political freedom, and humanitarian goals, as well as their promotion of national self-determination and their establishments of financial assistance mechanisms, would be a key symbol for the nations in the developing world as it broke away from colonialism. The Atlantic Charter had proclaimed "the right of all peoples to choose the form of government under which they will live." The UN Charter, moreover, promised that "human beings may be permitted to live decently as free people." These twin promises, political freedom and social security, were augmented in 1948 by the Universal Declaration on Human Rights; notable in the Declaration was an affirmation of women's rights owing to the efforts of the UN's Committee on the Status of Women.

Vietnamese nationalist Ho Chi Minh was one who hoped to free his country from colonialism on the principles of self-determination. A month after the Japanese Empire ended in August 1945 in the wake of the US atomic attacks, Ho used words borrowed from the American Declaration of Independence to pronounce his nation's right to fight the return of the French to imperial control there. But the US identified Ho and his Viet Minh organization as a Communist threat to the region. President Dwight D. Eisenhower believed that Vietnam was a "domino" that once turned to the Communist bloc, would knock over other regimes in Southeast Asia. Vietnam's independence — communist or not — was thus sacrificed to Cold War objectives, and the US entered into a deep military engagement there which long outlasted the French and cost almost 60,000 American lives and those of 1.4 million Vietnamese, Laotians, and Cambodians by the time it ended in 1975.

US attaché George F. Kennan declared in 1946 as the Cold War opened that "world communism is like [a] malignant parasite which feeds only on diseased tissue." Soviet ambassador Nikolai Novikov fumed in return that the US was bent on "world supremacy." As tensions rose, the US enacted two large aid packages to shore up anti-communist regimes and alleviate economic suffering in Europe and the Middle East: the Truman Doctrine (1947) for Greece and Turkey, and the Marshall Plan (1948), which offered $12 billion for 16 countries in Western Europe. But American funding could do little to stop a communist takeover in China, where Mao Zedong created the People's Republic in 1949, supported by the Soviet Union. In 1950, both communist giants encouraged Kim Il Sung of North Korea to attack South Korea (which was quickly defended by the United States and the UN) in the first major Cold War conflict.

Decolonization
It was during the Korean War, in 1952, that French demographer Alfred Sauvy coined the term "Third World." He saw the developing nations as reminiscent of the Third Estate, the commoners in France before the French Revolution. He wrote: "ignored, exploited, scorned... [the] Third World like the Third Estate, wants to become something too." Within two years, an independence movement in the French colony of Algeria emerged that would, like the Third Estate, eventually topple the French leadership. Those who represented the most oppressed in the United States also strongly identified with this struggle against colonialism: as W. E. B. DuBois of the NAACP, the biggest African-American civil rights organization, noted, "Until Africa is free, the descendants of Africa the world over cannot escape chains."

Truman understood the aspirations that Sauvy had identified. In his inauguration speech in 1949, the US president noted: "we must embark on a bold new program for making the benefits of our scientific advances and industrial progress available for the improvement and growth of underdeveloped areas. More than half the people of the world are living in conditions approaching misery....Their poverty is a handicap and a threat both to them and to more prosperous areas."

Truman's reference to the "threat" inherent in the developing world's suffering also marked these nations as a key Cold War concern. American assistance to them grew to $400 million by 1954 and evolved into such efforts as the Agency for International Development.

Yet despite this effort, most new nations in Africa and Asia adopted socialist models; this approach — state led, centrally planned, anti-capitalist and anti-colonialist — would long remain appealing to Third World leaders. From Nigeria to India, Arne Westad notes, "it promised modernity *and* justice; technology *and* social progress." To Kwame Nkrumah of Ghana, by contrast, capitalism was "slavery" and a form of neo-colonialism. Unfortunately, such stronger, centralized states also led to strongmen, like Nkrumah would be.

Suez and Cuban Missile Crisis

Egypt's Gamal Abdel Nasser, who came to power in 1952, sought a middle road between the two superpowers. At the Bandung conference of Asian and African Nations of 1955, he had embraced "positive neutralism," avoiding any Cold War alliances. Nasser, who had overthrown King Farouk and ended British occupation in his country, was wooed by President Eisenhower with aid and urged to join a pro-Western defense league, but he refused, instead using the US offers as leverage for assistance from the Soviet Union. Thus, Nasser obtained weapons from Soviet Czechoslovakia *and* Washington's promises of assistance for the Aswan Dam, a $1.3 billion project to increase Egypt's arable land and its power supplies.

But the US distrusted Nasser's ties with the Soviets and with Communist China; the Eisenhower Administration pulled aid for the dam on July 19, 1956. In response, Nasser nationalized the canal — infuriating the British and French, who still owned it. To reverse the nationalization they bombed Egyptian airstrips and were joined by the Israeli Air Force, who swept in taking arms and 6,000 soldiers around the canal zone. Moscow quickly demanded Israel, France, and Britain pull out, with a veiled nuclear threat that put the US Strategic Air Command on alert. At the same time, Soviet troops crushed an uprising in Hungary. Infuriated at his allies' neo-colonialism and wishing to make sure that Suez did not become a Cold War conflagration, Eisenhower pressured the European nations to leave Egypt. Nasser kept his canal and became a hero to Arab nationalists in the region. This example of Third World liberation underlined basic human rights, in Nasser's view: "I am speaking in the name of principles proclaimed by these countries in the Atlantic Charter," he tossed back at the British and French.

While Nasser flirted with both sides, in Latin America, the region's leaders hoped their Cold War loyalties would bring US support. But Secretary of State George Marshall, who came to a Bogota conference of the American States (soon to be known as the Organization of American States, or OAS) in 1948, offered only $500 million. His visit coincided with the assassination of a popular land reform supporter, Jorge Eliecer Gaitan, which led to riots and the deaths of thousands. The US saw Gaitanism and other populist movements like it as dangerous — fostering the expectations that would lead to Communism, and other Latin American governments agreed. The region would be dominated by right-wing dictators for the next several decades.

One of these, Carlos Castillo Armas, was installed by the US in Guatemala in 1954 after the overthrow of that nation's elected leader, Jacob Arbenz, following his land reform and nationalization measures which Washington saw as linked to Communism. A young Argentinian in Guatemala at that time was inspired by this event to spread revolution elsewhere: Che Guevara, who would later go to Cuba and support Fidel Castro.

Latin America's fate, it seemed, was inexorably tied up with the Cold War, bringing American-sponsored coups or interventions not only in Guatemala but also in Cuba (1961), Brazil (1964), the Dominican Republic (1965), Chile (1973), and Nicaragua (1981-6). At the same time, beginning in the Kennedy Administration the US and American firms sent over $22 billion in grants, loans, and investments under the auspices of the Alliance for Progress (1961-7) a program intended to mitigate poverty in the region and touted (at last) as the area's Marshall Plan. Unfortunately, economic and political circumstances in the region prevented much change for Latin Americans. Here was where Americans saw in closest proximity the Communist menace, real or not, and here the Soviet Union ventured the furthest to promote its goals, as the Cuban Missile Crisis showed in 1962.

By early 1960, the Eisenhower Administration, which had hitherto been open to Fidel Castro's new regime in Cuba, turned cold owing to his cozier relationship with Russia. In March, Washington began hatching plans to overthrow Castro. Fourteen hundred Cuban refugees in Guatemala and Nicaragua were trained to invade Cuba at the Bay of Pigs, but Castro was ready for the attack on April 17, 1961.

Khrushchev worried that the United States might try to harm his ally, Castro, again. Thus in 1962 the Soviet Union took the risky step of installing medium and long-range ballistic missiles in Cuba which could reach as far as Washington; they were identified by US spy planes in October 1962.

With the world suddenly on the brink of war (and the US did not even know these missiles had nuclear warheads), Kennedy established an Executive Committee of his National Security Council. The first option, an airstrike, was deemed too dangerous. The US instead implemented a 200-ship blockade, or quarantine, with the support of the OAS, and the nation was told on October 22. As tension was building, Fidel Castro privately urged a nuclear strike on the United States in a letter to Khrushchev. The Soviet leader instead asked Kennedy to remove the Jupiter missiles in Turkey, a request that could not reasonably be denied.

The Soviets agreed to take the missiles out under UN auspices only with the final secret agreement that the US would commit to leaving Cuba alone. Castro was furious at being made a pawn in the Cold War; he could, at least, be gratified that he remained a beacon to Third World revolutionaries for standing up to the United States.

Fortunately, the superpowers had avoided a horrific war, and also developed closer communications and soon a new treaty banning above-ground testing. But even then, the United States was about to be getting much deeper into another Third World war, Vietnam.

Reading: Global Institutions and the Stability of the Post-War World (Topical Essay)

Katherine Sibley has been researching and writing about Russian espionage and US counter espionage for nearly two decades and has a superb reputation for dragging the dramatic truth out of the archives. In her books and articles, Sibley has demonstrated that Washington's longstanding efforts to keep this topic under wraps has led to misunderstandings not only about how active Moscow's spies were in the United States, but to what extent the US government was knowledgeable and effective in stopping their penetration of American industry and technology. Sibley writes not only about spies, but also consults with the State Department's Historian's Office as part of its Historical Advisory Committee, which advocates for timely declassification of documents and responsible transparency.

This image is a mural in the Rincon Center Lobby of San Francisco by the artist Anton Refregier. Refregier painted the mural "War and Peace" in 1948. On the left is Fascism, the center is the Four Freedoms, which derives from a speech by Franklin Roosevelt, and the representation on the right depicts the various nations of the world seated at the conference table of the United Nations in San Francisco.

World War II was incredibly destructive; with more than 60 million deaths, its toll exceeded that of any other war in human history (this was approximately three percent of the 1940 global population). These chilling statistics have led historian Thomas W. Zeiler to call it "a war of annihilation."

At the same time, this cataclysm made possible a unified effort among the Allied powers: nations such as the US, Britain, France, China, and the Soviet Union, who moved to create lasting initiatives, structures, and agreements. These would not only check the kinds of nationalistic rivalries that made the war occur, but greatly improve the lives of those who survived World War II and their descendants — even if their war-forged unity did not last.

This essay will explore these institutions, World War II's diplomatic, economic, and humanitarian legacy for the postwar world: the United Nations, the Bretton Woods system, and the Universal Declaration of Human Rights. The men and women who envisioned these initiatives had survived not only the war but the Great Depression. They insisted on global cooperation to prevent future conflicts whether political or economic; their emphasis on "social security" or human well-being was a reaction to the horrors they had witnessed. At the same time, they were also dominated by a Western worldview that shaped their assumptions, especially on matters pertaining to the developing world, with sometimes problematic consequences.

While the input on these institutions would bear the stamp of many nations in the alliance, underlying all of them were the sentiments expressed in US President Franklin D. Roosevelt's "Four Freedoms" speech of January 1941. Roosevelt spoke of his hope for a world where all had freedom of speech and religion, and freedom from want and fear. Along with his clear espousal of US engagement in collective security against aggressors in the same speech — almost a year before Pearl Harbor — Roosevelt's freedoms were at the base of these institutions.

By August of 1941, with the war intensifying, the US president met his British counterpart Winston Churchill on the deck of the HMS Prince of Wales in Placentia Bay, Newfoundland. As the two men sang hymns they had known since childhood, they produced the Atlantic Charter. With its call for "social security," "economic advancement," as well as "freedom from fear and want," the Charter went beyond an agreement for "the final destruction of Nazi tyranny" to include social and humanitarian goals. Moreover, it also invited a "wider and permanent system of general security," an international organization to replace the defunct League of Nations.

Neither man could know what tragic events would bring them together again just four months later. On December 7, the Japanese military attacked the US naval base at Pearl Harbor, killing more than 2,400 people, and three days later, destroyed the Prince of Wales and another British ship, the misnamed Repulse, off Ceylon, killing 840 more. The US now joined Britain in the war.

On New Year's Day, 1942, more than two dozen nations fighting the Axis powers signed the "Declaration of the United Nations" in Washington, a document which drew closely on the Atlantic Charter and its call for economic and political security. Later in the war, representatives of the US, Britain, China, and the Soviet Union met at Dumbarton Oaks in Washington, DC, to set up plans for a new organization, the United Nations. Then in April 1945, with the war just concluding in Europe but still raging in Asia, representatives of 50 countries met in San Francisco to draft the UN Charter. Its preamble would echo the earlier meetings of the war: "to reaffirm faith in fundamental human rights...to promote social progress and better standards of life...[and] to unite our strength to maintain international peace and security." Once again, the Atlantic Charter's political, economic and humanitarian goals were evident.

The organization's leadership comprised a security council made up of Britain, France, China, the Soviet Union, and the United States. While the People's Republic of China replaced Taiwan as the China seat in 1971, these five World War II victors remain the most powerful members to this day, their permanent status and exclusive veto power a source of some controversy. Ten other nations also are elected to serve on the council for two-year terms; the rest serve in the General Assembly, which today includes 193 nations.

Despite its founding at a moment of World War II unity, the Cold War soon overshadowed the organization. When the UN refused to seat the People's Republic of China in 1949, for instance, the Soviets boycotted the Security Council, enabling UN troops to defend South Korea in its war with Communist North Korea in 1950, a decision the Soviet Union would have vetoed. While rescuing the South Koreans from the Northern regime, the Cold War also undermined other UN goals, propping up dictators like Castro in Cuba and Mobutu in the Congo when they served the strategies of either the United States or the Soviet Union.

Wars and territorial disputes have never ceased since 1945, and another key UN role is the dispatch of peacekeepers to troubled regions, often assisting civilians caught in the crossfire. Along with peacekeepers, made up of forces from member nations, the UN sponsors a vast range of programs from UNICEF to UN Women; refugees, sustainable development, and health are among its many priorities.

As its Charter confirmed, a chief function of the UN is economic security, which consumed the efforts of another wartime conference, in Bretton Woods, New Hampshire, in 1944. Since Depression-era "beggar thy neighbor" economic policies were blamed for the outbreak of war, deriving from such practices as manipulated currency valuations or protectionism, Bretton Woods created mechanisms to ensure cooperation to prevent these actions.

US Treasury economist Harry Dexter White drew up a plan with his British counterpart, economist John Maynard Keynes, and while the two did not agree on the US dominance of White's plan, their end result, the International Monetary Fund, would eventually provide stability to the global economy that helped it weather global crises like that of 2007-9. White also insisted that currencies would be tied to the US dollar, backed by gold. As the US held most of the world's gold, White prevailed, although later, debts from the Vietnam War, among other factors, would force President Richard Nixon to end the gold standard in 1971 and allow the dollar to float against other currencies. Along with the IMF and the gold standard, the Bretton Woods system also established the International Bank for Reconstruction and Development, known as the World Bank. Like the IMF, it is part of the United Nations. The World Bank has since loaned more than $300 billion to the developing world.

In 1946 White convinced Congress of the need for these financial instruments by pointing to the problematic effects of America's abdication of international involvement after World War I. Two years later, in 1948, White would speak to Congress again, with less salutary results. The House Un-American Activities Committee had called his wartime contacts with Soviet agents into question, and the stress of these hearings, along with his weakening health, induced a deadly heart attack just days later. Whatever his political leanings, White left a durable scaffold for the world's economy.

Initially, strict IMF accounting requirements were not flexible enough to deal with postwar devastation, and the US government found it necessary to directly loan $3.75 billion to Britain in 1946 (the equivalent of $57 billion in 2015). The first IMF loan, to France for $250 million, only came in 1948. That year, as formerly democratic Czechoslovakia became a Soviet satellite, the US also directly extended more than $13 billion to Europe in the Marshall plan, hoping to contain Communism.

Over the next six decades, the IMF would be an increasingly effective engine for preserving economic stability. However, the US and its Western bloc allies have long dominated the organization, and developing nations have lacked a voice. Since the 1980s, too, the Fund has employed measures on developing countries in economic crises which also reflect a Western bias, such as fiscal austerity, free market initiatives and globalization (often called the Washington Consensus). In 2015, the US Congress at last approved some long needed reforms in the Fund to enable more democracy in the organization as well as more influence by emerging economic powerhouses like China, India, and Brazil. At the same time, Chinese leaders launched the Asian Infrastructure Investment Bank, the first major regional alternative to the Bretton Woods system with nearly 60 members. Its website calls it a bank "conceived for the twenty-first century."

The Holocaust had a profound role in the declaration. The US and most other nations had done little to assist victims of Hitler's regime, and at war's end the evidence of Nazi atrocities and other depredations, including the plight of a million refugees in Eastern Europe, spurred action at last. Former First Lady Eleanor Roosevelt became a delegate to the UN General Assembly's first gathering in London, and her committee helped ensure these refugees would not be forcibly repatriated, as Soviet representative Andrei Vyshinsky wanted. As chair of the UN Commission on Human Rights, she would take a leading role in drafting the Universal Declaration in 1948, and see it adopted by 40 countries; the Soviet Union and its satellites refused, however, as did Saudi Arabia (which claimed its incompatibility with Sharia law) and South Africa. It included such principles as "freedom of thought, conscience, and religion"; the right to leave and re-enter one's country; the right to education and leisure; and prohibitions of torture and slavery. More than 150 nations have since signed the UN Covenants on Human Rights, which include the Covenant on Political and Economic Rights and the International Covenant on Economic, Social, and Cultural Rights, giving it the force of international law.

The Declaration has its flaws and its critics; it had no plank against racial discrimination, for example. At a sensitive moment in the Cold War, Eleanor Roosevelt knew such a statement would open up the US to attack from the Soviet Union, as well as raise the hackles of powerful Southern Democrats. As Carol Anderson has noted, the document's professions of "equality before the law" thus could raise charges of "hypocrisy" against the United States, something that US diplomat George F. Kennan also recognized.

African American lawyer Pauli Murray, on the other hand, applauded the Declaration as "the best of Christian-Judeo-Democratic culture." Yet as her endorsement shows, this is a Western standard that relies on the notion of individual rights within the context of the nation-state. Other cultures and religions emphasize the rights of the community over the rights of the individual, including Islamic and Confucian traditions. As the American Anthropological Association wrote in a protest submitted to the Commission in 1947: "Standards and values are relative to the culture from which they derive…postulates that grow out of the beliefs or moral codes of one culture…detract from the applicability of any Declaration of Human Rights to mankind as a whole."

The Declaration's tenets may not be universal, but its legacy has been far reaching all the same. By creating a standard of humanitarianism, it gave activists an instrument to promote change. It was the Declaration that motivated British lawyer Peter Benenson to form Amnesty International in 1961, when he discovered that Portuguese students had been imprisoned for "toasting freedom." The mission of Amnesty International, now a large NGO, is to ensure that the world's people "enjoy all of the human rights enshrined in the Universal Declaration of Human Rights." Its purview includes the US as well, where police brutality in Ferguson, Missouri and the detentions of suspected terrorists at Guantanamo Bay, Cuba have raised concerns. Since 1948, moreover, the UN has also more explicitly elaborated its understanding of human rights with planks against racial and gender discrimination, and in support of the rights of sexual minorities.

As this essay has suggested, the ideals which inspired and were made manifest in the Atlantic Charter of 1941, the United Nations Declaration of 1942, the Dumbarton Oaks and the Bretton

Woods Conferences of 1944, the UN Charter Conference of 1945, and the Universal Declaration of Human Rights of 1948, on topics ranging from peace to economic and social security to human rights have left a legacy for the world's people, and have continued to show the flexibility to accommodate a changing world.

Reading: The Cold War in the Third World and the Non-Aligned Movement, 1949-1973

China and Korea

Chinese Communist leader Mao Zedong and his forces had taken power in October 1949, after driving US-backed Nationalist Chinese General Jiang Jieshi and two million followers to the island of Taiwan. With Mao's declaration that he was "leaning to the side" of the Soviet Union, the US cemented its support to Jiang, whose much smaller island country would represent China in the United Nations until 1971.

Recriminations followed in the US as to who was responsible for the "loss" of China, part of a larger anti-communist wave in the United States in the late 1940s and early 1950s orchestrated by Senator Joseph McCarthy (R-WI). North Korea's attack on South Korea in June 1950 was also blamed on espionage agents; specifically, New York engineer Julius Rosenberg and his wife Ethel, whose passing of atomic secrets to Russia, US officials alleged, had enabled that war to start.

In contrast to this view, Secretary of State Dean Acheson had stated that Asia's future "lies within the countries of Asia and within the power of the Asian people." Nevertheless, the US immediately got involved in defending South Korea, leading a joint United Nations effort alongside troops from countries ranging from Britain to Thailand. Dropping more bombs on North Korea than it had on the Pacific front in World War II, the US nearly went to war with China when General Douglas MacArthur's troops got too close to its border. The conflict eventually ended in an armistice in July 1953 at the 38th parallel dividing the North and the South.

Just as the Korean War was ending, the US executed the Rosenbergs for conspiracy to commit espionage. Despite Washington's efforts to spin the deaths as justified, protests erupted from Tunisia to Indonesia. Rather than show the world that the United States was boldly standing up to Communist subversion, the executions instead painted Washington as heavy-handed, even hysterical. This was a blow to the new Eisenhower administration, which hoped to use rhetorical, psychological, and other propaganda to sway opinion abroad; the Third World, especially, was not convinced.

The Korean War set a precedent for hot Cold War battles in the developing world; it would shape the US response to the next, more complicated and longer lasting Asian Cold War conflict, in Vietnam. There, in May 1954, French soldiers, at last, surrendered at the siege of Dien Bien Phu. Two months later, the nation was temporarily divided between North and South by international agreement, with unifying elections planned for 1956. Instead of the elections, however, the United States made efforts to create a noncommunist South Vietnamese state, the Republic of Vietnam, under the leadership of Ngo Dinh Diem. The consequence was years of extensive military involvement by the US to counter the government of the Northern Communist Democratic People's Republic of Vietnam and its insurgents in South Vietnam. This war sharply divided American opinion and influenced the downfall of two presidents.

The Non-Aligned Movement

Many newly independent Asian and African leaders wanted nothing to do with either side in the Cold War. Their non-aligned movement included Indian President Jawaharlal Nehru, Indonesia's Ahmed Sukarno, Yugoslavia's Josip Broz Tito, and the leaders of Egypt and Ghana, and they met in 1955 in Bandung, Indonesia to affirm their neutrality, the first of several such conferences. They also called for further decolonization, peaceful coexistence, and an end to racial discrimination, especially in the apartheid state of South Africa.

Meanwhile, Nikita Khrushchev was working hard to win his own friends in the developing world. He traveled to Beijing in the late 1950s, sending Soviet "modernizers" to China's factories and laying the groundwork for that country's capitalist leap in the 1980s, doing so against the backdrop of China's own Great Leap Forward (1958-61), a disaster which led to the deaths of as many as 50 million people, largely from starvation. Khrushchev traveled to India, Burma, and Afghanistan as well, a move that alarmed Americans, worried about what *Time* magazine called a "lunge to the South."

Along with his cultivation of the developing world, Khrushchev also fostered a platform of peaceful coexistence with the West, in a Cold War thaw that brought him to the United States in 1959 and which, along with his earlier denunciations of Stalin's brutal methods in 1956, helped seal a long-standing split with China. Despite the thaw, President Eisenhower continued to send U-2 spy planes over Russia to check on their missile development (one of which was shot down in 1960) and maintained plans to overthrow Castro, an intervention to follow the previous Eisenhower coups against leftist governments in Iran (1953) and Guatemala (1954); less successful had been CIA support to a rebel force fighting the Indonesian leader, Sukarno, in 1958. By contrast, Eisenhower's successor, John F. Kennedy, wanted to re-engage with the Third World and show his support for neutralist countries; he invited Sukarno to the White House in 1961.

Vietnam War

Kennedy would be no neutralist on Vietnam, however, and remained strongly committed to continuing and expanding the US role there, especially as the Communist guerrillas in the South who supported a unified Vietnam under Ho Chi Minh became increasingly active in 1961. By the time of his death two years later, Kennedy had raised the number of advisers in South Vietnam to 16,000. The Soviet Union, meanwhile, sent assistance to North Vietnam, eventually amounting to more than $4 billion in economic and military aid, including surface-to-air missiles; Beijing also competed with Moscow to help Hanoi. These Communist efforts were constrained to some degree by fears of provoking the United States, and the US avoided pursuing all-out war in Southeast Asia for similar reasons.

The Vietnam effort notwithstanding, Kennedy's approach to the Third World was more sympathetic and nuanced than Eisenhower's, as reflected in his acceptance of the nonaligned movement and his creation of the Peace Corps; at the same time, he promoted civil rights at home more seriously than his predecessor. Still, he had not gone far enough, and in August 1963, the Reverend Dr. Martin Luther King, who had been imprisoned for protests in Birmingham, Alabama, a few months before, led an enormous march to promote faster change in the United States. At the same time, another civil rights demonstration was taking place on the other side of the world: Buddhist monks were protesting the US-backed government of Ngo Dinh Diem in Saigon, setting themselves on fire. The oppression of the Diem regime that these protests marked led Washington eventually to encourage Diem and his brother Nhu's opponents to oust them; the two were assassinated and subsequent regimes brought only continued instability to the US project in Southeast Asia.

Kennedy's own assassination came just three weeks after Diem's, and the war soon ramped up further; President Johnson, armed with an open-ended military resolution from Congress following a murky incident in the Gulf of Tonkin in the summer of 1964, had 400,000 US troops stationed in Vietnam by 1966, and 543,000 two years later. In response, antiwar activism and civil unrest expanded in the United States. The US Cold War consensus that had supported a hardline policy toward Communism was breaking apart, and the Third World was the catalyst.

Running for president in 1968 after Johnson had promised not to, Richard Nixon announced he would scale back the number of American troops and offered a "secret plan" to end the war. However, it took another five years before Secretary of State Henry Kissinger signed a treaty with

North Vietnam's Le Duc Tho, winning a Nobel Peace Prize for the settlement in early 1973. Tho refused the prize, and of course, the peace agreements brought no peace. In January 1975, the Democratic Republic of Vietnam invaded the South in a crushing blow and 150,000 South Vietnamese fled as best they could.

Reading: Vietnam and the 1960s
The Vietnam War and its surrounding circumstances are among the most important events in the 20th century. The conflict redefined much of the United States' internal politics and self-image. In many ways, America's involvement in Vietnam rattled the consensus politics of the 1950s and was a major driving force in Counterculture and reaction. Further effects rattled the world and helped spark a number of other conflicts and protest movements. Much of American history since has dealt with the complex legacy of the war in Southeast Asia.

Origins of the Vietnam War
The conflict in Vietnam was another example in the decades-long process of decolonization of much of Europe and Africa. Former imperial powers like France, Britain, and Portugal oversaw a number of turnovers to native peoples; some voluntary and others less so. Vietnam's case was more complicated due to the French colony's invasion and occupation by Japan in the Second World War.

Local forces led a sharp pushback against Japanese authority. In many ways, the occupation of 1940-45 created a national identity of resistance. Vietnam and wider French Indochina provided key similarities and differences to other states occupied by Imperial Japan.

Much of Vietnam's society split on the reaction to the Japanese invasion. Some welcomed France's abrupt exit while many others believed Japanese occupation was more brutal than that of the West. In particular, local militant groups including the Viet Minh led by Ho Chi Minh (1890-1969) remained a major foe of the Japanese efforts. Japan was careful to create an aura of continuation from the Vichy French forces. This ended in early 1945 as Japan sacked any remaining vestiges of French administration and colonial presence and replaced it with a puppet government under Emperor Bao Dai (1913-1997). This allowed a rapid rise of resistance fighters such as the Viet Minh. By the end of 1945, Ho's forces controlled much of northwestern Vietnam. The Viet Minh expanded into other portions of the country, rapidly gaining in numbers and credibility.

By the end of the war, Ho Chi Minh emerged as a central figure to many Vietnamese. After travels to France, the United States, and Britain, Ho joined a variety of left-wing and socialist movements. Ho's organization pushed for self-government of Vietnam at the Versaille peace talks but was not considered by the Allied Powers. However, Ho's stature grew and traveled to the newly formed Soviet Union and aided Chinese Communists before returning to Vietnam in 1941.

In the aftermath of the Japanese occupation, Ho played a shrewd game against other Vietnamese factions. By the end of the 1940s, the Communists emerged as the primary representative of Vietnamese political life. However, France would not grant independence to the fledgling movement, soon to be the Democratic Republic of Vietnam. Ho met with Soviet and Chinese leaders Josef Stalin and Mao Zedong, respectively. The Communist dictators pledged early support to Ho's movement.

France's recalcitrance was both a burden and opportunity for Ho. He served as president and prime minister of the People's Republic, commonly referred to as North Vietnam. French forces battled the Vietnamese during this first phase of the Vietnam War from 1946-54. The French often found themselves unable to adapt to a new style of warfare after the exhausting experience of the Second World War. By 1954 Vietnamese forces sharply defeated the French at the fortress of Dien Bien Phu. With the war seemingly unwinnable, France began its withdrawal from the country.

The Viet Minh and France signed the 1954 Geneva Accords, which effectively split the country in two, with the DRV dominating the north from Hanoi and the soon-Republic of Vietnam governing the south from Saigon. From this point on the United States became more involved in the situation especially after an effort for nationwide elections collapsed.

Vietnam's changing efforts came during an interesting time for the United States. The expansion of Soviet power in Eastern Europe and beyond led to sharper responses from the West. Communist victory in China (1949) and the Korean War (1950-53) further pushed the concept of Containment and the emerging Domino Theory. North Vietnam's aggressive actions included reprisals against landowners and an invasion of Laos in 1958-59, which led to the supply system known as the Ho Chi Minh Trail.

Early American Involvement

With Vietnam divided along the 17th parallel, the United States quickly became more involved as the 1950s continued. South Vietnamese dictator Ngo Dinh Diem (1901-63) was a staunch Catholic and anti-communist. His harsh repression of political and religious groups bred contempt among many non-communists in the country. Public order was difficult to maintain, especially after 1960 as the North sponsored the National Liberation Front, better known as the Viet Cong. Under President Dwight Eisenhower (1890-1969) the United States deployed hundreds of military advisors to South Vietnam to train local forces.

John F. Kennedy (1917-1963) won the 1960 presidential election bringing about a major change in policy. Outgoing President Eisenhower warned Kennedy about escalating issues in Indochina. The Kennedy Administration staunchly backed Diem's regime at first, including an increase of military advisors. By the time of Kennedy's death in 1963, this number increased to over 16,000. However, rebel attacks continued while South Vietnam's government appeared paralyzed.

As the number of American forces increased in the country, tactics changed as well. South Vietnam and the United States forces instituted the Strategic Hamlet Program, which relocated thousands of peasants into separate military-style camps. This program did not achieve its goals to separate the rural population from the Communists. As the conflict continued and South Vietnam's military and government struggled under pressure, the Kennedy Administration focused on Diem's leadership. Protests by Buddhists continued apace and violence against religious groups sharpened through paramilitary and government actions. The American government split on the prospect of removing Diem from power, with the decision finally in President Kennedy's hands. Vietnamese generals in contact with the CIA overthrew Diem on November 2, 1963. Instead of ending the violence, it accelerated, and guerilla activities increased.

Following President Kennedy's death in November 1963, President Lyndon Johnson (1908-73) rapidly escalated American involvement in the war. South Vietnam's government remained disorganized and was beset by another coup in January 1964.

Much of the reason for the escalation dates back to the Gulf of Tonkin Incident. On August 2, 1964, the U.S.S. *Maddox* fired upon several North Vietnamese torpedo boats which were following the American vessel. A similar incident was reported on August 4 between the *Maddox* and the U.S.S. *Turner Joy*. Historians still debate whether or not the North Vietnamese fired on American vessels or whether the Johnson Administration lied to Congress and the public. Regardless, the incident led to Operation Pierce Arrow, a bombing campaign, and the Gulf of Tonkin Resolution on August 7, 1964. This act of Congress gave President Johnson a free hand to wage war in and around Vietnam.

Early in 1965, the United States heavily increased bombing in North Vietnam. In March of the same year, the first American combat forces deployed to South Vietnam. By the end of the year, almost 200,000 American forces were in the country.

As American involvement increased, many of the truisms of U.S. military held since the Second World War changed rapidly. Viet Cong guerrilla tactics demoralized the South Vietnamese and damaged the American forces. Under the leadership of General William Westmoreland (1914-2005) direct American military involvement sharply increased. In addition, American allies including South Korea, Australia, and New Zealand sent troops to South Vietnam.

A Full-Blown War

American troop levels continued to increase during the Johnson Administration. The Tet Offensive proved to be a major shift in the conflict on either side. On January 30, 1968, North Vietnamese and Viet Cong forces broke the traditional truce surrounding the holiday Tet. Communist forces numbering over 80,000 attacked over 100 cities in South Vietnam. Perhaps the most telling visuals for Americans back home was a desperate firefight on the U.S. Embassy in Saigon.

The Tet Offensive was a tactical disaster for North Vietnam. It lost over 30,000 conventional and guerrilla forces and decimated much of the North Vietnamese Army and Viet Cong's organization. However, it proved to be a strategic success and a major component of the "Television War" horrifying Americans watching the nightly news. Over 1,000 Americans were dead across Vietnam, and meanwhile, public doubts about the war grew. By May 1968 Johnson approved peace talks between the US and North Vietnam to be held in Paris. These dragged on for months to no avail. In 1968, American troop numbers peaked in the country at over a half million. This was perhaps the height of American emotional trauma.

The situation rapidly destroyed Johnson's political career. Originally entertaining a second full term in 1968, Johnson's policy in Vietnam led to a yawning "credibility gap" between the reality on the ground and casualty figures. Johnson bowed to protest and internal pressure and dropped out of the 1968 race. Former Vice President Richard Nixon (1913-94) won the spirited contest. Nixon's victory was due, in part, to his vows to reduce American involvement in Vietnam. American troop levels began declining as he took office. Nixon vowed "Vietnamization" and training of local forces. American tactics changed, as well. U.S. and South Vietnamese forces began more aggressive anti-insurgency measures. In addition, Nixon opened relations with the People's Republic of China in 1972, splitting the two major communist blocs further.

Despite declining American troop numbers and casualties, the war escalated in other ways. In 1970, Prince Norodom Sihanouk of Cambodia (1922-2012) was overthrown by a pro-U.S. government. North Vietnam invaded Cambodia later that year. The United States and South Vietnam retaliated with its own incursion. American bombers carried out massive bombing runs on North Vietnamese forces and supply lines in the country.

These actions caused considerable dissent in the United States. Anti-war protests, declining with the smaller American presence in Southeast Asia, again spiked. Protesters at Kent State University at Ohio were victims of one of the most recognizable moments of the period. National Guardsmen opened fire on the crowd, killing four students and wounding nine. Four million students marched across the country in response to the killings. While the protests did not stop the American involvement in Cambodia, dissent against the war spiked.

In addition, South Vietnamese efforts to prevent communist activities in neighboring Laos were also a disaster. The Republic of Vietnam led a 1971 incursion into Laos to diminish guerillas' access to the Ho Chi Minh Trail, which ended in sound defeat.

Decline of the Conflict

Nixon's strategy of Vietnamization continued on track to mixed results. The number of American forces in the region continued to decline, falling below 200,000 in 1971. The South Vietnamese army grew in size but with limited capabilities. American airpower continued apace as a major support for the South's forces.

The drawdown coincided with several major American domestic political events. The largest was the 1972 election. President Nixon ran on a campaign he would later refer to as "peace with honor." His administration continued talks with the North Vietnamese government. The negotiations between National Security Advisor Henry Kissinger (1923-) and diplomat Le Duc Tho (1911-90) would eventually lead to 1973's Paris Peace Accords. Opposing Nixon was Democrat George McGovern (1922-2012), who ran on a platform of immediate withdrawal. A month before the November contest, the United States and North Vietnam reached a tentative ceasefire agreement. Nixon's victory was overwhelming, winning 49 of 50 states and over 60 percent of the vote.

North Vietnam leaked the contents of the diplomatic agreement after South Vietnam requested changes. President Nixon responded with Operation Linebacker II, a massive bombing campaign which lasted 11 days in December 1973. This move destroyed much of North Vietnam's ability to conduct the war. The president also threatened to sign the agreement without South Vietnam if its government did not accept the terms. The following month, on January 27, 1973, the United States and both sides in Vietnam signed the Paris Peace Accords. The Accords called for a cease-fire and a withdrawal of American combat troops. Both sides agreed to release prisoners of war and to respect South Vietnam's territory. The United States promised to replace material for South Vietnam if needed. The agreement also called for elections in both North and South and an eventual reunification of the country. Both Kissinger and Tho received the Nobel Peace Prize for their efforts.

Despite the agreement in Paris, the end of the Vietnam War did not proceed according to the Accords. The United States removed its final combat forces to the country and left a significant amount of military equipment for their allies. North Vietnamese forces and guerrillas remained in parts of South Vietnam. Instead of causing a collapse of South Vietnam, many of the guerrillas were pushed out of the Republic of Vietnam by local forces.

While North Vietnamese attacks and planning for a full assault continued, American ability and willingness to continue the war was over. President Nixon resigned the White House in August 1974 due to the Watergate scandal and was replaced with Gerald Ford (1913-2006). Between Democrats' control of Congress and Ford's newness, little aid was forthcoming to the South Vietnamese. Congress reduced aid to South Vietnam and sharply cut military operations in the region at a time that the Republic of Vietnam was in severe recession. A North Vietnamese offensive in late 1974 and early 1975 showed that the United States was in no position to return in any significant way. President Ford requested aid and supplies for the Republic, but Congress rejected his pleas.

Despite numerical advantages in military hardware, South Vietnam remained at a severe disadvantage. Morale collapsed as American aid ended and North Vietnamese victories seized more territory. By April 1975, North Vietnamese troops were on the doorstep of Saigon. President Thieu resigned from office and fled the country. On April 29, 1975 North Vietnamese forces seized Saigon, effectively ending the war.

Cultural and Political Effects

The physical and political effects of the conflicts in Southeast Asia garnered most of the headlines but there was an unmistakable, simultaneous shift in the culture of the United States. The rationale and conduct of American involvement bred a number of reactions, often resistance and cynicism. Youth culture and an emerging counterculture grew as the war and the draft continued. A reaction also emerged, perhaps best exemplified by President Nixon's November 1969 Silent Majority speech to the nation.

The anti-Vietnam War movement was perhaps the most extensive in American history. The anti-war movement borrowed from multiple strands in society, allowing it to grow in a unique manner. One powerful impetus was the large Baby Boom generation, born in the years after the Second World War. The young population formed the backbone of public protest against the conflict. Many of the protesters resented the draft that sent so many of their number to the jungles of Southeast Asia. Some of the more famous scenes of the era include young men burning their draft cards publicly.

The anti-war effort also dovetailed with the nascent Counterculture in the United States and beyond. Many of the protesters were also members of the rapid cultural changes, including the rise of hippies and opponents of the American version of capitalist democracy. Opposition to the war as a common cause accelerated hippies' communes, protest music, poetry, and 1969's Woodstock music festival, which drew over 400,000 young people.

The crescendo of both movements came together in the protests around the Democratic Party's convention in Chicago in 1968. Riots by the protesters were met with a crackdown by Chicago police. The messy violence outside the convention and the obvious split in the Democratic Party itself contributed to Republican Richard Nixon's victory over Democratic nominee Hubert Humphrey (1911-78).

Despite the vociferous outcry of anti-war protests, there was a significant pushback. Many Americans ended their support of the conflict after the 1968 Tet Offensive yet did not align themselves with the anti-draft or pro-North Vietnam tenor of some of the protests. Part of this is seen in the large shift toward Richard Nixon's 1968 Presidential campaign and during his administration. Many World War II veterans, union employees, and working class members swung their support towards Nixon's gradual withdrawal and "law and order" approach. By the time of Nixon's Silent Majority speech many geographic and demographic segments of the nation stood behind his approach. The end of the draft also severely reduced the number and intensity of the anti-war protests. By the 1972 election, Nixon actually carried the youth vote over George McGovern.

The Gulf of Tonkin incident, President Johnson's justification for American involvement in Vietnam, and the course of the war deeply harmed faith in the federal government. These, combined with a number of scandals such as Watergate and missteps of the Carter Administration changed the way Americans of every demographic saw Washington's power. Many in Congress gave Johnson the benefit of the doubt surrounding the Tonkin Resolution and the initial deployment of combat troops. Over time, more and more Congressional leaders and other public figures spoke out against the war.

Furthermore, President Nixon's oversight of the conflict further bred skepticism. America's involvement in Laos and Cambodia deeply countered stated goals of transparency in the region. One of the prime examples is the conflict over the Pentagon Papers. In 1971 the *New York Times* published a Department of Defense history of American involvement in Vietnam up to 1967. The papers discussed the Johnson Administration's movement toward intervention in the conflict, bombing raids in Cambodia and Laos, and other elements not released to the general public. The Nixon Administration attempted to prosecute the *Times'* author, Daniel Ellsberg, claiming he committed a felony for publishing classified documents. The charges were later dropped. The White House also pressured the *Times* to stop such publications, but was halted by the Supreme Court's 6-3 decision in *New York Times Co. v. United States.* The case showed an important distinction of press freedom and changed public perception of succeeding administrations' handling of the situation in Vietnam and beyond.

Through much of the Johnson and Nixon presidencies, media coverage of the conflict played an increasing role. Vietnam is commonly referred to in popular culture as the first "television war." Families watched footage of the war on their televisions each night, adding a visceral and realistic backdrop to fighting thousands of miles from home. Increasing attention also led to discovery of war crimes. The My Lai Massacre on March 16, 1968 was the most prominent. U.S. army soldiers opened fire on civilians in My Lai, South Vietnam, killing between 300 and 500. News of the slayings were published in the Associated Press in November 1969, leading to a major investigation and courts-martial but only one conviction. Further investigations by the U.S. government and the press uncovered dozens of similar yet smaller incidents. Both North and South Vietnam carried out large-scale killings.

In the aftermath of the war, the ghosts of the conflict haunted American policymakers. Vietnam veteran and future Secretary of State Colin Powell crafted the later-termed "Powell Doctrine" as a reaction to American involvement in Southeast Asia. Elements of overwhelming conventional military force was also used in the 1991 Persian Gulf War. In the aftermath of the swift victory with minimal American casualties, President George H.W. Bush said, "by God, we've kicked the Vietnam syndrome once and for all." Vietnam veterans Bob Kerrey, John Kerry, and John McCain all sought the White House. McCain, in particular, had been imprisoned by the North Vietnamese for five years.

World Effects

The Vietnam War and the reaction to it also affected youth movements across the world. The United States was not alone in having a large population of young people born since the end of the Second World War. The protests and discontent in the United States acted as both a microcosm and an impetus of larger protests around the world.

The protests had far and wide effects with large-scale movements across both Eastern and Western Europe. The two largest examples were the uprisings in France and Czechoslovakia.

In the former, two months of protests from May to June 1968 shook French society to its core. A number of protests, often led by young people, enveloped the country, including opposition to traditional capitalism, the French government, and American foreign policy. During the protests, over 10 million took to the streets or participated in workers' strikes. The general strike shut down the ability for President Charles de Gaulle (1890-1970) to act decisively. Police enforcement instead led to larger protests. At one point President de Gaulle fled to a military base and called for early parliamentary elections. While de Gaulle's allies won these elections handily, the tumult of the protests weighed heavily on him personally and politically. He resigned the presidency the following year and died in 1970.

In the case of Czechoslovakia, moderate reforms initiated by First Secretary Alexander Dubcek (1921-92) sparked an invasion by the Soviet Union and Warsaw Pact. Czech non-violence emerged against Soviet domination, and several major communist movements across the world opposed the invasion.

The end of American involvement also carried a number of major effects on Southeast Asia itself. The Khmer Rouge communist movement came to power in Cambodia, communists seized power in Laos, and threatened to do so in Thailand. In Cambodia's case, the Khmer Rouge massacred millions of civilians and precipitated a North Vietnamese invasion in 1978. This led to a punitive yet short Chinese invasion of Vietnam in March 1979.

Reading: Demise of the Cold War, 1973-present
Détente with China and Russia
As part of his plan to wind down in Vietnam, Nixon wanted to improve relations with the Communist bloc; he and his secretary of state, Henry Kissinger, believed that the support of Beijing would be important in making that possible, and early on made a plan to visit mainland China, then still unrecognized by the United States. Chinese leaders Mao Zedong and Zhou Enlai were open to re-engagement. With the Sino-Soviet split and then the Cultural Revolution, which Mao had launched in 1966 to purge his suspected enemies and rejuvenate the Communist Party, the country had become increasingly isolated. This initiative had mushroomed into a horror of civil war, torture, and even cannibalism among its adherents, and was responsible for the deaths of up to two million people. After experiencing bloody border clashes with Russia in 1969, Mao worried too about the possibility of a nuclear attack by the Soviet Union, and though he continued to rail publicly about the evils of imperialism, he was increasingly receptive to overtures from the West.

Nixon's approach to China was part of a larger policy called détente, or a lessening of tensions, that was aimed as well to improve relations with the Soviet Union.

Just before Kissinger flew secretly to Beijing to make arrangements for the president's visit, in July 1971, an American table tennis team also arrived in China. This exercise in "ping-pong diplomacy" showed the importance of direct cultural contacts as another path in moving forward official ties.

Chairman Mao and Premier Zhou warmly welcomed Nixon in February 1972 — "the week that changed the world" — and the men started a process of normalization of relations in the Shanghai Communique. This document included a plank for the "progressive development of trade," which jumped from five million dollars in 1972 to close to one trillion dollars today, most of it in Chinese goods. China's road to capitalism which spurred this vast growth was hardly predictable in 1972, but certainly this fraught moment between the Cultural Revolution and the Vietnam War that brought the US and China together had made it possible. Relations would be formalized in 1979.

Nixon and Kissinger soon succeeded in getting their desired second invitation, from Soviet leader Leonid Brezhnev, and this new relationship with the arch Cold War ally assisted in fostering arms negotiations, including the Strategic Arms Limitation Talks (SALT) of 1972. Agreements for both expanded trade with China and arms control with the Soviet Union were remarkable in such a short time, yet the Communist powers did little to assist the US in its predicament in Vietnam. After the fall of the South Vietnamese government to Hanoi, similarly, hard-line regimes also emerged in Cambodia and Laos, nations in which the US had earlier intervened to stop Communism's spread in Southeast Asia.

This series of sharp defeats for the United States in the Third World amplified domestic scrutiny for the détente policy. The Soviet role in Angola, newly independent from Portugal in 1975, also suggested that Communist influence was expanding. Unbeknownst to many at the time, however, that world was about to undergo a major transformation.

Mao died in 1976, and within two years, Deng Xiaoping, China's "paramount leader," began steps to take his nation toward a market-driven economy. China's growth exploded, and while slowing today, its GDP is now second only to the United States (or slightly ahead, depending on how it is measured). These market reforms offered another model for Third World development.

Final Cold War Conflicts
Détente had waned by the late 1970s, and hawkish groups like the Committee on the Present Danger resurfaced in the United States to decry rising Soviet military strength. Washington continued to support anti-communist interventions throughout this period, from Latin America to Africa. In 1973, the CIA secretly supported efforts to influence elections in Chile, where socialist president Salvador Allende had already nationalized several firms. The Agency asserted that

"Allende's election spells the end of democracy." Encircled as well by domestic foes like General Leigh Guzman, who called for the eradication of the "Marxist cancer from our fatherland," Allende killed himself during a coup that made General Augusto Pinochet Chile's right-wing dictator until 1990.

In 1978, however, an American-backed government unraveled in Iran. There, the Shah, first installed by US intervention in 1953, was increasingly resented for a variety of reasons, including his American ties and his repressive security service; with the encouragement of Shiite cleric Ruhollah Khomeini, a longtime critic who had been living abroad, protests spread. Islamic revolutionaries soon overthrew the Shah and by November 1979, seized 52 Americans working at the US embassy, whom they held for more than a year. President Jimmy Carter's attempt to rescue the hostages failed disastrously the following April.

If that wasn't damaging enough to US prestige, the Soviet Union's invasion of Afghanistan, also in 1979, was a further blow. In response to this attack, the Carter Administration canceled participation in the upcoming Moscow Olympics and cut off $2.6 billion in grain sales to Russia; Washington also sent military aid to Afghan *mujahideen fighters*, who in addition to being anti-Soviet were adherents of militant Islam. This aid continued through the Reagan and Bush I administrations, billions of dollars in support dispatched through Pakistani agents and augmented by Saudi Arabia's assistance. The mujahideen drove the Soviets out in 1989, but they were not the only anti-Soviet fighters in Afghanistan. Osama bin Laden and Maktab al-Khidamat, the forerunner to Al Qaeda, which would launch the 9/11 attacks on the United States, were running an operation there as well.

Meanwhile, in Latin America, further Soviet advances were underway, or so it looked to the United States. In 1979 Daniel Ortega's Sandinistas overthrew longtime right-wing strongman and friend of the United States, Anastasio Somoza, in Nicaragua. While President Jimmy Carter was receptive to Ortega and provided aid to his Sandinista party, Ronald Reagan's administration, alarmed by his growing links with Moscow and convinced that Cubans in Nicaragua were supporting a left-wing insurgency in neighboring El Salvador, wanted him gone. The CIA attempted sabotage operations and supported the anti-Sandinista Contra forces in that country. And both Carter and Reagan sent significant support to the Salvadoran military in its vicious war with the Cuban-backed insurrection, despite Salvadoran guards' rape and murder of four American nuns in 1980.

When Congress passed an amendment to stop any more American military aid to the Contras, individuals inside the administration secretly subverted it with an illegal scheme, using proceeds from Israeli arms sales to Iran, sales meant to promote the release of American hostages held in Lebanon. Later known as the Iran-Contra scandal, this arrangement starkly underlines the Third World's importance in this last phase of the Cold War.

In 1983, as the CIA airdropped a 15-page "Freedom Fighter's Manual" to the Contras and the US assisted other "freedom fighters" against Communism in countries from Afghanistan to Angola, US President Ronald Reagan called the Soviet Union an "Evil Empire."

But after a series of sclerotic Russian leaders died in quick succession, a new and dynamic General Secretary of the Soviet Communist Party, Mikhail Gorbachev, emerged in 1985, leading to a more hopeful turn in the superpowers' relationship. Gorbachev called for economic and political reforms with his policies of *perestroika* and *glasnost*. He and Reagan began discussions that led to something previously unimaginable; striking reductions in armaments, paving the way for the end of the Cold War (and the end of the Soviet Union as well, as the next section details).

One consequence was that Third World beneficiaries of the Cold War tension and its largesse, like Panamanian dictator Manuel Noriega, soon felt the cold shoulder. A well-paid client of the US since 1971, who had served as an intelligence source on Cuba and Nicaragua, Noriega now became less useful, and his role in drug trafficking and corrupt political practices in Panama more glaring. An

American invasion of 28,000 troops removed him in 1989, blasting him out of his hideout with music from The Clash and Jethro Tull, and underlining yet again the Cold War's heavy hand in the Third World.

The Fall of the Berlin Wall

Rock music also helped remove Erich Honecker of East Germany. In July 1988, Honecker foolishly invited Bruce Springsteen to East Berlin to assuage the country's restless youth with a concert. Springsteen told the crowd of 300,000, "I've come to play rock 'n' roll for you in the hope that one day all the barriers will be torn down." Sixteen months later, some of those same youth helped oust Honecker and tear the Berlin Wall to smithereens.

The fall of the Berlin Wall was a clear signal that the Cold War was ending and a transition to democracy in Eastern Europe was under way, and not just in East Germany. After almost 50 years, a united Germany joined NATO, but so too did former Warsaw Pact nations like Poland, Hungary, and the Czech Republic. The Baltic nations, long submerged within the Soviet Union, similarly broke away. Yet repressive Communist states continued to govern in China and elsewhere. Deng Xiaoping may have helped China move toward capitalism, but he did not tolerate political challenges; seven months before the Berlin Wall fell, a peaceful protest in Tiananmen Square was crushed and resulted in the deaths of thousands in similar protests around the country.

The Soviet Union itself disappeared on December 25, 1991, replaced by the Russian Federation. Boris Yeltsin, president for the Federation's first eight years, was succeeded by Vladimir Putin, a strongman who has been in power since 1999. Unlike Eastern Europe's experience, Russia's moment of democracy seems to have been fragmentary.

At the time, however, the end of the Cold War and the emergence of so many new democracies suggested for some the arrival of an entirely new era. Political scientist Francis Fukuyama suggested that this new spread of "Western liberal democracy" might be "the final form of human government." Yet even as he was writing, in the wake of China's crushing of protesters in Tiananmen Square, it was hardly clear that Western-style democracy was taking over the globe. And events since, including the most recent expansion of democracy, the Arab Spring of 2010-11, have also been marred by reversals in the last half-decade. In Egypt, six years after the overthrow of 29-year president Hosni Mubarak in 2011, military dictator Abdel Fattah al-Sisi has crushed press and political freedoms, and the terrorist group Isis (Islamic State in Iraq and Syria), a breakaway group and rival of Al-Qaeda, is making inroads.

Rise of Islamic Fundamentalism

The late Chalmers Johnson used the CIA term "blowback" to characterize the lasting and problematic consequences US interventions have among the Third World people who encounter them. An example of this was the turn of events in Iran in 1979, when Islamic protesters removed the American client, Reza Shah Pahlavi, and replaced him with a leader who denounced the United States. As Westad notes, Khomeini showed that no longer were Communists the main opposition to US influence; instead, "an ideology centered on the Third World itself" — militant Islam — had emerged to challenge both the Communists *and* the West. At the time, neither the Americans nor the Soviets realized fully the implications of this new development in the Third World. It was only some years after the unsuccessful Soviet intervention in Afghanistan, which began the same year as the Iranian Revolution, that both sides realized its sway.

The US helped the Afghan rebels, the mujahideen, kick out the Soviets with hand-held Stinger missiles. Once that war ended, however, and just as the Soviet empire also expired, these weapons remained behind, many now in the hands of extremists, some of whom planned an Islamic Afghanistan as part of a global *jihad*, or holy war. Benazir Bhutto, prime minister of Pakistan at the time, had earlier warned President George H.W. Bush that "You are creating a Frankenstein."

Although President George W. Bush would later admit that Iraq's leader Saddam Hussein had no connection with bin Laden's attack on the World Trade Center Towers on 9/11, that attack was a large part of the justification for a US-led multinational force invading Iraq in 2003, which ended Hussein's quarter-century of rule. The parliamentary democracy the US subsequently set up in Baghdad in 2005 faced challenges from the beginning, including a multi-pronged insurgency and corrupt leadership.

Today, the US-led Iraq war is long over, and the country is neither stable nor secure. Isis controls key cities, and battles for control with other groups, including Shiite militias; Iraq's military struggles to keep these factions in line, but its opponents have captured US weapons. The nation is challenged, moreover, by its history as a cobbled-together pastiche of many groups, a product of the imperialist 1916 Sykes-Picot agreement of World War I, which also created another unstable state, Syria.

Saddam Hussein kept things together for decades in his country by brutality and intimidation and outright murder, just as Moammar Gadhafi did in Libya for 40 years, and Bashar al-Assad and his father before him have done in Syria going back to 1971. "Across much of the Middle East today," writes Ali Khedery, who worked for the US in Iraq from 2003-9, "a sad truth prevails: decades of bad governance have caused richly diverse societies to fracture along ethno-sectarian lines." At the same time, disillusioned, marginalized young people have been radicalized and inflamed by extremists waging jihad.

Soon after rebels attempted to overthrow dictator Al-Assad in Syria in 2011, for instance, the insurgency there became a civil war, with crippling chaos amid the aerial intervention of the US and Russia; the war has cost the lives of 400,000. Nearly five million have fled the country, many attempting to reach Europe and the United States, where fears of them quickly aggravated populist, xenophobic tendencies and shifted political elections. Isis has further exploited the chaos in Libya following NATO's 2011 overthrow of dictator Muammar Gaddafi, a mishandled intervention which soon spiraled into civil war as well as the death of the US Ambassador, Christopher Stevens, in 2012.

As the current state of affairs in the Middle East suggests, with the end of the Cold War, the world's crises, once defined in polarized dimensions, have splintered into shards — Islamic fundamentalism, civil wars in Africa and the Middle East, resurgent nationalistic states like Russia, and environmental concerns. At the same time, the liberal international order which has preserved a sizeable portion of economic and military stability in much of the world since World War II, and assisted Third World development, is being questioned as never before, even by the US president, Donald Trump — who appears skeptical of the importance of continuing to fund long-term US treaty obligations in the world, such as NATO and the US-Japanese alliance. He has also emphasized China as a threat to American economic and security needs; by contrast, he appears to be unruffled by the expansionism of Vladimir Putin in Russia. Trump's election, which itself appears to bear the stamp of foreign intrigue, shows again a new age of global uncertainty. It remains to be seen what kinds of new challenges will emerge in this world that may now be moving beyond, in whole or in part, the liberal postwar order.

Unit 16: Globalization in the 20th and 21st Centuries

Manfred B. Steger, The University of Hawaii, Manoa

Reading: The First Wave of Globalization, 1890s-1914

The first modern wave of globalization was born in the late 19th century. It was the child of the ongoing Industrial Revolution that had transformed the social fabric of European countries and their overseas colonies. Powered by coal energy, first-wave globalization benefited from a series of technological innovations. For example, the invention and rapid development of steam-powered engines enhanced industrial production in factories and revolutionized transportation over land and sea.

Economy and Technology

The resulting shrinkage of distance was perhaps most spectacularly embodied in gigantic steamships like Germany's SS *Kaiserin Auguste Victoria* or Britain's RMS *Olympic*. These floating giants were capable of cutting the transatlantic crossing time from a month in the early 19th century to less than a week in 1912. Proliferating trains steaming along increasingly standardized railroad tracks transported growing volumes of goods and record numbers of people to their ever-expanding geographic destinations at ever-increasing speeds. The Trans-Siberian Railroad, the longest railway in the world, was constructed between 1891 and 1916. It connected Moscow with the Pacific city of Vladivostok over a record distance of 5,772 miles. Between 1906 and 1914, it facilitated the permanent migration of four million Russian farmers to Siberia.

Representing the first practical use of electricity, the commercial telegraph revolutionized the means of communication and stimulated the globalization of commerce and the news media. Additional applications of electricity proved to be an important conduit for the intensification of globalization. The 1890s and 1900s witnessed the electrification of "world cities" like London, Paris, and New York. Their inhabitants enjoyed enhanced mobility by means of trams, undergrounds, and escalators.

In 1866, the first commercially viable transatlantic cable enabled almost instant transcontinental communication albeit at the very high cost of $100 for 10 words. Only 20 years later, the rate had fallen to 12 cents per word. This price drop allowed millions of private and commercial consumers to take advantage of the new medium. In 1903, US President Theodore Roosevelt tested the recently completed global telegraph infrastructure by sending himself a round-the-world telegram. It arrived in less than nine minutes. The development of mass communication and the international dissemination of news was taken a step further at the turn of the century. It happened with the advent of international telephone connections and the first successful wireless radio signal transmissions. In 1914, there were 10 million telephones in operation in the United States alone.

Moreover, the rapid development of photography and the invention of film in the 1890s allowed ordinary people to get a realistic sense of faraway places and exotic cultures. Previously they had only a glimpse, and that through the filter of dry travel reports or the rich imagination of creative novelists. The combination of moving pictures and faster movement across geographic space made for a dramatic acceleration of the news cycle. In 1911, a special express train outfitted with a dark room was used to develop and transport a film about the investiture of the Prince of Wales. It left Carnarvon, Wales, at 4pm. The recording was ready for public viewing in London at 10pm.

But we are perhaps not as familiar with less known, yet equally important late 19th-century developments that gave substance to the first wave of globalization. One crucial achievement was the synchronization of global time. It was accomplished at the 1884 Prime Meridian Conference. It linked the entire planet in time, counting 24 hours around the globe with each hour aligned to "time zones" marked by longitudinal meridians east and west of London's Greenwich Observatory. This globalization of time into spatially distinct zones arrayed around the center of the dominant British Empire also encouraged the standardization of national time within most industrialized countries. After all, the adoption of stable, uniform time aided both the development of industrial capitalism and transcontinental colonial practices of political control.

Time also underwent important personal uses as it shrank to the size of an individual accessory adorning people's clothes. Millions of pocket watches snatched up by eager consumers in the 1890s and 1900s changed their sense of time to shorter and shorter intervals. "Minute-long phone conversations" or "fifteen-minute coffee chats" became commonplace phrases that measured social interactions in shrinking time. The rapid diffusion of pocket watches (and later wrist watches) not only accelerated modern life but also solidified the industrial norms of punctuality, calculability, and exactness.

This mechanical compression of time facilitated the rise of "Taylorism" — a production efficiency methodology that broke every factory job or task into small and simple segments. Such new forms of "scientific management" also offered industrial workers incentives for good performance. Thus they contributed to soaring levels of capitalist productivity and economic efficiency.

The new technologies of the industrial age climbed to a dizzying apex in the early 1900s. This occurred with the emergence of motorcars, airplanes, and superliners like the RMS *Titanic* — then the largest moving structure in human history. The economic, political, and cultural features of first-wave globalization had become clearly visible in what people began to refer to as the *Belle Époque* — the "beautiful epoch" from the late 1800s to 1914. It was characterized by optimism, regional peace, economic prosperity and technological, scientific and cultural innovations.

Economically, the most important first-wave globalization feature was the advancement of "free trade." It started in mid-19th century and rapidly expanded until the outbreak of World War I. British manufacturers, in particular, led the struggle to open up their domestic market to foreigners by reducing their country's trade barriers. Industrialists successfully defeated domestic agricultural interests when Parliament voted to eliminate the last vestiges of protectionist controls on foreign trade. They were aided by British international bankers who had made the City of London the world's first major financial center. Aiming at the creation of a basic international market, the British free trade movement was soon joined by other European and New World countries. As a result, the volume of international free trade quintupled between 1850 and 1900, as did European financial investment in the United States.

But trade liberalization did not mean that industrializing countries completely abandoned the use of tariffs. In fact, most economic internationalists also supported a system of social protection for the purpose of the continued industrial development of their nation. Indeed, the "world economy" created by first-wave globalization operated within the nation-state system of world capitalism. In other words, the pre-1914 economic integration was achieved through trade in goods and services between nationally based production systems. Nationally based capitalists organized national production. A national working class produced commodities within their own borders, and often used raw materials imported from the colonies. Thus, this shallow integration of the nation-based world economy produced by first-wave globalization differed markedly from the deep integration of the global economy in the early 21st century. The 21st century global economy involved the transnationalization of the production of goods and services.

Moreover, most international trade occurred within Europe and between Europe and North America and Australia. In the early 1900s, Japan emerged as the lone Asian industrial power. The expansion of world trade also stimulated the growth of international companies like Germany's Singer Sewing Machine Company or America's US Steel. It also enabled the rise of industrial titans like John D. Rockefeller, powerful financiers like Nathan Mayer Rothschild, and newspaper magnates like William Randolph Hearst. Brand name packaged goods like Coca-Cola drinks, Campbell soups, and Remington typewriters made their first appearance.

But the explosion of free trade and international business activity in the early 20th century would not have been possible without the willingness of most major industrial powers to join the gold standard. It guaranteed the exchange of a country's currency for gold at a pre-established rate. It provided stability and predictability to world trade and investment that thus facilitated the faster movement of goods, services, money, and people across national borders.

On the eve of World War I in 1913, merchandize trade output reached a level unmatched until the 1970s. This growth was driven by a massive increase in world population to 1.8 billion. To keep up with growing volumes of supply and demand, the expanding world economy relied on the transnational migration of skilled and unskilled laborers within and across continents. In 1910, global labor migration reached three million people per year. More than one million immigrants hailed from Europe and Asia. They were bound for the United States, Canada, or Australia. They were drawn to the New World by the promise of a brighter economic future as well as greater political and religious freedoms.

Politics
Politically, first-wave globalization was fueled by the renewed thrust of European colonial expansion. By 1910, the British Empire comprised a quarter of the land surface of the world and included more than a quarter of its population. Imperialist expansionism occurred simultaneously with the international movement of goods, capital, culture, and people. In fact, economic interests sometimes took the backseat to political rivalries among imperialist states.

At the same time, first-wave globalization also included attempts to reduce international tensions and improve humanitarian coordination. Seeking to preserve peaceful international relations, industrialized nations met at two international conferences at The Hague, Netherlands (1899, 1907). But these efforts to regulate international relations were blessed with only short-lived successes such as the banning of aerial bombing and chemical warfare. Attempts to provide a new institutional framework for settling international disputes led to the establishment of a Permanent Court of Arbitration in The Hague.

Similarly, socialist labor parties utilized their own international organization, the Second International Workmen's Association (1889-1914), to enhance communication, cooperation, and unity among the workers of the world. Other newly formed world organizations included the International Association of Seismology (1903), the International Office of Public Hygiene (1907), and the International Bureau of Commercial Statistics (1913).

Culture
On the surface, the expansion of European empires occurred in the name of pursuing a "civilizing mission." However, the cultural effects of these political practices of domination were far from noble. They included the spread and intensification of invidious racial categories and hierarchies that assigned essentialist forms of superiority to the European and North American colonizers. The diffusion of European languages, modes of education, dress, and manners elevated particular cultural forms to the status of universal standards. When Native peoples resisted the Christianization efforts of their colonizers it was interpreted as "proof" of the "blackness of their souls." They believed the Natives merely held a stubborn attachment to their "primitive" cultural traditions.

At the same time, the industrial core regions of the world could not help but be affected by the cultural practices of faraway regions. For example, Japanese, African, and Polynesian art began to exert a powerful influence on cutting-edge European Impressionist and Cubist painters like Paul Cezanne and Pablo Picasso. In Germany, so-called "colonial goods" (Kolonialwaren) like cocoa, rice, sugar, and tobacco imported from the European overseas territories ceased to be the privilege of the upper classes. They became readily available to the average consumer in Berlin and Munich. And the enticing photographic images of exotic and unspoiled "paradises" in the colonial world that appeared in high-circulation American and European newspapers spawned the beginnings of an organized international tourism industry.

Reading: The Second Wave of Globalization, 1945-75

Many of the new forms of global interdependence and connectivity that characterized first-wave globalization were undone by the collapse of the old international order in 1914. A large segment of the world's population was plunged into misery and dislocation. The unshackled forces of nationalist exclusivism and economic isolationism found their most extreme expressions in the Great War (1914-18), the Great Depression (1930s), and World War II (1939-45).

Economy and Technology

To be sure, globalization did not completely vanish during the three dark decades between 1914 and 1945. In fact, the expansion and intensification of warfare emerged as one of its distinct features. Many of the technological developments that fed second-wave globalization in the decades after World War II were the direct result of war-related activities. A short list of these innovations includes the microwave-generating magnetron, basic radar and sonar systems, synthetic rubber, super-sized ships made of welded steel, and streamlined production lines. Moreover, World War II accelerated the crucial shift from a coal-based framework of industrial development to a worldwide energy infrastructure run on petroleum.

Three additional war-related inventions proved to be especially important for the generation of the second wave of globalization. Airplanes powered by jet engines made their first regular appearance as Messerschmitt Me 262 turbojet aircraft in the German Air Force in 1944. During the 1950s, jet aviation technology greatly improved. It allowed production of commercial wide-body airliners. These were capable of transporting soaring numbers of goods and passengers to distant destinations in record time. In October 1958, Pan American Airlines ushered in the commercial jet age by starting its regular transcontinental service. Each of its Boeing 707 aircraft could carry more than 100 passengers and 11 crewmembers. The flight from New York City to Paris took only 8 hours and 41 minutes. It was affordable even for middle-class consumers at a relatively modest round-trip ticket price of $489.

Less than two decades later, French and British "Concorde" supersonic airplanes cut the trans-Atlantic crossing time to just under 3 hours and 30 minutes. Wealthy "jet-setters" holding Concorde tickets could enjoy lunch in a fine brasserie on the Seine and take friends out to dinner at a Manhattan steakhouse the very same day. By the mid-1970s, hundreds of jet airlines served nearly 500 million passengers annually. Many of them experienced new physical problems connected with such extreme forms of space-time compression. The most obvious effect was the body's inability to cope with swiftly changing time zones. This experience introduced a new term into the English language: "jet lag."

The second crucial World War II-related invention was rocket technology, initially applied to long-range guided missiles like the German V-2 rocket. At the end of the war, Wernher von Braun, Nazi Germany's leading rocket engineer, was brought to the United States to head up its burgeoning space program. After the establishment of NASA in 1958, von Braun and his large team of technicians and scientists successfully developed the Saturn V rocket. This rocket launched the three-man crew of Apollo 11 on their historic mission to the moon in July 1969.

The pictures of our "Blue Planet" snapped from outer space during the Apollo missions in the 1960s created in billions of people the first stirrings of a global imaginary. More than anything, the new space age gave physical concreteness to our borderless "global village." This popular phrase was coined by the Canadian communication scholar Marshall McLuhan. It sought to capture the complex dynamics of spatial "stretching" that made geographic distance much less of an obstacle in human interaction. Observing that the "mechanical age" of the Industrial Revolution was rapidly receding, McLuhan made a prediction. He anticipated that the "electric contraction" of space and time would eventually make the entire globe as open to instant and direct communication as small village communities in previous centuries had been. He was correct.

The third pivotal World War II impact on second-wave globalization involved the creation of digital electronic machines. A good example is Harvard University's Mark I computer, initially used by the US Navy for gunnery and ballistic calculations. The invention of magnetic-core memory and transistors in the 1950s made commercial computers viable. The 1960s witnessed a dramatic increase in the number of such computers, with deliveries tripling every year. One of the earliest solid-state commercial computers, the IBM 1401 emerged in the 1960s as the world's most widely used data processing system.

The ensuing decade saw an explosive growth of personal computers. In the early 1970s, Steve Jobs and Steve Wozniak exhibited their first Apple II machine at the First West Coast Computer Faire in San Francisco. Equipped with built-in BASIC programming language, color graphics, and a 4,100-character memory, the Apple II model went on sale in 1977 for $1,298. Even the most celebrated hallmark of third-wave globalization — the Internet — had its origin in secret US war communication projects. Many of these innovations underwent further development in the Cold War era in response to path-breaking Soviet satellite technology.

Politics

The political framework of second-wave globalization rested on a new postwar international architecture characterized by a steep rise of intergovernmental organizations (IGOs). It started in 1945 with the founding of the United Nations (UN), headquartered in New York City. The UN was committed to resolving conflict and ensuring peace through its permanent Security Council. To accomplish this they created sub-agencies dedicated to assisting political refugees, working for global disease control, promoting international economic development, and supporting children's welfare. Far from functioning as a world government, the new organization nonetheless served as a crucial catalyst for political globalization. In particular, the setting of international political and humanitarian standards exerted tremendous global influence. To some extent, the UN also stimulated the explosive growth of international non-governmental organizations (INGOs) from several hundred, in 1945, to thousands in 1975.

On the flipside, however, the victorious Allies had created a new international political order that divided the planet into two expansive "spheres of influence" separating the Soviet Union from the West by an "Iron Curtain." Still, Moscow and Washington were united in their support of the process of decolonization, which resulted in the creation of dozens of new nations in the Third World. As a result, the number of nation-states in the world increased from 81 in 1950 to 134 in 1970. At the same time, however, Washington competed with Moscow for political influence on these newly independent countries. Home to a quarter of the world's population, these "developing nations" remained politically and economically dependent on their former colonial masters. After all, the Cold War order relied on transnational policies of foreign aid coupled with the establishment of overseas military bases.

This dangerous dynamic pushed the world to the brink of nuclear war in 1962 when the superpowers confronted each other in the Caribbean for 13 days. This Cuban Missile Crisis reinforced the fact that the globe was now divided into three "worlds" or "blocs." The "First World" was dominated by Washington. The "Second World" was presided over by the Soviet Union and later joined by the People's Republic of China. The subordinated "Third World" nations were located in the global South. Many of these were not formally aligned with either Washington or Moscow. Yet, the political reality of the Cold War rivalry forced most of them to choose sides. Hence, second-wave globalization operated in a bipolar political world in which the cold hostilities between the two superpowers often played themselves out in hot proxy-wars in the Third World. Two major examples are the Korean War (1950-3) and the Vietnam War (1955-75).

The economic dynamics of second-wave globalization originated in the sleepy New England town of Bretton Woods. Led by the United States, the major economic powers of the West jettisoned the protectionist policies of the interwar period and struck a compromise that combined international economic integration with national policy independence. Their renewed commitment to the expansion of trade and economic cooperation reflected a shared belief in the effectiveness of global commercial interdependence as a bulwark against another devastating economic crisis or a new world war.

The successful establishment of binding rules on international economic activities resulted in the creation of a stable currency exchange system. Within this system, the value of participating currencies was pegged to the American dollar, worth one thirty-fifth of an ounce of gold. Bretton Woods also set the institutional foundations for the creation of three new international economic organizations. The International Monetary Fund (IMF) was established to administer the global monetary system. The International Bank for Reconstruction and Development, later known as the World Bank, provided loans for Europe's postwar reconstruction. In the late 1950s, its purpose was expanded to fund major industrial projects in the developing world. The General Agreement on Tariffs and Trade (GATT) became the first global trade organization charged with fashioning and enforcing multilateral trade agreements.

In spite of the continued existence of three separate "worlds," commercial activities and telecommunications often interconnected in sprawling networks that extended deep into the Soviet sphere of influence. Moreover, transnational economic alliances formed on both sides of the Iron Curtain. By 1973, the small European Coal and Steel Community (founded in 1952) had expanded into the formidable European Economic Community comprised of nine member states. Likewise, the Soviet-dominated Council for Mutual Economic Assistance showed a membership of nine countries by 1978.

In operation for almost three decades, the international Bretton Woods regime contributed greatly to the establishment of what some have called the "golden age of controlled capitalism." States pledged close economic cooperation but maintained control over their economic policies and money flows. Existing mechanisms of state control over international capital movements made possible full employment and the expansion of the welfare state. State-regulated capitalism delivered spectacular economic growth rates, high wages, low inflation, and unprecedented levels of material well-being and social security.

High taxation on wealthy individuals and profitable corporations led to the expansion of the welfare state. Rising wages and increased social services in the wealthy countries of the Northern Hemisphere offered workers entry into the middle class. More than half of the workers in the First World belonged to a union. An increasing number of people in the First World could afford to spend vacations abroad or even escape in "charter planes" to distant tourist zones. These had sprung up in the Third World and they became ever more integrated into the global economy.

By the early 1970s, however, the golden age of controlled capitalism ground to a halt. In response to profound political changes in the world that were undermining the economic competitiveness of US-based industries, President Richard Nixon abandoned the gold-based fixed rate system in 1971. This new world of "floating currencies" increased economic unpredictability and financial volatility. To make matters worse, a major energy crisis hit the world in the form of two "oil shocks" (1973 and 1979). It reflected the growing ability of the Organization of Petroleum Exporting Countries (OPEC) to control a large part of the world's oil supply. The price of petrol at the pump quadrupled overnight and contributed to a condition of "stagflation" — the simultaneous occurrence of runaway inflation and rising unemployment. During the next 10 years, the world economy tanked as it remained haunted by chronic price instability, soaring public sector deficits, and falling corporate profits.

Culture

The cultural aspects of second-wave globalization were deeply colored by these political and economic dynamics. The globalization of mass production and mass consumption in an ideologically divided world fueled the rise of a rather uniform Western "culture industry" largely based in the United States. Hollywood movies, french fries, McDonald's-style fast food, blue jeans, chewing gum, rock and roll music, American-English idioms like "OK" or "show time," and iconic American cars like the Ford Mustang or Harley Davidson motorcycles took the three worlds by storm. Even the sensational Liverpool-based band the Beatles only gained global superstar status after their record-breaking 1964 North American tour was launched by their first live US television appearance on *The Ed Sullivan Show*.

Indeed, the "Americanization of the world" relied very heavily on the growing power of the mass media to spread the gospel of consumerism through proliferating newspaper and magazine advertisements, and, most importantly, TV "commercials." Highly improved from its earliest manifestation in the 1930s, the TV set became an essential item in most First and Second World homes during the 1950s and 1960s. By 1972, the sale of color TV sets had surpassed sales of black-and-white sets. In 1976, Ted Turner launched his Atlanta-based WTCG "superstation" as the world's first basic cable network. Cable TV took advantage of cutting-edge satellite technology to offer consumers standardized subscription packages for multiple channels that beamed a steady diet of high-resolution, popular entertainment plus commercials into millions of households.

Superstar athletes like Pelé, Nadia Comaneci, and Joe Namath delighted their global TV audiences at transnational mega-sports events like the Olympic Games, the FIFA Football World Cup, or the American Football "Super Bowl" (played for the first time in 1967 in the Los Angeles Memorial Coliseum). And countless TV commercials delivered millions of viewers to quickly expanding "shopping malls" where they acquired the brand-name products used by their idols.

Yet, the consumerism and materialism of the second-wave culture industry also created a powerful cultural backlash in the form of alternative social movements and a spiritual yearning for a "New Age." The growth of protest culture started with the American Civil Rights movement in the 1950s and found its powerful climax in the worldwide social demonstrations of 1968. Unlike the prewar labor movements that had embraced primarily class politics, these new social movements often coalesced around identity positions opposed to racism, sexism, homophobia, and war.

The same logic applied to the new environmentalist movements of the 1960s and 1970s. This counterculture consisted to a large extent of young people who rejected centralized and bureaucratic models of political power while committing to forms of freedom and liberation that went far beyond purely material concerns. Expressing a fondness for participatory democracy anchored in ideals of individual agency, autonomy, and equality, alternative social movements emerged in both the First and the Second World. They emphasized direct political action and endorsed "spontaneous" desires and personal behaviors that ran afoul of established social norms, conventions, and hierarchies.

Reading: The Third Wave of Globalization, 1991-Present

The collapse of the Soviet Bloc in 1991 shattered the bipolar postwar order and triggered the gigantic third wave of globalization that made the world a far more interconnected and interdependent place. Within the next quarter century, the world would witness the rise of a new world order in which the hegemony of the United States was challenged by multiple "rising powers" such as China, Russia, India, and Brazil.

Economics and Technology

In addition to this novel political configuration, a "New Economy" of global reach was rapidly evolving, seemingly driven by irresistible market forces. Indeed, when "globalization" emerged as the buzzword of the 1990s, most people associated its meaning primarily to the expansion of trade and finance. The export volume of world trade exploded from $876 billion in 1975 to an astonishing $19 trillion in 2014. In that year, China, the world's rising economic power and leading manufacturer, was responsible for 11 percent of global exports while the US, the world's most voracious consumer, accounted for 13 percent of global imports.

The internationalization of trade in the 1990s went hand in hand with the liberalization of financial transactions. Its key components included the deregulation of interest rates, the removal of credit controls, the privatization of government-owned banks and financial institutions, and the explosive growth of investment banking. Globalization of financial trading allowed for increased mobility among different segments of the financial industry, with fewer restrictions and greater investment opportunities. The increasing power of transnational corporations (TNCs) like Exxon, Walmart, and Samsung was another major feature of third-wave economic globalization. Gigantic firms with subsidiaries in several countries, TNC numbers skyrocketed from 7,000 in 1970 to about 80,000 in 2012. Rivaling nation-states in their economic power, these corporations began to control much of the world's investment capital, technology, and access to international markets.

Third-wave economic globalization was greatly facilitated by the rapid development of information, communication, and transportation technology. This "digital revolution" was reflected in such innovations as desktop and laptop computers, the Internet, digital TV, wireless phones, standardized shipping containers, fiber-optic cables, electronic barcodes, and global commodity chains.

By the 2010s, these intensifying forms of technological connectivity had greatly expanded. It included all sorts of handheld mobile devices such as Cloud-connected smart wireless phones like the iPhone and tablets like the Kindle Fire. In addition, there were powerful Internet search engines like Google whose algorithms sorted in a split-second through gigantic datasets. There were also individual video-postings on YouTube, ubiquitous social networking sites like Facebook and Twitter, and the rapidly expanding "blogosphere." At home and at work, people could join in personal Skype and FaceTime conversations and online conferencing. And let's not forget devices used for entertainment like satellite- and computer-connected HDTVs and interactive 3-D video games. To be sure, the Internet assumed a pivotal function in facilitating third-wave globalization. The World Wide Web connected billions of individuals, civil society associations, and governments in millions of "online communities." The total number of websites grew from 10 million in 1996 to nearly 1 billion in 2014. Similarly, the number of Internet users worldwide exploded from 30 million in 1996 to 3.6 billion in 2016.

By the mid-1990s, insightful social thinkers like Manuel Castells referred to the post-Cold War era as a new "information age" characterized by the rise of a global "network society" that was built on the "flowing spaces" and "timeless time" of the new "information superhighways." Indeed, for the first time in human history, the compression of space and time generated new spatial and temporal dimensions: "cyberspace" and "real-time." Powerful microelectronic technologies connected multiple "virtual worlds" to the physical world in ways that made geographic space part of cyberspace and vice-versa. Major social media platforms offered personal and instant ways of accessing cyberspace in ways that sustained people's identities, interests, and social needs.

Constituting real-time markets for the exchange of information and knowledge, these autonomous virtual spaces also transformed and globalized higher education by enrolling millions of "distance learners" in new "online courses" and other "knowledge platforms." The same digital technologies also enabled the evolution of second-wave innovations that accelerated the shrinkage of geographic distance and the crossing of national boundaries. These included super-jetliners like the Airbus A380 or Boeing's Dreamliner, recreational and military drones, the international space station, and industrial and household robots. The technologies even reached into agriculture, where crops were genetically modified so that they could thrive in multiple climate zones.

Politics
But third-wave globalization unfolded not merely on the material planes of technology and commerce. It was also a direct consequence of novel "neoliberal" economic and political ideas that had been on the rise since the early 1980s. Two influential political leaders, British Prime Minister Margaret Thatcher and US President Ronald Reagan, had promised to lead their countries out of the economic doldrums of the 1970s by reducing the role of government.

Harkening back to the 18th-century liberal idea of the "self-regulating economy," such neoliberal doctrine was linked to a concrete set of public policies expressed in the "D-L-P formula." This stood for deregulation of the economy; liberalization of trade and industry; and privatization of state-owned enterprises. Related economic policy measures included massive tax cuts, the reduction of social services and welfare programs, and the use of interest rates by independent central banks to keep inflation in check even at the risk of increasing unemployment.

The collapse of Russian communism in 1991 seemed to vindicate Thatcher and Reagan's neoliberal ideas of the 1980s. Political parties in the West most closely identified with the model of controlled capitalism. It suffered a series of spectacular election defeats at the hands of political parties that advocated a neoliberal approach to economic and social policy. As free-market capitalism went global, neoliberalism morphed into "market globalism" — a worldwide free-market ideology built around the buzzword "globalization."

By the late 1990s, however, this capitalist vision of an economically integrated world was fiercely contested by a transnational "global justice movement" that first burst on the public stage at the large-scale demonstration against the World Trade Organization meeting in Seattle. Gathering steam throughout the 2000s, the global justice movement developed into a large network of NGOs that saw themselves as a "global civil society" dedicated to the protection of social justice, fair trade, the global environment, and human rights.

The adherents of this new global ideology of "justice globalism" also protested against what they saw as the pernicious role of international economic institutions in exacerbating the inequitable relationship between the global North and South. Starting in the 1990s, international economic institutions like the IMF and World Bank used the neoliberal principles of market globalism in the design of their development programs for the global South. In return for supplying much-needed loans to developing countries, the IMF and the World Bank demanded from their creditor nations the implementation of so-called "structural adjustment programs." Their official purpose was to reform the internal economic mechanisms of debtor countries in the developing world so that they would be in a better position to repay the debts they had incurred.

In practice, however, structural adjustment programs rarely produce the desired result of economic development. This is because mandated cuts in public spending translate into fewer social programs, and reduced educational opportunities. They also open the door for more environmental pollution, and greater poverty for the vast majority of developing countries. Given the dominant role played by the United States in the IMF and the World Bank, it was no coincidence that this program became known as the "Washington Consensus."

From a political perspective, third-wave globalization transformed the international society of separate states located in two spheres of influence into a global web of political interdependencies. It challenged conventional forms of national sovereignty. In 1991, at the conclusion of the Gulf War, US President George H.W. Bush announced the birth of a "new world order." In the new order, leaders would no longer respect the idea that cross-border wrongful acts were a matter concerning only those states affected. Such weakened state sovereignty meant that national governments had to answer to a broader global audience for their actions. This would be particularly so when it came to human rights, transnational threats to public health like AIDS or Ebola, and the environment.

Moreover, states found themselves challenged by increasing flows of goods, people, and environmental problems that made it difficult to control what occurred within their own borders. For example, during the Syrian civil war in the 2010s, millions of Middle Eastern refugees crossed into Europe, triggering a severe political crisis among European Union member states. Some commentators decried these dynamics of political globalization as leading to "the end of the nation-state." Others, however, saw them in more positive terms, enhancing the prospects for more effective regional and global governance structures.

However, the devastating al-Qaeda attacks of 9/11 seemed to confirm that diminishing national control had spawned new forms of insecurity. After all, transnational terrorist groups like al Qaeda and ISIS were not state-based actors but promoted an ideology of "religious globalism" through a global network of supporters. Moreover, their faith-based global vision rejected secular political structures in favor of a worldwide caliphate anchored in divine law. The long string of atrocities and mass killings committed by such groups in all parts of the world in the 21st century showed that they were prepared to use extreme forms of violence to achieve global domination.

Predictably, many nation-states reacted to transnational terrorism not only by committing to an open-ended "global war on terror," but also by developing new forms of electronic surveillance and enhanced security measures at spaces of global mobility such as airports, railway stations, and large-scale public events. The emergence of the "security state," in turn, encouraged the formation of transnational hacker networks like WikiLeaks. Claiming to protect democratic principles of transparency and accountability against state-based secrecy and surveillance, WikiLeaks penetrated sensitive national security sites and released classified information to the public. By the second decade of the 21st century, all sorts of "cyber attacks" were directed against state institutions, commercial enterprises, and private individuals.

Culture

From a cultural perspective, third-wave globalization seemed to enhance the second wave's tendency toward "homogenization" or cultural sameness. Rising to prominence in the 1990s, the phrase "McDonaldization of the world" captured the worldwide imposition of uniform Western standards on vulnerable cultures. There was certainly ample evidence of these homogenizing cultural tendencies of globalization. These appeared even in such mundane manifestations as Amazonian Indians wearing Nike sneakers, denizens of the Southern Sahara purchasing Texaco baseball caps, and Palestinian youths proudly displaying their Chicago Bulls sweatshirts in downtown Ramallah.

To a large extent, such Western "cultural imperialism" relied on commercial values disseminated by transnational media enterprises. During the three decades of third-wave globalization, a small group of very large TNCs came to dominate the global market for entertainment, news, television, and film. In 2014, the eight largest media conglomerates were Comcast, Google, Disney, News Corporation, DirecTV, Viacom, Time Warner, and SONY. They counted for more than two-thirds of the $1.5 trillion in annual worldwide revenues generated by the global telecommunications industry.

At the same time, there was also some evidence for the reassertion of cultural diversity such as the revitalization of indigenous cultural practices around the world. Rather than being totally obliterated by the Western consumerist forces of sameness, local difference and particularity still played an important role in creating unique cultural constellations. Indeed, third-wave globalization contained a complex cultural dynamic that involved not only manifestations of sameness and difference but also "glocalization"—the interaction of the global and local. In other words, global cultural flows also encouraged new forms of cultural hybridity. Examples include Bollywood movies, K-pop and "Gangnam-style" rap, the many variations of Hawaiian pidgin, and the culinary delights of Cuban-Chinese cuisine.

Cultural values also played an important role in the growing significance of the environment under the turbocharged condition of third-wave globalization. At the dawn of the 21st century, it had become impossible to ignore the fact that people everywhere on this planet were inextricably linked to each other. This happened through the air they breathed, the climate they depended upon, the food they ate, and the water they drank. In spite of this obvious lesson of ecological interdependence, the planet's ecosystems were subjected to continuous human assault in order to secure wasteful lifestyles. Hence, the environmental impacts of globalization were increasingly recognized as potentially life threatening for the planet and its countless species.

The unprecedented third-wave compression of the natural environment had significant results. Some of these were global environmental problems like human-induced climate change, transboundary pollution, and the reduction of biodiversity. They received enormous attention from research institutes, the media, politicians, and economists. These global ecological problems were compounded by the worldwide impact of man-made natural disasters such as the 2010 mega-oil spill in the Gulf of Mexico or the horrifying 2011 nuclear plant accidents at Fukushima, Japan. The increasing number of UN-sponsored environmental conferences reflected a growing consensus that solving the ecological problems of the 21st century required the formation of a global alliance of states and civil society actors.

Globalization is a powerful force that shaped people's lives in the 20th and 21st centuries. But it is neither an inevitable juggernaut nor an irreversible process destined to go on forever. In the 2010s, anti-globalization forces clinging to the national imaginary gathered steam. They reacted to increasing levels of insecurity and economic inequality in the wake of the 2008 Global Financial Crisis, the European debt crisis of the 2010s, and intensifying transnational terrorist attacks. Nationalist populists and economic protectionists, like Donald Trump in the United States, Marine Le Pen in France, or Nigel Farage, who led the successful 2016 Brexit campaign in the UK, have given voice to millions of people opposed to free trade, migration, and multiculturalism. In the years and decades ahead, the ongoing third wave of globalization will bring both new global crises and opportunities. Globalization's future viability depends on its ability to meet the three most daunting challenges facing humanity in the 21st century: the reduction of global inequality, the preservation of our wondrous planet, and the strengthening of human security.

Reading: From the National to the Global Imaginary (Topical Essay)

Manfred B. Steger is Professor of Global and Transnational Sociology at the University of Hawaii-Manoa. He is also an Honorary Professor of Global Studies at RMIT University in Melbourne, Australia. He is a pioneer in the emerging transdisciplinary field of Global Studies. Steger served as an advisor on globalization for the US State Department (2002) and as an advisor to the PBS TV series *Heaven on Earth: The Rise and Fall of Socialism*. Steger is also the author of 70 refereed articles and book chapters as well as the author or editor of 25 books on globalization, and social and political theory.

The image is a sculpture in front of the Union Station of the city of Toronto, Canada. It is called "Monument to Multiculturalism" by the artist Francesco Perilli. It was unveiled on July 1, 1985. There are four identical sculptures located in Buffalo City, South Africa, Changchun, China, Sarajevo, Bosnia, and Sydney, Australia.

The early 21st century is a challenging time of transition brought on by the dynamics of globalization. But what sort of transition are we talking about? This lecture argues that we are moving from the old divided world of self-contained nation-states to a new transnational social web of interconnected nations, localities, and regions.

Indeed, the transformative powers of globalization already reach deeply into all aspects of social life. For many observers, the most spectacular aspect of increasing global interdependence has been the digital revolution that has powered the gigantic economic and cultural flows of the global age. But globalization processes cannot be confined to the combination of economics and technology impacting the world "out there." The reality of intensifying connectivities is also deeply felt in people's consciousness "in here." This subjective dimension of globalization contains ideas, beliefs, feelings, and identities that are the stuff of what some social scientists have called the "social imaginary."

The National Imaginary

And yet, the social imaginary is a temporary form of social consciousness that exists in a concrete social context. It is, therefore, subject to change. At certain points in history, such change can occur with lightning speed and tremendous ferocity. This happened at the end of the 18th century when the scientific and social revolutions in Europe and the Americas transformed the previously dominant social imaginary in a dramatic way.

The old modes of understanding had reproduced divinely sanctioned power hierarchies in the form of tribes, clanships, trading city-states and, especially, dynastic realms. The republican experiments of the ancient world and the Renaissance had been short-lived. They were forgotten or actively erased from the collective memory. Things started to change after the European wars of religion in the 17th century and with the subsequent rise of the natural sciences. Between 1776 and 1848, there arose on both sides of the Atlantic the new template of the "nation" — now no longer referring to a feudal state hierarchy, but to a "general will" operating in free citizens. The political implications were as clear as they were audacious. Henceforth it would be "the people" — not kings, aristocrats, or clerical elites — that exercised legitimate authority in political affairs in the name of reason and its "natural laws."

However, after the failure of Napoleon's project of continental imperial rule in the early 19th century, the authority of the European and American people found concrete expression only within particular nation-states. Although the emerging principles of rights and justice were universalistic, the concept of the "people," in practice, meant the citizens of a particular state located in an "inter-national" system of warring states.

Throughout the 19th century, many people — patriotic citizens and mercenaries who fought for material compensation rather than their country — were still willing to sacrifice their lives for the divine rights of the dynastic rulers and aristocracy. Moreover, production remained based on land and agriculture. The speed of communication and transportation across the surface of the planet was limited to the velocity of humans, horses, and later, steamships and railways. Under these circumstances, the resources of the weakening aristocratic states were used to resist the new national categories of popular sovereignty. This struggle for the meaning of the "nation" also captured the imagination of historians, philosophers, and poets.

But how, exactly, did the rising national imaginary provide newly minted "citizens" with a solid sense of community, belonging, and shared values? Let us consider a concrete example: the public celebration of national holidays that became commonplace in the late 19th century. Let us picture a small town somewhere in Europe or the Americas. Here we find a smiling young woman waving a national flag as the marching band passes by playing patriotic songs. There stands at attention an old man on the side of the street, hand on his heart and mouthing the words that go along with these nationalistic hymns. Around the corner we can observe throngs of patriotically dressed children purchasing candy from street vendors. Behind the long row of excited onlookers we can make out two young men in uniform pointing proudly to a large cannon pulled by military horses.

In the blink of an eye, metaphors, images, symbols, space, and action flowed into each other in ways that made immediate sense to all participants. Our late 19th-century town dwellers did not expend any conscious effort in navigating their familiar national culture. After all, the social imaginary pervaded their holiday celebrations with a deep sense of "normalcy." This allowed for their meaningful participation as a national community of shared fate.

By the end of World War I in 1918, the struggle for the soul of the nation had been largely decided as the traditional powers of kings and emperors had been severely curtailed. The modern nation — both in the form of constitutional, limited monarchies and mass republics — had become the central category of human existence and belonging in the industrialized world. Seeking to remake their society according to the "national imaginary," citizens exhibited a restless energy that became the hallmark of the 20th century

These hyper-nationalistic tendencies intensified when the Great Depression of the 1930s led to unprecedented levels of mass unemployment and inflation. There arose extremist ideologies of Italian fascism, Japanese imperialism, and German National Socialism. They translated the national imaginary into aggressive programs that gave rise to the first truly global war in human history. World War II ended in the horrendous nuclear blasts that obliterated the Japanese cities of Hiroshima and Nagasaki and killed or injured most of their civilian populations. This result revealed the shortcomings of the national imaginary.

The Global Imaginary

Thus, World War II proved to be a watershed in the evolution of the global imaginary — people's growing consciousness of global connectivity. The 18th-century revolutions and the ensuing two decades of Napoleonic warfare in Europe had ushered in the national age. In the same way, the most destructive war of the 20th century served as a crucial catalyst for the birth of the global era. The three major Allied war conferences of Teheran (1943), Bretton Woods (1944), and Yalta (1945) laid the foundation of a global political and economic order. It was manifested in such international institutions as the United Nations and the International Monetary Fund.

At the same time, the Cold War divided the planet into expansive regions seeping across national borders. Still, people started to use the terms "global" or "world" to characterize these new geopolitical spheres. The First World comprised the Western democracies. The Second World encompassed the communist bloc. And the Third World consisted of colonial territories and newly independent countries in Asia, Africa, and Latin America.

World War II and its aftermath destabilized the Eurocentric system of Great Powers that had grown to maturity in the late 19th century. It also allowed the permeation of the dominant national imaginary by those ideas and practices that took the entire globe as their frame of reference. Even the yearnings for national liberation became globalized as decolonization movements in Africa and Asia generated new nation-states eager to assemble under the global umbrella of the United Nations.

But nothing captured the rise of the global imaginary as starkly as the dawning space age. Most of all, were the awesome pictures of an "Earthrise." These were first taken by Apollo 8 astronaut William Anders after the first-ever manned orbit around the moon on December 24, 1968. They did much to enhance people's awareness of our collective journey on Spaceship Earth. Our world is endowed with magnificent yet finite resources suited to sustain life on our precious planet. The fragility of the blue globe suspended in the vast cosmos was conveyed in these Apollo images. This perception loomed large in the emergence of transnational and countercultural "new social movements" in the 1960s and 1970s that centered on categories of ecology, indigeneity, race, gender, and sexuality.

The ascent of the global imaginary reached another threshold when the Berlin Wall fell in 1989. This marked the compression of the three "worlds" of the Cold War period into the one world of globally integrating markets and digital technologies. Ultimately, the civilian applications of wartime technologies culminated in the emergence of the personal computer and the Internet. The speed and intensity with which ideas, images, practices, people, and materials moved across national spaces was dramatically multiplied. Though still a long way from a full-blown condition of globality, the world was clearly becoming more integrated. Indeed, the growing presence of the adjective "global" in the news, advertising, policy circles, and the entertainment industry reflected this remarkable rise of a global imaginary.

However, the intensification of the global imaginary came with a slew of "global problems." These included growing disparities in wealth and wellbeing, and worldwide pandemics like Ebola and Zika. In addition were the issues of transnational terrorism, unprecedented migration flows, and global climate change. These problematic manifestations of globalization began to undermine the normality and self-contained coziness of the modern nation-state. This was especially so where deeply ingrained notions of community were tied to a sovereign and clearly demarcated territory containing relatively homogenous populations. Identities based on national membership were confronted with new global values of multiculturalism.

Like the forces of social change that shook Europe and the Americas more than two hundred years ago, today's destabilization of the national imaginary affects the entire planet. This is not to say that national and local communal frameworks have lost their power to provide people with a meaningful sense of home and identity. But it would be a mistake to close our eyes to the weakening of the national imaginary, as it has been historically constituted in the 19th and 20th centuries.

This tension between the global and national imaginary — between intensifying interdependence and a new dynamic of exclusion — has become the hallmark of our global age. More and more people around the world enjoy the benefits of global digital connectivity and information. But they also face unprecedented levels of surveillance and state control aimed at reducing the very forms of insecurity that come with the forces of globalization.

Likewise, we are witnessing the growing popularity of ecological, "green" political parties attuned to the new threats to our global environment. At the same time they are being challenged by the rising voices of national populists like Donald Trump in the United States. Trump has vowed to stop the forces of "globalism" by building border walls and returning "Americanism" to its rightful place at the center of people's communal aspirations. The intensity of this worldwide revolt against globalism has taken many pundits by surprise. It reflects the staying power of the national imaginary over crucial aspects of social life. Hence, to pronounce the nation-state dead would be both inaccurate and foolish.

But it would be equally myopic to ignore the power of the rising global imaginary and the new forms of cosmopolitanism and global cooperation it can inspire. Most likely, the 21st century will be a challenging time of transition in which the national and the global will continue to coexist uncomfortably. As the eruptions of the global continue to sear the national imaginary, they not only change the world's economic and technological infrastructure, but also transform our sense of self, identity, and belonging.

Our Authors

Unit 9: East Asia, 1350-1750
Kenneth J. Hammond, New Mexico State University

Kenneth J. Hammond is Professor of East Asian and Global History at New Mexico State University, where he has taught since 1994. He received his B.A. from Kent State University. While there he was active in the Students for a Democratic Society and the political events of the late 1960s-70s that included the May 4, 1970 shootings there. During the mid-1980s he spent five years in China learning the language. Following his time abroad, he attended Harvard University, receiving his Ph.D. in History and East Asian Languages. His major focus in the history of China is the Early Modern period, especially the 16th century. In addition, he works in global and comparative history, as well as urban history and cartography. He is the author of *Pepper Mountain: the Life, Death and Posthumous Career of Yang Jisheng 1516-55*, published by Routledge in 2007, and has edited three volumes on Chinese history, most recently *The Sage Returns: Aspects of Confucian Revival in Contemporary China* with Jeff Richey, published by the State University of New York Press in 2015. He is the author of many articles in academic journals and books. His expertise has led to lecture and teaching invitations at many universities in the United States, Canada, Mexico, Germany, Italy, China, and Great Britain.

Unit 10: The Early Modern West, 1500-1700
Paula Findlen, Stanford University

Paula Findlen is one of the leading scholars of the history of science and technology in 15th and 16th century Europe, especially Italy. She reminds us that the Italian mariner, Christopher Columbus, was no exception. Italy was the European center of science and technology, as well as the financier for exploration, in the age of discovery. Findlen has innovatively analyzed the impact on Europe of new geographic discoveries, objects, flora and fauna, images, and accounts brought back by sailors from the Americas and Asia. The new knowledge contributed more significantly to the development of modern scientific thinking and methods than we have understood before. Europe most certainly changed the Americas, but Findlen is one of an important group of historians who have shown that the Americas also changed Europe profoundly.

Unit 11: The Middle East and South Asia, 1500-1900
James D. Clark, American Institute of Iranian Studies

James D. Clark is a historian and scholar of the Middle East and Central Asia. He received a B.A. in History from Oklahoma State University (1981) and earned his M.A. in Arabic (1990) and Ph.D. in Middle East history (1999) from The University of Texas at Austin. His studies cover the areas of the Middle East and Central Asia.

Clark has taught in both the United States and the Middle East. He has lectured at the following universities and colleges: University of Nebraska—Lincoln (UNL), the University of Texas at Austin, the University of Nebraska — Omaha, Peru State College, Khojand State University, The Tajiki Institute of Management (TIM), and Tehran University. His teaching experience includes courses on Islam, the Middle East, Iran, world history, global studies, and American history. He has also taught Persian and Arabic language courses.

Clark's expertise has taken him abroad where he has held several administrative positions. During the 1990s he worked in Tajikistan as a cultural consultant for the University of Nebraska — Lincoln. In addition, he worked in Macedonia for the UNL Department of Management. From 2000 to 2006 he served as the director of the Tehran Project. There he supervised American doctoral students, promoted cooperation with Iranian institutions and academics, and worked with the University of Tehran, the International Center for Persian Studies (ICPS), and the Dehkhoda Institute. From 2007 to 2012 he was the program and site director of the Critical Language Scholarship (CLS) program for Persian in Dushanbe, Tajikistan.

Since 2000 Clark has been the Overseas Director for the American Institute of Iranian Studies (AIIrS), a non-profit consortium of US universities and museums, whose mission is to promote the interdisciplinary study of Iranian civilization and US-Iran cultural dialogue

Unit 12: Europe and the World, 1750-1914
J.P. Daughton, Stanford University
James P. Daughton began his academic career at Amherst College, Massachusetts, where he graduated with a bachelor's degree in European Studies (Magna cum laude) and Anthropology in 1992. Daughton went on to complete a Master's in Philosophy at Cambridge, UK, before his Ph.D. in history at the University of California, Berkeley, in 2002. Daughton's tenure at Stanford began in 2004.

Daughton is an historian of modern Europe and European imperialism. In exploring and presenting his findings he pays particular attention to the elements of political, cultural, and social history, as well as the history of humanitarianism, found in both. As can be expected, the breadth of his teaching repertoire reaches beyond European and world history. Some of the many courses he has taught include: Paris: Capital of the Modern World, The Ethics of Imperialism, Humanitarianism and Its Histories, and Capitalism and Its Discontents, to name just a few.

Daughton has exercised remarkable research and foreign language skills. For his many books, chapters, and articles, he has traversed the globe, analyzing documents in archives on multiple continents. He has conducted research in many countries including: France, 1996-present; Vietnam 1999-2000; England, 2003, 2009, 2015; Argentina, 2004; Australia, 2005; New Caledonia, 2005; Switzerland, 2007, 2009; New Zealand, 2010; Vanuatu, 2010; The Netherlands, 2011; Singapore, 2012; Cambodia, 2012; and Republic of Congo, 2015.

His first, prize-winning book is the perfect reflection of his academic and scholarly focus. An Empire Divided: Religion, Republicanism, and the Making of French Colonialism, 1880-1914, 2006, tells how poor relations between Catholic missionaries and republican critics shaped colonial policies, Catholic perspectives, and domestic French politics leading up to World War I. Daughton presents the thesis that many "civilizing" policies in the Empire were an outgrowth of missionary and anti-clerical republican discord. Indigenous communities — seeing this — exploited French disunity.

Daughton's work is internationally renowned. He has been an invited speaker and presenter in many countries. A sign of the continued influence of his work, the book Viet Nam: Borderless Histories, in which his essay, "Recasting Pigneau de Béhaine: French Missionaries and the Politics of Colonial History," (second printing 2008) will soon be available in a Vietnamese translation.

Unit 13: East Asia, 1700-1919
Hugh Shapiro, University of Nevada, Reno
Hugh Shapiro works on the history of disease in comparative context. The analysis of bodily experience is a powerful tool for grappling with historical transformation and his archival and fieldwork in China, Japan, and Taiwan focuses on how cultural practice, environment, and ideas inflect the way people experience illness, in particular neuropsychiatric distress. His recent work appears in volumes published

by Harvard University Press, Brill, Rowman & Littlefield, Kluwer and Globalyceum. Shapiro has enjoyed visiting appointments at Princeton University, at universities in China, Japan, and Taiwan, and at the Institute for Advanced Study in Princeton. Shapiro's other research and teaching interests include Sino-Russian-Central Asian relations and the history of de-colonization and authoritarianism. As a Smithsonian Journeys Expert, he has lectured in 20 countries in Eurasia. During his years of study and research in East Asia, he enjoyed diverse extracurricular experiences, such as working on an innovative Sino-Japanese television series for NHK. He received the Li-Qing Prize for the History of Chinese Science and won his University's highest teaching award.

Unit 14: World Wars and Decolonizations, 1900-1945
Pamela Radcliff, University of California, San Diego

Historian Pamela Radcliff is a noted expert in European history and the history of Spain. She began her studies at Scripps College where she earned her B.A. (1979) in history. She attained advanced degrees in history from Columbia University where she was awarded her M.A., M.Phil., and Ph.D. in 1984, 1985, and 1990, respectively. Radcliff's teaching fields include World History, Modern European History, European Women's History, Modern Spain, and Fascism. While at University of California, San Diego, she has embraced and promoted active learning pedagogy in her department. Her commitment to excellence in teaching is proven through student performance and university awards.

Radcliff continues her research specialties, writing interpretive essays and articles, and authoring books that reflect her new perspective on European history. Many of her writings have been printed in both English and Spanish, her articles appearing in the Journal of Social History, Gender and History, and the premiere Spanish journal for modern history. Radcliff's latest work, A History of Modern Spain, 1808-Present, draws on her 25 years of teaching and research experience and her extensive review of relevant secondary literature. This synthetic history charts the intricacies of local, regional, national, European, and international developments that created Spain's unique version of modernity.

Unit 15: The Bipolar World and its Demise
Katherine A. S. Sibley, St. Joseph's University

Soviet spies plagued the U.S. government before, during, and after World War II, but the secrecy surrounding the subject has created a huge challenge for American historians. Katherine Sibley has been researching and writing about Russian espionage and U.S. counterespionage for nearly two decades and has a superb reputation for dragging the dramatic truth out of the archives. In her books and articles, Sibley has demonstrated that Washington's longstanding efforts to keep this topic under wraps has led to misunderstandings not only about how active Moscow's spies were in the United States, but to what extent the U.S. government was knowledgeable and effective in stopping their penetration of American industry and technology. Sibley writes not only about spies, but also consults with the State Department's Historian's Office as part of its Historical Advisory Committee, which advocates for timely declassification of documents and responsible transparency. Recently she has turned her focus to First Ladies, and her last book was a biography of Florence Harding.

Unit 16: Globalization in the 20th and 21st Centuries
Manfed Steger, University of Hawaii, Manoa

Manfred Steger enjoys working with people of diverse social and cultural backgrounds in a collective effort to connect theory with socially engaged practice. As a global citizen embedded in the Pacific region, heI firmly believes that the acquisition and sharing of knowledge can go a long way in improving the lives of people that go hand in hand with ecological sustainable practices. His research focuses on social theory. In particular, heI explores the central role of ideas, beliefs, languages, images, and other symbolic systems in shaping the discourse on globalization in both academic and public arenas. Firmly committed to a transdisciplinary approach that crosses the artificial boundaries separating the social sciences and humanities, his internationally recognized scholarship brings together diverse geographic and methodological forms of inquiry. He has also made major contributions to the formation of Global Studies - a new field of academic inquiry organized around the study of globalization.

Made in United States
Orlando, FL
28 December 2021

12452599R00130